D1432539

Father Relations of War-Born Children

The Effect of Postwar Adjustment of Fathers on the Behavior and Personality of First Children Born While the Fathers Were at War

By LOIS MEEK STOLZ and

Edith M. Dowley
Erika Chance
Nancy Guy Stevenson
Margaret Siler Faust
Laverne C. Johnson
William Langdon Faust
Alberta Engvall
Leonard Ullmann
Joyce Marian Ryder
D. Bob Gowin

GREENWOOD PRESS, PUBLISHERS
NEW YORK 1968

Reprinted with the permission of the
Board of Trustees of the Leland Stanford Junior University

First Greenwood reprinting, 1968

Library of Congress catalogue card number: 69-10160

The investigation reported in this monograph was conducted within the Department of Psychology of Stanford University under a grant from the National Institute of Mental Health of the United States Public Health Service.

Printed in the United States of America

ACKNOWLEDGEMENTS

This has been a co-operative investigation in which each person in the major research group has had a specific responsibility but has contributed to many other aspects of the study as well. In addition to the authors of this monograph, many others either on the research staff or members of classes in child psychology have done part of the arduous task of collecting, recording, rating, or analyzing data.

It is difficult to acknowledge all our indebtedness, but we want at least to mention some of the large number who have given so generously and enthusiastically of time and energy.

First should be mentioned the fathers who were absent from their families during the war. The inspiration for the study came from them, and they were willing to try to relive earlier and not always pleasant experiences in an effort to contribute to our understanding of adjustments in family life. They and their wives must remain anonymous (all first and last names used in the text are pseudonyms), but it is no cliché to say that without them this study could not have been made. The generosity of the fathers and mothers who had had no war separation made possible a control group. To all these men and women and their children we owe a great debt.

The observations of the children in group situations was time-consuming and demanded the co-operation of many workers. We are indebted to Mr. Melville J. Homfeld, Superintendent of the Menlo Park, California, Elementary School District, for permission to observe children in kindergarten and primary grades; and especially to Mrs. Ina Porter, Principal of Encinal School, and Mrs. Elizabeth Mohun, kindergarten teacher, for their friendly forbearance of our intrusion. Thanks are due also to Miss Margurita Espinosa of Castilleja School, Palo Alto, California, and to Mr. and Mrs. Werner Warnbrunn of the Peninsula School, Menlo Park, California, who permitted us to observe in the kindergarten. Among the students whose recorded observations and interpretations added greatly to the study are the following: Dr. Jerome Oremland, Dr. Murray Thomas, Betty Kirkbride, Jared Fitch, Dale Cowgill, Ruth Wiles Howle, Robert Schaef, Charles Dilkes, Harvey Hutchison, Marjorie Gavin, Marlin Woodward, Patsy Kelly Shumway, Joyce Tappan, Theresa Hansel, Margaret Woollen Johnson, and Barbara Clar Turner.

There are several members of our research staff whose names do not appear in this monograph though the results of their efforts do. We greatly appreciate the contribution which each made. These include Helen Holmquist Halnan and Ramona Walker, who each served as major assistant during one year; Dr. Robert Wirt and Charles Nakamura, who assisted in rating protocols; Arlene Goodsteen Rosen, who assisted in making observations and in analysis of data in the Aggression Study; George Walker, who helped in recording behavior; and Sidney Siegel, who aided in the statistical analysis.

We wish to express our appreciation to Helen Dietz Pickering, who was secretary of the study for three years, and to Betty Griffits MacGillivray, who took over the work for the final intensive year. Their careful work contributed to the accuracy of the research and their friendly relations with staff and subjects helped to keep this complicated project running smoothly. We are especially indebted to Mrs. MacGillivray for her skillful preparation of the manuscript for publication, and to Alberta Engvall for attending to the many details connected with printing and publication.

As a research group we have needed constant advice by technical experts in the field of experimental design and statistical analysis. Our greatest debt is to Dr. Quinn McNemar for his generously given suggestions and counsel. We appreciate, also, the help we received from Dr. Douglas H. Lawrence and Dr. Lloyd Humphreys of the Department of Psychology at Stanford, and Dr. Fred Courts of Reed College, who was visiting professor of psychology at Stanford.

Dr. Donald W. Taylor helped with the plan for the psychological observation room and the initial installation of the recording equipment used in the experimental sessions. Dr. Paul Farnsworth made valuable contributions to the study of father perception. Dr. Paul Hanna and Dr. Fannie Shaftel helped in the planning of the program for mother interviews. Dr. Joseph Stone of Vassar gave us much encouragement while he was visiting professor at Stanford.

The research project was supported from April 1949 through June 1953 by grants from the National Institute of Mental Health, U. S. Public Health Service. We are grateful to Dr. Ernest Hilgard and Dr. Paul Farnsworth of Stanford University for their administrative help in the project, and to Dr. John C. Eberhart, Chief of Research Grants and Fellowships Branch of the National Institute of Mental Health of the U. S. Public Health Service, for his thoughtful consideration throughout the years of our work.

The major research group who are coauthors with the project director of this monograph were all graduate students at Stanford at the beginning of the study. In the first years of the research several of them were members of the research seminar which contributed to the planning of the overall study. The authors of this monograph have worked as a group for several years. It is difficult to define the limits of our respective contributions. We have planned together, helped each other collect data, and rated each other's protocols. Finally, in the preparation of this report, we have discussed, interrelated, and interpreted our joint findings. The enthusiasm and the high level of work of the junior authors throughout the years of the project have been major factors contributing to the worth of this investigation.

Lois Meek Stolz
Director of the Research Project and
Professor of Psychology, Stanford University

June 1, 1953

TABLE OF CONTENTS

IV. CHILDREN IN PROJECTIVE-PLAY SITUATIONS

V. SUMMARY AND INTERPRETATION OF STUDY

CHAPTER 1.
GENERAL DESCRIPTION OF THE FATHER RELATIONS RESEARCH PROJECT

The investigation presented in this monograph deals with the adjustments of father and first-born child to the stress occasioned by return of the father from overseas at the close of World War II. The study is a direct outgrowth of the social concern for the effect of war on the mental health of children which was prevalent during the 1940–50 decade.

The Social Setting

Concern for the Mental Health of Children During World War II

During World War II there was concern among parents and professional people regarding the effects which the war was having on children and the extent to which the strains of war on family life would have a lasting effect on the personalities of children. Even before the United States had entered the war, those who were responsible for children were visiting England and bringing back reports (22). These reports dealt with practical programs for children in wartime, stressing the all-important necessity of protecting children from death by bombing, starvation, disease, and exposure. In the midst of such pressing problems there was evidence of an interest and deep concern for understanding the effect that war, with its concomitant upheaval in the everyday living of children, might have on the emotional lives of these children. Dr. Martha Eliot said regarding the situation in England in February 1941 (22, p. 7):

> The immediate results in terms of saving children's lives are clear; what the effect will be on the emotional life of this generation of children is not yet known. That some children have been seriously disturbed in their emotional life by the experience of bombing is well known and surely to be expected. What is more surprising is the fact that so many children apparently face the situation with such a matter-of-fact attitude, regarding it pretty much as an adventure. How much this is just 'front,' put on because their parents are full of courage, cannot be gauged at this time. Only the future will tell.

In the fall of 1941 the Committee on Child Development of the Division of Anthropology and Psychology of the National Research Council met to suggest programs for research during the national emergency. Among the long list of suggestions there was some discussion of research of future significance made possible by the present emergency (88). This included a suggestion by Dr. T. W. Richards that "the present period of rapidly-shifting situations for most children provides an excellent opportunity to study the effects on individual children of environmental shifts of potentially very real importance." Among these he mentioned the changes that occur in the family configuration when the father suddenly goes to military camp, then returns after a year confronted with the task of readjustment to family life.

Immediately after Pearl Harbor new issues came to the fore. Attention was centered on the problems of how parents were to handle with their children the day-by-day situations which were arising because of the war. Government agencies, national organizations, and local groups began issuing pamphlets and arranging meetings to discuss what might be termed the mental hygiene aspects of family life during war (36, 73, 87, 89, 90). Topics such as parental anxiety, fears and anxieties of children, conversations about war, effect of radio war news on children, war games, and military toys were discussed over and over again. Once in a while there was mention of the effect on children of the absence of men in their lives.

In the meantime, bulletins and letters began to arrive from the Hampstead Nurseries in England, describing and interpreting the behavior of young children under wartime conditions. These bulletins were part of the research conducted by Anna Freud and her co-workers. Their purpose was "to do research on the essential psychological needs of children; to study their reactions to bombing, destruction, and early separation from their families; to collect facts about the harmful consequences whenever their essential needs remain unsatisfied, to observe the general influence of community life at an early age in their development" (28, p. 13).

The material from Anna Freud and her co-workers emphasized the psychological effect of separation and family stress on young children's personality development. Their observations focused upon how children respond to stressful situations and how they make use of changed but supporting interpersonal relations for their own development.

The observations relating to the reaction of children to early separation from their families emphasized, as might be expected, the relations with the mother. There was, however, from time to time some discussion of the father, but for the most part such observations concerned children who had known their fathers before war separated them. In a later publication, Dr. Freud examined in some detail children's relations to dead fathers, to absent fathers, and to phantasy fathers (29, pp. 101–16). Dr. Freud emphasized the role of the father figure in the instinctual development of the Oedipus complex, a figure so essential to the development of the child that he must be created if he does not exist in reality.

Gradually the emphasis shifted in the United States as it became evident that children were less in danger of suffering from an enemy attack than from neglect at home. The slow trickle of women into industry gained momentum and the care of children of working mothers became the focus of attention. Surveys showed the increasing migration of families to war industry centers, the crowded housing conditions, the rise in the number of women working outside the home, the decreasing number of boarding homes, the inadequate number of nursery schools, the lack of recreational facilities, and the decline in standards and provisions of schools.[1] Articles in popular magazines dramatized the effects of these social conditions on children (2). Until the end of the war, the federal government, state and local governments, and private agencies worked diligently on this practical prob-

---

[1]. An example of such a survey is: Kenney, Robert W. and Phillips, John. Report of the California State Interim Committee on Economic Planning (October 1942).

lem of child care. In every state and many communities the Civilian Defense Council, the Council of Social Agencies, the public schools, and many organized groups endeavored— in spite of the seeming apathy of legislators, of local inertia, and of professional competition—to provide facilities for the physical and psychological care of children of working mothers.

During this period there were analyses of changing social conditions and their effects upon children made by many people from different disciplines. Bossard (10, Chapter 23) made an excellent review of this material during the war. The data consist mainly of (a) analysis of social statistics, (b) social surveys of conditions of families and children, (c) observations of children's behavior by teachers, social workers, and psychologists, (d) discussions of mental hygiene implications by psychiatrists and psychologists.

There seems to be no doubt from the large number of discursive articles published during the war that professionally trained people were observing children and interpreting their behavior in light of war conditions. Several analyses of clinical case study material have been published. Early in the war Davis (16) and Clifton (14) and later Igel (43) presented material from case studies of social workers to illustrate the effects of the war on children. In 1944 Gardiner and Spencer (32) reported observations of 49 children referred to clinics or juvenile courts regarding their reaction to the enlistment of father or brother in the armed services. However, there were few attempts systematically to study by scientific techniques the effects of war on children. Two exceptions to this are noteworthy. Two experimental studies were conducted during the war in an effort to understand the effect on the feelings of children of their fathers being away at war. One of these by Sears, Pintler, and Sears (70) compared the aggression in doll play of three-, four-, and five-year-old children whose fathers were away at war with a control group whose fathers were present. The other, by Bach (6), compared the father fantasies of a group of children six to ten years old whose fathers were absent at war with a control group whose fathers were present.

Postwar Adjustments

With the end of the fighting, social concern for children shifted for the most part to getting back to "normal" and building up facilities depleted of personnel and equipment during the war. There were some evidences of continuing concern with the effects of the war on children. The most ambitious study was made in Iowa by Hill and his co-workers (40). This sociological investigation through interview data from 135 families analyzed the adjustment of families to the separation and subsequent reunion of the father due to war service. These were families well established before war brought the crises of father separation. Hymes (42) brought together informal observations made during the war on children at the Kaiser Child Service Centers whose mothers were working in the shipyards. These were interpreted in the light of general principles of mental hygiene to give teachers greater insight into the war experiences of children enrolling in kindergarten and primary grades. Underwood (83) reported an investigation of the relations of twenty veteran fathers with their children but the findings were not related to the war. However, in spite of the paucity of research, there were indications in modern fiction and cartoons that we were conscious of the problems that returning veterans were having with their children (77).

Continuing Social Concern

Social concern for the problem of war and children continues. The Preparatory Commission for the International Congress on Mental Health, through the special commission on the Effect of War on Children in the United States, requested groups in the United States to prepare papers summarizing their experiences and general conclusions regarding the effect of World War II on children (92). Some nineteen or twenty reports were submitted but these have not been published. The International Congress on Mental Health held in London in August 1948, had a special section devoted to the effect of war on children which considered theoretical analyses and some clinical data (91). In December 1950, the Mid-Century White House Conference on Children and Youth again focused attention on the problems not only of the effect of World War II on children, but the possible effect of the threat of renewed hostilities (76).

It is becoming evident that war is a common aspect of social life and that it plays an increasing role in influencing the personalities of people. As Bossard (10, Chapter 23) points out, "war phenomena are almost as common and normal as peace. Almost every generation in the past has been a witness or an actor in war." As modern warfare has become more dynamic and more disorganizing, we can expect increasing effects on the lives of parents and children.

The study to be presented in this volume is essentially related to the changes in social conditions of the 1940–50 decade in the United States which we have sketched. It deals with only a small part of the major problems of war and children, but it attempts to analyze some of the influences which family conditions occasioned by war can have on the developing personalities of children.

This study also throws light on the father as an influence on the developing personality of the child. The father role in child rearing has been largely taken for granted or ignored at times when the family setting was not disturbed. War-separation with subsequent return of the father high-lights the importance of the father. This has been alluded to in studies of the effect of broken homes on delinquency. Perhaps more important in this connection are the socio-anthropological studies concerning the perception of sex roles as affected by the father's participation in the rearing of the child.

Origin of Study

Married Veterans in College

In a sense the incentive for this study originated with the subjects rather than with the investigator. Following World War II, veterans flooded the campuses of most colleges in the United States. Stanford University had its share of these veterans as students. From 382 in the fall of 1945, the enrollment of veterans reached 2,090 by the spring, doubled the next year, and by the fall of 1947 reached the peak of almost 4,500. This was followed by a steady decline, until in the spring quarter of 1950 approximately 2,800 remained. In percentage of total enrollment at Stanford, veterans ranged from a low of 11 percent of the total enrollment in the fall of 1945 to a high of 57 percent in the fall of 1946.

Unlike the usual college student who is young, unmarried, and supposedly carefree, about one-third of these students were married, many with at least one child. In addition to their college obligations they had the responsibilities and the normal anxieties which come with maturity and family obligations in middle-class culture in the United States.

Stanford Village. Stanford developed its own special housing for veterans and their families by converting a war hospital into living quarters. This is known as Stanford Village, located three miles from the campus (38). Buildings in the Village were originally erected for temporary use and are of wooden construction. The entire area, covering 127 acres, contains 27 units of housekeeping apartments, with 14 apartments in each of the long one-story units. Each apartment includes a kitchen, bathroom, and one or two bedrooms. The apartments are arranged in rows of six on each side of a unit, with one apartment at each end.

Within the area one finds a wide variety of stores and recreational facilities including grocery store, post office, general store, soda fountain, barber shop, dry cleaners, sewing room, swimming pool, tennis courts, gymnasium, nursery school, chapel, and general administrative offices and maintenance plants. There is a theater, which features Saturday morning movies for the children. The roads in the Village are paved, the grounds around the buildings are filled in with lawn and shrubs, and the area is dotted with oak trees.

At the time of this study each family living in the apartments had at least one child. Behind the apartment units there are courts enclosed by fences which provide a play area for the children living in the two apartment units whose back doors open into the same court. This space is also used as a laundry drying area. The mothers co-operate in watching each other's children during the day and often "baby sit" for each other at night. The different courts have meetings at regular intervals to talk over common problems, which often stem from the quarrels of the many children who play together in the courts.

Stanford Village opened in 1946. The number of veterans housed there varied according to the facilities available as well as the general enrollment. The married veterans with children lived in the apartments. Their number varied from 97 in 1946 to 306 in 1949. No record was kept of the number of children in these families.

Child psychology course. In the fall of 1947 a number of these veterans were enrolled in a course in child psychology, offered for upper-division and graduate students. This course required observations of individual children as part of field work. Several veterans requested permission to observe their own children. Following these observations they came in for informal interviews, presumably about their observations. It became evident, however, that their interest was predominantly personal rather than academic. These men wanted to discuss their children in relation to themselves and in relation to their war experiences. Several of these veterans continued conferences throughout the year.

Nursery school. In the meantime a nursery school had been developed at Stanford Village to serve the veterans' families, under the auspices of the Departments of Education and Psychology of the University. Later this became an integral part of the Department of Psychology, as a laboratory for training and research in child psychology. This offered opportunity for observation and study of the war-born children of veterans.

Preliminary Plans

In May 1948, an analysis of three cases was made, using the interview material given by the fathers and the observations of the children made at the nursery school (75). On the basis of these three family situations, certain hypotheses were made concerning the relations of fathers with children born while they were at war and concerning the effect of these relations on the developing personalities of the children. Plans were made for an intensive study of father-child relations in a limited number of war-separated families. Due to unavoidable administrative delays funds were not available for the study until almost a year later. The present investigation was begun in April 1949. Data were collected between April 1949 and June 1952.

General Focus of the Study

The primary focus of our investigation was upon the relations of fathers with their first children, born while the fathers were away from home in the armed services, and the effect of these relations upon the developing personalities of the children. We have compared these families with families in which there has been no separation with subsequent reunion of the father.

In a study involving interpersonal relationships, it is not possible to isolate one segment without distortion and oversimplification. Although this investigation was designed to focus upon the father-child relation, and although each segment was analyzed independently, we have endeavored also to evaluate this relationship in the total family constellation.

As we began to evaluate our material, we found that some of the patterns of behavior, which are often referred to as problems, were found in the control, non-separated group as well as in the experimental, war-separated group. Our study then not only focused on an understanding of our initial question but took on a broader, and perhaps just as important, task. Our analysis was concerned with the similarities as well as the differences in our groups. It is our purpose not only to contribute to the understanding of war-born children and the later father-child relations, but to add new information concerning those families who are seldom seen in child guidance clinics or reported in clinical case histories.

We did not plan to develop or evaluate new research techniques, but rather to adapt known techniques to our specific task. We have used interviews, observations, and projective situations for collecting data, arranged to focus on father-child relations.

In this monograph we propose (a) to present the findings regarding these families as revealed by the several techniques used, and (b) to show the interrelations of these findings within one selected individual family.

A later publication, less technical in nature, will attempt to describe and interpret the individual family constellations and indicate certain pertinent implications for mental hygiene.

General Plan of the Study

Underlying Hypotheses

From the analysis of the three preliminary cases, certain hypotheses emerged concerning the characteristics of interpersonal relations within families to which the father had returned after being absent at war during the first year of his first-born child's life. These hypotheses were used as a general basis for the development of the study. Specific hypotheses for each part of the investigation were planned as the study proceeded.

In setting up the general hypotheses which were to be used as a base line for the study, we constructed a model on the basis of our original three cases. In other words, we anticipated that the families we investigated would have similar backgrounds and on this basis made our hypotheses.

Experimental model. We anticipated that marriages of the families we would study took place in the atmosphere of war and that the early months were spent in and around training camps, with separation, due to overseas orders, imminent. It was under these circumstances that the mother became pregnant with the first child. Before the child was born, the husband left for military duty.

We anticipated that the wife returned to the home of her parents or of her husband's parents and lived in a somewhat protected environment. Allotments from her husband combined with decreased living expenses in the maternal or paternal home, and sometimes free medical care from the government, gave her a measure of financial security. She did not have over-all responsibility for housekeeping but assisted as a younger and less experienced person. Fun and recreation were limited and she had to depend more upon older people for what social life she had. She had to accept a place of immaturity, a daughter's position rather than a wife's, with demands for flexibility in adjusting to the established family pattern.

We anticipated that when the first baby (often the first grandchild) was born into this grandparent-mother home, he became the center of family life. There may have been some conflict in the child-rearing methods of two generations, but despite inconsistencies, the general atmosphere was one of indulgence by mother and grandparents. The grandfather might play an important role in the baby's life. We assumed that there was an unusually high level of identification of mother with child. With few household responsibilities and no husband to care for, the mother devoted most of her time to her child. He became, in a sense, a partial substitute for the husband, filling an emotional void in the mother's life.

Even if the mother had maintained a separate home for herself and her baby, the bond between them was certain to be extremely close. Living alone the mother may have focused most of her attention on her child; he may have been overindulged and even overstimulated by the affection he received. He certainly would become more dependent on his relations with one person. In such a mother-child home the attachment between mother and child might become even stronger than it would in the grandparents' home.

We anticipated that during the period of the husband's absence, the mother tried to keep him informed about the baby through letters and photographs and tried to teach her baby about "daddy" by featuring him in frame and story. Thus, father and child (if old enough) built concepts of each other; concepts which later had to meet the test of reality.

We anticipated that when the father left his particular theater of the war to return home, he carried with him familiar, clear images of men, machines, and discipline, in sharp contrast to his vague, distant, almost unreal feelings about his family. He came with excitement and with some trepidation. He already had premonitions about the problem of getting a job and supporting a family for the first time; he may have wondered about re-establishing relations with his wife. He looked forward eagerly to seeing his own child but he did not sense the difficulties he might encounter in assuming his role as father.

General hypotheses. With such a model as an over-all background, we posed certain general hypotheses regarding the interpersonal relations which would develop in these war-separated families after the fathers' return.

A. The father in relation to his first-born child

1. The father will have difficulty in establishing his role as a father with his first-born on his return from the war. His child will see him as an intruder and will reject his eager but awkward advances, clinging to his mother as protector and solace.

2. The father will have difficulty in understanding the child's level of development; therefore, his expectancies in routine behavior, response to commands, and ability to learn will be beyond the child's maturity.

3. The father will be deeply hurt that his child does not accept him. He may feel that the child comes between him and his wife in the period of re-establishing relations. If his wife takes the side of the child, the father may feel isolated from the family. His failures with his child will contribute to his growing sense of inadequacy.

4. To defend his ego he will see the child as too babyish, too dependent on his mother, too much indulged ("spoiled"), and in need of being disciplined.

5. Before the father has established an affectionate relation with his child and before he has been accepted as a father, he will begin disciplining the child, emphasizing prompt obedience and using methods familiar to the military services, such as commands, set rules, severe punishment.

6. As time goes on, the father will be critical of the personality of his first-born, emphasizing the first-born's weaknesses rather than his strengths. This may be related to the father's own adjustment problems.

B. The father in relation to his second-born child

1. If there is a second child born after the father's return, the father may feel that this is really his first baby since he missed the infancy of

his first-born child. He will seek from this baby the love and acceptance he missed getting from the first child.

2. Since he is with this child from birth, he will understand his level of maturity better than he did the first child's and will be able to relate his paternal requirements to the child's developmental needs.

3. He will feel his second child is easier to get along with and easier to manage. He will be more accepting of his second-born's personality, seeing his strengths more clearly than his weaknesses. He will be more closely identified with the second child.

C. The first-born in relation to his parents

1. The first-born will have difficulty in relating to his father and in feeling warm and affectionate towards him. He will not feel secure with his father and will not accept him in a protecting, reassuring, assisting role. He will feel that his father does not accept him.

2. He will have difficulty in accepting his father in a disciplinary role. He will conceive of his father as harsh and punishing. He will be afraid of his father in relation to discipline.

3. He will be unusually dependent on his mother for sympathy, reassurance, and assistance and may look to her for protection from his father.

4. He will be jealous of his father's relations with the second-born, interpreting his father's preference for the second-born as an additional rejection of him.

D. General personality characteristics of the first-born. If we assume that the experiences which the first-born had during his early years of life acted as stresses molding his personality, we would expect each first-born to react idiomatically but we would also expect certain general characteristics to be found in the behavior and personality of all first-borns.

1. The first-born will have problems in relation to organic needs (eating, elimination, sleeping) since these were the primary areas of socialization at the time the father returned.

2. He will have difficulty in relating to men outside the home since he has had difficulty in relating to his father.

3. He will have anxieties regarding his own impulses (including overt aggressive acts) which have been unaccepted by his father and regarding discipline situations. He will therefore lack spontaneity.

4. He will have strong feelings of hostility towards his father.

5. He will tend to be dependent on and demanding of women teachers and other mother substitutes because of his close, dependent relation with his mother.

6. He will have a high level of chronic tension, due to the change in expectancies, discipline, and training methods when his father returned. His tensions may make him dependent on substitute comfort patterns or may be evidenced in tics, nightmares, chewing, excess motor activities.

7. He will have difficulty in his relations with other children because the grandparent-mother home tended to isolate him from other children and because of his difficulties in familial interpersonal relations. He may relate more easily to children with whom he can assume a domineering or ascendant role (younger, less mature, weaker).

8. He will be sensitive to the feelings of other children in distress but may show this only in anxiety rather than overt behavior of helping.

Selection of Subjects

There are 19 families which constitute our experimental group. Since the sample is small, the basis of selection is important.

Selection of experimental cases. In April 1949, we proceeded to locate families living in Stanford Village who might be available for this research. Beginning with the families of children registered in the nursery school, we interviewed either father or mother to secure adequate data for selection. We had hoped to find families which might meet the following requirements:

1. Families living in Stanford Village, the father either a student or a staff member of Stanford.
2. Father separated from family during mother's pregnancy with first child; returned after first child was at least two years old.
3. Mother with her parents during father's absence.
4. Second child born since family was reunited.

Thirty-nine families were interviewed in this preliminary survey. Of these, 6 had experienced no separation and in 2 families the father had been killed overseas and the mother had remarried. Table 1 summarizes the information for the remaining 31.

Table 1. Preliminary Survey Information

Time of Father-Separation		Time of Father-Reunion			Siblings		
Child's Age	Number of Cases	Child's Age (months) 0-6	7-12	25+	None	Younger	Older
Before birth	20	11	3	6	3	12	5
0-6 mos.	7	2	2	3	—	6	1
7-12 mos.	1	—	—	1	—	—	1
13-24 mos.	1	—	—	1	—	1	—
25+ mos.	2	—	—	1	—	2	—
Total	31	13	5	12	3	21	7

This information convinced us that we must revise our requirements for inclusion in the study if we were to find families available. We therefore reduced the length of separation, made no requirements regarding mother's residence during the father's absence, and omitted the criterion of a second child born after the father's return.

The criteria finally accepted for the experimental families to be investigated were as follows:

1. That the father was a participant in the armed services during World War II.

2. That he was absent from his family during at least the first year of life of his first-born child.

3. That the father was a student or staff member at Stanford University.

4. That the family was united at the time of the study and that they were living or had lived in Stanford Village.

There were only a few families in the nursery school that met even these revised requirements, but a survey of Stanford Village families located others. After a family was located, a letter was sent to the father inviting him to participate in the study. The families were offered free tuition for their child in the nursery school or in the club group organized for older children— to recompense in some degree for the time and co-operation given by the parents and children.

A total of 27 families were located in Stanford Village who on preliminary investigation met the revised requirements for inclusion in the study. This was about 9 percent of the veteran families living in the Village at that time. Of these, 21 were included in the father-interview study. Of the remaining 6, 1 family left campus before interviews could be arranged, 2 families were not invited because of limitations of time, and 3 fathers refused to co-operate. The reason given for refusing by two fathers was that they were too busy; the third father frankly said, "This sort of thing bothers me more than the dentist."

Only the original four cases participated because of problems with their children. Four additional cases initiated contacts with the interviewer and offered to contribute to the study after it was launched because of their general interest in the investigation.

Analysis was made of the data from 19 of these 21 cases since 2 cases did not meet all criteria. After interviews were under way, it was discovered that case 3 (a preliminary case) had not been separated from his family for more than a few months at any one period, and case 6 had been separated during the second rather than the first child's infancy.

Selection of control group. The control families were selected for each substudy to match the experimental families. They met all the criteria except that of father absence. They were from the same student and staff group, living in Stanford Village. They were similar in age, education and socioeconomic background. The families were matched as to number, sex, and age of children. The control subjects in the several substudies were not always from the same families. There were in all 51 families who served as controls for the 19 experimental families. A list of experimental and control families and the data secured from each is given in Appendix 1.

The two groups differed in family life history and in personality characteristics of fathers, mothers, and children. This, of course, means that the two groups differed in many other ways than the one variable of father absence. Because of the method of selecting cases it may be assumed that these important factors in interpersonal relations within the families were to some extent randomized between the two groups. One must keep this in mind in evaluating the results of this investigation.

Sources of Data

Three sources of data were used: the fathers, the mothers, and the children. Data from the experimental fathers were secured through a series of five intensive interviews; from the control fathers, through three interviews. Data from the mothers (experimental and control) were obtained through two interviews. Data from the children (experimental and control) were obtained through observations in group situations (nursery school, kindergarten, elementary school, or club group), and through responses to five projective play interview situations.

In addition to the data from experimental and control children, data were secured from a number of siblings of the experimental and control children. These were limited because in three experimental families there was no second child and in six others the siblings were too young to yield comparable data.

Description of the Experimental Families[2]

The 19 families who are included in our primary group for study had four things in common: the men had all been in the armed services; they had been separated from their wives during the war; they had been absent during at least the first year of their first-borns' lives; they had been reunited with their wives and their first babies after the war.

These experimental families had not been separated in the sense that this term is usually used sociologically. They were neither divorced nor legally separated, nor deserted by the fathers. They were temporarily separated during the war and subsequently reunited. These are families who have stayed together in spite of stress.

War Service

The men had been in different branches of the service, 13 in the Army, 6 in the Navy. The Navy men had been on ships patrolling the Atlantic, in the dreary isolated fog of the Aleutians or "sitting it out" like "Mr. Roberts." The Army men had been in the Battle of the Bulge, slugging it out around Aachen and the Rhine, or in England for three and a half years. They set up advance signal stations in Okinawa, or made the long march across Luzon. An O.S.S. officer moved along from Egypt to Italy to Yugoslavia. Two men moved into Japan, one into Korea, two into Germany, with the Armies of Occupation. Six had been in the Air Corps of these services: pilots of bombers on missions over Germany or in the Pacific; flying against the elements off Greenland; Dumbo-flying over the Solomons and Marshall Islands.

Thirteen of them ended the war as officers, six as noncommissioned personnel. They ranged in rank from private to Captain in the Army; from seaman to Lieutenant Commander in the Navy.

The length of their service ranged from 2 years and 1 month to 6 years, with an average of 3 years, 7.3 months. The median case served 3 years, 6 months. These were men who left their families at home to fight the war abroad.

---

2. The control groups will be described in each substudy as it is presented.

Socioeconomic Background.

The general background of the families can be estimated from the occupations of the fathers of the men in the study. Table 2 shows that the occupations were distributed in all seven classifications, but about three-fourths (74 percent) were in the first four groups (3).

Table 2. Occupational Level of Fathers of War-Separated Men

	Number	%	1940 Census %
I. Professional	4	21.05	2.71
II. Semiprofessional, managerial	3	15.79	7.16
III. Clerical, skilled trades, retail business	4	21.05	14.13
IV. Farmers	3	15.79	15.26
V. Semiskilled occupations, minor clerical positions and minor business	3	15.79	23.89
VI. Slightly skilled trades and occupations requiring little training or ability	1	5.26	14.56
VII. Day laborers of all classes (including agriculture)	1	5.26	22.29
Total	19	99.99	100.00

Three of these men had spent part of their childhood in publicly-supported foster homes. Five others were probably from lower-middle-class families from their descriptions. Here is the way some of these eight men described their situations:

"Mine was a poor family. I was the fourth of seven children. My father did this and that, general odd jobs around ranches. I picked cotton at five years. My mother died when I was seven."

"Both my parents died within a week. I was five years old. I had a brother, seven, sister, three . . . My grandparents raised us. My grandfather was a letter carrier . . . They did a lot for us, all they could do."

"Just after my father died, the crash came and that put us in a bad way. I was six years old and my brother a year younger. That left my mother in a bad fix with two kids and no income . . . We lived with various relatives and finally wound up in an orphan's home."

"We lived on a small farm but my father had to do work in the village to keep us going. My parents were never more than upper-lower-class in socioeconomic status."

"I had a job when I was in high school in a drug store. That was during the depression. I made $15.00 a week. I don't know if my father was making $15.00 a week himself. But, of course, we had what he used to call a 'subsistence farm.' He had a little income; he didn't worry."

Most of the other men came from middle-class homes; only one could be judged to be well-to-do and firmly established in the upper social group. Most of the families had felt the depression of the 1930's and had been forced to "tighten the belt" accordingly. Here are a few of their descriptions:

"I come from a very modest background. My father was unstable. He was an inveterate gambler . . . He always had a good job, but we've always lived moderately simply because he gambled it away . . . My mother was always working."

"We had a big— fairly big home. It was a large family, five children . . . My father worked on the railroads for years and years, in the mechanical end of it . . . The family went through stress during the depression. We never were in poverty, never were rich either. But during the depression things were very... tight as far as money was concerned."

"My mother and father were divorced when I was very young . . . I went to live with my father's mother who had a farm . . . Then my mother married a lawyer and we went to live with them."

All but four of the men in the study found it necessary to work while they were at Stanford studying. They had a variety of jobs including night clerk at a hotel, graduate assistant, manager of a circus, psychologist at a hospital, forester, athletic coach, teacher. Two men who had gone to Stanford before the war did not need to earn additional money to support their families. Two others were full-time members of the staff of the University.

Education

Before the men entered the service all but four of them had either graduated from college or were studying in college (see Table 3). The four men did not plan to go to college until the G.I. Bill of Rights opened the doors to them. They said:

"When I got out of school I wanted to go on to college but I couldn't get a job; and the folks couldn't afford to send me and my grades weren't sufficient to get me into a state school, and anyhow, I was out of money . . . After the war I got the chance to do something I had always wanted to do— go to college."

"I had never been to college— before the war. I had worked three and a half years as a salesman. I left that job to go into defense work to evade the draft which got me later anyhow. When I went back to the sales company after the war, they said my job was not available because I had gone into defense work . . . I had many doubts about going to college— I was 25 years old— but the professors advised it after I took the exams. I did free lance work in the evening. We got along all right."

"I had the G.I. bill so I thought I might as well go to college. My wife wanted me to. Prior to that I didn't think I could go to college and support my family."

After the war, but before this study began, 12 of them went to college, 10 obtaining degrees. Two of these were men who had been undergraduates at Stanford at the time they went into the services. When our study began all but 5 were enrolled for advanced degrees at Stanford. Three were under-

Table 3. Education of War-Separated Men and Wives

Status	Men: Before War	Men: After War	Men: At Time of Study	Wives: At Time of Study
H. S. Graduate	4	—	—	10[b]
Jr. College	—	2	—	—
Undergraduate	3	—	—	1
A. B.	10	4	3[a]	7
M. A.	1	4	1[a]	1
Ph. D.	—	2	3[a]	—
Ed. D.	—	—	6[a]	—
L. L. B.	1	—	2[a]	—
M. B. A.	—	—	2[a]	—
Faculty	—	—	2	—
Total	19	12	19	19

a Candidate for degree.
b Three had some college work.

graduates who had not been able to attend college before the war. Two had completed the Ph. D. degree at other universities and were on the staff at Stanford. The 16 who were seeking or had received advanced degrees had a range of professional interests: 6 in Education; 3 in Law; 2 in Business Administration; and 1 each in Psychology, Political Science, Sociology, Chemistry, and Economics.

Their wives were all homemakers and much less ambitious for education than their husbands. Ten were high school graduates, 7 were college graduates. Only one had a higher degree, only one was studying while her husband was studying at Stanford.

Marriage

These were war marriages in the sense that they were all made when war was imminent or had been declared. The earliest was four months before Pearl Harbor, the latest, a year before V-J Day. Two men did not believe that the war had influenced their marriages in any way. The war delayed the marriage of two men who were in Naval Air Corps training and hastened it for eight couples, three of whom eloped. Seven of the marriages were definitely war marriages in every sense. The couples met while the man was away from home in the armed services, the wedding took place hurriedly and under the cloud of impending separation. All of the marriages took place in the United States and all the wives were citizens of the United States.

Both men and women were young when they were married. Only three men and three women were over 25 years old. Most of the men (84.2 percent) were between 20 years and 25 years old; most of the women (84.2 percent) were between 18 years and 24 years old.

These were new families, only two had been together longer than 18 months before the war brought about their separation. Six families had been together 6 months or less.

Table 4. Marriages of War-Separated Families

	Range	Median	Average
Date of marriage	8/41-8/44	2/43	—
Age at marriage (years)			
Men	20-34	23	—
Women	18-31	21	—
Date of family separation	1/42-7/45	1/44	—
Months between marriage and separation	2-33	11	11.5
Months between separation and reunion	13-42	22	23.4

War Separation

The median family, which had been established for only 11 months, was separated by the war for 22 months. The shortest separation period was 13 months; the longest, 3 1/2 years. At the time of the reunion after the war, all but 3 of these families had been separated longer than they had been together. The length of this discrepancy varied from one familiy that had been united 2 years longer than they were separated to two families separated 40 to 41 months longer than they had been together. The median family was separated 14 months longer than they had been together; the average was 12.4 months longer.

In some cases there had been contact with the husband during the separation period. Two wives joined their husbands for short periods at a camp. Five husbands had short leaves with their wives. One father saw his wife for an hour on a hospital train; another was visited by his wife during a prolonged period of hospitalization. Three of the second-born children were conceived during such brief reunions.

Children

All but 3 of the first-born children were conceived while the wives were near training centers, camps, or ports to be close to their husbands. Twelve of the babies seem to have been planned, 5 were accidental, 1 was not planned but no prevention was taken, and for 1 there were conflicting reports.

Thirteen were born in the maternal home and 4 in the paternal home. There were only 6 girls among these first-borns.

The first child was born in these families from 10 to 31 months after marriage, all but two within 2 years. The median family had its first child within 16 months after marriage: over a third, within the first year.

When the families were reunited the children were between 10 and 33 months old; the average, 18 months old. Fourteen of the children were between 1 year and 2–1/2 years old.

Table 5. Description of Children of War-Separated Families

	Range	Median	Average
Months between marriage and birth of first-born	10-31	16	16.8
Age of first-born at reunion (months)	11-33	16	18.0
Months between reunion and birth of second-born	3-44	15	16.7

The second-born child was in most families born soon after the father's return. Of the 16 families who had a second child, 11 were born within 18 months; only 3 delayed 2-1/2 years or longer. Half of the second-borns were boys and half girls.

Five families had three children each. Four of these had all boys, one had all girls. The family constellations regarding sex of children were quite different (Table 6) and represented eight different combinations.

Table 6. Number and Sex of Children in War-Separated Families

	First M, Second F	First F, Second M	1M	2M	3M	1F	2F	3F
Number of Families	5	2	1	2	4	2	2	1

Living Conditions

Like most young families in the decade of the forties, these families had been on the move. Between marriage and war separation, all but one couple had lived in more than one place. Seventeen of the wives had followed their husbands to training centers and camps or had gone from port to port hoping the men might come in. They lived in an average of 2.7 places, the most itinerant near 7 different camps. But with their husbands overseas the wives settled down, 14 with their own fathers and mothers, 4 with their husbands' families, 1 in a port where her husband expected to return.

There was a period after the war when these new families were unsettled and moved about before they came to the temporary security of Stanford Village. Sixteen stayed for a while in the home where the wives had been while the husband was away. This was with the wife's family in 13 cases; with the husband's family in 2 cases; in the wife's temporary home in 1 case. One wife joined her husband overseas. Altogether they made an average of 4 moves but this average was weighted by one family that changed its place of living 13 times.

Age

At the time of the first interview the men ranged in age from 26 years to 40 years; 84.2 percent of the cases were between 26 and 33 years. Their wives were slightly younger, ranging in age from 24 years to 35 years; 79 percent of the cases were between 24 and 30 years. The median age for men was 29 years; for wives, 28 years.

Table 7. Ages of War-Separated Husbands and Wives

	Ages (years)					
	Husband			Wife		
	Range	Median	Average	Range	Median	Average
At marriage	20-34	23	23.7	18-31	21	21.9
At first interview with father	26-40	29	29.0	24-35	28	28.2

Comparison of Experimental Families with Model

In many respects the 19 experimental families were similar to the model on which we based our hypotheses. As has been shown, the marriages were all made in the atmosphere of war and the wives lived near training camps for the months preceding separation. It was in such situations that the first children were conceived. All but one of the wives lived in their own or their husbands' parental home during most of the time the husband was overseas, and the grandparents shared the responsibility of caring for the child.

The baby became the center of family life in each of these families, but in two he shared honors with a young cousin whose father was overseas. There seemed to be only three families in which there were strong disagreements between the grandparents and the mother regarding how the baby should be reared. Three who lived with parents of the husband reported that the grandparents had tried consciously not to interfere even when they disagreed with the methods the young mother was using. In each of the 19 families the mother or father or both testified to the strong bond that was established between the mother and her first-born while she was separated from her husband.

Each family also told of the letters and photographs sent daily or weekly to the absent father describing at first the progressions of pregnancy and later the sequences in the development of the baby. Every father reported that he was pleased and happy to get these reports, but the men who were in active duty at the front stated that it all seemed far away and remote from their lives.

In each case the mother tried to help her baby to understand about "Daddy," to learn to recognize his photograph, and to learn as soon as possible to say the magic word "da-da."

In these ways the experimental group closely resembled the model we had used in setting up the original hypotheses for the research project.

PART I. THE FATHER-INTERVIEW STUDY

CHAPTER 2.
DESCRIPTION OF THE FATHER-INTERVIEW STUDY

Purpose

The father-interview study was the basic study of this project. Our purpose was to gain information regarding the father's relation with his first child born during the war while the father was overseas serving in one of the armed services. Specifically, we wished to investigate (a) the areas of stress to which these returning veterans had to work out adjustment patterns, (b) the attitude of the father towards his first-born in significant areas of development, (c) the father-child relation as revealed by comparison of self- and child-perception.

Method of Collecting Data

In the preliminary cases several methods were explored for collecting data. At first, the father discussed freely and the interviewer made notes following the conference. Later, the interviewer wrote notes in longhand during the conference, transcribing them within a week. Two fathers tried writing their experiences. This proved a useful technique for obtaining straight factual data, but the censor was at work to keep out emotionally-toned material and there was a general tendency for the father to be brief, leaving out details which were meaningful. The written reports were then used as a basis for discussion with the father and thus were supplemented with data involving the father's feelings and attitudes.

Interview technique. On the basis of these experiences we decided to use an interview technique which was structured in broad areas but which left the father free to talk about his experiences and his feelings in his own idiomatic way.

Using the material from the preliminary cases as background, we developed an outline of the areas of discussion which we considered might be important in giving insight into the problem of father-child relations which we were studying.[1] The general areas included: (1) before-marriage history of father, (2) courtship, (3) marriage, (4) early marriage period, (5) pregnancy of wife, (6) birth of child, (7) father's early relation with child, (8) father's present relation with child, (9) the second child.

The outline was used as a guide for the interviewer. The father did not see the outline. He was not required to follow the items in any sequence but allowed to use his own structure and associations in talking with the interviewer. Following each conference, items were checked on the outline which had been discussed. On the basis of the material given, tentative plans were made for the areas which might be most fruitful for discussion at the next meeting. Each father was given an opportunity to discuss

---

1. The outline in detail is given in Appendix 2. Item Ia, before-marriage history of the wife, was not originally in the outline but was added because the fathers discussed it.

all nine areas. There was no attempt made to have each father discuss every specific item in the outline; rather, it was used as a general framework within which the father might be led to explore.

In addition to the areas in the general outline, the war-separated fathers were asked to tell about their war service and to discuss several specific questions relating to war experiences which seemed particularly pertinent to our investigation. These questions were asked in the final interview. They are listed at the end of the interview outline in Appendix 2. They are formulated to explore the following areas: extramarital experiences of the father during separation from his wife; the father's general feeling about the effect of the war on himself, on his relations with his wife, on his relations with his first-born, and on his relations with his second-born; the father's general appraisal of the strength and weakness of the character structure of the first-born. If any of these areas had been discussed in previous sessions, the questions were not asked in the final session.

Length and spacing of interviews. For the war-separated fathers we decided to have five interviews of one hour each, spaced a week apart, as a feasible, general plan. Most men would be able to give this much time and could give us the material we planned to cover in that time. For some it might be necessary to have more time; less voluble or fast talkers might take less.

The one-week interval was extended when obligations, illness, or vacations interfered. One father completed his conferences in ten days because he was leaving Stanford for a new job. In general, a week's interim seemed maximum; otherwise the men had to be reminded about the previous meeting and a warming-up period was necessary.

The one-hour limitation was often transgressed, sometimes because classes cut it short, sometimes because the men continued to talk after the signal had been given and they had started to leave. Those who have had experience will not be surprised that some of the most valuable material was given at just such times.

The non-separated fathers in the control group were given only three interviews each. This was done for two reasons. First, we had spent the greater part of two interviews with the experimental fathers discussing their war experiences and the immediate adjustment problems on return to the family. These discussions were not necessary with the control fathers who had not been separated from their families. Second, we had limitations imposed by time and money and because of these decided to eliminate any prolonged discussions of war experiences with the control fathers. This we regretted at the time and subsequently. The interview outline as planned was used to guide the control interviews in the same manner as the experimental.

Interview situation. Part of the interviews were conducted in the soundproof consulting room in the psychological wing connected with the nursery school in Stanford Village. It had an entrance which could be reached directly from the out-of-doors as well as a door connecting with the rest of the unit. This made it possible for fathers to be scheduled in series without coming in contact with each other. This seemed important in order to disguise as far as possible the identity of the participants. When it was more convenient for the father, the interviews were held in the interviewer's office at the University. In either case, two comfortable chairs, a desk, a small stand for ash tray, and carpet on the floor constituted the main furnishings. The office was somewhat more homelike than the consulting room, with books, curtains, and other office furnishings.

Recording. The interviews of the first eight war-separated fathers were recorded in longhand by the interviewer and subsequently transcribed. Beginning with case E9 an electric recording machine was available. The machine was put on the desk where the interviewer could operate it with a minimum of interruption to the conference. The two-way conference microphone was placed between the interviewer and the father. Most of the men were interested in the mechanism and it helped to make the first interview more informal and relaxed. The mechanical recording freed the interviewer to follow the discussion and to guide it into areas important for the study. It freed the father from the self-consciousness which often comes when someone is making notes. If the father continued talking after the Audograph had been turned off, the interviewer dictated a summary of this conversation onto the record after the father left. The records were typed by an assistant and edited by the interviewer before the next interview was scheduled.[2]

Methods of conducting the interviews. In every case except one, the interviewer had met the father before the first interview took place or had talked with him over the telephone to discuss the study and to plan the series of appointments. At the beginning of the first interview, however, the father was told about the purpose of the research, the confidential nature of the material, and the provisions for anonymity of the records. These included such precautions as: (1) no name to be put on audograph record, only case number; (2) no name to be put on typed records; (3) all identifying material to be disguised in any manuscript or publication.

Because of a question by one of the fathers early in the research program, each father was told that interviews with his wife would be with another person who would not have access to the material in the father's interviews. This seemed an important reassurance to most of the men.

The Audograph was explained and demonstrated. No father objected to the use of the recording machine; most of them displayed interest and seemed to enjoy having it used.

Following this, often the father would say, "Well, where shall I begin?" With a war-separated father, he was told something to this effect: "Suppose you begin by telling me something about your war experiences—when you went in, what you did, when you were separated from the services." With the non-separated father, the interviewer usually said: "Suppose you tell me about your family, how many children you have and what they are like." These seemed easy, natural beginnings for the men. It gave both the father

---

2. The machine used was a Gray Audograph, manufactured by Gray Mfg. Co., Hartford, Conn. This machine records thirty minutes on each side of the record. The record can be turned at the end of thirty minutes very easily and without much interruption to the flow of talk. A time indicator on the machine helped the interviewer to give warning and prepare for termination of the conference.

and interviewer a chance to get acquainted. It gave the men an opportunity to talk about something which was important and which they felt would be respected.

In general, it was planned that the five sessions for the war-separated men would be devoted to the following topics, though not necessarily in this order: (1) father's war experiences; (2) the first-born child; (3) father's life history; (4) the second-born child; (5) general questions relative to war and family. The three sessions with the non-separated men omitted the first and last topic.

As a rule, the interviewer did not ask direct, specific questions, but rather opened up areas for discussion by statements such as, "Tell me something about your father," or "Well, what about your second baby? I'd like to know about her, too." The father was allowed to talk as much as he wanted, with sometimes a comment from the interviewer to make the situation easy and natural. Every effort was made not to interrupt the course of the father's thinking, even to ask for specific data. Notes were jotted down and such questions were usually asked later. When the father finished what he had to say on any topic, a few specific questions might be asked or a new area opened up.

This method, structuralizing in general areas but allowing each father freedom to develop it in his own way, worked extremely well with these mature men. They thought the study important, they liked to talk and be listened to, they enjoyed the process of remembering and to some extent reliving experiences that had such meaning to them.

Interviewers. All the interviews with the war-separated fathers were conducted by L. M. Stolz. Originally, it had been planned that the same person would interview the non-separated fathers; however, as the project expanded this had to be abandoned because of limitations of time. The non-separated fathers were interviewed by E. Chance. We recognized the possiblities of error that this change in plans entailed; we believe that we have kept them to a minimum.

Both interviewers were women, both had previous experience in working with fathers in a consulting capacity. Both interviewers had already had considerable experience in using the semistructured interview technique. The second interviewer after preliminary instruction conducted three interviews with a practice case whose records were not used in the study. Following each session, Interviewer I checked the technique and discussed it with Interviewer II. This type of supervisoni was continued following each session with the first three control cases. There were no important differences in technique which could be discerned from the electrically recorded protocols of these three cases, so supervision was discontinued.

Description of the Subjects

There were 38 men in the father-interview study. The experimental group was composed of 19 men who had been separated from their wives because of the war before their first baby was born and subsequently reunited with their family when the baby was at least a year old. The control group was composed of 19 men who had not been separated from their families. The experimental families are described in Chapter 1.

The non-separated group was selected on the basis of the same criteria as the war-separated group (Chapter 1, p. 10) except that the fathers had not been separated from their families. They were matched with the war-separated group in socioeconomic status, number, age, and sex of children. We found as much difficulty in locating fathers who had not been separated from their families as we had found in locating fathers who had been separated until their first-born was at least a year old. It seems that the generation of young men who were in World War II were likely to have short absences from their families interspersed with reunions. They came home on leave, or their wives met them at ports or joined them at a camp. Most of the control fathers like the war-separated fathers were found through contacts with the Stanford Village Nursery School or through other local nursery schools.

In the non-separated group, 23 men were approached— in comparison with the 27 war-separated fathers who had been approached. Two of the non-separated fathers refused to co-operate because of pressure of work. Two had to be dropped after interviews had been initiated because it was found that they did not meet the criteria of selection.

All but three of the non-separated fathers were, like the war-separated fathers, either in college preparing for a profession or members of a profession (see Chapter 1). The three subjects who do not fall into this occupational category were two salesmen (both college graduates) and one technician. Actually, before the data were analyzed there was one man in the war-separated group who dropped out of college to become a technician and two who went into business following the award of the AB degree. The two groups were, therefore, quite similar as to occupational category.

In terms of aspirations, standards of living, and mores, all subjects can be said to come from a homogeneous group. Table 8 gives data concerning the fathers' age range, length of marriage, the duration of the fathers' absence on war service, and the age and sex distribution of the children for the subject-families.

Table 8. Description of Subjects of Father-Interview Study

	War-Separated Group		Non-Separated Group	
Fathers	Range	Median	Range	Median
Age at interview	26-40 yrs.	29 yrs.	31-53 yrs.	34 yrs.
Date of marriage	1941-1944	1943	1936-1948	1943
Age at marriage	20-34 yrs.	23 yrs.	21-47 yrs.	24 yrs.
Years between marriage and birth of first child	.83-2.5 yrs.	1.3 yrs.	1-7 yrs.	3 yrs.
Years in the armed services during World War II[a]	2-6 yrs.	3.5 yrs.	1-5 yrs.	3 yrs.

[a]Thirteen of the non-separated fathers served in the armed forces during World War II.

It can be seen from Table 8 that the non-separated group of fathers was somewhat older than the war-separated group. Although the median year of marriage is the same for the two groups, the non-separated fathers had a wider range. Three of the war-separated men were married just prior to Pearl Harbor, the others during the war; in the non-separated group two were married several years before the war, one a half year before Pearl Harbor, ten during the war, and six after the close of the war.

Whereas all of the war-separated group had been in the armed services during World War II, 2 of the control group had medical exemption from war service. Thirteen of the control group had been overseas in the armed services, 3 had been civilian employees of the armed services (2 overseas), and 1 had seen arduous duty in the Merchant Marine. In general, the war service of these 17 controls seemed similar to that of the experimental group (see Chapter 1).

The non-separated families had waited twice as long for their first child to be born. The 15 control families in which the man had served overseas in the armed forces during World War II had their first child after the father was reunited with his wife.

The Data Collected

Amount. The 19 protocols of the war-separated fathers represent a minimum of 95 hours of interview; the 19 protocols of the non-separated fathers represent a minimum of 57 hours of interview; a total of 152 hours.

There were differences in the amount of material in each case record. In the father-separated group comparisons can be made between the 12 cases electrically recorded. The least amount of material was 59 double-spaced typewritten pages in the protocol of Mr. Holman and the greatest was 156 pages in that of Mr. Wagner. The average protocol contained 93.4 pages (Table 9). The amount of material varied for each case in the five interviews. There was a tendency for the amount of material to increase through the fourth interview and to decrease in the fifth. The last three interviews found the fathers more voluble than the first two, probably an indication of increasing relation and perhaps due to increasing facility in recalling events and feelings of the past.

Table 9. Average Length of Father Interviews

	Number of Pages	
Interview	War-Separated Group[a]	Non-Separated Group[a]
I	17.2	21.3
II	16.6	20.1
III	18.5	18.2
IV	21.7	—
V	19.4	—
Total	93.4	59.6

[a] On the basis of the electrically recorded cases: 12 for war-separated group; 19 for non-separated group.

The protocols of the non-separated fathers are not as long since they represent only three interviews each. The average number of pages in each protocol was 59.6 pages. The averages of the non-separated fathers

Decisions Relative to Vocations

The initial stress of which these men seemed most acutely conscious concerned what they were going to do, what vocation they would follow. They felt this long before they returned. They thought about it overseas and on the return voyage were anxious about the imminent problems. These were young men who had not yet found their places in life. Their careers for the most part had not been interrupted but rather had been postponed. They were faced not only with finding a job but primarily with deciding what to do.

Types of Vocational Adjustment

Immediate peacetime jobs. There were two men who immediately received temporary civilian jobs related to the military work they had been doing during the war. This seemed to have some advantages in giving the men a feeling of adequacy while they were tackling other problems of adjustment within the family. For one man the job lasted several years and decided his future program for an advanced degree. For the other it was a short interim before continuing his work for the Ph. D. which the war had interrupted. But these men felt the pressures of vocational adjustment in civilian life, too, for different reasons each receiving a rating of 2 on a 3-point rating scale for anxiety associated with postwar vocational adjustments. Mr. Burgman was uneasy about his future. He said, "My wife had more confidence in me than I had felt in myself. That bothered me. I was afraid my wife might be disappointed." The other man, who showed definite signs of stress as he talked, said, "I fell into a job with considerable responsibility and I didn't have either the years or the training for the job. I felt, oh, well, just a bit insecure. And so I continued to pour quite a heavy amount of time and energy on the job and I think that contributed to the fact that I didn't participate as wholly as a father as I do now" (Mr. Harlow).

College expected. For six other men, returning to college to finish the education which the war had interrupted seemed expected by everyone, but five were faced with deciding what they should major in, one with what college to go to, and all were concerned with the financial difficulties involved. Mr. Marston and Mr. Wagner, quoted below, each received ratings of 2 on the anxiety scale; Mr. Holman received the extreme (high) rating of 3.

"I was very anxious to get back and to get into my training here. I had been associated with men who were older and the majority of them had their AB degrees. I had two years of college before I went in the service and I was very inexperienced about things. In the service I got to think like an older man and yet there was a sort of a gap. I wanted to get back and get that filled in! And more or less be a man rather than a boy. . ." (Mr. Marston).

"Perhaps if I'd been a little younger and I had a little more drive and hadn't been tied quite so much with the family, I would have tried to push the thing I was interested in (Ph. D. in physics) . . . There was nobody to advise me, nobody to see what I really wanted, and I just happened to miss it" (Mr. Wagner).

	Eating	Sleeping	Elimination
E1's	4.4	4.1	4.6
C1's	2.7	3.1	2.7
E1's vs. C1's, eating	t = 3.8	df = 19	P<.01
E1's vs. C1's, sleeping	t = 4.2	df = 19	P<.01
E1's vs. C1's, elimination	t = 2.2	df = 19	P<.05

play well with others. Fewer children in the E1 group were successful in playing with children than in the C1 group. All but one of the C2 children were reported as playing well with others, as were all but two of their older siblings.

Table 65. Means, t and P Values on Relations with Children

E1 vs. C1 $t = 2.2$, $df = 19$, $P < .05$
E1 vs. E2 $t = 1.8$, $df = 9$, P not significant at .05

More war-separated first-born children preferred to play alone than did children in any other group. Only four children in that group enjoyed playing with others much of the time. The eight first-born children in the war-separated group who preferred to play alone enjoyed books, crayons, paper dolls, erector sets, blocks, and collecting things more than they enjoyed play with children.

Children's Relations with Their Parents

The area of parent-child relations was clearly the most difficult area for mothers to discuss in their interviews. It was particularly difficult for them to express their feelings about the father-child relation when it was not a close one. Mothers were somewhat apprehensive about describing a relation which might show their husband in a poor light. It was difficult for mothers also to verbalize the ambivalences in father-child relations. These ambivalences in feelings were often extreme between the war-separated first-born children and their fathers. The picture which the mother presented of the father-child relation vacillated between a realistic presentation of the relation as she saw it, and an attempt to protect the family group by presenting the culturally approved picture of a close father-child relation. After describing a very distant father-child relation, mothers often felt they had to compensate and say something quite favorable. A section from one mother-interview shows a characteristic difficulty of describing an ambivalent father-child relation.

Q: Was there ever a particular adult whom she disliked?
"Well, I shouldn't say 'disliked,' but she's never been on too good terms with her father actually."
Q: It's hard for her to make a good, strong bond with him?
"Yes, it is. And right now she doesn't like anything to do with boys or men. She says she doesn't, anyway. I don't know whether she's getting into that stage already, but . . . Really, that wasn't the thing to say about her father. It isn't . . . She's crazy about him, but she isn't sure of him, and . . ."
Q: Is that something that has come up at certain periods or has it been true all through their relation?

seem to indicate that they talked less in each succeeding interview but only three cases followed this trend. For most cases the amount of material during the first two interviews was quite similar.

Content. One of the questions which immediately arises is whether the minimum-structured interview technique would yield comparable data from the several participants. As one preliminary test we analyzed the protocols according to the areas listed in the interview plan (see Appendix 2), tabulating only whether the area was discussed no matter whether briefly or at length, once or several times, generally or in great detail, with slight interest or with deep overtones of feeling. The analysis is shown in Table 10.

Table 10. Areas Discussed in Father Interviews

	War-Separated		Non-Separated	
	Number of Cases	Range of Subtopics[a]	Number of Cases	Range of Subtopics[a]
I. Before-marriage history of father	19	12-19	19	16-19
Ia. Before-marriage history of wife	18	3-18	16	12-16
II. Courtship	18	11-18	16	14-16
III. Marriage	19	15-18	19	16-19
IV. Early marriage period	19	8-19	17	12-17
V. Pregnancy of wife	19	11-17	18	12-18
VI. Birth of child	19	9-16	19	17-19
VII. Between birth and father's return	19	14-19	—	—
VIII. Father's return	19	17-19	—	—
IX. Father's early relation with child	19	13-19	19	19
X. Present relation with child	19	16-19	19	13-19
XI. Second child	16[b]	16[b]	16[b]	12-16
XII. General war questions	19	12-19	—	—

[a] Subtopics A, B, C, etc. In Outline, Appendix 2.

[b] Three families did not have a second child.

It can be readily seen that in the general areas, data were secured from all the war-separated fathers except one. There were four areas which were not discussed by all non-separated fathers. The areas of courtship, early marriage period, and pregnancy of wife were not considered as important for our study as other areas and the interviewer did not suggest these if time was getting short.

The area designated as Ia in Table 10 (Before-marriage history of wife) had not been included in the original outline, but since all but one experimental and three control fathers discussed this, it is reported here. However, the fathers varied in the subtopics under each area which they discussed. The greatest variation was in discussing the before-marriage history of the wife. Here, all but four fathers (one experimental, three controls) discussed his wife's family but only three experimentals had anything to say about her relations with peers. All but one of the fathers had something to say about the period of the wife's pregnancy with the first child, but only 25 mentioned the condition of the mother, and 29 discussed the anxieties (or lack of them) which they had experienced.

Although the relatively unstructured interview did not bring material from the fathers equally in each subtopic of the outline guide, the data were considered adequate for the analyses which we planned to make.

Analysis of Data

Our purpose in analyzing the data has been to gain from the material given by the fathers greater insight into the relations of fathers with the children who were born while they were at war. We wished to use the data from the fathers who had not been separated from their families as a base line for comparison. We have made three analyses. First, we have studied the areas of stress in the environments of war-separated men after the war when they returned to their families and made their first adjustments to their unknown child. Second, we have analyzed the attitudes of the fathers towards their first-borns in significant areas of development. Third, we have studied the father-child relations as revealed in each father's perception of self and of his first-born.

CHAPTER 3.
STRESS AREAS FOR FATHERS RETURNING FROM WAR

When the fathers in this study returned from war and were reunited with their families, they entered into what might be called an orientation period during which they had to work out adjustment patterns to a constellation of stresses peculiar to their situation. The problems they had to face can be grouped into three categories which relate to (1) selecting a vocation, (2) assuming the role of husband, and (3) assuming the new role of father.

Adjustments in relation to vocation were required of most married young men when they were separated from the armed services at war's end. Those who returned to their wives found that the reassumption of the role of husband made demands for adjustment. Only those, however, who were united with a first baby born while they were overseas had the complete constellation of stresses which our experimental group of fathers met on their return. The situation demanded that each accept obligation for his family, decide what occupation he was going to enter, renew his relations with his wife, and learn to live not only with his wife but also with a child, a child of his own for whose welfare he was responsible but of whom he had little acquaintance or understanding.

These areas were interacting, and difficulties in any one were likely to affect adjustments in the others. This interacting relation was felt by the fathers and was expressed in what might be called their adjustments to assuming the role of head of a family.

Adjustment to Being Head of a Family

The fact of having a family and being at the head of it became a reality to these men when they returned from war. There were only two families that had been married longer than 18 months before separation. In no case had the husband completely supported his wife economically, for either the wife had worked or the armed services had, from the beginning of marriage, provided compensation and special services. The returning veteran was somewhat suddenly precipitated into the role of being economically responsible not only for his wife and himself, but for his first child, born while he was at war. The men in this study were conscious of this as they returned and, in varying degrees, anxious about their competencies to fulfill this role. The following excerpts illustrate how they felt[1]:

"I went through a period of wondering whether I could live up to the responsibilities of a husband. I hadn't made a go of it overseas— I wondered what it would be like when I got back to civilian life" (Mr. Marston).

"At the beginning I was trying to establish myself as head of the family. I was anxious to get status in my own right . . . I probably overcompensated in trying to establish my role as breadwinner too soon" (Mr. Arnold).

"I had a period of adjusting as far as assuming responsibility was concerned. I hadn't had to worry about paying bills. The service took care of that. That was the first thing that hit me. It was pretty hard" (Mr. Wolf).

---

[1]. All names of subjects are pseudonyms throughout this monograph.

Decisions Relative to Vocations

The initial stress of which these men seemed most acutely conscious concerned what they were going to do, what vocation they would follow. They felt this long before they returned. They thought about it overseas and on the return voyage were anxious about the imminent problems. These were young men who had not yet found their places in life. Their careers for the most part had not been interrupted but rather had been postponed. They were faced not only with finding a job but primarily with deciding what to do.

Types of Vocational Adjustment

Immediate peacetime jobs. There were two men who immediately received temporary civilian jobs related to the military work they had been doing during the war. This seemed to have some advantages in giving the men a feeling of adequacy while they were tackling other problems of adjustment within the family. For one man the job lasted several years and decided his future program for an advanced degree. For the other it was a short interim before continuing his work for the Ph. D. which the war had interrupted. But these men felt the pressures of vocational adjustment in civilian life, too, for different reasons each receiving a rating of 2 on a 3-point rating scale for anxiety associated with postwar vocational adjustments. Mr. Burgman was uneasy about his future. He said, "My wife had more confidence in me than I had felt in myself. That bothered me. I was afraid my wife might be disappointed." The other man, who showed definite signs of stress as he talked, said, "I fell into a job with considerable responsibility and I didn't have either the years or the training for the job. I felt, oh, well, just a bit insecure. And so I continued to pour quite a heavy amount of time and energy on the job and I think that contributed to the fact that I didn't participate as wholly as a father as I do now" (Mr. Harlow).

College expected. For six other men, returning to college to finish the education which the war had interrupted seemed expected by everyone, but five were faced with deciding what they should major in, one with what college to go to, and all were concerned with the financial difficulties involved. Mr. Marston and Mr. Wagner, quoted below, each received ratings of 2 on the anxiety scale; Mr. Holman received the extreme (high) rating of 3.

> "I was very anxious to get back and to get into my training here. I had been associated with men who were older and the majority of them had their AB degrees. I had two years of college before I went in the service and I was very inexperienced about things. In the service I got to think like an older man and yet there was a sort of a gap. I wanted to get back and get that filled in! And more or less be a man rather than a boy. . ." (Mr. Marston).
>
> "Perhaps if I'd been a little younger and I had a little more drive and hadn't been tied quite so much with the family, I would have tried to push the thing I was interested in (Ph. D. in physics) . . . There was nobody to advise me, nobody to see what I really wanted, and I just happened to miss it" (Mr. Wagner).

"I went in the service with a vague idea, without knowing what getting a Ph.D. involved, of getting a Ph.D. after the war . . . My main concern on coming back was probably getting started in school. Concerned with how we'd finance school . . . I felt the terrific responsibility—going to school—overwhelming" (Mr. Holman).

Complicated decisions. The remaining 11 men had decisions to make which were even more complicated. In the process of coming to a decision each man not only had to make up his mind what he wanted to do himself and how he could support his family, but he had the difficult process of working out a decision that was acceptable to his wife as well. Sometimes both his own family and his wife's family brought pressure upon him and not always in the same direction. The men quoted below received the most extreme rating of 3 on the anxiety scale.

"The worst effect the war had on me, it chopped me out of four years—it put me behind in age. I'll be 31 when I get out of school and people will say, 'We don't want this old man around here.' And it's cut me out of a lot of other jobs, too. Most airlines chop you off at 26, 29—that's what I wanted to do, fly airlines . . . but I was too old . . . My wife and I had it a lot rougher after the war than during the war, I think . . . As soon as the war's over you've got just as many blocks as you ever had. You still gotta get a job and grub like the devil and work like the dickens and maybe then you don't get everything you want. And you change jobs a dozen times and then end up in business school" (Mr. Osborne).

"I had hoped of going back to school even before I got out of the services. I wanted to go right into industry, but decided I'd have to have some college first. But looking for a job was a sad disillusionment. (Long pause.) My wife wasn't interested in my going to college. I think she'd rather I got a job than go to college, especially when G.I. checks don't come in for a couple of months, like now" (Mr. Wolf).

"During the war I would wonder what I was going to do after this was over . . . The only pleasant memories I had were working on the road for my father-in-law. It seemed such a contrast to the Army life . . . I mean, that's as far as your thinking went. That ended all the problems; there wasn't anything after that. When you come home you see it's all different from that; the problems go right on when the war's over and the responsibility for wife and child grows. After a season on the road the whole character of the job changed. I hated to disappoint my father-in-law—going to school was the only way I could get out of it. And I always wanted to go to school but I felt too old for it. I knew it would be a sacrifice for my wife and Patricia for I wouldn't get much money. But my wife was willing and eager for me to go" (Mr. Irwin).

Three men toyed with the idea of remaining in military service where they had won social and economic status beyond previous levels and where the security offered seemed a simple and easy way to solve a difficult problem. The men quoted below received the most extreme rating (3) on anxiety.

"I was reluctant to return to civilian life. I felt those who had returned earlier would have a head start and it would be difficult for me to receive the type of employment and get the job I wanted. I was in favor of staying in the service. I had status, made good money. I hesitated some time. I was interested in establishing a home and enjoying my family. My wife was in favor of my staying in but she really didn't realize what it would mean to be a Marine officer's wife'' (Mr. Arnold).

''I was feeling temporary and uncertain about the whole thing . . . I had many decisions to make— whether to stay in the services for three years and later go to college comfortably or to go to school now . . . The service was easy; school was hard . . . My wife said she'd divorce me if I stayed in the service. I was tempted by the easy life and high income. I'd never had as much money'' (Mr. Mathews).

Comparison with Non-Separated Group in Vocational Adjustment

As we expected, the fathers who had not been separated from their families had to make vocational adjustments after the war, too. An analysis indicates that the types of situations they encountered were very similar to those of the war-separated group (see Table 11).

Table 11. Vocational Adjustment of Men After the War

	War-Separated	Non-Separated
War work led into peacetime job	2	4
Return to college expected	6	4
Complicated adjustment	11	11

Anxiety related to vocational adjustment. However, there seems to have been a genuine difference in the degree of anxiety which the two groups experienced in connection with these adjustments. The men who on returning from overseas had a baby as well as a wife to support indicate tension and uncertainty as they discuss their vocational adjustment. They use such phrases as ''felt insecure,'' ''lacked self-confidence,'' ''nobody to advise me,'' ''felt the terrific responsibility overwhelming,'' ''a lot rougher after the war,'' ''distraught,'' ''sad disillusionment,'' ''concerned about all the problems and responsibilities I had to face,'' ''problem deciding to go to school with wife and child,'' ''reluctant to return to civilian life,'' ''feeling temporary and uncertain.'' The non-separated fathers gave much less evidence of anxiety in relation to their vocational adjustments. They seemed to be able to make the adjustment to civilian life not without meeting some problems, but with greater feelings of adequacy to meet them. With three exceptions, they did not seem to feel overwhelmed by the situation they faced. We rated the war-separated and the non-separated fathers on a three-point scale regarding the degree of anxiety they experienced in relation to vocational adjustments after the war as they reported it. Using the method of chi square, we found a statistically significant difference between the two groups, with the war-separated group having greater anxiety: chi square equals 11.42, $P < .01$.

Summary of Vocational Adjustments

For the men in this study, the selection of a vocation was an area of primary adjustment after the war which took immediate precedence over other areas of life. It was involved with the problem of supporting their families, with the desire to meet up with the expectations of their wives as well as with the fulfillment in some measure of their own hopes and aspirations. The fact that the war-separated group showed greater anxiety than the non-separated group was probably due to their added responsibilities in providing for a child as well as a wife.

Adjustments with the Wife

The second area of stress for the returning veteran who had been separated from his family related to adjustments with his wife.[1] Even the man who had been married longest before separation felt anxious about this as the time of reunion approached. The adjustments included re-establishing love relations and sexual intimacy, working out routine ways of living together, acceptance of wife's family, and differences in methods of child rearing (see Table 12). This last was an area of adjustment which the non-separated group did not have to face.

Table 12. Adjustments with Wife of War-Separated Men

Areas	Problems	
	No	Yes
Love relations	12	7
Routines of living together	—	3
Wife's family	3	16
Methods of child rearing	—	19

Re-establishing Love Relations

Easy adjustments. Two-thirds of the men felt that although they had been apprehensive about their love realtions before they returned, the reunion went remarkably well and relatively quickly (Table 12). None of these 12 men acknowledged any extramarital relations during the war (see Table 13).

One father gave the war credit for having salvaged his marriage. He said that his marriage was about to go on the rocks when the war came; he had made a mess of it but he hadn't realized it until his wife wrote to him. He felt that they never could have talked about the things they wrote about, especially in the sexual area, and, therefore, their letters back and forth paved the way for their readjustment after he returned from overseas.

The examples quoted below are quite typical of those whose adjustments

1. Because of the confidential nature of this material, the quotations from fathers concerning adjustments with wife are not identified by pseudonyms.

The examples quoted below are quite typical of those whose adjustments with their wives went smoothly:

"In my job overseas married men did not associate with women because everyone knew them, the community was small. We had some merry times dancing and drinking. I was tempted; I guess I had a censor inside. I thought it might be a problem when I left home. I think the baby at home was a bond that helped hold me. We had no problems in sex relations when I came home; it came very easy" (Case E15).

"I had no trouble in emotional readjustment. We picked up where we left off. We had to really begin living together. We were never closely tied together before. We just started from scratch" (Case E9).

"No, I never went around with other women during the war. Certainly there were opportunities overseas for a couple of years. I wondered why. The compulsion was there; the desire was there, but it was suppressed. Certainly my wife had a good deal to do with that. I would hate above all to hurt her . . . If I ever considered that it would be a problem to re-establish intimate relations with my wife, it never became a problem. She understands me quite well and did the things that made it easy for me to slip back into relationships. It was much easier than I had thought it would be" (Case E11).

Difficulties in love relations. Seven men reported prolonged difficulties in re-establishing love relations with their wives; one of them temporarily had an extramarital affair; another had periods of separation from his wife. The three men who said they had become seriously involved with another woman while overseas all had difficulties in adjustments with their wives; two of them gave indications of having some guilt feelings (Table 13).

Table 13. Extramarital Relations of War-Separated Men During Absence From Wives as Related to Postwar Problems in Marital Adjustment

	Number	Problems in Love Relations with Wife
Promiscuous	—	—
Involved with one woman	3	3
Played around, nothing serious	2	—
Not interested	6	1
No opportunity	7	2
No report	1	1

The following excerpts indicate how the men felt about their problems:

"Before I got back the thought of re-establishing relations with my wife was quite a source of anxiety, it really was. Particularly as the months went on after I'd been gone so long and I felt definitely anxious about the situation . . . We lived with her family for a period after I got back. Adjustments got to be very difficult . . . I felt there was a change in our love relations that took almost a year to work out" (Case E12).

"I had never really known my wife. I just knew her superficially. She was different from what I had expected. There were some things that I wanted in a wife that she didn't have. I figured you can't have everything in marriage, I had to adjust . . . My wife and I had arguments every day. We weren't getting along very well. The whole situation was trying'' (Case E10).

''Our culture makes the veteran feel guilty about his experiences, the places he goes, the people he meets, getting drunk, sleeping with women. We begin to wonder about our taboos when other cultures approve of them. The only way is to start all over again when you get back, push your experiences back into the unconscious. Forget about them. The thing is not to talk about your war experiences to your wife, for they include dirt, filth, infidelity. When the time came for returning to the U. S. A., sometimes I was uneasy. It's odd how you feel. I loved my wife yet she seemed so far from me. Other things seemed more real. I knew other people better than I knew her. I was scared, I think— yes, I think I was . . . My wife felt _I_ was out of her life when I got back . . . I felt my wife was incapable of giving me the love I needed . . . It takes two full years for a man to get into his family again after military service'' (Case E1).

Routines of Living

One would expect that these young couples who on the average had been separated 12.4 months longer than they had been together would have had problems in getting together on the routines of everyday living. Only three of the men, however, mentioned this except as it related to the routines of living with the baby. One father, who was somewhat more mature than most of the men, said in summarizing the main effect the war had had on his family relations:

> ''It is hard to say but there is one thing I am pretty sure of and that is when people are first married, the early part of marriage means adjustments to each other's habits and ways of behaving. You take on some of your wife's habits and she takes on some of yours and you have little arguments and discussions about what should be done this way and what you should think about this and that. And the war interrupted this process for us and in a way delayed our adjustment, so that these things had to take place after I came back from the war. Otherwise we would have been all over that by that time'' (Case E15).

The report of a younger man reflects his difficulties in settling down and accepting the normal restrictions of family life:

> ''My desire was to get away from it all— away from restrictions. I wanted to go to a party every night, my wife didn't. My friends from overseas were heavy drinkers, my wife didn't like them . . . Any restrictions when I came back irritated me. We had to get up at 5:00 A. M. for the baby. I looked forward to spending a lot of time on the beach. But we had to take the baby. Then we had to bring him back for lunch and a nap. We never could enjoy the beach'' (Case E5).

Acceptance of Wife's Family

Only six of the men knew their parents-in-law well before they left their wives to go to war, and four of these had known them only as single men courting their daughters. Ten had only casual acquaintance and three had never met their in-laws. For all but two, then, this was an adjustment to be made after they were reunited with their wives.

It was somewhat surprising to find that 16 of the war-separated men were critical of their wife's family. In 13 cases the early difficulties between husband and wife were intensified by immediate adjustments the men

Table 14. War-Separated Fathers' Adjustments to Wife's Family

Problems	Number of Fathers
General disapproval of wife's family	16
Problems related to adjustment with wife	13
Problems related to rearing of child	13
Father disapproving of grandparents' relation to child	11
Grandmother came between father and child	7

had to make to their in-laws. These included 12 of the 13 men who had to live with their in-laws immediately after their return. The general criticisms included such matters as values, appropriate behavior, personality, economic status, and politics. Two excerpts illustrate this type of criticism:

"I always felt that if my wife had more discipline as a child, we would have been better adjusted in our marriage at that time. Her whole family was permitted to do what they wished and they had lots of involvements . . . In my wife's family there were no age boundaries in discussions at the table . . . They don't think a child is disrespectful if he talks back. They also let them do things they should not do and laugh about it . . . My wife's cousin is disrespectful to her father, but no one paid any attention to her" (Case E10).

"I have had differences of opinion with my in-laws. My wife's value system was different from mine. I was trying to wean her away from her family . . . The grandparents picked the baby up when she would cry and comforted her. I didn't approve . . . I didn't want them around our daughter too much but I was more afraid of the influence they had on my wife than on her . . . It made me just furious when my wife said she wanted to talk to her mother about what to do with our daughter. It cut pretty deep" (Case E8).

In relation to child. The problems in every case interrelated with the differences the men had with their wives in relation to the rearing of the child. In 11 families the man disagreed specifically with the methods of child rearing that the grandparents used, the grandparents being, in the father's opinion, too indulgent and too lenient. In 7 families the man definitely felt that the mother-in-law had kept him from making more adequate relations with his child when he first returned. The following excerpts show how these adjustments interrelated:

"I felt the grandparents spoiled our daughter and I began to feel they resented me. When I'd correct her, they'd always have an excuse for her. Sometimes they would even tell me I shouldn't talk that way to my daughter. That griped me, that sure griped me . . . Sometimes I felt they all would have been happier if I hadn't come home. I felt out of things, as if I didn't belong. They all seemed a tight little family with me on the outside" (Case E1).

"We did have conflicts over the parental situation, family interference. That was quite a source of conflict. I thought her parents, due to the living situation, had too great a part. So that was quite a source of conflict . . . I didn't agree with the grandmother's ideas about bringing up the baby at all" (Case E12).

"I felt my wife's mother kept me on the outside— she still does. Though she tried to put me at ease. If I did something wrong, as I often did, I'm sure she'd tell me I shouldn't do that . . . my practice was just to keep quiet . . . She is more lenient than I am" (Case E11).

"My wife's mother did everything for our daughter and I couldn't do anything for her . . . I feel that the grandmother kept me from being close to her. I was conscious of this from the beginning . . . She wasn't on my side in arguments about our daughter. She was there when the child was born and had more of a hand in it than I did" (Case E17).

Wife and Baby

There was only one man among the war-separated group who did not feel on his reunion with his family that the baby interfered in some way with his relations with his wife (see Table 15).

Table 15. War-Separated Fathers' Problems with Wife in Relation to First-Born

	Yes	No	Doubtful	No Mention
Child came between husband and wife	9	7	2	1
Too close bond between mother and child	14	2	3	—
Complications due to sleeping arrangements	6	4	9	—
Disagreements in methods of child rearing	19	—	—	—
Complications due to wife's family	12	4	1	2
Complications due to husband's family	2	—	—	17

Child between husband and wife. About half of the men felt that the baby really came between them and their wife by interfering with their privacy or keeping them from doing things together. Four of these admitted they resented the fact that they had to share their wife's attention with the baby, which was a different situation from when they had left home. Three men felt that the child played mother and father against each other. On the other hand, two other men mentioned that perhaps the child was a bond that held husband and wife together in the face of other stresses in their relationships. The following excerpts illustrate the problems as the nine men saw them:

"I had to share my wife's attention with the baby, which I hadn't had to do before—an adjustment I had to make" (Case E17).

"I was anxious to be with my wife every minute. I soon found there was very little privacy. Everybody was always around. Even in our room, the little girl was always busting in. She never let us alone a minute . . . Every time I sat down beside my wife, our daughter would want something and my wife would get up and leave me and do it. That irked me— especially when it seemed to me the baby was just doing it to be a nuisance" (Case E1).

Close bond between mother and child. About three-fourths of the men felt that the bond between the mother and her first-born was too close. Some of them saw this as one reason why the child had come between them and their wife. Others saw it as one reason why they had disagreements about child rearing. Even though some of them seemed to understand that this was probably a result of their absence and the wife's consequent loneliness, they still were disapproving.

Related to the close bond of mother and child was the fact that when the father returned, his wife and baby were sleeping in the same room, sometimes in the same bed. This was true in 15 families. The baby continued to sleep there after the father returned, as it was the only bedroom they had. Even when they moved to a place of their own, there was still but one bedroom. There was little privacy for the newly united couple. Six men mentioned this as one of the causes of their difficulties.

"When I first got back, he just didn't want to be left out. He cried a lot and everything when we put him to bed and left the room . . . He slept in the room with my wife while I was away and slept in the same room when I got back; it was the only room we had . . . One thing irked me. We'd put him to bed. He'd yell like mad . . . The first night I got back I started working on him" (Case E9).

"Our daughter slept in the room with us. She would crawl out of bed when she wet it and get in bed with us . . . There was another complication. She used to wake up more than by chance when we were having intercourse. We'd have to move very quickly . . . I'd get mad as hell. It was very frustrating" (Case E8).

"Oh, there was another thing we had a great deal of difficulty over. My wife and the baby had always slept together. When I got home, of course, I think the baby grew a little jealous of me when she saw me sleeping with her mother, and she would beat me to bed and get in there with her. She had her own bed but she just didn't want to stay in it . . . I spanked her. I felt the baby in our bed interfered with privacy with my wife" (Case E17).

Methods of child rearing. By far the greatest difficulties that these men had in their early relations with their wives were due to differences which they had in how to bring up their child. In all the families these differences led to some tensions between husband and wife but in 15 families the difficulties were great and prolonged. Only four men felt that these differences did not affect adversely their relations with their wife. One of these was case E19, who received rating 5 on a 5-point scale quantifying the men's reports of degree of disagreement with wife over methods of child rearing.

"I can't remember my difficulties with our daughter causing any special strain between my wife and me. It bothered me a good deal but it didn't affect adversely my relations with my wife" (Case E19).

The other 15 men felt that these differences brought difficulties in their relations with their wives, as illustrated by cases E10 and E17 both of whom received rating 5 on differences with wife.

"We almost separated over the fact that we didn't agree on how to raise children. If the boy and I got in an argument over how to eat, she'd stand up for him, right in front of him. We had many severe arguments every day. We weren't getting along very well. I felt as if I were an interloper. The whole situation was trying. It was really the first time we'd been together. I felt I should have something to say about my own child . . . I was emotional at times. The readjustment after the war—coming back and all . . . was probably difficult . . . My wife didn't understand my motives. Guess I do look mean when I get mad. She felt it was up to her to defend her child" (Case E10).

"My wife and I had quarrels over the baby. I thought she was stubborn. I tried to force her. My wife said, 'She's just a baby, you can't expect her to do things.' Probably I expected more of her than I should" (Case E17).

We rated the degree of differences between husband and wife in methods of child rearing during the early months of the man's reunion with the family. The 5-point scale ranged from no differences to extreme differences. We also rated the degree of differences in methods of child rearing between the husbands and wives of the non-separated group during the period before the child was 30 months of age. Although the situations were not alike, the comparison serves to highlight the problems which the war-separated families met in this area.

Because of the small sample, we tested the significance of the difference between the two groups by the method of chi square, making a three-by-two table by combining ratings 1 and 2, and ratings 3 and 4. Chi square equals 28; the difference between the groups is significant, the level of probability being less than .001. If the division is made between high and low groups combining ratings 1 and 2 and ratings 3, 4, and 5, chi square equals 30.76, $P < .001$.

It seems reasonable, therefore, to conclude that the husbands who had been separated from their families during the war had much stronger disagreements with their wives over child-rearing methods when they were reunited than did husbands who had not been separated.

Summary of Adjustments with Wife. The evidence shows that the father whose first child was born when he was overseas had problems in adjusting to his wife when he returned from the war. No man had problems in every area but, as is shown in Table 16, there were six different combinations of problem areas.

Three men reported problems in only one area, child-rearing practices. For the others, child-rearing practices were combined with other areas. The 8 men who had the most wide-spread problems, though not necessarily the most intense problems with the wife, all had problems relating to child-rearing practices and to the wife's family; 6 combined these with problems in love relations; 2 combined them with problems in routines of living. There were 14 men whose problems combined differences in child-rearing practices and adjustments to the wife's family.

Table 16. Areas of Problems of War-Separated Men with Wife after Reunion

	Number of Cases
Child-rearing practices	3
Child-rearing practices Establishing love relations	1
Child-rearing practices Routines of living	1
Child-rearing practices Adjustment to wife's family	6
Child-rearing practices Establishing love relations Adjustment to wife's family	6
Child-rearing practices Routines of living Adjustment to wife's family	2

Adjustments to the First-Born Child

The returning father's initial adjustment to the child who had been born during his absence was influenced by a variety of factors. We have analyzed five aspects of the situation: (1) the father's readiness to accept his unknown child, (2) the child's acceptance of the father, (3) the father's immediate attitude toward the child's behavior, (4) the methods of training or discipline which the father used in the early weeks and months, and (5) the child's attitude toward the father during the first year. In some ways these five were sequential. They were interacting and laid the foundation for the father-child relation.

Readiness of Father to Accept Child

The fathers varied in their feelings about the first-born as they returned from the war. They ranged from "bubbling with excitement" to "felt cold towards her" or "felt no connection." We rated them on a 5-point scale that went from enthusiastic through accepting, ambivalent, uninterested, to rejecting. We could not compare the feelings of fathers who saw their children for the first time when they were between 10 and 33 months of age with the feelings of the non-separated fathers who saw their children as newborns.

Acceptance. There were only six men who were ready to accept the child immediately and wholeheartedly. The quotations from Mr. Statler and Mr. Bryan indicate how the six who had enthusiastic acceptance (rating 1) felt. Four men were somewhat ambivalent about their feelings. The quotation from Mr. Irwin describes this approach.

"He seemed like my baby, very much so. Everybody told me how much he looked like me. I guess he did look like me. More like me than my wife. I had very much the feeling that he was my boy . . . I was quite excited to see him" (Mr. Statler).

"When I came back I was bubbling over with enthusiasm and anticipation . . . Within a few days I realized the moment that I had been anticipating for three years: I was face to face with my baby, my daughter" (Mr. Bryan).

"But as time grew nearer to arriving home I began to feel a little nervous. I didn't know . . . a picture is different from actually seeing a person, especially when you haven't seen them before, and I don't think I ever realized, ever experienced the feeling of being a father even until I got home. You know, I realized that I had a daughter, but I don't think it really sunk in. I mean, it was more a matter of fact than a matter of feeling, and I don't think—I can say that I wasn't really a father until I got home. You know, then it's different. You're there and you see your own offspring toddling around, and then you get the idea of the—the—I don't know—something of what you're here for, all that, you know. And, like I say, I was very nervous about it" (Mr. Irwin).

Uninterested and rejecting. Men who were rated at the other end of the scale indicated by remarks such as those quoted below that they were not ready to accept their unknown babies. Mr. Holman, Mr. Arnold, and Mr. Wagner received rating 4; Mr. Wycoff received rating 5.

"As far as my reactions to having a son when I was overseas, I don't remember—oh, I had a certain amount of mild elation, but it wasn't real. My son didn't mean too much to me. In fact, he didn't mean a great deal for quite a long while after I came home . . . It took me quite a long while to get acquainted with him, to get accustomed to the idea of having children. I really didn't know what it was like" (Mr. Holman).

"I felt I should like him better than I did" (Mr. Arnold).

"I can remember at the time I didn't seem to have any particular emotion one way or the other. I wasn't tremendously thrilled with the idea of seeing her and I didn't feel that she was any blight in my life either. I was just sort of noncommittal about the whole thing . . . I don't think I had the same feeling toward her that my wife did. My wife was deeply attached to her . . . I couldn't feel the same feelings. Alma was an older child to me to start with—sort of an adoption really" (Mr. Wagner).

"I will never forget the night I arrived home. I was anxious to get home. I remember feeling cold toward Ann. I didn't pick her up. She began crying. I was much more interested in my wife" (Mr. Wycoff).

Child's Acceptance of Father

According to the father's report, each child varied in his responses to "this strange man who had come to live with him." One father felt very definitely that his child of 20 months almost immediately accepted him as daddy. "There wasn't any of that experience that some parents had of his taking quite a while before the child would accept the father" (Mr. Harlow). This father had an important job that kept him extremely busy at the time of reunion and left him little time to be with either wife or child. At the other extreme was a child who would have nothing to do with her father, cried when he was in the same room, wouldn't let him touch her, and refused to let him do things for her. This was the response of the child to a father (Mr. Bryan) who was "bubbling over with enthusiasm" to see and be with his daughter.

Degree of acceptance. The behavior of the child towards the father on his return was rated on a 5-point scale according to the father's description of the child's degree of acceptance. Again, there was no comparable rating which we could make for the non-separated fathers.

Two children, Joe Weiss and George Osborne, are given rating 2 because the fathers stated that their sons accepted them all right; however, the behavior of the two children as reported by the fathers later led us to believe that these children were hesitant, too, about acceptance but that the fathers were insensitive to these cues of behavior.

The seven fathers who felt most rejected (child-acceptance rating 5) told about it in the following ways:

> "Don was 14 months old on my return. I remember I took him and pretty soon he was just hollering. He just wouldn't come near me. I was upset but didn't know what to do about it . . . I don't think he ever took to me. There was something there. I was just an unnecessary addition as far as he was concerned . . . It's always been hard for me" (Mr. Burgman).

One father told of the episode at the railroad station when he returned after three and one-half years overseas:

> "I had expected to see my wife, of course. But my in-laws were there with Mary. I realize now it was planned as a grand surprise for me, to let me see my daughter first. But it was upsetting. She would have nothing to do with me. The grandparents were hanging around her. I felt sorta embarrassed. I was kind of let down not to see my wife. Sometimes I used to wonder afterwards if my wife really wanted to see me . . . My balloon burst very soon. I, a stranger, was interference with her and her mummy . . . She cried because I was in the same room . . . She was unresponsive . . . She was interested in me and watched me but she wouldn't let me touch her or do anything for her" (Mr. Bryan).

Mr. Soule told of the persistent refusal of his daughter to accept him:

> "For a good many weeks or even months after I got home, Fran and I were not very close. She was suspicious of me. She usually kept her distance; she didn't receive my affections very well . . . as time went on it got me down a little."

Mr. Marston was less disturbed than some of the other fathers (child-acceptance rating 3). He said: "For the first day or two Ken was a little bit afraid of me. But there wasn't too much of a strain between us, at least for him. He didn't like to sit on my lap, he would squirm, didn't know what this strange character was. He had to size me up and be sure before he accepted me. I was more of a stranger to him than he was to me . . . He preferred his grandfather (paternal) to me. He got along fine with him."

Methods of rejection of fathers by children. The ways in which the children showed their lack of acceptance of the fathers varied but there were some forms of behavior that seemed particularly disturbing to the fathers. These are summarized in Table 17. It can be assumed that the number of fathers we found to be disturbed by such behavior is minimum, since no question was asked specifically on this topic.

Table 17. Behavior of First-Born Disturbing to War-Separated Fathers

	Number
Shy, aloof, indifferent to advances	8
Crying in relation to father	9
Refusal to let father do things for him	9
Refusal of affection from father	5
Fear of father	4

Such behavior as being shy, refusing affection or services, or even crying may seem to be very natural responses for young children to make to a stranger, but when that stranger is the young, inexperienced father who is feeling somewhat inadequate, such behavior is hard to take. All but three of the fathers admitted that they were disturbed; how long their disturbance lasted depended upon other factors.

Attitude Toward Child's Behavior

In the first weeks and months after the father returned he began to appraise the behavior of this new child of his. Mr. Weiss, whose child was 27 months when he returned, described his appraisal:

"I didn't take much responsibility for Joe when I first got back. For days and weeks I looked on while he was being brought up. He would take forever to eat his meals. My wife would beg him and promise him this and that and tell him to hurry up, but he just took his own sweet time and often he'd just refuse to eat altogether. She got upset and nervous. Then he would wet his pants. She never could catch him— looked like he was just perverse. He knew what to do, but would he do it? He sucked his thumb, too, not regularly but sometimes. It looked so silly to see a big boy like that sucking his thumb, that annoyed me. And he wouldn't obey my wife— no matter what, he just wouldn't obey. One of the biggest problems was to get him to go to bed. He'd cry and raise all kinds of fuss. After my wife got him in bed, he'd never stay there— out he would come."

We rated the father's early general attitude toward his child's behavior on a 5-point scale ranging from proud to extremely disapproving and critical. There was no comparable rating which could be made for the non-separated fathers. None of the fathers could be judged as proud or approving without reservations (rating 1 and 2). There were three fathers who were only slightly disapproving of the child (rating 3). Sixteen of the fathers were disapproving and critical of their child's behavior (rating 4 and 5).

Criticism by father. Since all of the fathers had some criticism of their first-born as they got to know him after the war, we studied the records to see of what it was they disapproved (Table 18).

Table 18. War-Separated Fathers' Criticisms of First-Born

	Number
Spoiled	16
Too close to mother	14
Specific behaviors	13
Personality characteristics	14

Most of the criticisms were focused on the child's relations with adults. Sixteen of the fathers thought their child was "spoiled" when they returned. They meant by "spoiled" that he always got what he wanted, he thought the world revolved around him, he lacked proper respect, he wouldn't mind, he wouldn't do what he was told, he was stubborn. As can be seen, they were concerned about the child's relation to authority figures. Fourteen of the group disapproved of the close bond with the mother and the child's dependence on the mother.

Thirteen men, like Mr. Weiss quoted above, criticized specific behavior of the children such as eating behavior, toilet habits, going to bed, and temper tantrums. The returning veterans seemed particularly concerned about any behavior which they considered babyish or sex-inappropriate such as crying, infantile speech, thumb-sucking, and late motor development.

Fourteen men criticized personality characteristics of their children. One father emphasized his dislike of his daughter's independence and aggressive assertiveness, and another was concerned about his son's shyness and lack of assertiveness. Seven of these 14 criticized their child for being unaffectionate, not liking to be cuddled, and being cold and unresponsive, behavior which had set a distance between the father and his child. All of them mentioned the child's overdependence upon his mother.

The following quotations show how these criticisms were interrelated in the father's mind. All of these men received rating 5 on father's attitude toward child's behavior.

"My wife was more like Allen's servant than his mother . . . The problems had to do with conformities, with not touching things, with not getting into things, not being messy, with sucking his thumb, with not minding . . . I thought he was spoiled. I thought my wife couldn't handle him. He would have temper tantrums. He lacked proper respect" (Mr. Statler).

"I talked to my wife about how spoiled Mary was and my wife was hurt.

She couldn't see it. She kept saying, 'She's such a little girl. She isn't naughty. She doesn't know any better.' But I didn't agree . . . She had to be the center of everything. She monopolized mealtimes . . . It was a great shock when I came back from the war to find she was so aggressive. I'd gotten snapshots of her but I hadn't realized she was so aggressive. I had pictured her quite different— more like my ideal of little girls" (Mr. Bryan).

"She did everything for Dan. If he wanted to be rocked, he'd cry, and she'd rock him. He got so demanding she didn't do anything but wait on him. He couldn't do anything for himself. I can't see placing all the emphasis on her being lonesome. She could have let him play by himself, let him think for himself or by himself; leave him develop his own interests along his own way, whether I was there or not . . . I'm not trying to hold her for everything, but I think it goes a long way towards developing a kid's reliability on himself— the way his mother treats him. If she's always cuddling him, always doing this and that and the other thing for him, he doesn't have to have any self-reliance. But if she's too busy and can't fool with him and he's left on his own, he develops it himself" (Mr. Wolf).

Father's Early Discipline of the Child

Most of the men assumed the role of father through disciplining. The father felt inadequate in changing diapers, feeding, bathing, and doing other routine care; inadequate not only in skills but in getting the baby to accept him instead of the mother. But in the area of disciplining, all but five of the men felt more adequate; in fact, here some felt more adequate than their wives. Mr. Wolf was typical of the group when he said, "I thought he was very spoiled and I realized immediately I'd have to straighten him out because his mother wouldn't." Three men admitted they felt inadequate, another evidenced tension and fear about it.

The fathers used punishment frequently. We rated both the war-separated fathers and the non-separated fathers on the discipline they used with their children in the early years. Since all of the children of the father-separated group were between 10 and 33 months when the father returned, the discipline used during that age range was rated for both groups. The 5-point discipline scale went from constructive through mild, firm, strict, to severe. This scale was developed on the basis of the descriptions given by the fathers and will be found in Appendix 3. Most of the fathers used several levels of punishment, but the rating was given at the level which seemed to characterize best the father's general approach.

The fathers who had been separated during the war used more severe discipline during the first year after their return than non-separated fathers did during a similar time in the life of their first-born. Because of the small sample, we made a three-by-two table by combining points 1 and 2 and points 4 and 5 in the scale. Chi square is 12.89; the difference is significant at the $P < .01$ level. This was checked by dividing matched cases into high-low groups; chi square is 8.62, $P < .01$.

No father of the war-separated group used what we have called constructive discipline, in which the father rarely punishes, but uses such methods as reasoning, adjusting of standards to child's level, compromising, or temporary removal from the situation. Two war-separated fathers were given rating 2 (mild), where the father tends to use disapproval, denial of privileges, and perhaps occasional very mild spankings. Both of these men felt ineffectual with their children. One of them (Mr. Harlow) said, "I recall instances when I felt quite inept as a father, particularly on discipline . . . my wife was much more successful . . . that bothered me." Neither of these men felt much a part of the family unit until about two years after they returned. Mr. Brown said, "I felt others had a hand in raising my child and I hadn't. I did in every way I could try to become a part."

The three men rated at level 3 (firm) were sometimes peremptory and impatient. They would scold and resort to a combination of several mild methods rather than using more extreme methods. They were likely to threaten and to argue with the child. None of these men felt that they were particularly strong as disciplinarians in the family. Mr. Holman said, "I'm impatient. I demand more of Ray than my wife does and it tends to justify; I demand more one way or another, perhaps not rightly. I'm quicker to punish than she is, I just am impatient. I think I have to justify what I do, to rationalize, but sometimes I lose my patience. I know that." This sounds very much like the non-separated fathers and nine of them were rated in this category.

The three war-separated fathers rated in level 4 were quite different. These men tended to be strict and uncompromising in discipline. Their demands were incisive. They used spanking in extreme behavior but relied more on strict orders that carried the threat of uncompromising authority. One of them belonged to the "cry it out" school. All of them believed in discipline strongly, as these excerpts testify:

> "I wanted Ken to hurry and grow up, to advance rapidly. I forgot he was not capable of understanding and doing these things. I tended to push him, to be strict . . . I thought he was spoiled. My parents told me I expected too much of him. They kept saying don't be so strict with him, remember he's just a little fellow" (Mr. Marston).

> "After I was discharged I can recall my training procedures; they were behavioristic—a slap was effective in training. I believed you spoiled babies by picking them up. I can recall feeding Ann when she was one year old and slapping her when she spewed food . . . One incident I remember which I have been ashamed of ever since—Ann was about 16 months old, she wanted to investigate a lot. We were on the train. Toward the end of the day I took her into the men's lounge. I was feeling rage. She was crying. I pushed her down roughly . . . I decided to train Ann for the toilet in a week. I put her on the potty and kept her there until she'd defecate. She responded with rage. I would too. She would get off the potty and defecate in the corner" (Mr. Wycoff).

By far the greatest number of the war-separated fathers (11) used what we have called severe discipline. The father spanked hard, spanked so it hurt. He might grab or shake the child roughly. He used force. He might yell or fight it out with the child. In general, his motive seemed to be to hurt or frighten the child. He relied on these methods frequently and seemed to be emotionally concerned with discipline, as illustrated in the following excerpts:

"I was filled with righteous indignation. My wife didn't believe in spanking. I felt it was the only way to make Allen conform. I spanked him . . . He would become emotional. He would fight with me. I felt he was my son and it was up to me to straighten him out—instinctively I felt that . . . I used to have the feeling he had his own way all day. I came home after work. Maybe I was irritable. I wasn't going to let him have his own way and that would cause conflict . . . He would throw himself around on the sidewalk. He'd kick . . . He'd overreact. It was mainly, I think, to get his mother on his side, which invariably would happen . . . " (Mr. Statler).

"The only way to make Joe behave was to discipline him. I decided I had better take over. If it was my time to put him to bed, I slapped him—then later I spanked him. That seemed to work; that was what he needed—someone strong to make him mind. Joe was really a hard child for my wife to bring up. Between two and one-half and four I took over and spanked him hard—it had amazing results" (Mr. Weiss).

"If her mother got out of her sight, Kate would scream, even when we were playing together. This made me mad; I felt she was spoiled. I spanked her. She used to get out of her play pen and crawl around the floor and get dirty. I didn't approve of this and I spanked her . . . She messed in her food; I said, 'No! No!' and spanked her hands . . . She cried if she wasn't rocked to sleep. I didn't approve of this. I let her cry it out for two solid weeks . . . She made a fuss at nap time. I spanked her" (Mr. Snyder).

"This was my first chance to really get acquainted with Rick. Guess I was very severe with him, especially in training in habits. He was learning to go to the bathroom. I had tried to break him of wetting—he was 14 or 15 months old. I went after him. He couldn't relax to release himself. I'd scold, spank him. I'd put him to bed and he'd whimper. I'd spank him—quite severe. I'd really throw fear into him . . . I was awfully severe with him" (Mr. Moore).

Discipline and disagreements with wife. In Table 19 we show the relation between the severity of the discipline which the father used on his return from the war and the degree of difference which the father reported between his idea of child rearing and his wife's. The correlation between the two ratings was not computed because of the small number of cases. As might be expected, there was most disagreement about child-rearing practices between husband and wife in those families where the father used the most severe discipline. Of the 14 fathers who reported using severe or strict discipline, all but one reported strong or extreme disagreements with the wife concerning child-rearing practices.

Mr. Marston, who was strict (rating 4) but did not have extreme disagreements with his wife (rating 3), thought his son was spoiled by his own parents when he returned. But his wife was not closely bound to the in-laws with whom she lived and easily made the transition to accepting her husband as head of the family. He said, "My wife said there was quite a difference when I came home. When I'd been away she could enter into that family—my mother and father—and become a daughter to them and let them be the head of the family and manage things. But when I came home, I was the family—she and I had the baby—and living with my parents, we were two separate families, and there was really quite a difference."

Two fathers, Mr. Mathews and Mr. Brown, were rated 2 and 3 as regards the kind of early disciplining of the child and had extreme disagreements with their wives (rating 5). Both of these men had difficulty in getting into the family picture. One stated that he felt much more criticism of his child than he could express and that he felt everyone had a hand in rearing his child but him. The other man seemed to feel that, in general, he was not as strong in discipline as his wife, he felt his wife was highly critical of his lack of initiative in this area, and he was critical of the methods his wife used when he returned.

Table 19. Relation Between War-Separated Father's Discipline of First-Born and Disagreement with Wife

Early Discipline of First-Born	Degree of Disagreement with Wife					
	1	2	3	4	5	Total
1						0
2			1		1	2
3			2		1	3
4			1		2	3
5				2	9	11
Total	0	0	4	2	13	19

Relation of early discipline to readiness for acceptance. Since the returning fathers varied in their readiness for acceptance of their unknown child it is possible that their attitudes affected the severity of discipline which they used with their children. However, inspection of Table 20 reveals no consistent relationship.

Table 20. Relation of War-Separated Father's Discipline of First-Born to His Readiness to Accept Child

Early Discipline of First-Born	Father's Readiness to Accept First-Born					
	1	2	3	4	5	Total
1						0
2		1	1			2
3		1	1	1		3
4		1		1	1	3
5	2	1	2	4	2	11
Total	2	4	4	6	3	19

The two fathers who were most enthusiastic about their children on return, Mr. Bryan and Mr. Statler (rating 1), used very severe discipline (rating 5). However, the nine fathers who were least ready to accept their children all used strict or severe discipline except one. This exception (Mr. Holman) reports that he, also, would have used more severe discipline if he had not accepted his wife as the dominant person in relation to his child.

Relation of discipline to child's acceptance of father. As might be expected, there was a closer relation between the child's initial acceptance of the father and the severity of the father's discipline. Table 21 shows this relation. The two cases which show the child accepting (rating 2) and the father severe (rating 5) are the two cases (Mr. Weiss and Mr. Osborne) mentioned earlier, in which the data as a whole would deny the fathers' statements that the children accepted them readily. The other case of wide discrepancy (discipline 2, acceptance 5) was the father whose child definitely rejected him but who did not feel he was allowed by his wife or her parents to take on his father role (Mr. Brown). Correlations were not computed because of the small sample.

Table 21. Relation of War-Separated Father's Discipline to Child's Acceptance of Father

Early Discipline of First-Born	Child's Acceptance of Father					
	1	2	3	4	5	Total
1						0
2	1				1	2
3			1	1	1	3
4			1	1	1	3
5		2	2	3	4	11
Total	1	2	4	5	7	19

Discipline and father's attitude toward child's behavior. The relation between the father's attitude toward the child's behavior during the first weeks and months of his return and the kind of discipline the father used can be seen in Table 22. It is evident that there is a tendency for the two to be related. The only father who had a discrepancy of more than one point on the scale was Mr. Brown, whom we have mentioned before as feeling it was impossible for him to discipline his child as he would have liked to do. Correlations were not computed because of the small sample.

Table 22. Relation Between War-Separated Father's Discipline and Attitude Toward Child

Early Discipline of First-Born	Attitude Toward Child's Behavior					
	1	2	3	4	5	Total
1						0
2			1	1		2
3			2	1		3
4			1	1	1	3
5				2	9	11
Total	0	0	4	5	10	19

Child's Attitude Toward Father in the Early Years

During the weeks and months following the father's return, the child was developing attitudes toward his father, who had now become a permanent fixture in the family group. This was the time when the father had assumed his role as father mainly as a disciplinarian. A second child had not been born.

We rated the attitude of the child toward the father as reported by the father during the early years for the war-separated and the non-separated group. We used a 5-point scale ranging from 1 (close, warm relations) to 5 (rejection and fear).

Because of the small sample, for statistical analysis by the method of chi square we rearranged the scale into three levels joining points 1 and 2 and points 4 and 5. Chi square equals 12.66; the difference between the attitudes of war-separated and non-separated first-borns is significant at the level $P < .01$. If the method of matched high-low groups is used, chi square equals 8.92 and the difference is significant at the same level.

The first-borns of the war-separated fathers did not respond favorably to the returned father even after they had an opportunity to get to know their father better. The fathers were conscious of this and sensitive about the situation, as the following excerpts from war-separated fathers, who were rated 4 or 5, testify:

"Mary was interested in me and watched me, but she wouldn't let me touch her or do anything for her. When she wanted something I could very well do, she would insist on having her mother or one of her grandparents . . . Later, when we had moved, we'd go back to my wife's house for weekends. She would run to her grandfather, hold on to him and sob. She'd say, 'This is my daddy,' She would cling to her grandfather— nearly always make a scene. She would say over and over again, 'I love you, I love you, I love you.' I felt embarrassed, I felt everybody knew Mary didn't like me. I was hurt, too— to have this happen at all, but especially before my wife's parents . . . Gradually she got so she ignored me, she did things that irritated me just on purpose. My wife said she was good when I was away but as soon as I'd come home she started up" (Mr. Bryan).

"Fran had trouble getting used to me. She wouldn't accept just ordinary affection. She just wanted to keep her distance. She'd talk about me, talk to me, smile at me, but I couldn't come close. She just wasn't trusting . . . She wouldn't go out with me without her mother along. I tried to help with her bath, with her food, but usually she wouldn't let me. This went on until she was over three. Even after we became friendlier there was always that limit, never go beyond it" (Mr. Soule).

"My wife was always trying so that Don would feel more for me, but I don't think it ever worked . . . He wouldn't let me do things such as changing diapers and feeding him which I had learned to do. This irritated me. He didn't need me for anything . . . Even when he was two or three years old he just wouldn't let me come close to him. I didn't like it, I didn't like it a bit" (Mr. Burgman).

The contrast of the relations of the non-separated fathers is well illustrated by the excerpts from Mr. Garrett, Mr. Stone, and Mr. Murray, who received ratings of 1 on the attitude of child toward father.

"In the mornings when I was home, we'd play. Herbert always was inseparable from me. I couldn't get the car out of the garage without taking him along. He was always going shopping with me. We'd ride around, go to see the trains, or out in the country" (Mr. Garrett).

"Every time I came home Harry would run out and want a surprise or want to go on a drive or something . . . He has always been closer to me than to my wife" (Mr. Stone).

"Luke and I have had quite a bit to do with each other, I'd say, since he was born. Little excursions here and there . . . If I couldn't come out in the yard, he'd come in" (Mr. Murray).

Summary of adjustments to first-born child. Two-thirds of the fathers were not ready to accept their unknown children when they returned from the war. Their offspring seemed no more ready to accept them, behaving as young children are likely to do to strangers. All but three of the fathers were disturbed by this and felt pushed out or rejected.

Sixteen of the fathers were disapproving and critical of their child's behavior. They thought the children were "spoiled" and were too dependent on their mothers. Fourteen made specific criticisms of behavior or personality characteristics.

Most of the men assumed the role of father through disciplining, using significantly more severe discipline than the non-separated fathers. The severity of the war-separated father's discipline shows a tendency to be related to the degree of difference with his wife in methods of child rearing, to the child's nonacceptance of the father, and to the father's early negative attitude toward the child's behavior. These relations could not be tested statistically.

These early experiences with the father as he assumed his role of disciplinarian affected the developing attitudes of the first-born. The war-separated children tended to have significantly greater negative feelings for their fathers than the non-separated group did for their fathers. In the war-separated families emotional distance between father and child increased in the first years and the barriers to affectionate interpersonal relations became stronger.

Interpretive Summary

This analysis indicates that the men who returned after the war to a wife and a first child born while they were overseas were faced immediately with situations which precipitated the formation of adjustment patterns in several areas of life. We have studied in this chapter those related to vocation, to wife, and to the first-born child.

There is evidence that the men had anxieties in regard to their careers greater than the non-separated group ($P < .01$). These men who had been "in another world" faced the necessity for adjusting to civilian life, choosing a career, and supporting a family with a deep sense of inadequacy. The continuity and sameness of their lives had been disturbed and they were forced to seek self-stability in uncertain fields. It may be that the men who went to college after the war felt this more deeply than men who immediately got a job. It is, perhaps, more difficult to combine the status of student with the roles of breadwinner and head of family. Where a sense of inadequacy and feelings of insecurity exist already, integration of these roles will be particularly difficult.

The men were anxious, too, about re-establishing intimate relations with the wives from whom they had been separated. Although this was soon resolved for most of them, a third had difficulties that continued over the years. The adjustment with the wife became complicated with adjustments to the first-born child.

Our evidence seems to point to the fact that the assumption of the role of father had many hazards for these men. The problems became interwoven with adjustments to the wife and consequently became more threatening to the man. His feelings of inadequacy were increased because of his inability to gain affection from his baby, to take care of him, or to control him. In some cases the presence of in-laws interfered with the father working out his family relations in privacy.

The war-separated fathers were critical of their children and used more severe discipline than the non-separated group used with their children at similar ages ($P < .01$). The criticism and severe discipline which the father expressed seem to have been adjustive mechanisms to the stress situation. Criticism may have been a method of justifying the expression of the hostility he felt towards a situation which had increased his feelings of inadequacy and had isolated him from warm interpersonal relations.

The behavior of the war-separated fathers toward their first-borns soon alienated their children from them. The war-separated children were more rejecting of their fathers than the non-separated children at similar ages ($P < .01$). For some men this increased their feelings of loneliness, of isolation from the family, and of personal inadequacy.

CHAPTER 4.
FATHERS' ATTITUDES TOWARD FIRST-BORN CHILDREN

The interviews with the fathers contained information regarding the characteristics of the first-born child as the father saw him. We wished to find out whether the attitudes of the fathers who had been separated during at least the first year of life of their children differed from the attitudes which the non-separated fathers had toward their first-borns in certain areas of the children's development. We did not know whether the descriptions these fathers gave of their children had validity in the sense that they would be verified by other people, such as the mother; but that was not our present concern. We were interested in whether in the eyes of their fathers the first-borns of the war-separated and non-separated groups differed, and in what ways and in which areas they differed.

The analysis seemed to us important because it would relate specifically to some of our original hypotheses. We expected that the war-separated fathers in comparison with the non-separated fathers would consider that their first-borns had more serious behavior problems, and that they would be less worried and more annoyed by these problems. We expected that the war-separated fathers in comparison with the non-separated fathers would be more distant from their first-borns and more critical of them as persons. We expected that the war-separated fathers would see their first-borns as closer to the mother and the second-borns as closer to the father.

Method of Analysis

On the basis of preliminary study of the interviews, three general areas in the development of children were selected for analysis. These include: behavior of the child in certain significant areas of development, personality characteristics of first-born, interpersonal relations within the family. Under behavior of the child there are six subtopics: eating, elimination, sleeping, dressing, tensions and comforts, and social relations with children. Under interpersonal relations within the family are included relations of first-born child with sibling, with mother, and with father.

The material relevant to each of these topics was excerpted from the series of interviews of each father and typed on separate sheets. The material on each topic was arranged in two columns: column one listed all statements referring to the child as he was previously, and column two, all statements referring to the child as he was at the time of the interview.

The excerpts on each topic were rated on a 5-point scale representing a continuum from "no problems, well-adjusted" (point 1) to "serious problems, extreme difficulties in adjustments" (point 5) (see Appendix 4). The data of the 38 cases were distributed to cover both ends of the scale; that is, the children with the least problems in the sample were rated 1, the children with the most serious problems in the sample were rated 5. This scale was used, also, in rating data from the mother interviews (Chapter 7) and in a comparison of mother and father interviews (Chapter 8).

Reliability for the ratings was determined by the agreement between two raters. Rater A had not read the interview protocols. His ratings were used as the basic ratings and were checked by Rater B, who had conducted the interviews with the war-separated fathers.[1] These two raters had previously used the same scale in rating data from the mother interviews with a high degree of reliability (see Chapter 7). Two sets of excerpts from the father-interview data were rated: those concerning the father's attitude toward the child's eating behavior and toward the child's eliminative behavior. The Pearson r between the two sets of ratings for eating behavior was .846 and for elimination behavior was .917. The reliability seemed adequate so that no further checks were made.

In addition to the adjustment scale, ratings were available on two other scales developed by Engvall in the comparison of mother- and father-interview material. These were scales on the degree of worry shown by the father, and the annoyance value of the behavior to the father. These scales and their reliability are described in Chapter 8. The scales will be found in Appendix 7.

The differences between the war-separated group and the non-separated group on all scales were obtained by the t technique for related groups (54). Because we could not assume underlying continuity of the scores we have required a P of .01 or less for significance, thus accepting differences as significant only when they are rather rigorously established.

Behavior of First-Born Child

Eating Behavior

The father's description of the child's eating behavior includes such items as attitude toward food, likes and dislikes, amount of food, manners at table, as well as other specific behavior that annoys a particular father.

Table 23. Eating Behavior Criticized by Fathers

	War-Separated	Non-Separated
Likes and dislikes	10	9
Amount of food eaten	5	3
Manners at table	10	5
Dawdling	8	7
Refusal to eat	14	4

It can be seen in Table 23 that both groups of fathers criticize the same aspects of eating behavior but there are fewer non-separated fathers than war-separated fathers who complain about the child's refusing to eat and the child's table manners.

When the excerpts are rated according to degree of seriousness of the eating behavior, the mean rating for the war-separated group is 3.84; for the non-separated group, 2.47. The mean difference between the groups is statistically significant at the level of $P < .02$ (see Table 24). Ratings of extreme seriousness were given to 12 war-separated children but only to 4 non-separated children. Only one war-separated child was rated as having no problems in eating, in contrast to six in the non-separated group.

1. Rater A, L. Johnson; Rater B, L. M. Stolz.

Table 24. Father's Attitude Toward Eating Behavior of First-Born

Scale	Mean		t	Significance
	War-Separated	Non-Separated		
Seriousness of problem	3.84	2.47	2.64	$P < .02$
Worry	3.32	1.79	4.03	$P < .001$
Annoyance	3.68	1.95	3.87	$P < .02$

The difference between the groups in the seriousness of the child's problem seems to be closely related to the father's attitude toward the child's behavior. This is well illustrated in the father's descriptions of the child's likes and dislikes in food. The non-separated fathers say, "there are some things he doesn't like," "he gets tired of dry cereal," "he won't touch anything new," or "sometimes she's choosy," but they are not very disturbed about it. The war-separated fathers, on the other hand, are disturbed about similar behavior of their children and try to make the children eat what they do not want. This difference in attitude is even more striking when they discuss dawdling: the non-separated fathers complain about the child's slowness in eating, his excess conversation at the table, and his delay in coming to meals; but they do not make an issue of the situation which upsets the whole meal, as the war-separated fathers are likely to do.

The war-separated child who refuses to eat seems to be reacting to the father's forcible methods of feeding. Holding food in the mouth and refusing to swallow, spewing or vomiting food, not chewing, are effective means of resistance which these children use. On the other hand, the four non-separated children reported under food refusals in Table 23 are described as going through stages of not wanting to eat, or of not wanting to eat breakfast, or, in one case, of having thrown the food in the wastebasket. Here the difference lies in the fact that the war-separated fathers seem to be reporting "food battles" in which the father and child each uses extreme methods of getting his own way.

There seem to be two aspects to the problems in regard to manners while eating. The war-separated fathers were likely to expect a child to eat properly even when quite young. Two fathers reported slapping their daughters' hands at 13 and 16 months "because she put them in the food"; two criticized their babies when under two years for knocking things over; one made his son leave the table because he played with his food at 16 months. The war-separated fathers did not like their children to be messy, to play with things at the table, to bring toys to the table, to wriggle and not sit still— all rather normal types of behavior for young children. Four of them mentioned particularly the child's poor behavior in restaurants. As the child has become older there seem definitely to be attempts of the child to annoy the father deliberately through "laughing and silliness," "playing at the table," "leaning on elbows," and other such indirect techniques. Of the five non-separated fathers who report problems relating to table manners, three complain about messiness, one about general poor table manners, and one about manners in restaurants. However, their complaints are in the nature of "I wish he wouldn't" rather than the "He makes me so mad" of the war-separated fathers.

A few excerpts from the discussions of the war-separated fathers illustrate the differences in the father's attitude which seems to be basic to the child's problems. All of these cases were given rating 5, indicating serious problems in eating behavior.

"Eating is still an emotional matter with Albert, who is five years old. Now it is dawdling: continual conversation, laughing, silliness between him and his brother. Mealtime is a highly emotional scene" (Mr. Mathews).

"Rick (at six-and-one-half years) has table manners that aren't too good. He will lapse into manners of younger kids, does silly things—fantastically silly for a child of his age. He leans on his arm when he eats . . . He draws things in the air with his spoon . . . He eats slowly . . . Rick always asks for dessert first. The trouble is, he is underweight and he doesn't eat enough. I put big servings on his plate. If he doesn't want it, he acts foolish. He wastes food" (Mr. Moore).

"Ann (four-and-one-half years old) has been an eating problem for some time now. For a long time she didn't want to eat. This has been a problem. My wife believes that diet is really everything and this makes Ann's reluctance to eat hard to take . . . Ann uses eating to control us. When we don't press her, she will usually eat" (Mr. Wycoff).

"Dan (just over four years old) changes his mind too much. He says he wants a soft-boiled egg, then he doesn't want it, he wants candy instead. She will give it to him . . . Dan takes a big plate of stuff, then leaves it. Doesn't take more than two bites out of it. So we've tried everything— threats, bribery, being sweet about it, and everything else" (Mr. Wolf).

"Kate (three years, seven months) dawdles over meals, often refuses to help herself, toys with tableware or food, or eats only her favorite foods. She often delays coming to the table, invariably has to go to the toilet during the meal . . . This has been going on since she was two . . . Kate drinks cream in her milk and has large portions of butter on vegetables which may dull her appetite . . . She doesn't eat between meals . . . Kate undoubtedly senses our concern over her eating habits and, perhaps, she comes to the table in an overly emotional state . . . We put things on her plate, small servings and tell her, 'If you don't eat, you are sick, so you must go to bed.' This caused extreme resistance and crying" (Mr. Snyder).

Contrast the attitude expressed in the following statements which are typical of the non-separated fathers. Mr. Goldman's description was rated 3, Mr. King's and Mr. Rowell's were rated 2, Mr. Gibson's and Mr. Martin's were rated 1.

"Lisbet's not the best eater, but I wouldn't say that she's an eating problem. She'll dawdle over her food. It's nothing that has ever worried us. At times it's annoying if she doesn't want to eat this or that . . . I object when she refuses to eat many things" (Mr. Goldman).

"Leonard's quite a slow eater. He will just sit there and go over the events of the day and take his time, which is typical of him—he isn't hurried about anything . . . He eats very, very good, a substantial meal, and he has quite an appetite'' (Mr. King).

"Eats satisfactorily. Quite a normal child . . . Marty's a very slight child, probably always will be. And that's satisfactory, so there are no great feeding problems . . . He dilly-dallies a lot. Particularly with eating. It's purposeful, mischievous'' (Mr. Rowell).

"At breakfast Sally won't each much: juice and milk. She'll ask for a certain kind of eggs, then not touch them . . . Eats a huge lunch, huge dinner, and in between, everything she can get her hands on, including candy . . . Sally tries everything we try. There are things she doesn't like which she won't eat and we never force her to eat anything because she is such a good eater, she really is'' (Mr. Gibson).

"Wonderful appetite. Breakfast varies. Sometimes it will be very good indeed, sometimes only fair. Always eats something . . . If there are other people at the table with food, Otto has to share. So, therefore, he will eat his dinner at five-thirty and then again with me when I come home'' (Mr. Martin).

These excerpts also illustrate our findings that the war-separated fathers were significantly more worried about and more annoyed by the eating behavior of their first-born than the non-separated fathers (see Table 24). The mean rating on the scale for worry for the war-separated group was 3.32; for the non-separated group it was 1.79. The mean difference between the groups was significant at the $P < .001$ level. On the annoyance scale the mean rating for the war-separated group was 3.68; for the non-separated group, 1.95. The mean difference between the groups was significant at the $P < .02$ level.

Elimination

According to the fathers' reports, all but two of the war-separated children were in the process of learning control of bladder when the father was reunited with the family. This may have affected the degree of seriousness of their problems in this area. The contrast is striking since 8 fathers in the war-separated group and only 1 in the non-separated group reported that the first-born had extreme problems. At the other end of the scale there are 5 of the war-separated and 15 of the non-separated who had no or only slight difficulties.

The mean rating on the scale of seriousness of problem for the war-separated group was 3.00 and for the non-separated group, 1.74. The mean difference between the groups was statistically significant at the level of $P < .01$ (see Table 25).

Table 25. Father's Attitude Toward Elimination Behavior of First-Born

Scale	Mean		t	Significance
	War-Separated	Non-Separated		
Seriousness of problem	3.00	1.74	3.19	$P < .01$
Worry	2.47	1.53	2.97	$P < .01$
Annoyance	1.95	1.32	2.19	$P < .05$

At the time of the interviews, according to the fathers' reports, five of the war-separated children (two girls and three boys) were persistent bed-wetters. Their ages ranged from three years, seven months to six years, four months, with only one child below four-and-one-half years old. In addition, two girls of six years and one boy of four years, three months still had "accidents" at night. Two boys in the war-separated group still had daytime "accidents" at four years, eight months and five years, seven months of age. In the non-separated group only one child still regularly wet the bed and she was just three years of age; three others between three and five years had "accidents" at night; none had daytime "accidents."

It is evident that the war-separated fathers felt they had had a hard time training the first-born but the non-separated fathers felt it went rather easily. Seven of the war-separated group admitted to using spanking and other rather severe punishment in training their child. The mean difference between the groups on the scale of worry is statistically significant at the level of $P < .01$. The mean rating for the war-separated group is 2.47; for the non-separated group, 1.53 (see Table 25).

On the annoyance scale the mean difference between the groups approaches significance ($P < .05$) with the war-separated group tending to evidence greater annoyance (see Table 25).

Sleeping

The problems related to sleeping discussed by the fathers deal with problems of routine and problems connected with disturbances during sleep (see Table 26). The first include the child's attitude toward going to bed, rituals connected with going to bed, length of sleep, and attitude toward getting up. There are eleven war-separated and five non-separated fathers who report problems in this area (ratings 3, 4, 5). Disturbances to sleep include fear of dark, nightmares, restlessness of sleep. Five fathers in each group report severe problems of this nature. In addition, although not included in this rating, the discussion of elimination shows that persistent bed-wetting caused sleep disturbance with eight war-separated and four non-separated children, according to the fathers' reports.

Table 26. Sleep Problems of First-Born

	War-Separated	Non-Separated
Routines	11	5
Sleep disturbances	5	5
Routines and disturbances	5	2
Persistent bed-wetting	8	4
Routines, disturbances, bed-wetting	3	0

More war-separated fathers report problems of a serious nature in every area except sleep disturbances. There are eight children seen by war-separated fathers as having complicated sleep problems such as having problems in both routines and disturbances or these two in connection with bed-wetting. In contrast, only two children were reported by the non-separated fathers as having complicated problems.

When the excerpts are rated on the 5-point scale for seriousness of problems in routines, the mean rating for the war-separated group is 3.26; for the non-separated group, 2.11. The mean difference between the two groups is statistically significant at only the $P < .07$ level.

For problems in relation to sleep disturbance the war-separated group has a mean (1.95) slightly more than the non-separated group mean (1.89), but this difference is not statistically significant. If persistent bed-wetting had been included in the ratings of sleep disturbances, there would be a greater difference between the groups.

On the scale of father's worry, the mean of the war-separated group is only slightly higher than the non-separated group and the mean difference is not statistically significant (see Table 27). On the scale of annoyance the mean rating for the war-separated group is 3.00 and for the non-separated group, 1.50; the mean difference is statistically significant at the level of $P < .01$ (see Table 27).

Table 27. Father's Attitude Toward Sleep Behavior of First-Born

Scale	Mean		t	Significance
	War-Separated	Non-Separated		
Seriousness of problem				
Sleep routines	3.26	2.11	2.04	$P < .07$
Sleep disturbances	1.95	1.89	.10	–
Worry	2.30	2.10	.52	–
Annoyance	3.00	1.50	3.36	$P < .01$

The descriptions of Kate Snyder and Ann Wycoff given by their fathers which are cited here illustrate the tendency for some of the war-separated children to have complicated problems in relation to sleep. Both girls were persistent bed-wetters at the time of the study. Kate is rated 5 on seriousness of problems relating to routine, 1 on disturbances. Ann is rated 4 on routines, and 5 on disturbances. Both fathers evidence above average worry (rating 3) and considerable annoyance (4 and 5).

"When I first came home Kate was spoiled, she would not go to sleep without being rocked, a habit her grandmother had instilled. I felt she needed discipline and spanked her several times . . . I didn't approve of her taking toys to bed with her. She used to take a blanket to bed with her and I didn't think that was necessary . . . We often had difficulty with her at nap time. Kate always made a fuss and I would spank her . . . Afternoon naps no longer appeal to her, but she is held to them even though she doesn't sleep. Even without a nap she objects to going to bed at night and seldom retires without complaining or even crying" (Mr. Snyder).

"Ann was never afraid of the dark until two summers ago when we left her for a few days. I don't know what happened but when we came home, from then on she has been afraid of the dark. Once she wakened frightened and said she'd seen something in the room . . . About three weeks ago she had a night terror. I couldn't comfort her. My wife went in and held her for some time . . . She likes the door open and she had a light in her room for a long time . . . When she wets she crawls out of her bed and gets in with us— usually her mother'' (Mr. Wycoff).

Dressing

It is evident that the war-separated fathers are less concerned with problems that relate to the child's behavior in getting dressed and undressed than are the non-separated fathers. Ten of the war-separated group have practically nothing to say about this area, whereas only one non-separated father is as disinterested. There are only three war-separated fathers in contrast to six non-separated fathers who consider that the first-born has serious problems in dressing.

Table 28. Types of Problems in Dressing Behavior

	War-Separated	Non-Separated
Dependent, lacking skills	4	8
Slow, dawdling	4	6
Delaying getting dressed	1	5

The fact that the child lacks skills and is still dependent on his parents for getting dressed is the problem mentioned most often by the fathers (four war-separated, eight non-separated). However, none of the war-separated fathers describe this as a serious problem and none is either worried or annoyed by the dependent behavior. Of the four non-separated fathers who consider this a serious problem, three are worried and two are annoyed.

Mr. Irwin's description of his daughter, who was five years, four months old, illustrates the war-separated father's unconcern about this; Mr. Martin's description of his boy, four years and two months old, illustrates the non-separated father's somewhat greater tendency to worry and annoyance.

"Her mother dresses Patricia in the morning after I leave. Sometimes I dress her at noon for kindergarten. It goes pretty well if she is concentrating on it. She can dress herself to a certain extent, can put her shoes on but not tie them . . . I make her stand still'' (Mr. Irwin).

"Otto's not good about dressing. His mother has not made him dress himself to my satisfaction. I think he's delinquent there. I think he should be much further along than he is. He does a part job. He does it when he's properly motivated. But it's difficult to motivate a child when he's smart enough to know that if he doesn't dress himself, he will be ultimately dressed . . . In general, it is not a satisfactory situation. We've got to get it cleared up pretty soon'' (Mr. Martin).

The next most frequently mentioned problem is that the child has the skills to dress himself but he dawdles and is too slow. Of the four war-separated fathers who mention this, three are annoyed by it; of the six non-separated fathers, two are worried and three annoyed. Excerpts from one war-separated father, Mr. Wolf, illustrate this father's annoyance at a problem considered not serious.

"Dan seems to dawdle most when you want him to dress in a hurry. Whenever you're in a big hurry to get somewhere he can't seem to get dressed, can't find his shoes and socks . . . It gets us both nervous and irritated. Ends up with his mother dressing him or threatening him with a spatula and he hurries up and does it."

There are five non-separated fathers and one war-separated father who say their children do not want to get dressed in the morning. These situations are considered serious problems by all the fathers but they vary greatly in the degree of worry or annoyance which they evidence. Mr. Snyder is extremely annoyed (rating 5) but only slightly worried (rating 2) about this habit in his three-and-one-half year old daughter; Mr. Stone, a non-separated father, has extreme ratings on all three scales in regard to his five year old son, Harry.

"Kate's slowness in dressing in the morning and liking to go about in robe and slippers irritates me. I realize it is a result of her living with her ailing grandmother for so many months while I was away. In my family if anyone donned a lounging robe, it was interpreted as a sign of illness. But Kate likes to prolong the pajama-and-robe period as long as possible" (Mr. Snyder).

"We fight to get Harry through breakfast and then it's fight again trying to get him dressed to go outside to play. Often times it's ten o'clock or so before my wife gets him dressed. Every day this happens . . . Seems that about every time we finally have to get angry about him and really put our foot down before he'll actually start to get dressed . . . The things that are most irritating are his lounging around in his pajamas and not wanting to change" (Mr. Stone).

Although the mean rating on the seriousness of the problem in dressing is smaller for the war-separated group than for the non-separated group, the mean difference is not statistically significant (see Table 29).

Table 29. Father's Attitude Toward Dressing Behavior of the First-Born

Scale	Mean		t	Significance
	War-Separated	Non-Separated		
Seriousness of problem	1.79	2.53	1.39	–
Worry	1.26	2.21	2.33	$P < .05$
Annoyance	1.58	2.11	1.08	–

There is a tendency for the non-separated group of fathers to be more worried than the war-separated group about their first-born's behavior in relation to dressing ($P < .05$).

Neither group of fathers indicated much annoyance over dressing behavior, but the mean of the non-separated group is larger than that of the war-separated group. However, the mean difference is not statistically significant.

The fact that there is a tendency for the non-separated fathers to be more concerned about dressing behavior than the war-separated fathers may be due to the fact that the non-separated fathers take more responsibility for the dressing routines of their first-borns. According to the mothers' reports the war-separated children are less independent in dressing than the non-separated children. However, the mothers also report that the war-separated fathers take less responsibility for the care of these first-born children than the non-separated fathers do (see Chapter 7).

Tensions and Comforts

All but seven war-separated fathers and six non-separated fathers reported some kind of tension or some form of comfort which their children displayed. Table 30 lists the types of behavior which are reported as problems.

Table 30. Tensions and Comforts Reported by Fathers

	War-Separated	Non-Separated
Whining, crying	7	4
"Nervous"	3	3
Chewing, biting	2	1
Blinking, staring	—	1
Thumb- or finger-sucking	6	4
Masturbating	2	2
Milk, bottle	2	1
Toys in bed	2	2
Blanket	1	3
Rocking, stroking	2	1

The fathers in both groups reported relatively few forms of tensions, whining and persistent crying and general "nervousness" being the most frequent. They reported far more comforts, with thumb- or finger-sucking being the most prevalent.

There seemed to be a tendency for the war-separated fathers to report tension or comforts only if they were problems. All but 1 of the 12 reporting received ratings of 3, 4, or 5 on seriousness of problem. In the control group, only 7 of the 13 reporting received such ratings. However, as can be seen in Table 31, the difference between the mean rating for the two groups is small, with the war-separated group slightly higher. The mean difference is not significant.

Table 31. Father's Attitude Toward Tensions and Comforts of First-Born

Scale	Mean		t	Significance
	War-Separated	Non-Separated		
Seriousness of problem	2.84	2.47	.75	—
Worry	2.16	1.95	.50	—
Annoyance	2.37	1.58	1.57	—

Seven of the war-separated fathers and five of the non-separated fathers indicate they are worried about these behaviors. The mean ratings are smaller for both groups than on the seriousness scale with the war-separated showing greater worry than the non-separated group. The mean difference is not significant.

The war-separated group is more annoyed about these problems than the non-separated group. Seven war-separated and only three non-separated fathers received ratings indicating definite annoyance (ratings 3, 4, 5). The mean of the war-separated group is 2.37 and of the non-separated group, 1.58; but the mean difference is not statistically significant. Of the three war-separated fathers who are most annoyed (rating 5), two of the children have combinations of problems and one sucked his thumb persistently. Ann, an only child, has an extreme form of masturbation and an unusual desire for skin stimulation; she has regressed recently to sucking a bottle and other forms of infantile behavior at four years. Her father is quite tolerant of these behaviors but it is her whining and persistent crying that annoy Mr. Wycoff intensely. Mr. Statler, who is both worried and annoyed by his son's extreme form of thumb-sucking, is one of the fathers who is concerned about his boy's general sex-inappropriate behavior.

Relations with Other Children

To all the fathers except one (Mr. Mathews) in the war-separated group, the first-born's relations with other children seem an important yardstick for evaluation. Many of them describe in great detail the activities, behavior, and status of their children with peers.

There are four different categories into which most of their remarks can be grouped: whether the child seeks or withdraws from other children; whether he is friendly or aggressive; whether other children accept or reject him; whether his behavior is sex-appropriate or inappropriate. Table 32 gives the number of children described in positive or negative terms in each of these four categories. In each category more non-separated fathers mention positive traits and more war-separated fathers mention negative traits.

Table 32. Social Characteristics of Children

	War-Separated	Non-Separated
Positive		
Seeks children	7	14
Friendly	8	16
Children accept	6	16
Sex-appropriate	—	2
Negative		
Withdraws from	12	5
Aggressive	5	3
Children reject	10	3
Sex-inappropriate	10	5

In describing their children, 14 non-separated fathers use phrases such as "likes to be with other children" and "isn't shy at all," whereas only 7 war-separated fathers use such terms. In contrast, 12 war-separated and only 5 non-separated fathers use phrases like "doesn't like to be with other kids," "won't go out and play," "afraid of other children," "is shy," "likes to be alone."

One of the greatest contrasts seems to be in the non-separated fathers' emphasis on the friendliness of their children. Such statements as "is very friendly," "is willing to share," "makes friends easily," "never aggressive," "has good social techniques," "is diplomatic" are used by 16 non-separated and only 8 war-separated fathers. Even though five of these non-separated children sometimes quarrel, are selfish, or too bossy, the feeling of the fathers is that they are predominantly friendly in their relations. Among the children described as aggressive, three of the war-separated children and only one of the non-separated are viewed as extreme.

As one might expect, the children described by the father as friendly and outgoing are also described as being liked by other children. Those described as aggressive or withdrawn are more often described as being rejected by other children. The non-separated children usually are described as being accepted and more war-separated children are described as being rejected.

Among the fathers of the 26 boys in the two groups, there are 15 who are conscious of the sex-inappropriateness of their child's behavior. The characteristics which concern ten war-separated and five non-separated fathers include playing with girls or younger children, being shy, being afraid of other children, and especially not being able to fight. There is one war-separated father, (Mr. Bryan) who considers that his girl is too aggressive with other children, not gentle as a little girl should be. Such inappropriate characteristics disturb the fathers a great deal. The men report that they try hard to teach their boys the necessary skills so they can hold their own in a fight. The war-separated father thinks his son is gentle and lacks courage because the boy was brought up by women while he was overseas. Several descriptions of first-borns who are considered to lack "manly" attributes are cited here.

"Allen likes to play with girls . . . He has trouble in school. There are two boys who are awfully strong for their ages. I say he should fight them but he says he's going to get hurt. I'm sure some circumstance will make him fight some time and he'll get over it . . . I've talked to Allen about being a sissy. I don't want to have anybody picking on him. I want him to fight back if he has to" (Mr. Statler).

"Ray wouldn't hold his own in the group at all. Any aggression at all on the part of others would result in a retreat or tears or giving up what he had. Very little spunk. That used to worry me quite a little. Ray wasn't aggressive enough, an innate 'shyness' . . . I expect I had a feeling that Ray was a 'sissy' . . . I had a heart-rending experience yesterday. Ray came in complaining about the boy next door. I said, 'Don't tell me about it, go out and handle it yourself.' Ray said, 'What shall I do?' I said, 'If he hits you, hit him back.' Well, Ray went out and took a terrible licking from that boy. I didn't know what to do. I felt terrible. Instinctively he won't lash out—I don't know why" (Mr. Holman).

"Have you ever seen Bruce fight anybody? You never will. I've never even seen him defend himself. Ever since we moved down here he certainly is the scapegoat. The children annoy him. Bruce knows how to fight but I've never seen him do it and he can just be tormented. Someone will come up and swing on him and he won't fight back . . . I used to be afraid of boys and I don't want this to happen to Bruce'' (Mr. Arnold).

"Ken plays with the smaller ones. Probably Ken has played with more little girls than boys. He tries to keep up with the older boys who tease him, get him to cry. If a boy pushes Ken, he will never fight back, he'll come home'' (Mr. Marston).

"When he was a little boy everybody would push Don around. Even a smaller boy could push him around. All he knew was to cry . . . It bothered me very much that Don could not fight back. We didn't insist much, just told him the way he should go . . . I think this may be due to the fact that I was away at war and Don was in a feminine, protected environment. . . Don doesn't fight. He isn't belligerent. I have had trouble teaching him to defend himself. When he loses, he feels sorry for himself and cries. I hate to see other children pick on him. I hope Don will be less shy as he gets older. I am really worried about this'' (Mr. Burgman).

Table 33. Father's Attitude Toward Behavior of First-Born with other Children

Scale	Mean		t	Significance
	War-Separated	Non-Separated		
Seriousness of problem	3.11	2.00	2.49	$P < .04$
Worry	2.74	1.95	1.66	–
Annoyance	2.11	1.68	1.20	–

The ratings of the fathers' descriptions of the relations of their first-borns with other children on the three scales are shown in Table 33. On the 5-point scale evaluating the degree of seriousness of the problem as described by the fathers, the mean for the war-separated group is 3.11; for the non-separated group, 2.00. The mean difference between the groups tends toward statistical significance with $P < .04$. The mean ratings on the fathers' worry is in the same direction with the war-separated group evidencing more worry but the mean difference is not statistically significant. This same tendency is shown in the ratings on annoyance.

The evidence points to the fact that all young children have difficulties in learning how to get along with other children but that the circumstances surrounding the lives of children whose fathers were absent during the early years increased their difficulties in this area. As is shown in Chapter 7, the mothers report that the war-separated children had fewer contacts with other children in the early years than the non-separated group. The close relation with the mother and the general feminine atmosphere in which they lived, perhaps, also contributed to their being less able to adjust to the hurly-burly of young children's group play. The excerpts cited here illustrate how the fathers of the war-separated children see many problems in their children's social behavior and how the non-separated fathers view their children as much better adjusted. Mr. Osborne, Mr. Wolf, and Mr. Weiss are fathers who have extreme ratings on the seriousness of the problem and on the degree of the father's worry; Mr. Wolf also has an extreme rating on annoyance. Mr. Soule has a medium rating on all three scales.

"George knows a lot about kids. He just knows all what they're liable to do before they do it. He knows enough when a bunch of kids are rolling a top not to go over and play with it because they'll just bat you. He'll just kind of slink into line because they'll just push you around . . . At school George plays with little boys . . . He plays with Ann at home all the time. They fight all the time and play all the time . . . He's the most bossy kid I ever saw. He's always got somebody in tow. Has to run the whole thing. That's why he won't play with bigger kids at school. They won't let him run everything . . . If Ann doesn't do what he says, he won't hit, he'll push, he'll say, 'All right, I don't like you.' He doesn't get into fights. He uses any other tools rather than going after them with his fists. Snobbishness, taking toys, saying his daddy will do this or that. He doesn't bring me in particularly because he knows I won't fight his battles" (Mr. Osborne).

"Dan doesn't want to go to parties. He's got to stop picking on little kids. He's got to learn to be unselfish with stuff . . . The kids used to call him 'Diapers.' Dan didn't care. He'd go on howling every time something would happen. He still does . . . He always wants to be it. He sometimes exploits kids—always being pulled in the wagon, never pulling . . . If the big kids took his things, Dan just cried. Now he's hitting back. He doesn't come to tell me about his trouble because I punished him for that . . . He's inclined to lay the blame on others when he does something" (Mr. Wolf).

"Joe gets in groups and tries to lead but he's not accepted. The children leave him out of their play. He looks unhappy . . . Some of the children in the Village are tough and Joe has a hard time. The children near us bully him and he is afraid of them" (Mr. Weiss).

"I hope as Fran grows older she will be more outgoing than she is now. She still shows in her relations with children in the neighborhood a lack of ability to stand up for herself, assert herself, make her own way. She relies on us too much. She comes running in for help if things go against her, crying because she can't have her way. I hope she will be a little more extroverted than she is, to be able to go out into a gang and give and take, not being as sensitive if things go a little bit against her" (Mr. Soule).

The quotations below have been selected to illustrate the tendency of the non-separated fathers to see their children as having more satisfactory relations with other children. Mr. King and Mr. Park were rated 1 on all three scales.

"I think Leonard was pretty well liked by the kids at an early stage. I know there were always a lot of kids who would come around and want to play with him . . . He is not antisocial at all. He likes to have a lot of friends and he likes to even up his time with his friends . . . Leonard isn't much for telling on something that somebody else has done that's wrong. He keeps those things to himself pretty well. He doesn't squeal on the other fellow . . . I think one of the reasons why the kids like Leonard is that he's natural. He doesn't have any artificial attitudes about things. He likes good healthy play and never tries to pit one friend against another. I really believe he's a pretty balanced boy'' (Mr. King).

''Winston's a little advanced for his age (four years, four months). Mostly he's been playing with older children and he's picked up a little bit more than he would ordinarily . . . Winston's a very friendly child. He's been able to mix with other children very easily. I think he's able to adjust himself very quickly . . . Not that he doesn't have any fights, he does. I've made him pretty rough because I play with him pretty roughly, fight with him after supper and things like that. I tell him not to back down in a fight with other children, but he doesn't take a fresh attitude either . . . Winston's very diplomatic for a child. When he wants to get something from another child, he'll talk his way around until he usually gets it, and he seldom grabs or takes something . . . He tends to be a leader, he's more or less one of the gang. In the neighborhood he plays with all the children. He doesn't tie to any particular one . . . Now he doesn't want to go with my wife and me if we are going someplace, he'd rather stay home and play with the kids . . . Winston doesn't tattletale. Matter of fact, he'll protect a kid'' (Mr. Park).

Personality Characteristics of First-Born

As we have shown, the war-separated fathers as a group are more critical than the non-separated group of their first-borns' behavior in eating, elimination, and relations with peers, and tended toward being more critical in sleeping behavior. There is no war-separated father who isn't extremely critical of his child in one of these areas and some are critical of their first-borns in several areas. In addition, the war-separated father is more critical of his child's personality.

In Chapter 5 we present an intensive analysis of the personality traits of the father and his first-born child. Our analysis here gives only a brief summary of the father's attitude toward the child's personality. Toward the close of the series of interviews each father was asked, ''What do you think are the strongest characteristics of your first-born? Are there any ways in which you would like to see him change in the coming years?'' The excerpts on the father's feeling for child included the father's discussion of these questions. Only these excerpts were used in this analysis of the father's attitude toward the personality characteristics of his child.

Table 34 gives the personality traits most frequently criticized and approved by both groups of fathers. Every one of the war-separated fathers has something to criticize in his child, but seven of the non-separated group give no criticisms. The war-separated group criticize, on the average, 3.3 traits per child and the non-separated, only 1.5 traits. More war-separated fathers than non-separated fathers mention every trait listed as criticized in Table 34. The traits most often criticized are being a ''sissy'' (for boys), being unresponsive, and being highly emotional (nervous, sensitive).

Table 34. Father's Attitude Toward
Personality Characteristics of First-Born

Traits	War-Separated	Non-Separated
Criticized		
Highly emotional	7	5
Unhappy	2	—
Stubborn	5	4
Disrespectful	3	—
Selfish	3	1
Demanding	3	—
Unresponsive	7	—
"Sissy"	9	5
Other	16	11
Total	62	29
Approved		
Intelligent	11	17
Verbal	4	5
Creative	1	3
Disciplined	3	5
"Good"	2	8
Self-reliant	2	5
Sense of humor	3	5
Friendly	3	10
Good natured	1	3
Interested	1	5
Other	3	8
Total	34	74

Table 35 shows the number of traits criticized by each group of fathers. One war-separated father mentions eight, another six, and two others five different traits that they do not like (see Table 35). Mr. Wolf says his oldest son is fearful, sissy, indecisive, dependent, selfish, noisy, show-off, and self-centered. Mr. Moore says his boy is scatterbrained, selfish, nervous, untrustworthy, and inconsiderate. Mr. Bryan says his five-year-old girl is bossy, disrespectful, too independent, stubborn, self-centered, and unresponsive.

Analysis of the personality traits fathers approve of in their first-borns shows an opposite trend. The war-separated fathers mention on the average less than half as many characteristics which they approve (1.8) as the non-separated fathers (3.9). More non-separated fathers than war-separated fathers mention each approved trait in Table 35. Each non-separated father has at least two traits and some as many as seven traits which he mentions on these excerpts as desirable, whereas three war-separated fathers could think of nothing and eight mention only one trait (see Table 35).

Table 35. Number of Personality Traits of First-Borns Criticized and Approved by Fathers

Number of Traits	Criticized		Approved	
	War-Separated	Non-Separated	War-Separated	Non-Separated
0	—	7	3	—
1	5	5	8	—
2	6	4	3	4
3	4	1	1	4
4	—	1	2	2
5	2	—	—	3
6	1	—	—	3
7	—	—	—	3
8	1	1	—	—

One gets the impression that approved traits are mentioned by the war-separated father somewhat grudgingly but are referred to with genuine enthusiasm by the non-separated father. This is well illustrated by Mr. Burgman, a war-separated father:

"We don't see any extraordinary characteristics. Just a normal child for his age. We were a little afraid that he was a little slow before but all of a sudden he catches up. Nothing as yet has crystallized to indicate any superior ability, just normal."

In both groups, more fathers were proud of their child's intelligence than of any other trait, but in the war-separated group 7 fathers could think of nothing else, while all of the 17 non-separated fathers who mention this discuss other qualities as well. In mentioning the first-born's intelligence the war-separated father is likely to be somewhat apologetic but there is no evidence of this in the non-separated group. Mr. Ford, for example, says, "Ned learns quickly, he is eager to learn. He may not be brilliant— his father isn't."

The non-separated fathers mention friendliness often, emphasizing the qualities of being warm, sympathetic, generous, kind to other people. Only three war-separated fathers describe their first-borns in these terms.

Interpersonal Relations Within the Family

It is in the area of interpersonal relations within the family that the fathers' reports show the greatest differences between the war-separated and non-separated groups.

Father-Child Relations

We have attempted to get at the basic feeling between the father and his first-born by a rating of the father-child relation. The material for this evaluation included all statements of the father concerning his general attitude or feelings for the child and all statements he made concerning the child's attitude toward the father.

We believe that this material epitomizes the interpersonal relations between father and first-born. As we have shown, the war-separated fathers do not seem more concerned with certain specific areas such as dressing than the non-separated fathers, but there is no father who is not deeply concerned with his relations with his first-born. The excerpts for this rating are much longer than any of the others (including eating behavior, a behavior of much concern to fathers).

The excerpts were rated on the 5-point scale of seriousness of problem. The mean rating for the father-separated group is 3.34 and for the non-separated group is 1.68. The t value is 4.39, the mean difference being significant at the $P < .001$ level.

Only one father in the father-separated group was given a rating of 1, indicating warm, positive, supporting relationships, whereas 12 of the non-separated fathers received this rating. This war-separated father (Mr. Harlow) is the one mentioned in Chapter 3 as having had an important job related to his wartime service when he and his wife were reunited. He participated little in family life and had no responsibility for his child. He has kept this aloofness from responsibility for his child during his years of graduate study. Thus he still maintains something of the "Santa Claus" quality which Bach describes in his study (6).

At the other end of the scale, four in the father-separated group and one in the non-separated group received the rating of 5, indicating serious difficulties in father-child relationships. The quotations we cite illustrate how the war-separated fathers feel, and the contrast in the feelings of the non-separated fathers. Mr. Burgman was rated 4; the other war-separated men quoted were rated 5 in father-child relations. Mr. Tipton and Mr. Moffett, both non-separated fathers, received ratings of 1. Since the excerpts contained so much material, it is difficult to select a short quotation that presents adequately the feeling of the father. The depth of feeling shows when the father says the same thing over and over again in different ways and with different illustrations.

"Rick is scatterbrained at home . . . He irritates me no end . . . He can't be trusted . . . I blow hot and cold with Rick. I'm not too consistent. When it comes to loving, I try to be as good as I can . . . I have to hold myself in . . . He doesn't have too many lovable traits. Things he does are antagonizing, annoying . . . He is scared of me. He doesn't show too much affection. He has a speech impediment which shows when he says blessing or talks to me . . ." (Mr. Moore).

"The response from Mary is not there. She never runs to me when I come home. She is busy listening to the radio. I have to take the initiative— she is unresponsive . . . She doesn't want me to do things for her. We never do anything together . . . I think Mary will be the executive type. I now accept it; before I didn't like it" (Mr. Bryan).

"I think that something is wrong somewhere— that he has not adjusted well to me in general . . . My wife is the main one in his life. I don't think he's ever really accepted me. It is better now. I can do things for him my wife can't do and he's beginning to see a father's worth something. But mother is first . . . Even now there are instances when he excludes me. If he says something at the table and I say, 'What did you say?' he will answer, 'I wasn't talking to you!' "(Mr. Burgman).

The excerpts that follow are typical of the affectionate, close relations of the non-separated group.

"We purposely waited on having children until I was out of the Navy . . . We get along pretty well together I think. Howard wasn't a cuddly baby but he likes my affection now, seems to want it . . . It's hard to say whether he feels closer to me or to my wife. He looks forward to my coming home a great deal and he enjoys spending as much time as he can with me on weekends . . . It's usually me who will give him a shower. I don't have to do anything for him, he justs wants somebody to talk to him at the time . . . Howard loves to get me in a game that involves pretending. We can pretend we are on a rocket ship or something; we do that when we are driving. . . All in all we get along pretty well together, I think" (Mr. Tipton).

"I've always been rather fond of babies. Cathy was a great thrill. She was very cute . . . She was always responsive. Always liked to be with people and she was aware of them . . . I'm not only reconciled to having two girls but I consider myself very lucky that it panned out so well. Strictly from the parents' point of view, I think it's probably a lot easier to start with girls than boys . . . Oh yes, they were planned. We wanted two right close together, then some more later on . . . We think they're pretty wonderful kids. I think we're very lucky . . . I couldn't honestly say there's any difference in Cathy's attitude toward me or my wife. I'm good for certain things, and mother's good for certain things . . . I'm inclined to be more sentimental with her, and to baby her more than her mother does" (Mr. Moffett).

Father's Discipline of First-Born

In 13 of the war-separated families, the father says that he is considered the disciplinarian in the family by the first-born and he feels that this makes a difference in his relations with his first-born child. From our analysis of the first year of the father's contact with his first-born, it is evident that the war-separated fathers used much more severe discipline than the non-separated group (see Chapter 3, p. 43). Although there is evidence that they have changed their methods as the children have developed, their severity still seems to be greater than that of the non-separated fathers. Ratings on a 5-point scale of the severity of the father's punishment (including data regarding later methods of discipline as well as in the early years) gives a mean of 3.68 to the war-separated group and a mean of 2.26 to the non-separated group. The t value is 3.85 and the mean difference between the groups is significant at the $P < .005$ level.

First-Born's Relations with Mother

All but two of the war-separated men feel that even after the years they have lived with their first-borns, the children are still much closer to their mothers. Mr. Burgman puts this very well when he says of his five year old, "My wife is the main one in his life. I don't think he's ever really accepted me." It might be considered natural for a young child to be closer to his mother, but most of the non-separated fathers do not feel that way about their first-borns. Table 36 shows the difference between the war-separated and non-separated fathers in this regard. Seventeen of the war-separated fathers feel the mother is the main person in the life of their first-born, while only 5 of the non-separated fathers feel that way. One of the most interesting findings is the high proportion of non-separated fathers who feel the child is equally close to mother and father. In finding the significance of the difference between the two groups, cells 2 and 3 in Table 36 were combined in order to obtain the required expected frequency per cell. Using the method of chi square, the difference between the attitudes of the first-borns toward their parents is statistically significant at the level of $P < .001$; chi square equals 15.5.

Table 36. Relation of First-Born to Mother and Father as Reported by Father

	War-Separated	Non-Separated
Child closer to mother	17	5
Child equally close to father and mother	1	11
Child closer to father	1	3

The excerpts which are cited tell how the war-separated fathers feel about the relations of the first-borns to mother and father.

"Whenever Kate wants anything special she asks her mother for it . . . Goes to mother when I direct or punish her . . . Mother continues to spoil her . . . Kate prefers her mother to go to her at night" (Mr. Snyder).

"His mother has been closer to Albert than I will ever be. Albert is her boy, Leslie is mine . . . If Albert wants something fixed, he goes to his mother. When he is most worried it is about his mother's affection and the threat of its loss . . . Albert looks to his mother for direction . . . When he goes to the neighbors to visit, the man is just another man; he makes relations with the woman" (Mr. Mathews).

"Sometimes I have felt George's more his mother's boy and Alvin is more mine because Alvin is rough and tough. George's nature hates to use force— a little more mama's boy" (Mr. Osborne).

"I feel Pattie and my wife are close, like my wife and her mother. I felt left out in the early days and I feel left out now" (Mr. Irwin).

"Dan's more of a mother's baby . . . He runs to his mother if I swat him hard. If he's gonna bawl, he runs to her . . . The only reason I think he's his mother's boy is that she had most of the bringing up the first two years. He still looks to her . . . Dan's jealous of his brother as he's gotten older. He seems to be vying for his mother's affection" (Mr. Wolf).

Father's Relation to Second-Born

There were 16 families in each group in which there was a second child.

In one war-separated family the second baby was born during the course of the interviews with the father. Table 37 shows how the fathers feel toward their first- and second-born children. All the war-separated fathers except two say that they love the second child better than the first. One of these two fathers (Mr. Statler) certainly shows a difference of feeling for his second child though he stoutly denies it; the other father's second child was only a few days old (Mr. Holman). This differs from the non-separated families, in which five fathers feel closer to the first child than the second and seven felt equally close to both children. Cells 1 and 2 in Table 37 were combined to obtain the significance of the difference by the method of chi square. The difference between the two groups of fathers is statistically significant at the $P < .001$ level; chi square equals 12.7.

Table 37. Father's Attitude Toward First- and Second-Born Child

	War-Separated	Non-Separated
Closer to 1st than 2nd	—	5
Equally close to 1st and 2nd	2	7
Closer to 2nd than 1st	14	4

In the family constellation for the war-separated group the first-born is the mother's child and the second-born is the father's child. The non-separated father is likely to say, "When the second one came, the first became much closer to me, I took over a lot of his care," whereas the war-separated father is likely to say, "When the second baby was born I did a lot for him as I'd missed it with the first and this gave my wife more time for the first-born."

The attitude of the war-separated fathers is well illustrated in the following quotations from their interviews.

"I don't feel the same affinity for Rick as I have for the other children. Probably due to the fact I saw Teddy (the second child) born. Maybe because I'd learned from Rick how to treat Teddy . . . Teddy is such a sweet kid" (Mr. Moore).

"Alice seems like a first baby—I feel like a first-time father. She's getting all the attention I would have lavished on Fran if I'd been around . . . Fran shows jealousy when I play with Alice, it's a big problem" (Mr. Soule).

"I often wonder, am I as attached to Alma as I am to the other two children" (Mr. Wagner).

"In my mind, Edward (the second boy) is my baby. I often call him Babe, my baby, see? . . . My wife says that the younger boy is my child." (Mr. Arnold).

Mr. Marston has difficulty in feeling the same towards both his boys. He describes it in this way: "I've always felt I've known Leslie (the second child) right from the start and with Ken (the first child), really, I didn't have much to do with him until he was a year old . . . I think I sometimes favor Leslie and then try to compensate for Ken. We're constantly trying to resolve these things and be the same to both of them." This is especially interesting since Mr. Marston is the father who was more like the non-separated group in his perception of self and first-born (Chapter 5, p. 96). He was relatively nonrejecting of Ken and did not use phobic projection as the other war-separated fathers did.

It seems pretty clear that the war-separated father has tried deliberately to build a warm, close relation to his second child because he feels he has lost out with the first child. Mr. Burgman describes this situation with feeling:

> "I missed Don when he was one to fourteen months, and I just didn't know how a baby looked, so when Maria was born I showed more concern, more interest with her. All the little things that she was learning which were not new to my wife but new to me . . . Maybe I did try a little harder to play up to her because I was a little afraid I had lost my Don. And Maria, when she became 'socialized,' when she got out of her crib to look around and become a member of the family, I was there—and she had adjusted to me and I had adjusted to her."

Sibling Relations

The second child was born to the war-separated families, on the average, 16.7 months after the father's return. This meant that many of the first-borns had to adjust to a sibling during the period of greatest adjustment to the father. The war-separated children ranged in age from 19 to 64 months when the second child was born, an average age of 34.1 months. The non-separated first-borns had a narrower range in age at the birth of their siblings (13 to 52 months), the average age being 3 months younger than the war-separated group.

All the fathers except one non-separated father discussed the relations of their first and second children.

The number of fathers in the two groups whose descriptions of the relations between first and second child are given extreme ratings (3, 4, 5) are similar for the scale of <u>seriousness of problem</u> and <u>worry of father</u>. However, six of the war-separated fathers and only one non-separated father were extremely worried about the situation.

The two groups talk almost equally about quarrels and hitting, competitiveness and selfishness. The war-separated fathers more often than the non-separated fathers say their first-borns have regressed or are unhappy or that they dominate the second-born. More non-separated fathers mention teasing (a mild form of conflict) and more mention the protective role the first played with the second.

The analysis of the ratings of the excerpts on the three scales are given in Table 38. On each scale the war-separated group is rated higher than the non-separated group, but the mean differences are not statistically significant for <u>seriousness of problem</u> or <u>worry of father</u>. The mean difference of the ratings on the scale of annoyance tends toward significance with a P which is less than .04.

The greater annoyance of the war-separated fathers is probably related to the fact that these men were closely tied to the second-born and resented any relation of the first to the second which was detrimental to the second.

They were not equally protective of the older child's rights. Mr. Arnold, for example, had insisted that Edward (second-born) have every privilege and opportunity parallel with Bruce, the first-born child. He even resented the fact that Bruce was admitted into nursery school earlier than Edward, who was two years younger. The second year, when Edward was admitted, Mr. Arnold insisted that they be in the same group. Bruce was quiet and shy; Edward, vigorous and extremely social.

Table 38. Father's Attitude Toward Behavior of First-Born with Sibling

Scale	Mean		t	Significance
	War-Separated	Non-Separated		
Seriousness of problem	3.25	2.94	1.53	–
Worry	2.50	2.06	1.79	–
Annoyance	2.19	1.50	2.29	$P < .04$

Mr. Osborne showed this same tendency. He did not want George to go to nursery school before Alvin, who was 19 months younger. Even when George was in kindergarten, his father did not want him to be friends with Ann if it meant Alvin was left out. He said, "Every place George goes, Alvin's got to go, too. I won't have Alvin left out. He can hold his own any place."

Summary and Interpretation

Ratings of excerpts from the father interviews showed several differences between the war-separated and non-separated fathers in their attitudes toward the first-born's behavior. In eating, elimination, and sleep behavior, the war-separated fathers considered that their children had more serious problems; the fathers were more worried and were more annoyed about this behavior. All these differences were either statistically significant or tended in that direction.

In only one of the routine care items which we analyzed was the non-separated group more concerned than the war-separated group. This was in dressing routines, where the only significant difference was in the father's degree of worry. We believe that the tendency for the non-separated father to be more worried about his first-born's ability to dress and undress himself is due to the fact that these fathers participated more in the care of their children than the other group did. In the war-separated group it was the mothers who took the responsibility for the dressing routine and who, therefore, were more concerned about it (as shown in Chapter 7).

The war-separated fathers had higher ratings on all three scales regarding tensions and comforts, but the differences between the groups were not statistically significant. The war-separated group seems somewhat insensitive to these manifestations of insecurity since in the mothers' reports the war-separated children show more tensions than the non-separated children.

In relations with other children, the war-separated fathers, in comparison with the non-separated fathers, saw their children as having more serious problems and they tended to evidence more worry and annoyance about their behavior. Only the difference in the degree of problem tended toward statistical significance, however.

The war-separated fathers also seem to be more critical of their first-born's personality. Evidence for this was not analyzed statistically here. Quantitative analysis on this topic will be presented in Chapter 5.

It is in the area of father-child relations that we find the greatest differences between the war-separated and non-separated groups. The ratings on father's relations with first-born, father's discipline of first-born, mother's relations with first-born, and father's relations with second-born all show significant differences between the war-separated and non-separated fathers. These differences were at the $P < .001$ and $P < .005$ levels of significance. The war-separated fathers tend to perceive their first-borns as having more difficulties with their siblings and they are more annoyed about their behavior. None of these differences between the groups regarding sibling relations was statistically significant, though annoyance tended to be ($P < .04$).

The picture of the war-separated group shows a father and first-born who are distant and have serious problems in their interpersonal relations. The father uses severe, though somewhat modified discipline with the first-born whom he has never really accepted and whom he continues to find difficult to manage. The mother and first-born have kept their close relation while the father has found his compensation in his warm, intimate relation with the second-born. Mr. Wolf summed up the situation quite clearly when he said:

> "I think to be there from the time he was born up to his first or second birthday would be the most important for making the father feel closer. Oh, like Raymond now. He's just at the stage when he starts to learn to walk and to learn to talk and to learn to do this and to do that; and if you're there, I guess you feel closer to him, as if you had a hand in shaping their mannerisms. But if you come back and he's there and he's developed everything he's going to, well, you just haven't had a part in it. That's the answer . . . The stuff you learn in the first two years is the primary basic stuff, and you just can't get out of it in a couple of years. I think it'll take 10-15 years for Dan gradually to mold and until he gets what I want him to be. I guess every guy has his standard pattern what he wants his kids to be like. The first one has a disadvantage when you're not there to mold him right from the start. You have to start with something that's already there and kind of re-mold it back to your way; whereas when the second one comes and you're there you can mold him the way you want right from the start."

CHAPTER 5.
FATHER'S PERCEPTION OF SELF AND FIRST-BORN CHILD

by Erika Chance

Theoretical Orientation

The preceding analysis indicated that the war-separated fathers were under considerable stress in having to adjust simultaneously to their roles as breadwinner, husband, and father.

Since previous studies had indicated that stress is revealed in terms of change in perception, we were interested in comparing patterns of self- and child-perception in the war-separated fathers with those of non-separated fathers.

Dynamics of the Father-Child Relation as Revealed by Self-Perception and Child-Perception

We selected trait correspondence between the father's self-perception and his perception of the first child as a crucial factor in father-child relation (13). This decision was based on a number of considerations. The first of these was the observation that the fathers tended to mention this factor spontaneously as if they themselves felt that the perceived similarity between themselves and the first child presented the high lights of their relation. A second group of considerations arose from a survey of recent studies in perception and from psychoanalytic postulates concerning the dynamics of the parent-child relation.

Psychoanalytic theory postulates that the mother tends to see the child as an extension of herself—cf. Freud, the child as a penis substitute (30); Levy, the overprotective mother (51); Erikson, the attitude of the daughters of United States pioneers toward their sons (24). These postulates appear to deal somewhat inadequately with the question of the significance of the child for the father. Psychoanalysis holds that the child will be perceived by the mother as endowed with personality tendencies which she herself cannot integrate. The question arose, therefore, whether the same mechanism might be found in fathers.

In contrast, folk custom as well as philosophic and fictional literature suggest that the father tends to perceive the child as an extension of that part of the self which has been integrated and crystallized into a social role. This trend is illustrated by the use of such terms as "Junior," by the role assigned to godfathers, and by the recurrence of such phrases as "chip off the old block." It is possible that such customs serve to provide a sense of continuity beyond the father's own lifetime.

Analytic hypotheses, popular postulates, and the findings of recent studies in perception could be reconciled along lines indicated by the writings of Erikson. He holds that one of the crucial stages of ego-development is the development of a sense of identity, i.e., "the accrued confidence that the inner sameness and continuity are matched by the sameness and continuity of one's meaning for others . . ." (24).

Hilgard (39) has stated that maintenance of a stable perceptual frame of reference is a primary goal of individual functioning. This could be interpreted as a more widely applicable phrasing of the need for continuity which Erikson describes. Correspondence between self-perception and child perception might be understood as an expression of the need to maintain such a stable frame of reference and a sense of identity.

Focus of this Study

This study is especially concerned with the question of what happens to self-perception and child-perception when the stability of the frame of reference and the individual's sense of identity are threatened, either by inadequate intrapsychic integration or by external circumstances. Erikson (24) has given a number of clues as to the type of defense mechanism one might expect. Particularly pertinent is his statement regarding men with war neuroses that "what impressed me most was the loss of a sense of identity." Another clue is in his discussion of role diffusion as the juxtaposition of isolated (or dissociated), incongruous perceptions of the self. His description of overidentification in the adolescent who is faced with the danger of role diffusion is also suggestive.

The hypotheses outlined below attempt to evaluate to what extent the father's perception of the first child might be interpreted as an expression of the need to maintain a sense of continuity and identity. The father's return from the war is assumed to be a situation which represents considerable threat to ego-identity in that he is under stress to adjust simultaneously in the areas of vocation, marital relations, and child relations. The first child who was born in his absence is expected to be the focus of perceptual defense mechanisms in that the manner in which he is perceived can either reinforce a sense of continuity or threaten it considerably. The hypotheses assume that perceptual processes will reinforce the sense of continuity, but that their defensive nature will be revealed by the patterns and accompanying affective tone in which the first child is perceived.

If the experience of war-separation and the subsequent return to a new family constellation is more potent as a conflict-producing factor than developmental factors, then a group of war-separated fathers should tend to perceive themselves more negatively and to show more conflict concerning their evaluation of themselves than fathers not so separated. We would expect this group to show a larger number of defensive perceptual patterns than the non-separated fathers.

On the basis of analytic theory and perception studies, the following perceptual patterns were selected as possessing a defensive function:

Parataxis or transference.[1] If the trait correspondence assists in maintenance of a stable frame of reference and of a sense of continuity, we would expect individuals showing intrapsychic conflict, as defined above, to see themselves reflected in their perception of the first child more than individuals not so conflicted.

1. In a previous study (12), E. Chance investigated "transference," defined as ". . . the tendency to respond to the therapist with feelings, attitudes, and behavior which are stereotypes . . . of his childhood experience in relation with the parental figure . . . important in his development." It is possible that correspondence between self- and child-perception is a manifestation of the same process.

Rejection. An alternative perceptual defense consists in distancing and isolating the perceptual object from the perceiver. Disapproval can be understood as one way of separating oneself socially from a threatening perceptual object. If disapproval functions as a defensive perceptual pattern, we would expect that a conflicted group of fathers will tend to disapprove more of their first children than a group not so conflicted.

Phobic projection. The assumption that there will be correspondence between the "perceiver" and the "perceived" is found in perception studies, in projective tests, and in the analytic literature, and is based on the concept of projection in the broadest sense. This definition includes projective processes which are accompanied by either positive or negative affect. Phobic projection, in which the individual perceives negatively in another those traits about which he himself is in conflict, represents one of several types of projective processes. We defined phobic projection for the purpose of this study as disapproval by the father of those traits perceived in the first child about which he has shown conflict in perceiving himself. We would expect this pattern to occur more frequently in those cases where fathers show high intrapsychic conflict than in those not so conflicted.

Method of Analysis

Requirements for devising a systematic method of analyzing interview material fall into two groups: first, the choice of basic units of analysis or the kind of categorization to be used; and second, a series of dimensions along which the basic units can be grouped and systematically ordered.

The Categorization of Material

Requirements for categorization. If personality is defined as "the relatively enduring pattern of interpersonal relationships"— Sullivan (79)— then the basic units of analysis must represent an ongoing interpersonal process or action tendency. The unit of categorization, therefore, is an act performed or experienced by the individual.

Current conceptual systems in psychology tend to emphasize selected central variables which are, of course, hypothetical. Dichotomous classification is prevalent and does not do justice to the complexity of personality functioning. We wished to find a method of categorization in which the central variables would be predetermined to a lesser extent than is usual and which would do justice to the complexity of personality. Therefore, empirical classification at the phenomenological level seemed indicated. It was necessary that the number of categories be sufficient to allow for multiple grouping and also for some choice in the use of existing systematic frames of reference. We wished to define our categories so that empathic rating from the subject's point of view would be possible (7).

Grouping of categories. It is assumed that the frequency and the intensity with which a given category occurs represent the degree to which an individual is preoccupied with that category. Categories can, therefore, be grouped according to the degree of preoccupation.

Any one unit of analysis will represent an interpersonal process or experience perceived by the individual. The process or experience can be perceived as desirable or undesirable by the subject and can be so rated. Categories can, therefore, be grouped into those which tend to be accepted and those which tend not to be accepted.

Since categories represent interpersonal processes as perceived by the subject, they can be grouped into those which stand for positive interaction or movement toward people and those categories which stand for hostile and negative interaction— that is, according to the direction of the process.

Interpersonal processes and experiences as perceived by the subject may represent active participation by him or an experience which he perceives as a relatively passive one.

Lastly, interpersonal processes can be grouped according to the object which is perceived as functioning in a given manner. For the purpose of this investigation, categories perceived by the subject will be ordered around two main objects: self-perception and perception of the first child.

Categories used. The categories as shown in Table 39 are an extension of the system of interpersonal mechanisms as described by Freedman et al (27). Whereas these writers used 16 categories (see Figure 1), the present investigation added 4 categories, expanding the system to 20. These additions were made in order to facilitate multiple grouping. We wished to describe the father's perceptual pattern of self and of child as predominantly active or predominantly passive. Therefore, an active outgoing "love" category and a passive recipient classification were substituted for the single category of "love" used by Freedman et al. Similarly, opportunity was provided for classifying both active and passive forms of hatred separately (e.g., hate vs. resentment). Similarly, the addition of positive and negative forms of dominance (bossing vs. directing) and of submission (conforming vs. submitting) makes it possible to describe an individual as predominantly friendly and moving toward people, or tending to be hostile and to move against people. (The additions are indicated by an asterisk in Table 39).

These additions allow for a fourfold grouping of categories: positive active, negative active, positive passive, and negative passive. The relationship between categories has been well described by Freedman, Leary, and Ossorio by placing them upon a circle (see Figure 1). This illustrates their underlying continuity as well as the complementary character of categories at opposite points of the circle.

Scoring system. The scoring system used by Freedman et al consisted of scoring in terms of frequency and intensity. Intensity was rated on a 3-point scale, where a score of 1 represented a statement of mild intensity, possibly an understatement; a score of 2 represented moderate or appropriate intensity; a score of 3, strong intensity. This scoring system was adopted with one important addition. Statements were also rated according to whether the subject perceived the interpersonal experience or process as desirable (plus rating) or undesirable (minus rating). The addition of this variable permits ordering of the data along a further dimension.

Unit of classification. The unit of classification was the smallest possible unit in the typed interview material connoting an interpersonal process or experience with reference to the subject or the subject's first child. Rating in each case was, however, contextual, i.e., the place of the unit in the flow of the interview was taken into account.

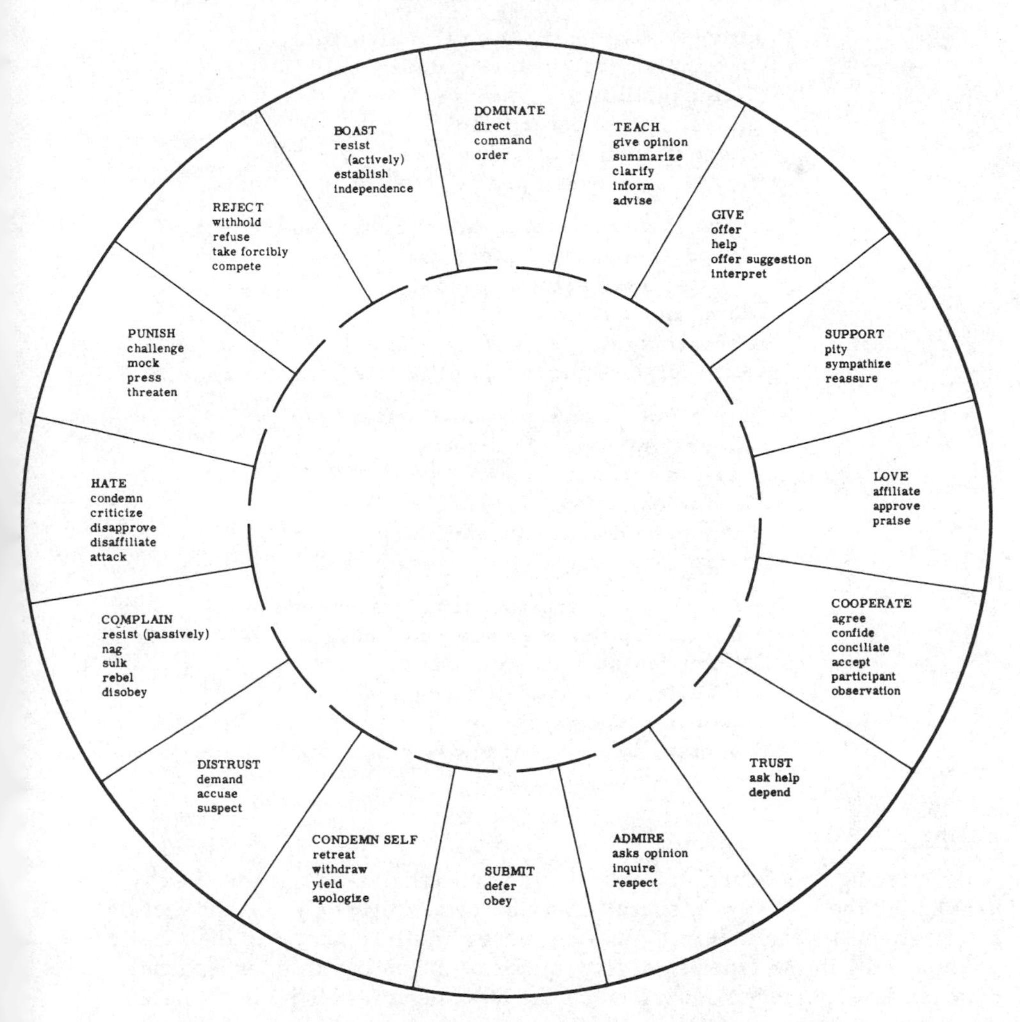

Figure 1. Categories for classifying father-interview material—from Freedman, Leary, Ossorio, and Coffey (27).

A sample of categorized material is given in Appendix 5. This will illustrate the uses as well as the limitations of this method of analysis, since it will be apparent that even 20 categories do not provide for classification of all interpersonal processes perceived by the subject. It must be expressly stated, therefore, that measures of correspondence and relationship between the pattern of self-perception and the perception of the first child can only refer to the processes classified here and to higher order processes which represent composites of these.

Table 39. Categories Used for Classifying Father-Interview Material

Positive Active Interpersonal Statements
- Dominates, directs, is independent
- Teaches, informs, advises
- Gives, helps, interprets
- Supports, pities, sympathizes
- *Loves, approves, praises

Positive Passive Interpersonal Statements
- Cooperates, conciliates, agrees
- Trusts, asks help, depends
- Admires, asks opinion
- *Conforms, obeys
- Appreciates, praises, loves

Negative Active Interpersonal Statements
- *Bosses, dominates, directs
- Resists actively, boasts
- Competes, takes, refuses
- Punishes, mocks, threatens
- Hates, condemns, criticizes, attacks

Negative Passive Interpersonal Statements
- Complains, resists passively, nags
- Distrusts, accuses, demands
- Retreats, apologizes, condemns self
- Submits, defers, obeys
- *Resents, hates, condemns, criticizes

Rating Procedure

The rating procedure throughout each case analysis first involved bracketing the unit of classification which had reference to the subject or his first child. The unit of classification was defined above as the smallest possible unit in the typed interview material connoting an interpersonal process or experience described by the 20 categories listed in Table 39. As shown in Appendix 5, different types of brackets were used for those units descriptive of the father's self-perception and those descriptive of his perception of the first child. Following this, each unit was rated in one of the 20 trait categories, according to the degree of intensity and whether perceived as desirable or undesirable.

Scores of the 20 traits shown in Table 39 are based on two main types of judgments: those concerning the frequency with which statements indicative of a given trait occur; and those concerning the intensity of these statements. Each of these can be further analyzed into: (1) statements rated plus, (2) statements rated minus, and (3) summed score irrespective of sign.

Method of Testing Reliability

The three cases which presented the greatest difficulty in rating for

Rater A (E. Chance) were selected in order to test the reliability of this method of analysis. These were Mr. Irwin and Mr. Wolf, war-separated fathers, and Mr. Murray, non-separated.

Rater B (C. Nakamura) was given a copy of Table 39 which lists the 20 categories used for classification. In addition, the basis for intensity ratings and for positive ratings was explained. Rater B then rated two easier cases for practice purposes. He conferred with Rater A to discuss questions about the use of the categories. Finally, he proceeded to the rating of the three difficult test cases.

Each set of ratings consisted of 40 total category scores, 20 for categories descriptive of self-perception and 20 for categories descriptive of child-perception. The 40 total category scores were further analyzed into two main groups: scores based on frequency and scores based on frequency weighted by intensity for each of these two main groups. Three subscores were computed for each group as follows:

1. The positive rating scores, which are based on the number of units (weighted by intensity for the intensity scores), include the statements per category which imply the father's approval of a trait or category.
2. The negative rating scores include those statements conveying disapproval of a trait or category.
3. The total category rating scores are based on the scores of positive and negative ratings summed regardless of sign.

Three types of scores for each case were thus obtained. Correlations by the product-moment method were obtained between the two sets of independent ratings for these three types of scores as shown in Table 40.

The fact that the r's obtained for total category rating scores are not appreciably lowered even where there is low agreement in negative rating score, is due to the small number of scores involved in the negative ratings which are, of course, part of the total category rating.

Table 40. Correlations Between Ratings of Two Independent Raters

	Positive Rating Scores	Negative Rating Scores	Total Category Ratings
		Frequency Correlations Obtained	
Mr. Murray	r = .96	r = .52	r = .97
Mr. Wolf	r = .98	r = .83	r = .97
Mr. Irwin	r = .96	r = .82	r = .96
		Intensity Correlations Obtained	
Mr. Murray	r = .96	r = .43	r = .95
Mr. Wolf	r = .98	r = .84	r = .96
Mr. Irwin	r = .97	r = .78	r = .97

The correlations of the two raters on the positive rating scores and the total category scores for the three cases range from .96 to .98 for frequency ratings and from .95 to .98 when frequency ratings are weighted by intensity ratings.

For the negative rating scores, which required the more difficult judgment as to whether the subject perceived that the trait was undesirable, correlations ranging from .78 to .84 were obtained for Mr. Wolf and Mr. Irwin. In the negative rating of Mr. Murray, special difficulty was encountered in that the subject used a good deal of circumlocution so that the context became unusually important for the detection of the implied undesirability of a trait. This partially accounts for the relatively low agreement on negative ratings obtained for Mr. Murray.

These three cases had been selected because they would represent the greatest difficulty in rating. It was argued that if satisfactory reliabilities were obtained here, the other cases would present less difficulty for reliable rating. Since the extreme degree of circumlocution exhibited by Mr. Murray appeared to be a feature peculiar to his case and the scale proved reliable in other respects, it was decided to adopt this method of analysis.

Predictions Regarding Perceptions of War-Separated Fathers

Differences in Projective Process

Correspondence in perception. The first task was to demonstrate the existence of trait correspondence between the perceiver and the perceived with respect to the father's self- and child-perception.

Emotional involvement. If this could be demonstrated, it was expected that the war-separated fathers, as compared to non-separated fathers, would show greater emotional involvement in their first-borns, manifested by a higher degree of trait correspondence between self- and child-perception and by a higher average intensity in interpersonal statements about the first child.

Intrapsychic conflict. It was assumed that war-separation and the father's subsequent return to the family would represent an experience resulting in intrapsychic stress and conflict. Three criteria of intrapsychic stress and conflict were selected: self-rejection, range of inconsistency, and degree of conflict in self-evaluation. It was predicted that the war-separated group of fathers would differ significantly from the non-separated group of fathers in respect of self-rejection, range of inconsistency, and degree of conflict.

Father's perception of first child. We predicted that war-separated fathers would tend to reject their first-borns more than non-separated fathers. We predicted, in addition, that war-separated fathers would tend to reject those traits in the first-borns about which they themselves were in conflict. This phenomenon was termed phobic projection.

Differences in Projective Content

It was expected that the content of self- and child-perception for the two groups would differ. This was determined by an analysis of the content of self- and child-perception for the two groups as described by the use the 38 fathers made of the four groups of 20 categories employed for analysis of the interviews. The war-separated fathers were expected to be less secure in terms of their ego-identity, but no prediction was made about the manner in which the content of self-perception would reveal threat to ego-identity.

Correspondence of Father's Self-Perception and Perception of First Child

The basic assumption of this study, that the father's self-perception will tend to show some correspondence with his perception of the first child, was investigated by means of establishing correlation coefficients between scores for self-perception and child-perception for each of the 38 cases. Two kinds of correlation coefficients were computed for each case: one measuring trait correspondence in terms of frequency of statement per category; and one measuring trait correspondence when the frequency of statement per category was weighted by the intensity with which a statement was made.

The concept of trait correspondence is illustrated in the analysis of the interview series for Mr. Moore. The trait-correspondence score based on frequency of statements per category is r = .58. When scores are weighted by intensity, the trait correspondence is r = .61. These figures are obtained because Mr. Moore describes himself and Rick as engaged in similar interpersonal relationships. Of the 20 categories the following are used for description of himself as well as Rick.

Positive Active Categories
- Positively directing others
- Teaching, explaining, advising
- Actively loving, praising

Positive Passive Categories
- Passively loving, appreciating
- Co-operating, conciliating
- Trusting, asking help, depending
- Admiring, asking the opinion of others
- Conforming

Negative Active Categories
- Bossing, negative direction of others
- Competing, boasting
- Punishing, threatening, mocking
- Hating, attacking

Negative Passive Categories
- Resenting, hating passively
- Complaining, resisting passively
- Distrusting
- Retreating, condemning oneself

In view of the fact that Mr. Moore perceives similarities between himself and Rick in 16 of the 20 categories used for analysis, it is not surprising that he has a relatively high trait-correspondence score indicated by r = .61.

The 76 correlations obtained by the two methods for war-separated and non-separated fathers were considered to represent two ways of measuring the amount of trait correspondence. The 38 correlations based on frequency scores range from .03 to .82 with the median at .495. Their distribution is approximately normal. The 38 correlations based on frequency scores weighted by intensity ratings range from .05 to .90, the distribution approximating the normal curve with the median at .51.

The findings suggest that the group of correlations obtained from frequency scores weighted by intensity ratings represented a somewhat more sensitive measure of trait correspondence in that these r's tended consistently to be somewhat higher than the correlations based on unweighted frequency scores. These results tend to support the basic assumption of the study that there is a tendency for fathers to perceive self and child similarly.

Emotional Involvement, Intrapsychic Conflict, and Child-Perception

Results concerning differences in self-perception and child-perception between war-separated and non-separated fathers are shown in Table 41.

Table 41. Findings Concerning Differences in Self- and Child-Perception

Scores Used for Comparing the Two Groups	Differences Found Between the Two Groups	
	t	Significance
A. Criteria of emotional involvement		
1. Trait correspondence between self- and child-perception		
a. in terms of frequency	0.81	—
b. in terms of intensity	0.40	—
2. Mean intensity of child-perception	1.52	—
B. Criteria of intrapsychic stress or conflict		
1. Self-rejection scores	2.94	$P < .01$
2. Range of inconsistency scores	2.74	$P < .02$
3. Degree of conflict	0.10	—
C. Father's perception of first child		
1. Child-rejection scores	2.77	$P < .02$
2. Phobic projection scores	chi square = 4.90	$P < .05$

Emotional Involvement as a Differentiating Factor

We expected that war-separated fathers would show more emotional involvement in their first child than non-separated fathers as indicated by two criteria: (1) a higher trait correspondence between self- and child-perception, and (2) a higher mean intensity of child-perception. However, our findings were negative, the t's shown in Table 41 indicating that the two groups do not differ significantly on the measures devised here. The conclusion suggested by these findings— that war-separated fathers and non-separated fathers do not differ in degree of emotional involvement with their first children— must, however, be limited to differentiation when these criteria are taken singly. They may not apply when score constellations for the two groups are examined.

Intrapsychic Conflict or Stress as a Differentiating Factor

Self-rejection. It was hypothesized that war-separated fathers would tend to perceive themselves more negatively (reject themselves more) than non-separated fathers.

The concept of self-rejection was defined operationally as the ratio of negatively evaluated interpersonal statements concerning the self to the total number of interpersonal statements about the self (weighted by intensity).

Negative evaluation of an interpersonal statement about the self could be implicit in the context. Statements drawn from records for Mr. Moore, a war-separated father, will illustrate the kind of verbalization on which self-rejection scores are based. "I felt jealousy . . . I always wanted people to like me, I think I always had an inferiority feeling . . . I want to compliment, but I cannot . . . With jobs I do well at first, but after a while things don't go so well. Concerning Rick, I scold him a lot . . . I take a lot out on him. I guess I expect too much of him." For Mr. Moore, the ratio of negative statements such as the above to the total statements about the self was .16.

Testing the difference between the mean self-rejection scores for the two groups revealed a t of 2.94 which indicates significance at the .01 level. The war-separated fathers were more self-rejecting than the non-separated fathers.

Range of inconsistency in self-evaluation. As a second criterion of stress or conflict, a measure of the consistency with which the father tended to evaluate himself was devised. It was expected that war-separated fathers would tend to show inconsistency of self-evaluation over a wider range of categories than non-separated fathers.

Range of inconsistency was defined operationally as the number of categories receiving both negatively and positively evaluated statements about the self, as illustrated by the cases of Mr. Olsen and Mr. Wagner.

Mr. Olsen, non-separated, implies negative evaluation of only one interpersonal category in which he also implies self-approval. This is the category of active criticism or attack. His range of inconsistency score is, therefore, 1. Mr. Wagner, a war-separated father, evaluates himself both positively and negatively on 14 of the 20 categories, indicating some conflict on all forms of interpersonal relationships with the exception of supporting and pitying, loving actively, appreciating, depending, admiring, and conforming. He receives a score of 14 for range of inconsistency.

In testing the difference between the mean range of inconsistency scores for the two groups, a t of 2.74 was found which indicates significance at the .05 level. The war-separated group showed inconsistency in self-evaluation over a wider range of categories than the non-separated group.

Degree of conflict in self-evaluation. It was further expected that war-separated fathers would show a greater degree of conflict per trait in that they were expected to produce more nearly equal positive and negative evaluations in respect to traits perceived for the self.

Degree of conflict in self-evaluation was considered to be represented for each case by the average ratio of the difference between positive and negative judgments concerning the 20 categories to the total score per category. Frequency scores were weighted by intensity for this measure.

For the war-separated fathers, Mr. Moore's material, part of which was quoted above, will illustrate the phenomenon which the concept of "degree of conflict" attempts to represent. "My brother and I became very self-sufficient. We never had experienced real care. We missed it as soon as we were old enough to realize. We built up a very broad concept of life. We developed certain selfish attitudes."

This excerpt contains two positive statements concerning independence from others ("self-sufficient," "broad concept of life") and one negative statement concerning the same category ("selfish attitudes"). This man is somewhat ambivalent concerning self-sufficiency. His score of .52 may not do justice to the severity of the conflict he experiences in some areas since it is an average of the discrepancy between positive and negative evaluations for all 20 categories.

A t test of the difference between the means for the two groups does not reveal the predicted significant difference in degree of conflict in self-evaluation.

Child-Perception as a Differentiating Factor

Child-rejection. It was predicted that war-separated fathers would tend to evaluate the traits perceived in their first-born more negatively than non-separated fathers. Child-rejection scores were constructed in the same manner as self-rejection scores. They were based on the ratio of negatively evaluated statements concerning the child to the total statements concerning the child (weighted by intensity).

An illustration, again from Mr. Moore's records, would be, "He irritates me no end . . . he gets upset, he cries a lot, he won't obey. He is unhappy because we can't afford a new radio."

The mean child-rejection scores for the two groups were found to differ significantly at the .05 level, t being 2.77. The war-separated fathers reject their children more than the non-separated fathers.

Phobic projection. Furthermore, it was expected that war-separated fathers would tend to show more phobic projection than non-separated fathers, i.e., they would tend to perceive those traits negatively in the first child which they perceived in themselves with ambivalence.

Illustrative of phobic projection in war-separated fathers are such statements as Mr. Wolf's: "I am a quiet, reserved person. I like to keep myself to myself. The neighbors are a rowdy lot. Sometimes I wish we were more sociable . . . Dan is a sissy, he does not seem to get on with the other kids. When they have a party, he cries."

Mr. Moore (war-separated father) states that he wished he could tell people how he felt; he wished he could compliment them, but that it was hard to be frank. However, it is good to be self-sufficient. Rick irritates him because when he is scolded for something he did not do, he won't tell his father. Rick has a speech impediment at home, but not in school. Rick seems unable to express his affection.

Thus, conflict in both self- and child-evaluation concerning the same trait was not considered sufficient indication of phobic projection. Complete rejection of self and child concerning the same trait was also not considered an adequate criterion. Phobic projection was held to be present only where there was conflict in the father's self-evaluation for a category in which the child was perceived in a disapproving light.

Since the distribution of differences between the scores for the two groups did not follow the normal curve, the hypothesis was tested by means of chi square, a non-parametric test. The difference was found to be significant at the .05 level, chi square being 4.9. The war-separated fathers tended to evaluate negatively in the first-born, traits which they perceived in themselves ambivalently.

Self-Perception and Child-Perception Irrespective of War-Separation

In order to ascertain interrelations between patterns of self- and child-perception for the entire sample, making allowance for the "effect" of war-separation, data were analyzed using the covariance within-group r. This technique makes it possible to state the degree of relation between the various factors for the entire sample irrespective of whether fathers were war-separated. Results concerning patterns of self-perception and child-perception for the sample of 38 cases are shown in Table 42.

Table 42. Findings Concerning Patterns of Self-Perception and Child-Perception for the Sample of Thirty-Eight Cases

A. Interrelation of the criteria of emotional involvement.
   1. Relation of trait correspondence to the mean intensity of child-perception. $r = .23$

B. Interrelation of the criteria of intrapsychic stress or conflict.
   1. Relation of self-rejection to range of inconsistency in self-evaluation.
      covariance: within-group $r = .61$ — $s_x = .06$, $s_y = 3.18$
   2. Relation of self-rejection to the degree of conflict.
      covariance: within-group $r = -.33$ — $s_x = .06$, $s_y = .33$

C. Interrelation of self-rejection and child-rejection.
   1. Relation of self-rejection and child-rejection
      covariance: within-group $r = .71$ — $s_x = .06$, $s_y = .17$

Emotional involvement. It was assumed that the criteria for emotional involvement used here would tend to be associated. A product moment correlation between trait correspondence based on weighted frequency scores and mean intensity of child-perception yielded an r of .23, suggesting that the criteria used here do not tend to be closely associated.

Intrapsychic stress. Self-rejection, range of inconsistency in self-evaluation, and degree of conflict were selected as criteria of intrapsychic stress or conflict. It was expected that self-rejection would tend to be associated with range of inconsistency and with degree of conflict as measured here.

Covariance technique, used to make allowance for the found difference between war-separated and non-separated cases, revealed a within-group r of .61 for self-rejection and range of inconsistency. For the relation between degree of conflict and self-rejection, a within-group r of -.33 was obtained. The negative correlation here is explained, of course, by the scoring system which is so designed that minimal conflict will yield maximal scores and vice versa. An inverse relation between self-rejection and degree of conflict scores was therefore expected.

The findings in this section tend to support the hypothesis that self-rejection, range of inconsistency, and degree of conflict are associated.

Self- and child-rejection. It was expected that high self-rejection would tend to be associated with rejection of the first child. This hypothesis was supported in respect to the 38 cases by a covariance within-group correlation of .71.

Use of the Twenty Categories in the Description of Self- and Child-Perception

The foregoing sections have dealt with perceptual patterns in terms of their interrelations. Such interrelations as trait correspondence, approval or disapproval of a trait in the self or the child may be a manifestation of intrapsychic processes such as identification, isolation, rejection, and phobic projection. However, they tell us little of the psychic content which is "identified with," or "projected upon." The content of self- and child-perception as described by the use subjects have made of the 20 categories is summarized in Table 43.

An analysis of the kind of categories most characteristically used in self- and child-perception reveals that when the findings for both groups are summarized, the 38 fathers tend to see themselves predominantly as positive and active in their interpersonal relationships. The first child is seen as predominantly passive. This would correspond to the stereotypes which the culture provides for the definition of father- and child-roles.

An interesting difference in the conception of these roles, however, is revealed when data are further analyzed, as in Table 44, and a comparison is made in the content of self- and child-perception between war-separated and non-separated fathers.

Non-separated fathers tend to see themselves almost twice as much involved in positive active interpersonal relations as war-separated fathers. This group of categories is most characteristic of their self-perception, 40.7 percent of the total scores being devoted to it.

The war-separated fathers, on the other hand, tend to see their interpersonal experiences as more evenly distributed among the four clusters of positive active, positive passive, negative active, and negative passive categories. The highest percentage for any one cluster is 27.7 percent for the positive passive group of categories.

The first child is seen as predominantly passive by both groups, but more so by the war-separated fathers than non-separated fathers. For the non-separated fathers, there is a marked differentiation between positive passive interpersonal relations, and the child is seen as predominantly

Table 43. Subjects' Use of Categories for the Description of Self- and Child-Perception Shown as the Means of Percentages[a]

	Self-Perception		Child-Perception	
	War-Separated	Non-Separated	War-Separated	Non-Separated
Positive Active				
Dominate	5.5	9.3	4.9	8.3
Teach	1.7	4.0	.3	.8
Give	5.4	10.1	1.6	3.5
Support	2.4	1.3	.7	.5
Love	10.6	16.5	4.0	4.4
Total	25.4	40.7	11.5	17.4
Positive Passive				
Appreciate	8.0	6.7	10.9	8.2
Cooperate	14.9	15.3	14.2	17.0
Trust	.7	.6	5.8	5.2
Admire	1.6	1.3	.6	.9
Conform	2.6	1.8	5.0	5.1
Total	27.7	25.8	36.3	36.4
Total Positives	53.1	66.5	46.8	53.8
Negative Active				
Boss	2.8	2.3	2.3	1.8
Resist	1.2	1.6	5.7	6.6
Compete	1.3	1.2	1.9	3.5
Punish	3.8	3.0	.2	.9
Hate	12.1	10.5	7.2	7.1
Total	21.2	18.4	17.3	19.8
Negative Passive				
Resent	7.8	4.2	10.6	6.7
Complain	6.0	2.9	11.2	7.8
Distrust	1.3	.5	2.6	5.0
Retreat	7.4	6.8	9.0	5.1
Submit	2.5	2.7	3.3	2.1
Total	25.0	15.2	36.7	26.2
Total Negatives	46.2	33.6	54.0	46.0

[a]The percentages shown are derived by calculating percent frequency scores weighted by intensity for each case and then obtaining the mean percentage per category.

appreciating, co-operating, trusting, whereas negative passive traits receive a smaller percentage score. In contrast, the war-separated fathers devote all of 73 percent of the child's scores to a description of his passivity in interaction with others. Half of this is seen as positive passive interaction (appreciating, co-operating, etc.), and half as negative passive (resenting, complaining, whining). This finding may well serve to illustrate the war-separated father's ambivalence in relation to the first child.

Some dynamic theories of personality use the concept of interlocking role systems for the explanation of "normal" personality functioning and assume that relations between two or more people are based on complementary roles (11, chapter 10; 59). The leader-follower and protector-dependent role constellations would exemplify the concepts used in these theories. In this connection, the complementary nature of self- and child-perception for the non-separated fathers (positive action vs. positive passive) makes an interesting contrast with the war-separated fathers' lack of such a complementary pattern.

Table 44. Summary in Means of Percentages of Subjects' Use of Categories in Terms of Category-Clusters[a]

	Active		Passive		Totals	
	W-S	N-S	W-S	N-S	W-S	N-S
			Self-Perception			
Positive	25.4	40.7	27.7	25.8	53.1	66.5
Negative	21.2	18.4	25.0	15.2	46.2	33.6
Totals	46.6	59.1	52.7	41.0		
			Child-Perception			
Positive	11.5	17.4	36.3	36.4	47.8	53.8
Negative	17.3	19.8	36.7	26.2	54.0	46.0
Totals	28.8	37.2	73.0	62.6		

Differences Between War-Separated and Non-Separated Cases

1. Positive active categories in self-perception $t = -6.33$ P .001
2. Negative passive categories in self-perception $t = 3.92$ P .001
3. Positive active categories in child-perception $t = -2.7$ P .02
4. Negative passive categories in child-perception $t = 2.5$ P .02

[a]The percentages shown are derived by calculating percent frequency scores weighted by intensity for each case and then obtaining the mean percentage per cluster of categories.

As shown in Table 44, war-separated fathers tend to see themselves significantly more in negative passive and less in positive active terms than non-separated fathers. Likewise, they perceive their first-borns significantly more in negative passive and less in positive active terms than the non-separated fathers. The differences are significant at the .001 and the .02 level.

Idiomatic Patterns as Illustrated by Case Analysis

Individual Patterns

Score constellations for the extreme cases on all measures for the two groups were examined and a number of typical and atypical cases were selected in order to test the usefulness of this method in contributing to the understanding of idiomatic patterns of personality dynamics.

In selecting three war-separated and three non-separated fathers to illustrate the score constellations shown in Tables 43 and 44, it was felt that the selection of two typical cases from the war-separated group should be counterbalanced by an atypical case which would illustrate the danger of overly facile generalizations based on group trends.

Accordingly, the two cases representative of the war-separated group, Mr. Moore and Mr. Wagner, have high scores on phobic projection, child-rejection, self-rejection, and range of inconsistency. For purposes of comparison, two cases from the non-separated group, Mr. Stone and Mr. Moffett, — who have a similar score constellation and are, therefore, deviates from the score pattern of the non-separated group— are presented. In addition, two cases are presented which share low phobic-projection, child-rejection, self-rejection, and range of inconsistency scores. One of these, Mr. Marston, a war-separated father, presents a picture which stands in sharp contrast to the general pattern of the war-separated group. The other, Mr. Arno, a non-separated father, is representative of his group.

In order to make possible comparison by means of graphs, raw scores on all measures were converted into Z scores based on the means of the non-separated group.[2] The means of Z scores for the war-separated group were calculated and are shown as a heavy line in Figure 2.

In the detailed discussion of each case the interviewer's impression given prior to the quantitative analysis will first be described. We will proceed to a discussion of score constellations and to an evaluation of the father-child relation as it is revealed in the course of the interview and through analysis of the material.

Mr. Moore, typical war-separated father. Mr. Moore is a man of medium height, somewhat stocky and muscular. He has blonde hair, wide open blue eyes, ruddy, healthy looking skin. During the interviews he usually had some difficulty in getting started, saying "I don't know where to begin." Once started, however, he talked rapidly, sometimes for as much as thirty minutes without interruption. His words came with intensity, he seemed eager to "blurt it out." His first interview dealt mainly with his war experiences; the second picked up almost as a serial story telling about his own childhood, then about his first-born. He seemed definitely in need of talking to someone; yet, combined with a real eagerness, there was some difficulty in relating to the interviewer as a person.

When he discussed his first-born, Rick, there was anger in his voice, tension in his whole body. His attitude toward Rick was completely negative, there seemed to be no time when he softened, felt sorry for Rick, or even saw anything good in him. He always compared him unfavorably with the second child.

2. The Z score or standard score is the deviation of the individual score from the mean of the non-separated group of fathers. The mean of the non-separated group is given a score of 50, each standard deviation a score of 10.

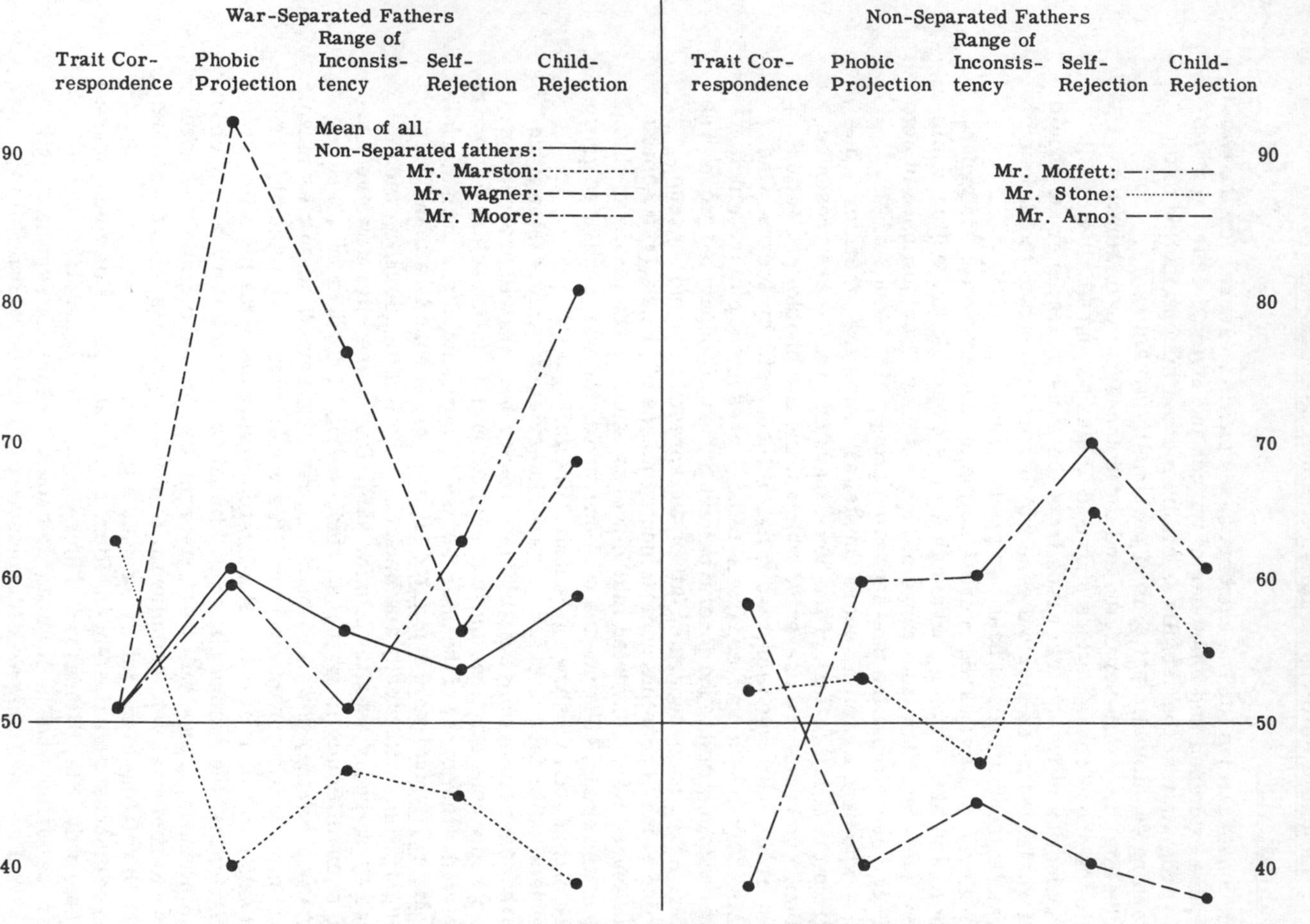

Figure 2. Z scores of three war-separated and three non-separated fathers on trait correspondence, phobic projection, range of inconsistency, self-rejection, and child-rejection. These Z scores (standard scores) are based on the scores of the non-separated group; they have a mean of 50 and a standard deviation of 10.

When he talked about his own early childhood or his own personal problems, he showed definite anxiety. Over and over he talked about his ineptness in personal-social relations. He told of his parents' deaths when he was very young and the subsequent loneliness. Even being "good" had not brought him the affection that had come so easily to his brother. One felt that he longed now as he longed in childhood for close personal relations. His feelings of unhappiness and frustration had left a residue of hostility which permeated all his social relations as well as his attitude toward himself. He said of his parents, "My brother and I have thought it was probably a good thing they died, they both smoked and drank wine and now we are in the church, we think perhaps it was an act of God."

The interviewer felt as she listened to this father that his harsh view of himself and his hostile feelings toward people were related to his anger with Rick. In his relations with Rick he dared to express overtly the hostile feelings he had to repress with his peers. It seemed as if his baby had added to the feelings of inadequacy of this highly disciplined good churchman.

The analysis of Mr. Moore's material supports the interviewer's impression that this man is extremely insecure. He has a self-rejection Z score of 63 and tends to perceive himself as always having been inadequate, as unable to express affection or maintain relationships. It is probable that his manner of producing material, which was accompanied by so many signs of tension and anxiety, was related to the fact that the very interview experience was a situation which he both feared and desired. He was eager to relate to the interviewer and yet found this difficult.

Fifty-eight percent of the statements descriptive of this man's self-perception show Mr. Moore involved in hostile interpersonal relations, and the largest single category in describing himself is that of active criticism, hatred, and attack, which receives 18 percent of the total self-descriptive statements. These figures are in line with the interviewer's impression that Mr. Moore showed strongly hostile tendencies.

Mr. Moore's feelings toward Rick fit into this pattern insofar as his child-rejection score is the second highest for the entire sample of 38 cases (Z score = 80). He sees Rick as resentful, whining, and complaining (37 percent of the statements descriptive of the first child). The relation between his own aggression and Rick's tearful ways appears to be lost to him as shown by such statements as, "I told him I won't have him cry when I correct him," "If I scold him for anything, he cries . . . I won't have it . . . it doesn't get him anywhere to cry."

The trait-correspondence score for this case is relatively low (Z score = 52) and the phobic-projection score, relatively high (Z score = 61). Insofar as Mr. Moore sees 58 percent of his own and 68.9 percent of Rick's interpersonal relations as hostile, this suggests that he tends to reject in Rick those characteristics of his own which he indicates stand in the way of satisfying human relations.

Since this man is so insecure already and tends to use hostility as a means of dealing with others, it may well be that he uses child-rejection as a point of anchorage which will give him, at any rate, some sense of superiority. In order to achieve this, however, he cannot permit himself too great a feeling of closeness to the child. This reasoning may explain the relatively low trait-correspondence score.

This process appears to leave Mr. Moore with a bewildered feeling that all is not satisfactory. In his own words, "I don't feel the same affinity for Rick as I do for the other children. The wife often asks me whether I love him. I do . . . but other kids are more loveable."

In summary, the interviewer's impressions agree with the quantitative analysis in that Mr. Moore is described as extremely insecure, hostile, and child-rejecting. It is suggested that this man's pattern of hostility toward others and rigid disciplining of himself are related to his longing for warm, interpersonal relations. Being "a good churchman and moralist" may well have been his manner of seeking approval. Since he has been unable to establish warm and secure relationships with others, he seeks self-approval through a puritan pattern of self-restraint. Rick, who fails to provide the warmth which Mr. Moore craves and who represents a threat to his father's defense mechanisms as shown in the above analysis, becomes the focus of Mr. Moore's hostility.

Mr. Wagner, typical war-separated father. Mr. Wagner is a tall, handsome young man. He has the blonde hair, ruddy complexion, and strong body of a Nordic type. His strength and vigor were evidenced in every session. He talked more than any other father (the longest typed protocol) and he spoke more intensely. He seemed to enjoy the sessions immensely, talking freely for the full hour with few remarks from the interviewer. In four of the five sessions he continued to talk for 10 or 15 minutes after the recorder had been turned off. He showed a tendency as the sessions progressed to have more insight into his early behavior and to suggest to the interviewer generalizations that might be made about the effect of war on fathers.

It seemed to the interviewer that his relation with his first-born was primarily characterized by a struggle for dominance. He set out to make his little girl behave the way he wanted her to behave, even if he and the child both died in the attempt. He was persistent, uncompromising, and punitive. Here indeed was a straight-forward authoritarian, disciplining, as John Dewey puts it, "by beating with unremitting blows a foreign substance into a resistant material."

On the surface this man seemed, in general, to be pretty sure that he and his own childhood family combined most of the virtues. However, one sensed that after he left his small rural home community, he had had to readjust his perception of self and to accept a role of lesser importance than he had held before. This brought into the discussions some ambivalence in his attitudes toward self. The interviewer felt that he perceived his first-born daughter in a highly negative way. The positive qualities he seemed to find came, in general, as a result of his strenuous working on her during the early years.

Mr. Wagner illustrates the pattern associated with extreme phobic projection. Since this father has a trait-correspondence score of only 50.9 (Z score), the fact that he received the highest phobic-projection score argues that the perceived trait correspondence between himself and the child is used very largely for the rejection of the child. Mr. Wagner scores near the mean for the entire sample on self-rejection. His inconsistency

Z score is 68. This suggests that insofar as he has any doubts about evaluating his own characteristics, these same traits seen in the child become undesirable without a doubt.

This father has problems which appear to give rise to a defense mechanism best described as an isolation of the self from the threatening person or situation by lack of affect or rejection. His pattern is illustrated by such statements as, "I just sort of went into a shell when I went overseas . . . didn't get terribly impressed one way or another." Or, concerning a quarrel with his wife, "It didn't upset me too much, I guess I was still living in a shell . . ." Or, on seeing his first-born, "I can remember that I didn't seem to have any particular emotion . . . I was just noncommittal about the whole thing . . . it was a bit of a disappointment . . . I wasn't tremendously impressed."

It is notable that his child-rejection score is among the seven highest for the entire sample. That the low trait-correspondence score he receives may be a somewhat unsuccessful attempt at isolating himself and his problems from the perception of the child is indicated by such statements as, "I am quite stubborn and the child is stubborn too," and his frequent reference to the forceful manner with which he recurrently deals with the child's resistance as "having a round about that" as if it were a boxing match.

This father sees himself as predominantly positive active in interpersonal relations, but he shows some inconsistency in evaluating himself in such roles as positively directing others, teaching, and giving. He shows even greater ambivalence on all ten of the categories describing the self in negative relations with others. His high projection score is derived largely from the fact that he perceives the first child as similarly involved in eight of these negative relationship categories. He disapproves of this decidedly in the case of all but one of the eight categories, that of submission to force, which receives 4.2 percent of the total statements descriptive of the first child. This is not surprising in view of the fact that his habitual manner of dealing with the first child is characterized by what he calls "brute force."

This man thinks of himself as a disciplinarian and one who likes to submit to discipline. He has but little notion that his relation with his first-born may not benefit from these techniques, as illustrated by such statements as, "I began to form ideas of what she should and should not do . . . probably aggravated her stubbornness." "I am the only one for whom she would eat, I would just hold her and force the food down . . . it worked and now we get along fine."

The outstanding features of this case as seen through the interviewer's eyes and in the light of the quantitative analysis appear to lie in Mr. Wagner's great rigidity, which makes it necessary for him to attach those of his own characteristics about which he is in doubt, to his daughter. In this context he can punish and reject and at the same time feel approval of himself as a disciplinarian. The interviewer's reference to Mr. Wagner's "authoritarian" outlook on life is supported by his liking for meting out and receiving discipline. His typically flat affect in new situations which require a spontaneous feeling reaction, his need to dominate the very interview situation, and his inability to tolerate self-doubt without projection, all suggest a very rigid personality organization in which relations will be distorted by use of perceptual defenses.

Mr. Marston, atypical war-separated father. The interviewer was immediately struck with the smallness of Mr. Marston. He is about five feet and two inches tall with small bones and well-proportioned body, but on an unusually small scale. He has nice features, attractive brown eyes, well-shaped head. He has a friendly but somewhat shy approach, a warm smile when he is at ease. He has a poised well-bred manner, speaks in clear, simple style with excellent vocabulary.

During the interview he referred to his size several times, first, in connection with his concern about what the armed services might do with him, again in talking about his likeness to his father, and finally in discussing his first-born boy. One felt that identification in size was important to him and explained partly why he modeled his life after his father's and why he saw so many ways in which he and his first-born were alike.

In spite of Mr. Marston's evident concern with his lack of physical size, the interviewer was impressed with the poise of this young man, not only in interpersonal relations during the session, but also in discussing himself and his family. He impressed one as a person who had had problems to meet, who had sometimes failed, but who each time had grown through the experience. He said once that when he returned from the war he had been hard on Ken because he wanted him to grow up too fast. The interviewer felt that the father also had pressed himself to grow up and meet life's responsibilities earlier than most men. This may have been a compensation for his size, but it may also have come from his own ego-ideals absorbed so early from his responsible, friendly, successful father.

The interviewer felt that Mr. Marston identified closely with the son who had been born during his absence. His initial difficulties were due more to his lack of understanding than to his rejection of the boy. He tried to be fair to him, to explain his problems. On the other hand, he was firm in discipline, holding his son to the same ideals he had held for himself. His strictness was born of conviction of what was desirable rather than of hostility toward his son or of feelings of self-inadequacy.

Quantitative analysis of the material revealed that Mr. Marston differs strikingly from the war-separated group of fathers. His child-rejection score and self-rejection score are among the four lowest for the entire sample. He also has a relatively high trait-correspondence score (Z score = 62) which suggests that he sees the child in much the same terms in which he perceives himself. In accordance with the interviewer's impressions, these scores indicate a good deal of positive identification with the first-born.

Furthermore, the interviewer's feeling that this man was well able to integrate experiences is born out by the fact that Mr. Marston appears to have little conflict in evaluating himself (range of inconsistency Z score = 47.4). He has less need to use this conflict for phobic projection than any of the war-separated fathers.

Whereas the foregoing section of the analysis would tend to describe Mr. Marston in terms which are typical for the non-separated group of fathers, closer examination reveals that he differs from the non-separated group in some important respects.

The content of his self-perception shows that he sees himself as predominantly passive. Sixty-one percent of the total statements descriptive of self-perception fall into this group. Forty-one percent are devoted to positive passive interpersonal statements such as, "I like it . . . I have a great attachment for . . . there were very few men (in the forces) for whom I had any dislike," and 20 percent fall into the negative passive cluster of categories illustrated by such phrases as, "It was hard . . . it was tough . . . I got discouraged but I stuck it out." This predominance of the positive passive categories in self-perception is atypical of the non-separated father and somewhat contrary to the masculine role assigned to the father by our culture. It is interesting to note that the interviewer's comment on this case described a man of unusually small stature, somewhat unmasculine in appearance. This father's comment, "I feel that physically I couldn't compete with a lot of men doing the fighting," suggests that he was quite conscious of this factor. One questions to what extent the percentage score for the category of positively directing and dominating others (12 percent) may represent a compensatory trend for his lack of physical stature.

As the high trait-correspondence score (Z score = 62) suggests, Mr. Marston sees the child in very similar terms as predominantly positively passive (62.5 percent). He verbalizes his feeling of identification with his first-born as, "I've always been one to sit back and let things come to me . . . rather than step out. Ken takes after me, I think; he is more quiet . . . likes to tag along after a playmate . . . When the older boys tease him, get him to cry, he'll go back and try something that isn't quite so strenuous . . . When you tell him something, he tries hard to do the right thing. He is pretty tractable." One wonders whether this man would have been equally accepting of a child perceived as more boisterous, aggressive, and resistive.

In summary, the interviewer's impressions and the quantitative analysis agree in suggesting that this man has little inner conflict and is well able to integrate new experiences, and that he shows considerable identification with his first-born. In all these respects he is somewhat atypical of the war-separated fathers.

It is suggested that Mr. Marston's relation to his own father, as described here, together with his unusually small stature, may have contributed to a self-perception pattern which falls predominantly into the positive passive categories; and that his preoccupation with relations in which he has a positively directing role of friendly disciplinarian may well represent a compensatory trend.

<u>Mr. Stone, atypical non-separated father.</u> Mr. Stone is a slender young man of medium height. He has a round face, smooth brown hair, and at times a rather vacant expression. In the interview series he produced material very slowly, interspersed with frequent and long silences which he would finally terminate with such questions as, "And what else?" This manner of production might well be interpreted as passive resistance.

Most of his material in the first interview was devoted to criticism of Harry, his first-born, but in this as well as the subsequent interviews, this man made many disparaging statements about himself. In comparing context and tone of self-critical material with material containing criticism of Harry, it appeared as if he were far more ready to condemn himself than to reject the child. Areas in which the father perceives similarity between his own faults and Harry's point up the possibility that he uses criticism of the child not in order to reject Harry, but to enhance his own sense of inadequacy.

The quantitative analysis of interviews with Mr. Stone indicates that he is among the six cases with the highest self-rejection score (Z = 65) for the entire sample. His range of inconsistency score is 47.4, which suggests that he has few qualms in so rejecting himself. That he has a decidedly poor opinion of himself is borne out by such statements as, "I always tend to pick out faults in other people, probably a complex I have, an inferiority complex . . . the only time I don't is when I hit it off just right with people."

This is a realistic self-criticism insofar as 18.8 percent of the total statements descriptive of himself fall into the category of active criticism, attack, and hatred. His basic desire to be accepted is represented by an almost equal percentage (19 percent) of statements which fall into the category of outgoing love and praise.

In his perception of the child the father's intrapsychic conflict is less clearly reflected than one might anticipate from the high correlation between self- and child-rejection obtained for the entire sample. His Z score for child-rejection is 55 and 53.3 for phobic projection. It is possible that the fact that this father sees only an average degree of similarity between himself and Harry (Z score for trait correspondence = 52.1) makes it easier for him to perceive Harry as relatively separate from himself. Where such similarities in undesirable characteristics are perceived, they appear to be accompanied by a different affective tone.

Thus Harry Stone, like Alma Wagner, is seen as predominantly negative and passive (44.6 percent) in interaction with others. Of the interpersonal statements in this cluster, 23.3 percent are devoted to describing him as resentful, resistive, and complaining, but such statements as those below do not imply rejection.

"He used to be whiny . . . but, well, I think he is improving." Or "When he gets bullied at all, he'll come running away before the boy would maybe even touch him . . . he'd get terrified . . . it was kind of pathetic to watch . . . but last time he took it well."

These statements suggest rather that Mr. Stone, who has conflict in positive relationships as suggested by the equal balance of critical and loving roles which he assigns himself and by his high self-rejection score, can accept Harry in terms of the child's ability to develop and change. As he states it, "I think Harry is changing right now. I think he is getting more independent . . . it's difficult to tell because of that. I used to think he was quite a baby, but I think he's coming out of it."

The quantitative analysis of this case supports the interviewer's impression that this man's chief difficulty lies in strong feelings of inadequacy, but that these are not reflected in his relation with the first-born in terms of child-rejection. Two factors are suggested which might be important in reducing child-rejection for this case. One is the average trait-correspondence score and the other consists in the father's perception of the child as a developing personality constantly growing toward better adjustment. It may well be that such observations could re-enforce the father's own feeling of inadequacy in that he cannot, at this stage, see himself making equal strides. This may contribute to the fact that the self-rejection score for this case is higher than the child-rejection score.

Mr. Moffett, atypical non-separated father. Mr. Moffett is a young man in his thirties, of medium height and slender build. He was most co-operative in the interview series and appeared anxious to give the right kind of material. He talked in an even tone, implying that he deliberated about each point he had in mind before formulating his ideas.

The interviewer felt that this man has always been anxious to conform and adapt to his environment and that his ideals and standards for adequacy in the role of father as well as in other relations might well be hard to live up to. Where relations would not follow the culturally approved or ideal pattern, Mr. Moffett would tend to blame himself rather than other people involved. He seemed at the same time, however, to gain a great deal of satisfaction from his constant striving toward more positive and giving relations.

The quantitative analysis bears out the interviewer's impressions concerning this man's tendency to criticize himself. His self-rejection score is the second highest for the entire sample of 38 cases. There are some indications that his tendency to see himself in an adverse light tends to "spill over" into his perception of Cathy, his first-born. This is suggested by his relatively high scores on child-rejection (Z = 61.2) and phobic projection (Z = 60). It is possible that the low trait-correspondence score (Z = 38.8) represents an attempt to confine his problems to himself.

This is most clearly indicated by the context of his criticism of Cathy, which suggests that he has a good deal of guilt around his demands on the child. Thus he says, "Probably Cathy is more like I am. She is impatient. I should know better." Or, "The children are so good that once they get out of line we don't give them enough leeway . . . when they began to get tired, instead of realizing that was natural, we said, 'Well, you were so good the other night . . . why can't you be good now?' " Or, "So I think perhaps we are a little too demanding." These comments suggest that although Mr. Moffett is critical of his first-born, the context and tone of this criticism is much less harsh in relation to Cathy than in relation to himself. In this pattern he resembles Mr. Stone, who showed a similar trend.

That child-rejection tends to be related in Mr. Moffett's case to a discrepancy between his ideals versus Cathy's, but particularly his own performance, is suggested by the great difficulty which this father had in dealing with lying and deviousness of his first-born.

He sees Cathy largely as negatively passive in interpersonal relationships (34.8 percent of the statements descriptive of her fall into this cluster). But when he discussed instances of dishonest behavior, the bulk of the blame is allotted to himself. Thus, "We have been able to trace these incidents to a possible need for reassurance, possibly because we both lost our patience . . . or were short with her . . . to a point in the evening when she was not sure where she stood."

These instances of self- and child-criticism indicate that Mr. Moffett is like the non-separated group. This is supported by the fact that he tends to see himself as predominantly positive and active in relation to others, with 34.1 percent of the statements descriptive of himself in the categories of giving, helping, and praising. It is evident, therefore, that although his scores on self-rejection, child-rejection, and phobic projection are more akin to the war-separated group, the total constellation of scores derived from process and content of perception show him to be more like the non-separated group.

Interviewer and quantitative analysis agree in suggesting that Mr. Moffett's self-rejection and child-rejection are related to his striving for ideals which are difficult to achieve and that where he or his first-born fail in this respect the father's sense of inadequacy tends to be enhanced rather than his wish to blame the child.

Mr. Arno, typical non-separated father. Mr. Arno is a tall, young man with pleasant regular features. He talks easily with little evidence of tension, but throughout his interviews a considerable restraint and formality in choice of words was noted. For instance, his use of "positively oriented" for describing affectionate feelings, or "negatively oriented" for describing dislikes appeared to the interviewer to represent a toning down and distancing of personal feelings. It was as if abstract and intellectualized language would make them a little more remote.

The interviewer felt that this man experienced some conflict around conforming to conventions and rebelling against them which he might strive to resolve by achieving control of situations through academic detachment or personal dominance. He appeared to be very sure of his capacity of control even in adverse situations.

Thus, although he acknowledges the birth of both children as a burden and a possible threat to his own life goals, his handling of the children suggested that he had the situation well in hand and that his feelings in this area need no ventilation in terms of child-rejection. His need to control situations did not appear, however, to be reflected in his perception of Sarah, since he seemed to stress her independence and her dominant qualities.

Mr. Arno has a score pattern like the group of non-separated fathers but below the average. His self- and child-rejection scores fall among the three lowest for the entire sample and his phobic-projection score is zero.

The content of Mr. Arno's self-perception is also typical of the non-separated group of fathers in that he sees himself as overwhelmingly engaged in positive active interpersonal relations. Of the total statements about himself, 48.5 percent fall into this cluster of categories. When the cluster is further examined, it is found that the highest percentage score goes to the category of positive dominance and the giving of directions. Complaint or resentment would indeed be alien to such a person as is borne out by the fact that the ten categories descriptive of negative interpersonal relations receive only 24.1 percent of the total statements about the self. Furthermore, this man tends to evaluate his own and Sarah's relations with others in an extremely positive light. He makes negative evaluations on only 13 occasions out of a possible 348. One might well conclude that Mr. Arno is "so positively oriented" that he may tend not to perceive negatives.

Preoccupation with control of relations is suggested by his own high percentage scores for dominance and the fact that Sarah is also described as positively directing and controlling. Twenty percent of the statements descriptive of her relations with others fall into this category. The trait-correspondence score suggests that Mr. Arno sees Sarah as a chip off the old block in this and other areas (Z score = 58.2). The possibility of conflict arising between dominant father and dominant daughter is reduced by Mr. Arno's allotting 50 percent of the statements descriptive of Sarah to the positive passive cluster. He describes her as, "Really completely subtle, persuasive . . . well, just in a very direct positive manner . . . telling everyone else (peers) what to do first . . . She likes to get her way, but without the unpleasantness of being disliked." This might well apply to Mr. Arno's own interpersonal relations as well, insofar as his percentage scores on dominating and directing are almost equal to those describing him as conciliating and co-operating.

In summary, it is notable in this case that the quantitative analysis substantiates the points which struck the interviewer as characteristic of the father and his perception of the first-born. These consist in an outstanding "positive orientation" in terms of perceptual content and evaluating process which appear to be used to control living circumstances. This father has little doubt that both he and his first-born are able to achieve such control.

Discussion of Illustrative Cases

The case discussions presented here serve to illustrate the use of quantitative analyses of interview material as well as their limitations and make the deficiencies of a mathematical representation of clinical material all too evident.

The problem of score constellations is more amenable to a descriptive clinical approach than to mathematical representation. This is shown by the very different meaning of a low correspondence score for Mr. Moffett and Mr. Wagner. In Mr. Moffett's case the low r is interpreted as the man's attempt to confine his conflicts and doubts to perception of himself and illustrative material shows that he uses self-rejection in his father-role rather than reject the child. In contrast, Mr. Wagner uses his low trait-correspondence score very largely to reject in his child those traits about which he is ambivalent in himself. Thus, a low trait-correspondence score appears in one case to enhance empathy and identification with the child, whereas, in the other, it serves to further alienate father and child.

Similarly, although the within-group r between self-rejection and child-rejection is high (r = .71) for all 38 cases and indicates a tendency to correspondence between inner-directed and outer-directed processes of rejective perception, this does not entitle us to predict low child-rejection where self-rejection is low. In Mr. Wagner's case, where self-rejection is near the mean of the combined distributions of war-separated and non-separated cases, child-rejection score reached an extreme. This father seemed to use perceptual distancing through rejection as a defense mechanism. This is suggested by the total score constellation (low trait-correspondence, high phobic projection), and by the content of material quoted which illustrates his tendency to flat or hostile affect and his lack of insight into the effect of punitive child-handling.

The converse is illustrated in the interviews of Mr. Stone and Mr. Moffett where, contrary to the established group trend, high self-rejection is associated with low child-rejection. Here, again, context of the scores and content of the material is essential to a correct interpretation of their meaning.

Mr. Marston and Mr. Arno have in common low self- and child-rejection scores and from this point of view might be considered similar. But a closer examination reveals Mr. Arno as an active, outgoing person, somewhat preoccupied with "getting his way without the unpleasantness of being disliked," who perceives the child in similar terms. In contrast, Mr. Marston sees himself as submissive and passive and his first-born as a follower, as one who is "pretty tractable."

The analysis of group trends enables us to state that Mr. Arno is representative of non-separated fathers and Mr. Moore, of war-separated fathers, but the above discussion will serve to demonstrate that the selection of only one variable such as self-rejection as basis of prediction would lead to quite erroneous conclusions when applied to the individual case.

The uses of this method of analysis lie rather in pointing up the importance of the total constellation of scores in relation to the content of the material produced by any one subject. The discussion on trait-correspondence in the context of two contrasting cases indicates that the same factor may be related to two opposite "effects" according to the context in which it occurs. This is the psychoanalytic model of hypotheses concerning personality.

The Method of Analysis— Its Uses and Limitations

As was pointed out in an earlier section, the categorization of interview material, even when as many as 20 variables and several dimensions are used, still makes for the omission of many data which, though relevant, do not lend themselves to this particular classification. Statements which one might regard as clinically very revealing and symbolic of the individual's self- and other-perception can frequently not be used.

An example of this is the concern of Mr. Marston, war-separated, with his stature, and his recurrent statement, "I am a small man." Another instance is the description given by Mr. Wolf, a war-separated father, with considerable feeling, of a scene in which he looks down from the deck of a battleship onto a number of smaller vessels. In the context of the case the interviewer and the investigator felt that this scene represented much of that subject's habitual feeling concerning all "that could be looked down upon," but they did not feel justified in using such data.

All direct statements about complex interpersonal relations could not be rated. Thus, many fathers stated spontaneously that they saw themselves reflected in the first child. The method of classification used here is a tool for testing the hypothesis that such correspondence between self-perception and child-perception tends to occur but it could not make use of statements so directly in support of it.

The categories employed here dealt with the components of complex interpersonal relations rather than with the relations themselves. It was hoped that frequency and intensity of the components would yield a pattern representative of self- and child-perception and that this could be adequately described by scores based on such simple operations as adding, subtracting, and averaging.

An examination of the method of analysis and the scoring system will bear out our contention that the mathematical representation of psychological processes, even if based on an empathic rating method which has shown some reliability, still falls very short of the subtleties of actual human experience.

An instance of this is the 3-point intensity scale used here largely for the purpose of weighting the frequency score for a category in order that it might approximate the emotional emphasis with which that category may be used by the subject. It would appear that a 3-point scale is not adequate in differentiating between the child-perception of war-separated and non-separated fathers when the comparison is based on group means. It is possible that a 5-point scale might have made the differentiation, but this might have lost in unreliability since the discrimination required would have presented greater difficulty.

Another instance is the use of average discrepancies to represent degree of conflict between positive and negative evaluations of the same trait as perceived in the self. These scores also do not differentiate between war-separated and non-separated cases.

These findings raise questions concerning the use of the method of averaging for an investigation which employs a multivariable classification. If, as is the case in the 20 categories used here, the categories receive very uneven scores for each of the 38 case analyses, the average might serve to hide group differences instead of revealing them when the group means of the case averages are used for comparison.

It would appear from the findings of this study that measures based on proportions such as the self- and child-rejection scores, the range of inconsistency scores, and the table of percentages describing the content of self- and child-perception are more informative and also more useful in differentiation between war-separated and non-separated cases. It must be stressed that the restricted nature of the sample limits the application of conclusions derived from the study to populations which are similar in socioeconomic status.

Summary and Discussion of Findings

Differences in Intrapsychic Conflict

The war-separated fathers consistently show significantly higher scores than non-separated fathers on measures indicative of intrapsychic conflict and stress. This finding supports the underlying hypothesis of the research project that war-separation and subsequent return to a family constellation different from the one left behind will affect the feelings and attitudes of fathers. The impact of the challenge to adjust simultaneously in the areas of marriage relations, vocation, and father-role, as discussed in Chapter 3, seems causally related to the greater intrapsychic stress and conflict of war-separated fathers.

The non-separated group also presented a number of other features which one might expect would make for increased stability of their frame of reference and a reduced susceptibility to feeling threatened by the role demands of fatherhood. As shown in Table 8, Chapter 2, the non-separated group tended to be chronologically more mature at the time of interview. Furthermore, a greater number of the war-separated group contracted war marriages and the conception of the first child occurred relatively soon after marriage. The non-separated group, on the other hand, although they show the same median date of marriage, have a much wider range of marriage dates. In the non-separated group, the conception of the first child occurred after a longer period of marital adjustment.

It is probable that the lower rejection and conflict scores for self-perception of the non-separated group are related to these factors as well as to the fact that they could adjust more gradually and naturally to the role of father.

Differences in Self- and Child-Rejection

Fathers from both groups tended to see themselves reflected in the first-born and this tendency was measured in terms of trait correspondence between self-perception and child-perception. The difference between war-separated and non-separated fathers was not statistically significant.

The measures of various types of projective processes which were devised showed significantly greater incidence of rejection of self and child in the war-separated group. The greater incidence of phobic projection found in the war-separated group serves to illustrate the defensive character of child-perception in this group.

Interpretation of Low Trait Correspondence

The analyses of individual cases in this chapter suggest that trait correspondence in self and child may be a function of the score constellation and the content of perception. A low trait-correspondence score indicates that the father tends to see his first-born in different terms than himself. It can be interpreted in a number of ways, depending on the context of the trait-correspondence score.

First, it may be explained in terms of his ability to accept differences in the first-born, where it is accompanied by a low child-rejection score and perceptual content which indicates positive relations and would thus represent an illustration of "tolerance."

Second, it may be explained as a defense mechanism operating toward confining the father's problems to himself and separating child-perception from his own characteristics if the low trait-correspondence score is accompanied by a high self-rejection and range of inconsistency score. This kind of defense mechanism would work toward improvement of father-child relations where the father tends to disapprove of himself, as is illustrated in the description of Mr. Stone. This constellation could be interpreted as representing negative perceptual patterns oriented around the defense of the child against the father.

Third, it may be explained as a defense mechanism where there is a high phobic projection or child-rejection score. In such a case, the father cannot permit himself perception of too great a similarity between the first-born and himself, since this would enhance his own insecurity (Mr. Wagner). This last constellation is self-defensive in orientation.

In the light of the theoretical discussion which precedes the account of this investigation, one may be tempted to interpret these findings in terms of popular postulates concerning non-separated fathers, in that they tend to see the first child as endowed with characteristics approved in themselves and derive from this a sense of continuity. War-separated fathers, on the other hand, appear to present a perceptual pattern frequently postulated by psychoanalytic theory for mother-child relations. They tend to endow the child with characteristics which they are unable to approve or integrate in themselves so that the child becomes the focus of perceptual defense mechanisms which derive from the father's conflict and ambivalence.

Patterns in Descriptions of Self and Child

An analysis of the categories most characteristically used in the description of self-perception and child-perception shows that the contents of the perceptual patterns for the two groups differ.

The self-perception of war-separated fathers is more evenly distributed among the positive active, positive passive, negative active, and negative passive clusters of categories. In contrast, the non-separated fathers show a more clearly defined sense of their role as individuals who direct positively, who teach, help, support, and praise. The positive active cluster contains 40.7 percent of their scores.

It is possible that the non-separated father's perception of the first child as predominantly positive passive (appreciating, co-operating, trusting, and conforming) reduces the need for perceptual defense such as isolation by rejection. This is because the child is seen in a role complementary to the father's.

In contrast to this, the war-separated father's perception of himself is as predominantly passive, a role which is contradictory to the cultural norms. This, together with his perception of the child as predominantly passive (half positively and half negatively), might be expected to lead to enhancement of intrapsychic conflict and need for perceptual defenses such as isolation by rejection. It is almost as if these men were trying to ward off the dangerous parallels between the content of their self-perception and their perception of the first child by means of child-rejection and phobic projection.

PART II. THE MOTHER-INTERVIEW STUDY

CHAPTER 6. DESCRIPTION OF THE MOTHER-INTERVIEW STUDY

by Edith M. Dowley and William Langdon Faust

The role of the mother in father-child relations is always important. When war separates fathers from their children and delays their acquaintance beyond the period of infancy, the mother's role is crucial. Rearing a child in his father's absence and protecting him until the father's return throw a great burden of responsibility on the mother. The problems of reunion for father and child raise problems also for the mother, problems for which she must constantly seek solutions. Sometimes she finds herself between father and child, each of them wanting her all for himself, each resenting her attention to the other. The primary concern of this study is not the mother and her problems, however. This study, like all studies in this monograph, is primarily interested in the effects on the child of father-separation and later reunion. It differs from the other studies in only one major respect. It attempts to look at the war-born child through his mother's eyes; to see him as she saw him when an infant, and as she sees him now behaving and relating to persons, places, and things in his everyday world.

Purpose of the Study

The purpose of this study was to gain further insight into the effects of father-absence in infancy on first-born children through data reported by the mother. We hoped to learn from mothers in what ways the father's absence and later return affected children in these three general areas:

1. The children's experiences in relation to child-rearing practices and to circumstances of living in the war and post-war years,
2. The children's behavior in relation to these child-rearing practices, to people and to events in their lives,
3. The attitudes of fathers and mothers toward these children.

General Plan of the Study

For our purpose it seemed necessary to study not only the first-born children, but also second children born to the same families after the father's return. Comparisons could then be made to see in what ways these siblings were different. However, when we were asked, "Are not all first-born children different from second-born children anyway?" we thought it advisable to include in this study two kinds of families: (1) a group of families with the father absent during the first year of life of the first-born child and present during the life of the second-born; and (2) a second group of families, with the father present throughout the infancy period of both the first- and second-born children.

We believed that although all first-born children may be different from second-born children in some respects, first-born children whose fathers were absent during their infancy would be different from other first-born children as well as from their own younger siblings.

Primarily, in this study we were interested in those children whose fathers were absent during the child's first year of life. In order to see these children in the correct perspective, it was thought necessary to compare them with children whose fathers were not absent during the child's first year. Three control groups were therefore planned for purposes of comparison with the experimental group in the study. The primary control group consisted of first-born children whose fathers were present during the first year of life. Throughout the study it will be known as the non-separated first-born group (C1). The second control group was made up of the second-born siblings of the war-separated children. This group will be called the war-separated second-born group (E2). A third control group used the second-born children of the non-separated families. They will be called the non-separated second-born group (C2). The father-separated group will be referred to in the study as the war-separated first-born group (E1). We call the E2 children "war-separated" here in order to identify them as members of the war-separated (experimental) families. Actually, of course, these second-borns were not themselves war-separated; they were born after the reunion of the father with his family.

Methods for Collecting Data

An interview technique was used to secure data from the mothers. Although schools, physicians, and many social agencies have routinely used the mother-interview for obtaining information about children useful to their purposes, very few research studies of children were found which used the interview method for obtaining data. In 1938 Jean Walker Macfarlane (52) included the interview method as a research technique in a longitudinal study of children from infancy through adolescence. Recognizing its drawbacks, such as lack of uniformity and objectivity, she worked out a methodology and a set of guiding principles which "avoided the invalidities of too rigid procedure and the inadequacy of unsystematic data collection." Pyles, Stolz, and Macfarlane (65) reported on the validity of such interview material. Mothers of 252 children in a superior urban community who were reinterviewed after one and two years were more than usually accurate when their reports were compared with records kept of physical examinations of their children. These mothers tended to err slightly in the direction of suggesting precocity of first-born children, showed a slight tendency to forget some of the difficulties in child training, and a tendency to forget the illnesses and disturbances they suffered in pregnancy.

In spite of the inaccuracies which mother-interviews are known to have, we wanted information about children which would cover the entire period from conception to a present level of maturity. For most children the only source of such information is the child's own mother. This we felt to be especially true for children whose fathers were not with them until they were one to two years of age.

Selecting the Content of the Interview

In developing the interview schedule for use with the mothers it was necessary to select from the wide range of possible areas of investigation those which would seem most pertinent for this particular study. The basis used for selection was threefold:

1. Areas which other studies (research and clinical) had emphasized as important in determining or revealing characteristics of children.
2. Areas which seemed to be especially important in the lives of war-separated children as revealed in the father-interviews made by Stolz in this project.
3. Areas which seemed to be important on the basis of our experience with and observations of young children born during the war.

Content of the Interview Schedule

The interview schedule consists of three parts: I, the life history of the child; II, a comparison of mother-attitudes toward first- and second-born children; and III, the effects of war-separation on children. The complete schedule will be found in Appendix 6.

Part I, the life history of the child, consists of 111 questions on the developmental progress of the child, the methods used in rearing him, and other conditions which may have influenced his development. Other studies have shown that much insight can be gained regarding the personality and present behavior of children through knowledge of the conditions surrounding their births, the child-rearing practices of their parents, their opportunities for physical, mental, and social development, and the emotional atmosphere of their early years (17, 19, 41, 61, 86). Each mother was asked the questions in Part I, first about her first-born child and later concerning her second-born child.

Part II, a comparison of mother-attitudes toward first- and second-born children, consists of 11 questions, the answers to which might show differences between the mother's first- and second-born children as she saw them and might reveal important differences in the life space of the two children. We hoped that the answers to these questions would provide evidences of parental acceptance or rejection of children and of identification of children with their parents. Part II compared first- and second-born; and it was used at the end of the interview concerning the first-born child only.

Part III, the effects of father-separation on children, consists of two questions concerning the effects of father-absence on the war-separated child as they appeared to the mother. Consequently these two questions were asked only in the interviews with mothers of war-separated children.

Form of the Interview Structure

The form of the interview was determined by the needs of the study itself. Since this was to be a comparative study, we felt that a certain amount of specific data was essential. The interviewer would therefore of necessity determine the areas to be discussed. At the same time, however, since the study was also one of attitudes, feelings, and relationships, the mother should have freedom to talk on the subject given to her in any order she wished. For this purpose, a combination of structured and nondirective interview techniques was used. Flexibility in the order of discussion was made possible by the use of the questions listed on the interview schedule which could be checked off by the interviewer as the mother was talking. Questions not answered could then be asked at the end of her discussion of each area.

Mothers were encouraged to talk freely and fully on the subject-area under discussion while the interviewer was responsible for keeping the interview on the subject, within the time allotted, and always moving forward. Such encouraging devices as smiling, nodding agreement or sympathy, saying "Mm mm mm," "And you felt . . . ," "You said you thought . . . ," were used to keep the mother talking and developing the topic she was discussing. Occasionally, when the mother seemed anxious or emotionally disturbed because of the material she was handling at the time, it seemed important to reassure her. In such cases the interviewer made short comments such as "Sometimes it does seem difficult," "But children recover quickly," or "They forgive us most things, don't they?"

As far as possible we avoided asking questions which might be answered merely by Yes, No, or other single-word answers. Instead, many of the questions used attempted to get the emotional concomitants of an experience or event by being worded in such ways as, "How did you feel . . . ?" "Do you remember anything special about . . . ?" or "Did you enjoy . . . ?" Throughout the interview there were questions asked which required the mother to repeat certain data in different ways and in different connections. This insured re-checks on answers which might be misunderstood without repetition or restatement.

Order of the Interview Questions

It was planned to ask for life-history data before asking the mother to make a comparison of her two children. This was based on the assumption that the comparisons would have greater accuracy following the mother's review of her child's development in the life history.

The questions concerning the effects of father-separation were placed at the end of the interview. By that time it was assumed that the mother would have made a confident relationship with the interviewer and could talk to her about father-child relations with greater ease. We also felt that the life-history discussion of the child would give the mother more insight into the father-child relation.

The order of the questions in the life-history part of the interview schedule was determined by the order found most successful in the interviewer's past experiences in interviewing mothers. Such order is determined by: the necessity for establishing a good relation between the mother and the interviewer; the desirability of stimulating and sustaining the mother's interest; the necessity for encouraging and guiding the conversation so as to get the data wanted; and the need to stimulate the mother's memory for the details required by the study.

For this purpose the chronological order is often less desirable than one contrived by the interviewer which starts with a dramatic area or time in the life of the child and ends with an area which the parent may find less easy to talk about because of its highly personal and intimate nature, or because she has not thought about it before and would find it difficult to remember without some preliminary discussion. For these reasons, for instance, pregnancy and labor were put last on the life-history interview, and nursing and weaning, first.

The interview was planned so that it would take approximately one hour for a mother to discuss each child. Each mother was interviewed twice. The first interview concerned her first-born child; the second interview, her second-born child. The two interviews were scheduled within ten days of each other. Each mother was asked at the beginning of the first interview for her permission to record electrically the interviews.

Description of the Families

Criteria for Selection of the Families

The criteria for selection of the war-separated and non-separated families were the same as the criteria used in the larger research (see Chapter 1, p. 10), with the additional requirement that there be a second child in the family. In the war-separated families the second child was born after the father's return from the war.

Originally it was planned to select families in which the ages and sexes of the first- and second-born children in the war-separated and non-separated families were matched. However, this was found to be impossible in the families living in Stanford Village.

The Families Selected

There were 12 war-separated families and 11 non-separated families found which met the criteria. The 12 war-separated mothers were all wives of the war-separated men studied in the father-interview study reported in Part I of this monograph. Three of the non-separated mothers were wives of the non-separated men studied in the father-interview study; the other non-separated mothers were from different families.

Description of the Children

Chronological Age

There was a total of 46 children in the study, ranging in age from 6 months to 88 months at the time of the interview with the mother. Appendix 1 gives complete data for each child.

The 12 war-separated first-borns ranged in age from 52 months to 88 months, with an average age of 67.7 months. The 11 non-separated first-borns had a range in chronological age from 44 months to 77 months, with an average age of 58.2 months.

The 12 war-separated second-borns ranged in age from 6 months to 65 months, with an average age of 33.7 months. The 11 non-separated second-borns had a range in chronological age from 19 months to 50 months, with an average age of 30.2 months.

It will be seen that the war-separated first-borns were somewhat older than the non-separated first-borns, a difference of 9.5 months between the average ages. However, the range in ages in the two groups was very similar, 36 months for the war-separated group and 33 months for the non-separated group.

The average chronological age of the war-separated second-born group was only 3.5 months greater than the non-separated group but the range was much larger, 64.5 months compared with 31 months.

Sex

Of the 46 children, there were 25 boys and 21 girls. The war-separated families had 16 boys and 8 girls; 10 boys and 2 girls among the first-borns and 6 boys and 6 girls among the second-borns. The non-separated families had 9 boys and 13 girls; 4 boys and 7 girls among the first-borns, and 5 boys and 6 girls among the second-borns.

Intelligence

The average Intelligence Quotient of the war-separated first-borns was 122, with a range from 106 to 138. For the non-separated first-borns the average Intelligence Quotient was 119.6, with a range from 96 to 133, indicating that mentally the two groups were comparable.

Comparisons cannot be made with the intelligence of the second-borns because many of the children at this time were too young to be given the Stanford-Binet. Of the 6 war-separated second-borns who were given the intelligence tests, the range in Intelligence Quotients was from 100 to 136. The range of the 7 non-separated second-borns was 111 to 151.

Data Collected

A total of 46 interviews was held with 23 mothers; one for the first-born child and one for the second-born in 12 war-separated and 11 non-separated families.

The interviews were all electrically recorded by the Audograph Recording Machine. The data included 38 hours and 40 minutes of recording, an average of 1.7 hours per mother. The average length of the interview with the war-separated mothers for the first child was 8.6 minutes longer than the average for any other group.

The typewritten data include 1,332 double-spaced pages. There is an average of 36.0 pages and 26.1 pages for first- and second-born children, respectively, of war-separated mothers; and an average of 32.9 pages and 25.7 pages for first- and second-born children of non-separated mothers. The war-separated mothers were more voluble (by 160 pages) than the non-separated mothers, about one-third of this being for the second child. This was probably due to the two additional questions asked them concerning the effect on the first child of father-absence.

All mothers responded to all of the questions in the interview schedule. There were no overt refusals. The war-separated mothers seemed better oriented and somewhat more at home than the non-separated mothers. This was probably due to the fact that their husbands had previously been interviewed for this research project by Stolz, and several had expressed a desire to be interviewed, too. In general, the mothers seemed to enjoy the interviews. As one mother said, "I love to come. No one ever gives us mothers a chance to talk about our children."

Analysis of Data

Analysis of the data has been focused on studying three aspects of the effect of the father's absence and subsequent return on the life of the first-born child. We have studied the effect of father-absence on the child in regard to (a) the early life experiences of the child, (b) the behavior of the child, (c) the interpersonal relations of the child. In these analyses the first-born has been compared with other first-borns of non-separated families and with his own sibling. In addition, comparison has been made of the attitudes of the mother and the father toward the first-born.

CHAPTER 7.
CHARACTERISTICS OF WAR-BORN CHILDREN AS REVEALED BY MOTHERS

by Edith M; Dowley and William Langdon Faust

Predictions Regarding Differences Between Groups of Children

When this study was undertaken, we anticipated that there would be great differences between war-separated children and other children. We presumed: First, that the factor of father-absence would of necessity make the early life experiences of the E1 children different in many respects than the early life experiences of the children in the other three groups. We thought that the circumstances connected with the conception and birth of the E1 children might provoke parent dissatisfaction or rejection, or arouse feelings of extreme possessiveness and protectiveness in the mother. We also thought that the early feeding and weaning experiences of these children and their experiences in relation to the other child-rearing practices of their parents would differ significantly from the experiences of their younger siblings and from the experiences of children in the non-separated families. Second, as a result of these less favorable experiences, we thought that the behavior of the war-separated children would be different from the behavior of the other children. We expected to find these differences manifested especially in their behavior in relation to eating, elimination, and sleeping; in fears; in dependence on adults due to emotional immaturity or lack of competence in manipulation; and in the manifestations of tension as evidenced in tics and comfort patterns. Third, we predicted that these children would have more difficulties in their relations with their parents, with other adults, and with children.

Early Life Experiences of the Children

We were surprised to find that except for the factor of father-absence itself, the early life experiences of the E1 children did not differ significantly from those of the other children. On the contrary, as may be seen in the following discussion, we found that in some ways the early life experiences of the E1 group were more favorable than were those of the other three groups. We found very few differences in the circumstances surrounding conception and birth or in the mothers' attitudes toward their pregnancies. We found more similarity than difference between the child-rearing practices and parent expectations of E1 and C1 children and between E2 and C2 children. Second-born children on the whole, had more favorable experiences in terms of parent permissiveness and understanding, and of parent expectations appropriate to their developmental levels than did first-born children.

Conditions Associated with Birth

In studying the attitudes of mothers toward their first- and second-born children we wished to know something of the conditions associated with pregnancy, labor, and child-birth as well as of the mother's feelings regarding these experiences. This seemed important in a study of children conceived at a time of impending husband-wife separation because of war (first-born war-separated children in this study), and of children conceived after the reunion of the husband and wife at the war's end (second-born war-separated children).[1] The question: "When you first knew you were pregnant, how did you feel? Were you worried, frightened, pleased?" was often sufficient to elicit a large amount of informational data.

Mothers' reactions to pregnancy. All except 3 of the 23 mothers in the study became pregnant with the first child when the husband was waiting for orders to report for military service outside of this country. As it happened, eight of the husbands were not subsequently separated from their wives, although at the time that their wives became pregnant, they expected that they would be separated.

Only two of the expectant mothers were displeased with their pregnancies. One of these mothers was in the non-separated group and the other in the war-separated group. There were also two mothers who were displeased when they found that they were pregnant with their second-born children. These were not the same mothers, and, again, one was a non-separated and one a war-separated mother.

However, in no case did the mother make any reference to her husband's impending departure as a reason for her to worry about her pregnancy. One mother, who had not known she was pregnant when her husband left for overseas, said she "was feeling very disappointed" because they both had "wanted a baby when he was gone." She was consequently "very pleased" when she found that she was pregnant.

Mothers' reactions to length of labor. The mothers were asked, "Were you in labor long? In pain long?" as another possible means of evaluating their attitudes toward their children.

More mothers in this study thought their labor time short than long. They considered their time in labor long for only 17 of the 46 babies. Of the periods in labor considered long, eight were for war-separated first-born children, five for non-separated first-borns, one for a war-separated second-born child, and three for non-separated second-born children.

Although more mothers of war-separated first-borns reported being in labor for a longer time than mothers of non-separated first-borns, the difference was very small. Both non-separated and war-separated mothers tended to remember being in labor longer with their first babies.

Mothers' reactions to the pains of labor. In each group mothers reported more severe conditions during labor for the first child than for the second. Twelve mothers (seven E1's and five C1's) remembered severe labor with their first babies, while only five mothers (three E2's and two C2's) remembered the conditions of their labor with their second babies as severe. However, more mothers in the war-separated first-born group reported

---

1. As is noted in the previous chapter's discussion of the composition of the groups studied in this section, the children here designated "second-born war-separated children," or E2's are members of the war-separated families but were not themselves separated from their fathers.

severe pain in labor than mothers in any other group. Seven of the 12 mothers in this group reported their labor pains as severe, five as normal, and none thought it easy. One mother in this group said, "I remember saying I thought at that time I would never have another child." Another mother in this group reported, "I can remember it like a nightmare. It's a terrible way to have children. There must be better ways." A third mother of a war-separated child, in telling of the end of labor, said, "I got frightened after a while. It was worse than I expected. I hadn't heard much about it hurting or anything and I just didn't expect it to hurt like it did." All three of these mothers were alone in the hospital as their husbands were gone and they were far from their own parents' homes.

Factors related to the sex of the baby. The results of this study show that a surprising number of parents feel that they know in advance what sex the baby will be and are surprised and occasionally disappointed when it turns out to be the opposite. Of the 46 babies in this study, the sex of 21 of them was a surprise to their mothers, who had expected the opposite of what they were. No differences could be found between the attitudes of mothers in the war-separated groups and the attitudes of mothers in the non-separated groups toward the sex of their children.

Disappointment in the sex of the child occurred more often with second-born children than with first-born. Out of the nine mothers who admitted they were disappointed in the sex of the baby, seven referred to second-born children and two to first-born.

Experiences in Relation to Organic Needs

Infant experiences, such as feeding and toilet training, clearly depend upon parental attitudes and primarily upon the mother's attitudes. Parental attitudes often change with prevailing social attitudes. Also, attitudes and related techniques change through raising a first child. Therefore it was considered that the analysis of the important infant experiences of the E1's should take account of these family changes in attitudes and techniques by considering the differences between the E1's and the E2's in light of the differences between the C1's and C2's. The statistical analysis used in this chapter depends upon rating the differences between the first- and second-born war-separated children and also the differences between the first- and second-born non-separated children.

The rating scale used was a 3-point scale from +1, meaning that the first-born child had better experiences in the light of currently recommended practices in child-rearing than did the second-born sibling; through 0, indicating that both children had similar experiences; to -1, where the second-born child had the more favorable experiences. For example, in feeding, breast feeding was considered a more desirable experience than bottle feeding in early infancy. A +1 rating was given to that pair of siblings in which the first child was breast fed, but the second child was not. The rating was given to that pair in which both or neither were breast fed. The -1 rating was reserved for the case where the first-born was not breast fed, but the second-born child was breast fed.

Material from which these ratings were made came from the answers which the mothers gave to specific questions. The first tabulations of these answers were made by Dowley (21) by comparing all four groups with each other. The present material on experiences is a retabulation of the material, reorganized to make use of the difference scores between the first- and second-born children in the war-separated and non-separated groups.

Early feeding experiences. Nursing: The practice of breast feeding for a period of at least the first six months, where at all possible, has been strongly advocated by psychologists and anthropologists. Although all but three mothers in this study planned in advance of birth to nurse their babies, only twenty children were breast fed for more than one month. Only eight children in this study were breast fed for six months or more.

The first-born children in the war-separated group had the advantage over C1's in this regard. However, this advantage was not statistically significant. The mean for the difference in experiences between E1's and E2's was +.33. This means that more E1's were breast fed than were their siblings, E2's. The mean of the differences between C1's and C2's was 0, which indicates that first- and second-born children in the non-separated group tended to be treated alike. Since assumption of underlying normality and continuity of the scores clearly could not be made, these means were treated by a distribution-free statistic, Festinger's d (25). Using this statistic, we found that the difference between these means of the war-separated and non-separated groups is not significant. Although the differences between the siblings in the war-separated group were not significant in light of the non-separated group differences, more E1's were breast-fed than were children in any other group. The E2 group had the next largest number of children who were breast-fed.

The higher incidence of breast feeding in the war-separated first-born group may be explained on the assumption that the mothers in this group had more time to spend with their babies, since their husbands were away, and many of them were living with relatives who either freed them from, or shared with them the responsibility of running a home. Some mothers reported, "I had nothing else to do but take care of the baby." In addition to the time factor, many mothers in this group derived their primary emotional satisfactions from their babies. One mother explained it: "If you don't have a husband to show your affection to, you give it all to your baby."

Early feeding schedules: With the emphasis on a return to breast feeding and to other forms of natural child nurture and rearing, feeding children on a regime of self-regulation has been strongly advocated both in the professional and popular literature for the past 12 to 14 years (34).

All but 3 of the 12 E1's and 3 of the 11 C1's were fed on a strict schedule in infancy while the opposite was true of the second-born children. Eight E2 children and 9 C2 children were fed "on demand" in infancy.

The differences between the first- and second-born children of both groups in relation to feeding schedules are marked. The explanation for this great difference most probably lies in the time-lag between the publication of the arguments for self-regulation by such authors as Gesell (33), Aldrich (1), and Ribble (66) and the practice of it by the general public. Here again when the mean of the differences between the war-separated siblings is compared with the mean of the differences between the non-separated siblings, using Festinger's d, the differences are not significant. When family differences are taken into account, the E1's were not fed on stricter schedules than were the C1's.

Time of beginning and accomplishing weaning: There is no significant difference between the four groups of babies in this study in the time of beginning and the time of accomplishing weaning. The mothers reported that the methods used in accomplishing weaning were more permissive in most cases for second-born children than for first-borns. A few more first-born war-separated children were weaned abruptly by their mothers and more war-separated second-born children were allowed a longer, more gradual weaning experience.

In the area of feeding and weaning the experiences of E1's were not significantly different from other groups. More of the E1's were fed on stricter schedules than were their siblings, but this was also true of the C1's and seems to be a factor associated with the change in prevailing attitudes.

Experiences in relation to elimination. Current writing on the subject of elimination training shows a definite trend away from early, coercive methods to an approach that recognizes the importance of developmental factors in learning bowel and bladder control (53, 81). Watson (85), who advocated a "conditioning" regime in the teaching of habits of cleanliness, was a powerful influence in the 1920's and 1930's. Because of his teachings, parents often measured their success as parents by the age at which their child accomplished toilet training. Research in the cultural demands made of young children in the area of elimination control reveals that "the middle class child often has to pay a heavy price in intimidation for his early and strict training. There is no doubt also that he often has to win parental acceptance at too high a cost in anxiety" (17, p. 103).

Age of beginning training in control of elimination: There was a considerable variation among the 46 children in this study in the time of beginning bowel and bladder training—from the earliest, 4 months at the time bowel training was started, to the latest, 26 months at the time of beginning training for both bowel and bladder control. First-born children were started on their training much earlier in most cases than were second-born children. Many of the second-born children had not completed their training at the time of the mother-interview, and four of them had not even begun their training. Of these four, two war-separated second-borns had had no training at all; one war-separated second-born had completed bowel training but had not started bladder training; and one non-separated second-born had not started any training.

The mean of the difference between war-separated siblings in age of beginning bladder training is -.54 and for age of beginning bowel training is -.45. In both trainings the E1's were begun earlier than their siblings. Similar means for non-separated siblings are -.54 and -.72. Again the first-born children were begun earlier. When the differences between the means for bladder training are compared, using Festinger's d, no significant difference is found. The differences between the means for bowel training are not significant either.

Age of accomplishing control in elimination: Although their training in learning bowel control was started later than that of the first-born groups (by from 2.5 to 4 months), the war-separated second-born children achieved bowel control a month earlier than either first-born group. And in like manner, in bladder training, the second-born non-separated children whose training was begun from 3.5 to 5.5 months later than either of the other three groups of children, achieved bladder control from 2.2 to 4.7 months earlier. The time of accomplishing both bowel and bladder control seems to follow a familial pattern. Both groups of war-separated and both groups of non-separated children are more nearly alike in this respect than are both groups of first-borns and both groups of second-borns.

Table 45. Age of Beginning and Completing Bowel and Bladder Training (in months)

	Number	Bowel Training		Bladder Training		Bed-Dryness
		Begun	Accomplished	Begun	Accomplished	Accomplished
E1	12	8.1	20.3	13.9	28.4	37.0
C1	11	9.6	20.7	15.7	25.9	34.5
E2	8	12.1	19.2	15.7	28.2	29.6
C2	7	16.0	21.1	19.2	23.7	23.6[a]

[a]Based on 6 cases.

Duration of the training period: For the children in this study the earlier the training was started, the longer it took to accomplish, and the later the training was started, the shorter the training period. In the group whose training was begun earliest, the war-separated group of first-born children, it took an average of 16.2 months to learn bowel control, and 14.5 months to accomplish bladder control. In the non-separated second-born group where training was started latest, the bowel training was effected in 5.1 months and the bladder training in 4.5 months average. In general, mothers whose first-born children took a long time to acquire habits of elimination, postponed the training of their second-borns.

Experiences in relation to sleeping. In the interviews on which this study is based, questions were asked concerning the amount of sleep, in infancy and at the present time; the length of time the child slept; his behavior before going to sleep and upon wakening in the morning; the quality of his night sleep and his behavior during the night.

Forty of the 46 mothers were satisfied with the amount of sleep that their children were presently getting. Of the 6 who were not satisfied, 2 were in the war-separated first-born group, 2 in the war-separated second-born group, and 2 in the non-separated first-born group. Again, all the mothers of the non-separated second-born children were satisfied with the amount of sleep these children were presently getting.

Experiences in relation to locomotion and manipulation. Mothers frequently deter their young children from climbing, jumping, investigating, exploring, and even from walking and crawling for fear of the possible harm that may result from such activity. They may in some cases deprive the infant of experiences that are necessary in learning to protect himself from physical injury at a later day. Some children learn late to cope with such potential hazards in the environment as stairs, radiators, and open doorways. Such restriction and deprivation of opportunity for learning are almost always the result of parents' anxiety for the safety and well-being of the child.

Freedom for locomotion in infancy: Mothers varied in the amount and kind of activity they provided for their children in the period of development between the time of learning to sit up and the time of competence in locomotor ability. Some children were given "the run of the house" from an early age, while others were like Raymond Wolf, who was "kept in his crib or in a doorway swing most of the time."

The mean of the differences between the war-separated siblings in the area of motor freedom and restriction is -.19. This means that more E1's than E2's were restricted. The mean for the non-separated siblings is +.19 which indicated that fewer C1's than C2's were restricted. Although E1's had different experiences in this area than the C1's, when these groups are compared with their siblings this difference is not significant when tested by Festinger's d.

The war-separated first-borns were allowed the least amount of freedom of space and opportunity for activity of any of the four groups of children, with their younger siblings having the next least amount. The non-separated first-borns were given the most freedom, their younger siblings having the next most. There is no indication of greater freedom being a privilege of first-borns which is denied to second-borns because of the difficulty for parents to watch two young children. Even though there are fewer second-born non-separated children allowed freedom than first-born non-separated children, there are slightly more second-born war-separated children who were given freedom than first-born war-separated children.

Learning about the environment through touch: One of the periods in a child's development which parents consider most difficult is the time when the child is learning to walk and is touching, breaking, and tearing objects within his sight and reach about the house. Some mothers seem able to guide the young child during this period by consistently using positive, permissive approaches such as substitution, satisfaction, and interpretation; other mothers use restrictive negative controls such as slapping, spanking, scolding, and saying, "No, no!"

Twenty-six mothers used negative controls in teaching their children not to touch certain objects around the house, while only 19 used positive approaches. The positive approaches seem to have yielded better results, however, since they were used for 16 out of the 24 children called easy to teach, and for only 3 of the children thought of as difficult; while negative controls were used for 18 out of the 21 children considered difficult to teach, and for only 8 of the children who were considered easy to teach.

The mean of the differences between war-separated siblings is -.36. This indicates that more E1's were restricted than E2's. The mean for the non-separated siblings is -.09 which shows that slightly more C1's than C2's were restricted in manipulation. The difference between the means is not significant when tested by Festinger's d.

Mothers considered the first-born children easier to teach not to touch things than the second-born children. There is no significant difference in the number of children considered difficult nor in the number of mothers using negative controls, between E1 and C1 children.

Experiences and Relations with Adults

The early lives of the war-separated first-born children were different from the early lives of the children in each of the other groups in at least two respects. These children not only lived the first year or so of their lives without knowing their fathers, but also lived as visitors with their mothers in families largely or entirely made up of adults. These adults, in many cases, were as important to the war-separated child as his mother. They went to him when he cried, changed him, fed him, played with him, fondled him, and disciplined him. In some cases they were responsible for the training methods mothers used with their children.

Experiences with close relatives. All of the war-separated first-born children lived with relatives for at least part of the first year of life. Eight of them lived with grandparents for the entire time before their fathers returned from war, and one war-separated family lived in the grandparents' home until the second-born child was more than two months old. In the non-separated groups there were only two children who lived with other than parental adults.

Therefore the war-separated first-borns had opportunities to know intimately grandparents or relatives with whom they had daily association. This was not true for any other group. On the other hand, the war-separated first-borns were the only group deprived of contacts with their fathers.

Experiences with adults other than close relatives. In spite of the fact that they lived with relatives, mothers of war-separated first-born children frequently reported that these children lived rather sheltered lives and did not know adults other than their own mothers and grandparents. From the reports of the non-separated mothers, a majority of their first-born children lived in populous neighborhoods when they were babies and they often knew well and occasionally stayed with adult neighbors for an afternoon or evening when their mothers were out. Thirteen of the second-born children in this study, 3 war-separated and 8 non-separated children, had lived in Stanford Village from the time they were tiny babies. These children knew many adults and knew them well.

More non-separated children went places with their parents as babies than did war-separated children. Mothers had fewer baby-sitters for first-born babies than they did for second-born babies.

Father's help with the care of children. The mothers reported that their husbands shared with them the care of 33 of the 46 children in this study. Mothers were not helped very much by fathers in the care of 13 of the children. This, the mothers reported, was for such reasons as, "He has always been too busy to help much," "He's not very handy around children," or because the children insist on having "mommy do it."

The mean of the differences between the war-separated siblings in relation to father care is -.54. This indicates that the war-separated fathers more often helped with the care of the second-born than with their first-born children. The mean for the non-separated siblings is +.27, which indicates that the non-separated fathers more often helped with the care of their first-born children. The Festinger's d = 3.4. This value is significant at the .05 level. This difference between treatment of war-separated siblings taken in light of the difference between non-separated siblings points to the fact that war-separated fathers reversed the usual procedure of being more likely to help with the care of their first-born children.

Since there is a higher incidence of fathers helping with the care of non-separated first-born and war-separated second-born children, according to the mothers' reports, this would suggest that fathers found it very satisfying to do things for the first child they knew from infancy. This satisfaction is perhaps superseded by other interests such as work or study by the time the second child is born. War-separated fathers did not know their first-borns as infants, and when they returned to their homes at the end of war their children were often so used to the ways their mothers had of handling them, they were unwilling to let their fathers take over. These fathers often derived great pleasure from their second-born children because they had so little opportunity to do things for their first-born children. More war-separated second-born children were cared for by both of their parents than were children in any other group. Eleven of the 12 war-separated fathers helped with the bathing, dressing, putting to bed, and general supervision of their second-born children. Only five of these same fathers helped with the care of their first-borns. In the non-separated groups, fathers shared the care of 10 of their 11 first-born children, and of 7 of 11 second-borns.

Children's Experiences with Other Children

In discussing early experiences of the children in this study the mothers answered several questions concerning their children's opportunities for being near and playing with other children during infancy and early childhood. It was found that children who lived in the homes of their grandparents during the first year or more of life had fewer opportunities for knowing children than children who lived with their two parents in neighborhoods made up of young families. The mothers were asked, "Were there other adults and children living with you in the home? Did he know many adults and children well?"

Only 20 children, or 43 percent of all the children in this study, knew many other children well as babies. There were fewer children in the war-separated group (only one child) who knew many children than in any of the three other groups. In the non-separated first-born group there were the next fewest, with 5 children. There were more children in the non-separated second-born group who knew other children as babies. Eight of these children, or 72 percent of the group, knew other children as babies. The war-separated second-born group had the next most. From these figures it would appear that second-born children had more opportunities to know other children as infants than first-born children, and the war-separated first-borns has the least opportunity of all.

Comparative Behavior of the Four Groups

Method of Analysis

In analyzing the early life experiences of the children we considered the direct answers which mothers gave to specific questions. These answers, concerning the child's experiences such as whether he was breast fed or not breast fed, were easily dichotomized. The mother's description of her child's behavior, however, did not lend itself to simple dichotomous tabulation. Rating scales which took into account the degree and quality of the child's behavior had to be devised. Scales were constructed for the rating of nine areas of behavior.

In analyzing their childhood experiences, we compared the two siblings of each family in order to discover which of the two had the more desirable experiences. In the analysis of the children's behavior, however, difference scores between the first- and second-born siblings in each family were not used. Instead, all groups—E1, E2, C1, and C2—were contrasted. Special emphasis was placed on the comparison of the E1's both with the E2's, their second-born siblings, and with the C1's. This made it possible for us to judge whether the behavior was to be expected of all first-borns, whether it might be expected of all children in war-separated or non-separated families, or whether it was found only in the war-separated first-borns.

The material to be rated in each of the areas of behavior was excerpted from the extensive recorded interviews with each mother and then typed onto individual cards. On each card, together with the description of the child's behavior, his age, and sex, was a number coded to disguise the child's identity. These excerpts did not include all of the statements which the mother made about her child's behavior in any area. The summaries from the mother-interview were usually direct quotations which characterized her child's behavior in a given area. In some cases a summary of the mother's description was written instead of using verbatim excerpts in order not to distort the meaning. That was done when a few sentences quoted from the material would not give, by themselves, a complete picture of what the mother intended.

The scales used to rate each of the different areas of behavior included only five possible ratings. Essentially the scales used to rate the different areas of behavior were similar, but the specific wording of the scales varied, depending upon the behavior characteristic to be rated. The instructions given to the raters concerning these scales are in Appendix 4.

The scale which was constructed did not specify the type of behavioral description which was to be classified under each rating, but instead depended upon the individual rater's evaluation of each behavior excerpt as compared with the other behavior excerpts. Such a scale has the advantage of making the greatest possible use of raters who have had extensive experience in observing and evaluating children's behavior. The technique is useless, however, unless such holistic ratings are reliable between raters. For this reason the scales used to rate behavior were carefully checked to ascertain whether they were reliable. The first characteristic to be rated, "eating problems," was rated by three separate persons (raters were:

1. E. Dowley; 2. L. M. Stolz; 3. L. Johnson). Rater 1 was familiar with both the material and the children. The other two persons did not know the material except as anonymous protocols. The intercorrelations among these three raters are: .91 for Rater 1 vs. Rater 2; .90 for Rater 1 vs. Rater 3; and .90 for Rater 2 vs. Rater 3. These correlations were accepted as indicating that the scale was reliable. These correlations also gave evidence that persons having only excerpts from the total mother-interview would rate these excerpts in the same way as a person familiar with both the entire mother-interview and with the children. As the study continued, Rater 2 and Rater 3, neither of whom knew the protocol material, both rated other scales for continuing checks on their reliability. Correlations between their ratings ranged from +.86 to +.90. These correlations were considered high enough to indicate that the scales were reliable.

The ratings gathered by these rating scales were arranged in an analysis of variance design (9). According to the pattern of this design the sources of variances are the war-separated children vs. non-separated children; the first-born children vs. the second-born children; between families; the interaction between first-born vs. second-born against war-separated vs. non-separated; and the residual. In this analysis the residual term is used to test the interaction and the first-born vs. second-born main effect. The variance due to families was used to test E vs. C. The difference between the means of the E1's and the C1's was analyzed using the t technique. The variance due to families was the error term used in the t test of the differences between E1's and C1's. The difference between the means of the E1's and the E2's was also treated using the t test and the residual variance was used as the error term.

Since some of the second-born children in this study were too young to evidence the behavior on which they could be rated on some of the various scales, these children were given a rating of "A" meaning too young to rate. When this rating was given to a child on any scale, that child and his first-born sibling were eliminated from the analysis of that scale. The size of the groups used in each analysis of variance differs depending on the number of pairs dropped. Such ratings of "A" were given to only two children, both in the E2 group (Lois and Lucille). Whenever both (Lois and Lucille) were given "A" ratings at the same time, one pair, chosen at random, was dropped from the control group.

Eating Behavior

Analysis of the problem behavior in relation to eating as reported by the mothers in this study shows two principal kinds of eating behavior which are of concern to parents. The first manifests itself in such ways as refusal to eat, decided food prejudices, and refusal to conform to meal patterns established in the family. This behavior is frequently, if not always, associated with parent-forcing due to a lack of awareness of a child's readiness or capacity for food. The second kind of problem behavior associated with eating seems to be due to a general immaturity of some children in their ability to chew and swallow solid foods, or to take over the responsibility for feeding themselves. This becomes a problem when parents expect and sometimes demand more mature eating behavior.

One child, Fran, had neither of the above difficulties but her problem was rather an almost insatiable desire for food. Delays in getting food frequently resulted in crying, tantrums, and repeated declarations that she was not loved.

The mothers' reports of their children's eating problems were rated on a five-point scale (see Appendix 4). The scale took account of the seriousness of the child's eating problems as described by the mother.

The various sums of squares, degrees of freedom, variance estimates, and appropriate F and P values for the ratings of eating problems are presented in Table 46.

Table 46. Variance Table for Data on Eating

	df	Variance Estimate	F	P
Total	43			
1st-2nd	1	19.1	13.6	.01
E-C	1	19.1	9.6	.01
Family	20	2.0		
Interaction	1	2.7	1.9	—
Residual	20	1.4		

The main effect of first-borns vs. second-borns is significant at the $P < .01$ level. The mean of the first-born is higher than the mean of the second-born children. This would lead to the conclusion that first-borns have more serious eating problems than second-borns. Also, the war-separated group as a whole differs from the non-separated group as a whole at the $P < .01$ level. Since the war-separated group as a whole has a higher mean rating than the non-separated group, we infer that the war-separated children have more eating problems. The meaning of the difference between the war-separated and non-separated groups will be discussed later when the groups are compared on their independence in eating (see p. 132).

Table 47. Mean Scores and t and P Values for Data on Eating Scores

	1	2
E	4.46	2.64
C	2.64	1.72

E1 vs. C1 $t = 3.08$, $df = 21$, $P < .02$
E1 vs. E2 $t = 3.64$, $df = 10$, $P < .01$

The E1's differed from both the E2's, their second-born siblings, ($P < .01$), and from the C1's ($P < .02$). As can be seen from the mean scores (Table 47), the E1's had more eating problems than either of these groups.

Elimination Behavior

Physical maturation of the musculature of the human infant is an important factor in learning bowel and bladder control (53). Until a child has reached the appropriate level of maturity, he cannot learn "self-control" even with the most consistent training methods. The chronological age at which this maturation takes place may differ widely from individual to individual. Usually daytime competence is achieved by the age of two-and-one-half years, night competence sometime around the fourth birthday (20). Some mothers in this study reported training accomplished for their children as early as 18 months of age by day, while some considered their children "very slow" if they had not finished training by 2 years of age.

The problems reported by the mothers of the first-born children fall into three main categories: those connected with bowel control, those connected with bladder control, and those which seem to show some anxiety about elimination as evidenced by unusual modesty in toilet habits.

Bed-wetting and retarded learning in bladder control are problems found in both the war-separated and the non-separated groups and may be thought to be associated with late development. An examination of the details of these problems as reported, however, reveals some differences in their seriousness from one child to another.

The scale used in this area rated the child's problems in elimination behavior. This scale was identical with the scale used for rating eating problems except that the words "problems in elimination" were substituted for the words "problems in eating." Since control in elimination is more dependent on developmental factors than on training methods in the very young child, raters were instructed to take into consideration the age of the child when rating problem behavior in this area.

The various analysis of variance functions are presented in Table 48. As can be seen, only the differences between first- and second-born chil-- dren are significant.

Table 48. Variance Table for Data on Elimination Scores

	df	Variance Estimate	F	P
Total	39			
1st-2nd	1	34.2	34.2	$< .001$
E-C	1	3.0	1.6	—
Family	18	1.8		
Interaction	1	2.1	2.1	—
Residual	18	1.0		

The various means for the four groups (see Table 49) indicate that the E1's have more problems related to elimination than do the other groups. The differences between the means of the scores for the E1's and C1's are not significant. On the other hand the E1's did have significantly more problems associated with elimination than their siblings, the E2's.

Table 49. Means, t and P Values for Elimination Scores

	1	2
E	4.1	1.8
C	3.1	1.7

E1 vs. C1 $t = 1.6$, $df = 19$, P not significant at .05
E1 vs. E2 $t = 5.1$, $df = 9$, $P < .001$

Six E1 children were reported by their mothers as having problems related to elimination. Don at 4 years, 11 months had only just achieved night dryness, and was still soiling his clothes several times a day; Dan at 4 years, 8 months, Ray at 4 years, 11 months, and Rick up until he was 6 years of age wet their beds every night. When she was 4 years old Fran refused to urinate, and would often go for 12 to 16 hours without urinating "and then she would become angry and irritable, of course." Ray resisted bowel training until he was three and one-half. "He refused to defecate in the toilet but went on the floor in a dark room or closet or in his bed." When his mother "at six month intervals tried to train him," he would resist going at all and would retain his feces for three or four days at a time. His mother reported that Allen at 6 years, 4 months would not use the bathroom at school "because they don't have doors in the boys' bathroom and he doesn't like it."

In the C1 group four children were reported as having problems. Jill frequently had wetting accidents by day until she was past 4 years of age, and was still wetting her bed at night until she was six and one-half. At 4 years, 8 months Connie wet her bed at night whenever she was punished or when she was upset because of stresses or strains in the family. When Lisbet was in kindergarten she regressed to bed-wetting at night for several months and during that same year, she wet the floor at home and at school when she was annoyed with her mother or her teacher. Once she defecated on the floor "on purpose." Roger at 80 months doesn't like to use the bathroom at school. His mother thinks he avoids going there because he is afraid of the bigger boys who "persecuted" him there.

The larger incidence of problems and the larger number of children having problems in the war-separated group seems less significant in this study than the types of problems in each of the groups. The problems of the war-separated children are more complex and more difficult for them to live with than are those of the non-separated children. This may be accounted for in many ways such as the over-training by the mother because she had "lots of time" and not much else to do when her husband was away; the lack of stability in the early lives of these children who moved frequently during the training period; or perhaps it might be due to the sterner discipline of the returning father in the period when this training was being carried on.

Problems Related to Sleep

The four groups of children were also compared on the problems associated with sleep. Two types of disturbances which mothers reported in connection with the sleep behavior of the children in this study seem revealing. One is the form of disturbance which is manifested in bad dreams and nightmares; the other, in wanting to get into the parents' bed in the middle of the night.

Mothers were asked to describe the behavior of children in sleep which might indicate they were dreaming or having nightmares. Such behavior as crying, screaming, sleepwalking, or prolonged anxious talking in sleep were considered by the raters as problems related to sleep. Again the rating scale was the same as that used in rating problems in eating. The phrase "problems related to sleep" was substituted for "problems in eating."

The variance table (Table 50) for the ratings of sleep problems shows that the difference between the first- and second-born children is significant at the $P < .01$ level.

Table 50. Variance Table for Data on Sleep

	df	Variance Estimate	F	P
Total	39			
1st-2nd	1	15.6	14.2	<.01
E-C	1	5.6	3.5	—
Family	18	1.6		
Interaction	1	13.3	12.1	<.01
Residual	18	1.1		

The war-separated first-born children had a much higher mean number of nightmares than did any of the other groups of children. They had as many nightmares in fact, as the three other groups combined. This would obviously suggest greater emotional disturbance in the war-separated children which manifested itself in sleep.

It should be noted that the first vs. second times E vs. C interaction is also significant. This significant interaction indicates that the difference between the first- and second-born children is greater in the war-separated group than it is in the non-separated group. The means of the four groups (see Table 51) indicate that the interaction arises from the discrepancy between the means of the war-separated first- and second-born children. The E1's have the most problems associated with sleep while the E2's have the fewest.

The significant interaction is highlighted by the differences between the means of the E1's and the E2's and the C1's. Both these differences are significant beyond the $P < .01$ level in the direction of the E1's having more problems associated with sleep than the other groups.

Ten of the 12 first-born war-separated children, their mothers reported, frequently had bad dreams and nightmares. Only three children in each of the other three groups were reported as having bad dreams. As

Table 51. Means, t and P Values for Problems in Sleep

	1	2
E	4.60	2.20
C	2.70	2.60

E1 vs. C1 $t = 3.3$, $df = 19$, $P < .01$
E1 vs. E2 $t = 5.3$, $df = 9$, $P < .001$

the mothers described them, the nightmares of the E1 children were often severe and upsetting. They were characterized by loud prolonged screaming and crying and a need for comforting by their mothers.

Some of these children went through periods when their dreams recurred night after night over a long period of time. Fran and Albert dreamed of things jumping on them in bed. Dan dreamed of a he-witch who was trying to pull his mother under the bed. When George was 18 or 19 months old, his parents often took 15 or more minutes to quiet him after his nightmares, which recurred night after night.

Some children's nightmares were so severe that the parents brought the child into bed with them for the rest of the night. Rick's mother described his night terrors: "Sometimes he wakes up and is delirious and doesn't know me for a few minutes." Don's mother said of his dreams, "If you can manage to waken him and put him back to bed, he's all right."

Problems Related to Organic Needs

These three areas of eating, sleeping, and elimination are often thought of as the area of organic needs. Following such a line of thought, we combined these three areas in an analysis of variance design. For this purpose the first-born war-separated children were compared only with the first-born non-separated. The same ratings which had been used in the previous analysis were used here. The analysis of variance design was somewhat different than that used for the previous analysis (see Table 52).

The variance due to individuals was used to test the main effects of war-separated (first-born) vs. non-separated (first-born). The F of 32.0 is significant far beyond the .001 level. Again we are led to conclude that

Table 52. Variance Table for Data on Eating, Sleeping and Elimination

	df	Variance Estimate	F	P
Total	59			
E-C	1	35.2	32.0	<.001
Tests	2	.05	.04	—
Tests × E-C	2	1.1	1.0	—
Individuals	18	1.1		
Individual × Tests	36	1.7	1.5	—

there is a difference in behavior between the war-separated first-born children and the non-separated first-born children. This difference clearly shows that the E1's have more problems in the area of organic needs.

Table 53. Means, t and P Values for Area of Organic Needs

	Eating	Sleeping	Elimination
El's	4.4	4.1	4.6
Cl's	2.7	3.1	2.7
El's vs. Cl's, eating	t = 3.8	df = 19	P<.01
El's vs. Cl's, sleeping	t = 4.2	df = 19	P<.01
El's vs. Cl's, elimination	t = 2.2	df = 19	P<.05

As we have noted before, the E1's differ from the C1's in the degree of severity of problems which they have in eating and sleeping. This is borne out by the present analysis (see Table 53). The interesting point here is that the area of elimination which previously had not been significant at the .05 level now becomes significant at that level. This is undoubtedly a function of the difference in the variance estimates used to compute t. Since the two methods are at odds, it seems most reasonable to consider a difference between E1's and C1's in the area of elimination as at best only suggestive. Another study would have to be conducted before any confidence could be placed in the findings.

Fears and Tension and Comfort Patterns

In comparing the personalities of the children in this study it seemed important to know something about their fears; their modes of behaving when under tension or strain due to fatigue, frustration, or worry; and their ways of comforting themselves when they were hungry, ill, or unhappy. The mothers in this study were asked some specific questions relating to fears, comfort patterns, and expressions of possible tension. They also revealed in their statements about their children in other areas of behavior much information which throws light on these three.

Fears. In estimating the importance of fear as it influences human personality it would probably be necessary to know the causes of the fears, the other factors associated with the feared object or event, and the intensity of the child's response to the feared object. For obvious reasons, such as insufficient interview time, the dimming of mothers' memories with the passing of time, and a lack of complete knowledge of the event on the part of the mother, it was not possible to get this background data. In this study an attempt was made to find out the kinds of things the children feared and the intensity of their fears. The fears which mothers ascribed to their children in this study fell into 12 categories: animals, strangers (predominantly men), the child's own father, older children, toy guns or knives, masks (Hallowe'en), the dark, loud noises, water, falling, punishment, and being alone.

The fears most common to all the groups of children were fears associated with loud noises, fears of animals, and fears of masks, in that order. The ratings for this area were made on the same type of scale as used for rating problems in eating, sleeping, and elimination.

Table 54. Variance Table for Data on Fears

	df	Variance Estimate	F	P
Total	43			
1st-2nd	1	15.4	8.5	<.01
E-C	1	5.9	3.3	—
Family	20	1.8		
Interaction	1	1.4	1.2	—
Residual	20	1.2		

Fears as ascribed by their mothers to the first-born children were significantly greater and more serious than those ascribed to second-born children (see Table 54). The war-separated children as a group do not differ significantly in fears from the non-separated group.

On the other hand, if the E1's are compared with the C1's, the difference is significant at the $P < .05$ level (see Table 55). The E1's do have more disturbing fears than C1's.

Table 55. Means, t and P Values for Fears

	1	2
E	4.18	2.64
C	3.00	2.27

E1 vs. C1 $t = 2.2$, $df = 21$, $P < .05$
E1 vs. E2 $t = 3.2$, $df = 10$, $P < .01$

As would be expected from the over-all differences between first- and second-born children (see Table 55), the difference between the E1's and E2's is significant ($P < .01$).

Tension and comfort patterns. One of the important areas in which conflict between the father and child should show up would be in the child's manifestations of tension and his use of comfort patterns. The rating scale for this area was devised to take account of these two factors. The scale was the same as that used for rating problems in fears except that the words "tension and comfort patterns" were substituted for "fears."

The difference between first-born children and second-born children is significant at the $P < .001$ level (see Table 56). As can be seen from the means in Table 57 the first-born children manifested more serious tensions and had extreme comfort patterns. The differences between the war-separated group as a whole and the non-separated group does not reach the $P < .05$ level of significance.

Table 56. Variance Table for Data on Tension and Comfort Patterns

	df	Variance Estimate	F	P
Total	43			
1st-2nd	1	19.1	21.2	$<.001$
E-C	1	3.9	3.5	—
Family	20	1.1		
Interaction	1	1.8	2.0	—
Residual	20	.9		

As would be expected, the E1's differ significantly from the E2's. Also, the E1's differ from the C1's. The E1's show more serious signs of tension and have more comfort patterns than any of the other groups. Two specific types of behavior in this area should be discussed: thumb-sucking and crying.

Table 57. Mean Scores, t and P Values for Tension and Comfort Patterns

	1	2
E	4.46	2.73
C	3.46	2.54

E1 vs. C1 $t = 2.36$, $df = 21$, $P < .05$
E1 vs. E2 $t = 4.55$, $df = 10$, $P < .01$

Children who sucked their thumbs or fingers: Thirteen of the 46 mothers in this study reported that their children "never" sucked their thumbs, "not even for a day." Some mothers reported thumb-sucking for "a day or so," or "just when teething," or for as much as the first two or three months of life. Nine children stopped sucking their fingers before they were six months old.

The war-separated group of first-born children has the fewest thumb-suckers. Only three of these children ever sucked their thumbs or fingers. There is also a difference between the war-separated and the non-separated families in the numbers of children who sucked their thumbs. From the evidence given by the mothers in this study, there seems to be more of a tendency for thumb-sucking to follow a familial pattern than for it to be a characteristic of first-born or of second-born children. Seventy-two percent of the non-separated first-borns and 72 percent of non-separated second-borns sucked their thumbs, while only 25 percent of war-separated first-borns and 42 percent of war-separated second-born children sucked their thumbs.

War-separated first-born children were considered by their mothers to do more crying and whining than the children in any of the other three groups. The non-separated second-born children cried the next most. The war-separated second-born children cried least easily of the four groups. The greater incidence of crying in the war-separated first-born group over the war-separated second-born group is not in harmony with the findings of Jersild (46, p. 363) who reported "a sharp decline with age in crying."

Competence in Manipulation

Eagerness for independence. Observations made in nursery schools, kindergartens, and first grades have impressed us with the great differences children show in dependence or independence of adult help in eating and dressing. Some children are eager to cut their own meat or to learn to tie their shoes before leaving the nursery school, while some first graders need help in buttoning their coats and putting on their rain boots.

The mothers were asked questions concerning the eagerness of their children in learning to feed themselves and in learning to dress themselves. Independence in eating and independence in dressing were both rated on similar scales except that the word "dress" was substituted for the word "feed."

Independence in eating. No difference was found between first- and second-born children (see Table 58) in their eagerness to feed themselves.

Table 58. Variance Table for Data on Independence in Eating

	df	Variance Estimate	F	P
Total	43			
1st-2nd	1	6.5	3.8	—
E-C	1	14.2	6.3	$<.05$
Family	20	1.7		
Interaction	1	.1	.1	—
Residual	20	.8		

There is, however, a significant difference ($P < .05$) between the war-separated group and the non-separated group, the former being less independent in eating. This is extremely interesting in light of the fact that the only other time that we found a significant difference between the war-separated group and non-separated group as a whole was in eating problems (see p. 124). These findings are important in the light of our characterization of the war-separated families. We have pointed out previously that the E1's were somewhat indulged in the amount of mothering they were given. Certainly the mothers of E1's did not force their children toward independence to a greater extent than is usual with first-born children before the father's return. When the E fathers returned from service, many of them demanded a great deal more independence and self-reliance in eating than their children were used to. In many cases these fathers demanded greater independence than the child could handle at his stage of development. In addition, the return of the father to the family often meant that the mother had less time for her child and the child was suddenly pushed toward more independence. The father's demands for independence along with the mother's sudden inconsistency only created anxiety and sometimes regression in behavior; rarely did they produce psychological adequacy. The child often rebelled against being independent. On the other hand, many of these same fathers overcompensated in the treatment of their second-born children. When the second child came along the father indulged him as he wanted to have this child love and accept him. The war-separated father was successful in promoting an excellent relation with his second-born child (see p. 138 and Chapter 4) and often considered the E2 as "his child." In their interviews some of the fathers recognized this difference with some statement like, "I guess I'm easier on Johnny (E2) than . . . " The response of both the first- and second-born war-separated children has been to be less independent in eating than are the children in the non-separated families—the E1's because they were suddenly forced beyond their development, and the E2's because independence has not been expected or, in some cases, desired of them. Not only are the war-separated first-borns less independent, but these war-separated children pay another price besides dependence in eating. As a group they have more problems in eating than the non-separated group (see p. 124).

Not only do we find differences between the war-separated and non-separated groups, but the E1's are significantly less independent in eating ($P < .05$) than either the E2's or the C1's.

Table 59. Means, t and P Values for Independence in Eating

	1	2
E	3.55	2.73
C	2.36	1.77

E1 vs. C1 $t = 2.2$, $df = 21$, $P < .05$
C1 vs. E2 $t = 2.2$, $df = 10$, $P < .05$

Independence in dressing. In the area of independence in dressing the first-born children do not differ significantly from second-born children nor do E's differ from C's (see Table 60).

When the mean for the E1's is compared with the mean of the C1's, however, the difference is significant at the $P < .05$ level (see Table 61). The E1's are less independent in dressing than are the C1's. The E1's do not differ significantly from their siblings, E2's, in independence of dressing.

Table 60. Variance Table for Data on Independence in Dressing

	df	Variance Estimate	F	P
Total	35			
1st-2nd	1	8.1	3.5	—
E-C	1	3.4	3.1	—
Family	16	1.1		
Interaction	1	4.6	2.0	—
Residual	16	2.3		

Table 61. Means, t and P Values for Independence in Dressing

	1	2
E	4.00	2.33
C	2.67	2.45

E1 vs. C1 $t = 2.8$, $df = 17$, $P < .05$
E1 vs. E2 $t = 2.2$, $df = 8$, P not significant at .05

Children's Behavior in Relations with Adults

Children's reactions to adults. Mothers were asked to tell about the responses of their children in meeting new people, and of their relation with adults other than their parents and those relatives whom they may have known well. Thirty-five of the children in the study were thought by their mothers to be "friendly, outgoing" children, and only 11 children were not. The scale used to rate the child's relations with adults was a 5-point scale ranging from good relations with adults to serious difficulties in relations with adults.

Table 62. Variance Table for Data on Relations with Adults

	df	Variance Estimate	F	P
Total	39			
1st-2nd	1	4.2	3.5	—
E-C	1	5.6	3.1	—
Family	18	1.8		
Interaction	1	1.3	1.1	—
Residual	18	1.2		

There is no significant difference between the first- and second-borns or between the children of war-separated and non-separated families (Table 62). In addition, when the mean for the E1's is compared with the means for E2's and C1's, no significant differences are found (see Table 63).

If instead of rating the degree of the child's difficulties in relations with adults, the rater considers only the response to the direct question, "Did your child ever dislike any adult intensely?" an interesting difference is found. In response to this question, mothers of ten children spontaneously

Table 63. Means, t and P Values on Relations with Adults

	1	2
E	3.10	2.80
C	2.70	1.70

E1 vs. C1 $t = .9$, $df = 19$, P not significant at .05
E1 vs. E2 $t = .6$, $df = 9$, P not significant at .05

replied in the affirmative and described the adult and the child's reasons for disliking that adult. Of the ten who disliked an adult intensely, seven were war-separated first-borns, two were non-separated first-borns, and one was a non-separated second-born child. These numbers are too small to test statistically but are interesting as they show a trend. There were no war-separated second-born children who ever were reported as having disliked an adult. In the E1 group, mothers reported that three of the children disliked their own fathers and had frequently said, "I hate Daddy!" One mother said her boy disliked "all men, without exception." Alma was said to dislike her maternal grandmother, Albert disliked his uncle who teased him, and Bruce disliked "anyone who does anything he thinks is unfair, and he has never forgiven a woman who broke down the door of his play house over a year ago."

Children's Success in Playing with Other Children

Mothers were asked if their children got along well with other children at the present time. A variety of answers was given to this question when mothers had doubts about the social aptitudes of their children. They answered in such ways as, "Well, he doesn't seem very interested in playing with children," "He's very bossy and children don't like that," "I think she prefers to play alone," "He wants to play with children but he says they don't like him and won't let him play with them." When mothers felt their children were successful they replied, "Oh, he gets along just fine," or "He can hardly wait to get out to play and he wants to be with children every minute."

The scale used to rate these responses was the same as that used to rate "relations with adults" with substitution of the words "relations with children" for "relations with adults."

Table 64. Variance Table for Data on Relations with Children

	df	Variance Estimate	F	P
Total	39			
1st-2nd	1	3.0	1.1	—
E-C	1	4.2	4.2	—
Family	18	1.0		
Interaction	1	1.3	.5	
Residual	18	2.8		—

As can be seen in Table 64 the differences between E's and C's and between first- and second-born children are not significant.

Comparison of the means of the E1's and the C1's (Table 65) shows that the E1's have poorer relations with children (at $P < .05$ level) than do the C1's. The E1's are not significantly different from their second-born siblings in this area of relations with children, however.

Mothers reported that most of the children in this study were able to play well with others. Fewer children in the E1 group were successful in playing with children than in the C1 group. All but one of the C2 children were reported as playing well with others, as were all but two of their older siblings.

Table 65. Means, t and P Values on Relations with Children

	1	2
E	2.90	2.00
C	1.90	1.70

E1 vs. C1 $t = 2.2$, $df = 19$, $P < .05$
E1 vs. E2 $t = 1.8$, $df = 9$, P not significant at .05

More war-separated first-born children preferred to play alone than did children in any other group. Only four children in that group enjoyed playing with others much of the time. The eight first-born children in the war-separated group who preferred to play alone enjoyed books, crayons, paper dolls, erector sets, blocks, and collecting things more than they enjoyed play with children.

Children's Relations with Their Parents

The area of parent-child relations was clearly the most difficult area for mothers to discuss in their interviews. It was particularly difficult for them to express their feelings about the father-child relation when it was not a close one. Mothers were somewhat apprehensive about describing a relation which might show their husband in a poor light. It was difficult for mothers also to verbalize the ambivalences in father-child relations. These ambivalences in feelings were often extreme between the war-separated first-born children and their fathers. The picture which the mother presented of the father-child relation vacillated between a realistic presentation of the relation as she saw it, and an attempt to protect the family group by presenting the culturally approved picture of a close father-child relation. After describing a very distant father-child relation, mothers often felt they had to compensate and say something quite favorable. A section from one mother-interview shows a characteristic difficulty of describing an ambivalent father-child relation.

Q: Was there ever a particular adult whom she disliked?

"Well, I shouldn't say 'disliked,' but she's never been on too good terms with her father actually."

Q: It's hard for her to make a good, strong bond with him?

"Yes, it is. And right now she doesn't like anything to do with boys or men. She says she doesn't, anyway. I don't know whether she's getting into that stage already, but . . . Really, that wasn't the thing to say about her father. It isn't . . . She's crazy about him, but she isn't sure of him, and . . ."

Q: Is that something that has come up at certain periods or has it been true all through their relation?

"Well, I don't know . . . I suppose he came (home) at a hard time for her. She was very attached to my father and when her daddy came we moved away from our house to his folks' house and I think it was hard for her to accept him. But she is just crazy about him. But she never knows just how he's going to react. I mean, sometimes he can accept her love and shower her with love and sometimes he . . ."
Q: Sometimes she's rebuffed . . .
"Yes, if she's sick, he can never administer to her— never take her temperature or give her medicine. And he feels that, I think . . ."

Although the mother describes the child as both not being on "too good terms with her father, actually" and then later as "crazy about him," it is clear from other data in the father-interview and in an incidental observation in the home, that both of these statements are true of the father-child relation. It is believed that although all mothers present this material on parent relations in a careful and somewhat protective manner, it is essentially a true picture of how they see the relations between husband and child.

Children Who Have Personality Traits That Annoy Their Parents

Mothers and fathers frequently refer to personality or behavior characteristics of their children which they find particularly annoying. Often these are highly revealing of the way a mother or father feels about a child. The mothers were therefore asked, "Does this child have any personality traits that annoy you?" and "Any that annoy his father?"

Traits that annoy mothers. The 23 mothers reported that 27 of the 46 children had traits which annoyed them. These traits in the order of emphasis were: general irritability such as is manifested in crying, whining, fussing, squealing, and tantrums; insistent demanding; slowness; bossiness; and rudeness.

Some mothers found it difficult to think of traits that annoyed them, but feeling they should tell something, tried hard to recall a past irritating situation with a child. Two mothers replied, "I can't think of any. Is that bad?" Several mothers felt certain their children had no such traits.

Traits that annoy mothers were rated on a 5-point scale from few to numerous and very disturbing. As may be seen in Table 66, there are no differences between the war-separated and the non-separated families nor between the first- and second-born children on this scale.

Table 66. Variance Table for Data on Traits that Annoy Mothers

	df	Variance Estimate	F	P
Total	43			
1st-2nd	1	5.1	3.0	—
E-C	1	1.9	1.0	—
Family	20	1.8		
Interaction	1	.2	.1	—
Residual	20	1.7		

Table 67. Means, t and P Values on Traits that Annoy Mothers

	1	2
E	2.82	2.00
C	3.01	2.44

E1 vs. C1 t = 0.3, df = 21, P not significant at .05
E1 vs. E2 t = 1.5, df = 10, P not significant at .05

When the differences between the various means are considered (see Table 67) it can be seen that there are no significant differences between E1's and either E2's or C1's.

There is an interesting point here. Although the difference is not significant between E1's and C1's, this is the only case in which the E1's are given "more desirable" ratings than the C1's. This, of course, is the characteristic and the only characteristic on which it was anticipated that the E1's would not be given least desirable ratings.

Traits that annoy fathers. Fathers were reported as being annoyed by the traits of 24 of the 46 children. Traits that annoyed them were whining and crying, stubbornness, carelessness, rudeness, insistent demanding, deceitfulness, arguing, teasing, and loud talking.

Mothers of E1 children found it somewhat easier to recall the traits that annoyed the fathers. Perhaps these traits were more obvious and more serious. It is also possible that more attention was focused on them by the returned fathers. Allen's "habit of feeling sorry for himself" when scolded or punished by his father was extremely annoying to his father. Albert's use of silly language "irritated his father no end." Mr. Wagner found Alma's stubbornness and slowness in eating so annoying that "he spanked her more than I think he should have," Mrs. Wagner said. George's sneakiness, Fran's messiness, Ken's whining and crying, and Bruce's slowness to obey were sources of continual annoyance to their fathers, according to their mothers.

Ten of the 12 E1 children had traits that annoyed their fathers while only 2 of the 12 E2 children were reported as having such traits. Often the mothers said of these war-separated second-born children, "His father can't see anything wrong with him," or "He thinks she's just right."

The traits that annoy fathers were rated on the same scale as the traits that annoy mothers with the word "father" substituted for the word "mother." The analysis of variance indicates that although the war-separated group as a whole did not differ from the non-separated group, there was a significant difference between first- and second-born children at the $P < .001$ level (see Table 68).

The interaction between E vs. C as compared with first- vs. second-born children is significant at the $P < .05$ level. The various means for the four groups must be considered before the differences can be understood.

As can be seen in Table 69 the significant interaction indicates that the difference between the E1's and E2's is significantly greater than the difference between the C1's and C2's. The war-separated fathers saw a greater difference between their first- and second-borns than did the non-separated

Table 68. Variance Table for Data on Traits that Annoy Fathers

	df	Variance Estimate	F	P
Total	39			
1st-2nd	1	27.2	20.9	<.001
E-C	1	.00	.0	—
Family	18	1.4		
Interaction	1	10.1	7.8	<.05
Residual	18	1.3		

fathers. It is extremely interesting that war-separated fathers saw many more annoying traits in their first-born children while their wives saw more annoying traits in their second-born children.

Traits annoying to both parents. Frequently a child was found to have traits annoying to both parents. This was true of 63 percent of the non-separated first-borns, 58 percent of the war-separated first-borns, and 45 percent of the non-separated second-borns. No war-separated second-born children were found to have traits annoying to both of their parents. First-born children had more personality traits annoying to both of their parents than had second-born children.

Table 69. Means, t and P Values on Traits that Annoy Fathers

	1	2
E	3.80	1.20
C	2.80	2.10

E1 vs. C1 $t = 1.8$, $df = 19$, P not significant at .05
E1 vs. E2 $t = 4.8$, $df = 9$, $P < .001$

Comparison of annoyance to mother and father. Mothers reported more children with personality traits that annoyed them than annoyed the fathers in all groups except the war-separated first-borns, where more children had traits annoying to fathers than to mothers. The two first-borns in the war-separated group who were reported as having no traits annoying to their fathers are Don and Ned.

Mothers of non-separated children tended to report the same children as having traits that were annoying to both fathers and mothers. They reported little difference in the numbers of first- and second-born children who had annoying traits. Two fathers in this group were reported as feeling that the first-born daughter was "the apple of his eye."

Punishment

Mothers were asked, "Was this child ever punished severely?" They were encouraged to describe the methods of control used by mothers and fathers and the effectiveness of their methods. Data which they gave in other parts of the Interview Schedule (particularly in the areas of elimination training, behavior in relation to eating, sleeping, and manipulation, relations to people, and in personality traits found annoying to adults) were also used in making up the data on punishment.

Mothers reported that 17 children in all four groups were punished by their mothers with severe measures (usually hard spankings); and 17 in all four groups were punished severely by their fathers (not all the same children). A few more first-born children were punished by both parents than were second-borns in this study. Except for the war-separated first-borns, there is a noticeable tendency for mothers to report themselves as the frequent punishers rather than to attribute this to the fathers. With the war-separated first-borns, however, mothers reported that fathers did more punishing of their children than did the mothers.

There were degrees of severity in the father's punishment, as reported by the mothers. The fathers in the war-separated group were more severe in punishing their first-borns than they were in punishing their second children or than the non-separated fathers were in punishing their children.

Excerpts of mothers' descriptions of punishment by fathers were taken from all the mother-interviews and submitted to the raters to rate on a 5-point scale. The rating scale was a continuum from rarely punished by father, to often severely punished by father.

Table 70. Variance Table for Data on Punishment by Fathers

	df	Variance Estimate	F	P
Total	39			
1st-2nd	1	2.5	4.0	—
E-C	1	10.0	4.3	—
Family	18	2.3		
Interaction	1	6.4	10.3	$<.01$
Residual	18	.62		

The main effects shown in Table 70 are not significant. The first-born children as a group were punished no more severely than were the second-born children; and war-separated children, as a group, were punished just as severely as non-separated. However, the interaction between first- and second-borns with E vs. C is significant at the $P < .01$ level. The importance of this significant interaction can be appreciated by looking at Table 71.

Table 71. Mean, t and P Values on Punishment by Father

	1	2
E	3.50	2.20
C	1.70	2.00

E1 vs. C1 $t = 2.6$, $df = 19$, $P < .05$
E1 vs. E2 $t = 3.7$, $df = 9$, $P < .01$

The significant interaction indicates that although the C2's were punished somewhat more severely by their fathers than were the C1's, the opposite is true in the war-separated group—that is, the E1's were punished more severely than the E2's. From the means of the non-separated group it would seem that first-born children usually are not punished as severely as second-born children. Yet in the war-separated group the fathers punished their first-born children much more severely. These fathers punished their first-born children more severely than they punished their second-born children ($P < .01$) and more severely than the non-separated fathers punished either their first-born or second-born children ($P < .05$) (see Table 71).

Five mothers in the war-separated group reported that they felt their husbands were too severe in punishing their first-born children. They did not feel that these same fathers were too severe in punishing their second-born children. It should be noted here that in these five families, four families had first- and second-born children of the same sex. In the fifth family the first-born child was a boy, the second-born was a girl. No mother in the non-separated families felt that her husband was more punishing than she was herself. Four non-separated mothers felt that they punished more often and more severely than did the non-separated fathers.

The following descriptions taken verbatim from the mother-interviews illustrate the kind of punishment used by the five war-separated fathers whom the mothers considered most severe in their treatment of first-borns. Their punishment of the first-borns is here contrasted with their punishment of the second-borns.

George Osborne (E1): "(His father) has always been hard on George. When he was little his father used to lose control of himself and treat him much more roughly than he should. He didn't know what to expect of a child when he came back (from the war) for one thing, and he would do anything that came into his head. He'd shake him or dangle him by his heels and let him flop upon the bed from a distance and that would knock the breath out of him . . . He frequently spanked him, but I don't think he ever took a stick to him, though he might have."

Alvin Osborne (E2): "Well, he's been spanked and shaken and things, but not to be bruised or anything . . . He thought I should be spanking Alvin and doing severe things to him because of his pants-wetting, but I wouldn't, so he said he was going to; but I notice he didn't get around to it very much. He spanked him a couple of times. He hasn't been very hard on him. He has more sympathy for Alvin and feels Alvin is a good-hearted little child, which he is."

Dan Wolf (E1): "He's had some bad spankings from his father, but his father is doing less of that now. We disagreed on so many points (about Dan) that finally his daddy said that if I felt that way about it, I should go ahead and train him any way I thought and he wouldn't say any more about it . . . When he was only three, one time he ran away from me across a busy street. That time his daddy spanked him very hard and left some bruises on him. I was very unhappy about it. I thought he should be spanked, but not as severely as that. I think it made him afraid of his daddy and of other men."

Raymond Wolf (E2): "He's spanked when it's necessary. He hasn't been severely punished. His daddy has spanked him and I've spanked him, too."

Alma Wagner (E1): "I thought her father sometimes used to spank her a little too much. He thought she was awfully stubborn about eating, I think, and she had little tantrums about things. He kept up a pretty high standard of how he wanted her to behave. I think he expected a little bit too much of her. She responded to spankings very well. She seemed to realize that he meant business and she would behave very well after that."

Pauline Wagner (E2): "She's not punished very often. She's corrected more than she's punished. She was very special to her daddy for quite a while when she was a baby. He never expected much of her, but just let her be a baby. If you spanked Pauline, it upset her terribly. She would be broken-hearted and you'd have to love her and love her, while with Alma it would be like water off a duck's back to some extent."

Rick Moore (E1): "I thought his father was quite severe in spanking him. Sometimes Rick was upset even though he didn't talk too much about it . . . He (his father) was very severe with him (in toilet training). He used to spank him even at night, you know, to try to make him wet when he got him up, that is if he wouldn't do it, but he just kept crying. Of course I didn't approve."

Teddy Moore (E2): "With Teddy his daddy just spanked him occasionally. I don't think he was ever severely punished in his life."

Allen Statler (E1): "His father expects a high level of behavior all the time with Allen. He's pretty firm on discipline and he'll call him on everything." (He gets spanked for being rude, bossy, or disobedient, and even for running in the Village store with other boys.) "He doesn't think he should get away with anything. I'm inclined to feel sorry for him. I hate to see him picked on by his father . . . His father doesn't have much of a temper. I mean, he punishes just to punish. He spanks hard and talks quite loud and severe."

Louise Statler (E2): "Her father isn't as strict with Louise. He thinks with a girl it's different . . . He's getting a little more strict with her now. He's getting exposed to her a little bit."

Relations with Fathers

No one question could be thought of which would, we felt, elicit from the mothers the child's feelings about his father or the father's feelings about his child. Throughout the interview, however, mothers revealed through answers to questions in relation to eating, elimination, fears, nightmares, language, and other behavior and relations, the way the child and his father behaved and felt toward each other. Therefore, the entire interview for each child was searched and mothers' statements about father-child relations were put on cards for raters to rate. There were three questions which usually revealed the most data about father-child relations: "Does your husband spend much time with the children?" "Does he (the child) have any personality traits that annoy his father?" "Which child is easier for your husband to get along with?"

The scale used for rating relations with father was similar to the scales used to rate relations with adults. The scale ranged from <u>good relations with father</u> to <u>very serious difficulties in relations with father</u>.

The interaction between first- vs. second-borns times E vs. C is significant at the P <.01 level (see Table 72). The meaning of this significant interaction can be found by looking at Table 73.

Table 72. Variance Table for Data on Relations with Father

	df	Variance Estimate	F	P
Total	43			
1st-2nd	1	23.2	17.8	<.001
E-C	1	.0	.0	—
Family	20	1.0		
Interaction	1	13.2	10.1	<.01
Residual	20	1.3		

The significant interaction indicates that the war-separated fathers differ in their relations with their first- and second-born children to a significantly greater degree than do the non-separated fathers. The war-separated fathers have an extremely poor relation with their first-born and an extremely good relation with their second-born children. On the other hand, the non-separated fathers, who have a somewhat poorer relation with their first-born children than with their second-born children, do not have as poor a relation with these first-borns as do the war-separated fathers. Nor do they have as good a relation with their second-born children as do the war-separated fathers.

The war-separated fathers, according to the mothers' reports, had difficulty in relating to the children born during their absence. They found it difficult to get close to these children when they were united with them and afterwards made demands on them which were beyond their developmental ability. As a consequence they were often critical of these children, whom they described as spoiled, stubborn, babyish, noisy, and disobedient; and found it easy to scold and punish them. Children so treated resented the harsh discipline their fathers brought into their lives; they learned to fear and avoid their fathers and frequently learned to dislike them. On such a foundation of mutual distrust and criticism it has often been almost impossible to build a good father-child relation. On the other hand, most of the war-separated mothers were more indulging and permissive with these first-born children. They allowed them to be dependent longer in feeding and dressing. They tended to do less punishing of these children than of their

Table 73. Means, t and P Values on Relations with Father

	1	2
E	4.00	1.46
C	2.81	2.45

E1 vs. C1 $t = 2.8$, $df = 21$, $P < .02$
E1 vs. E2 $t = 6.0$, $df = 10$, $P < .001$

second-born children and less than the control mothers did. They did not reveal many personality traits of these children which annoyed them and several of them said of their first-born children in the interviews, "Oh, he (or she) is really my boy (or girl); his brother (or sister) is closer to his daddy."

General Comparison of the Four Groups

In order to get a picture of the four groups of children used in this study for purposes of comparison, a profile was made of the four groups based on the ratings of their behavior and relations (Figure 3). The mean ratings for each group were charted on a graph showing their mean scores for eating, elimination, sleep, fears, tensions, independence in eating, independence in dressing, relations with adults, relations with children, punishment by father, traits that annoy father, traits that annoy mother, and relations with father. The mean scores of the war-separated children (E1) are in the higher, less desirable end of the scale. There is no overlapping of their scores with those of the other groups except for the mean scores on traits that annoy mothers. The three other groups show considerable overlapping, with the predominance of their mean ratings falling in the middle of the scale on the graph. The second-born non-separated children (C2's) receive consistently low ratings, it will be seen, and their profile is the best of the four groups. The war-separated second-borns (E2's) show more fluctuation in their mean scores from one rating to another than do the other two groups used for comparison with the war-separated group. The profile of the non-separated first-born group (C1's) shows consistently a higher rating than do either of the second-born groups. This, again, shows the tendency for first-born children to have more problems in behavior and in relations than second-born children.

General Summary and Interpretation

In the interviews, the mothers of the war-separated children indicated that they felt their first- and second-born children differed from one another in many characteristics. The mothers of the non-separated children, also, saw a difference between their first- and second-born children. Over and above these differences between the siblings, however, it is evident from our analysis that the E1's were exceptional in that they differed from all of the other three groups of children in many ways. This group of war-separated first-borns was found to differ from other children more in terms of certain aspects of their behavior and social relations than in their early life experiences. Although there are differences, and some of these may be important differences, our data did not show any statistically significant differences between the groups in the reactions of mothers to pregnancy, their reactions to the conditions of their labor, and their reactions to the sex of their babies. We do not mean to imply that the factors associated with birth are not important in affecting behavior in the areas which we studied, but no significant differences were discovered which could be related to the differences in behavior which we have found among the groups.

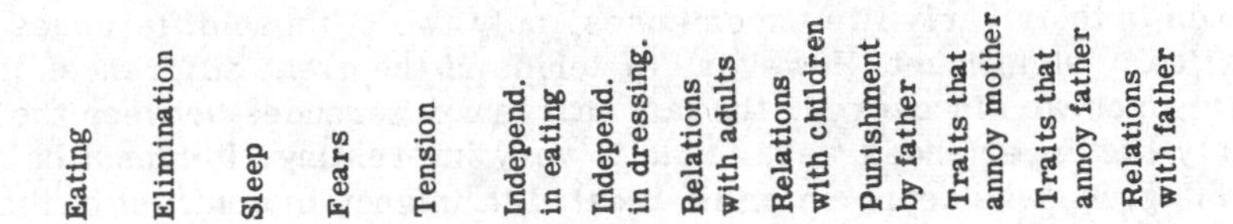

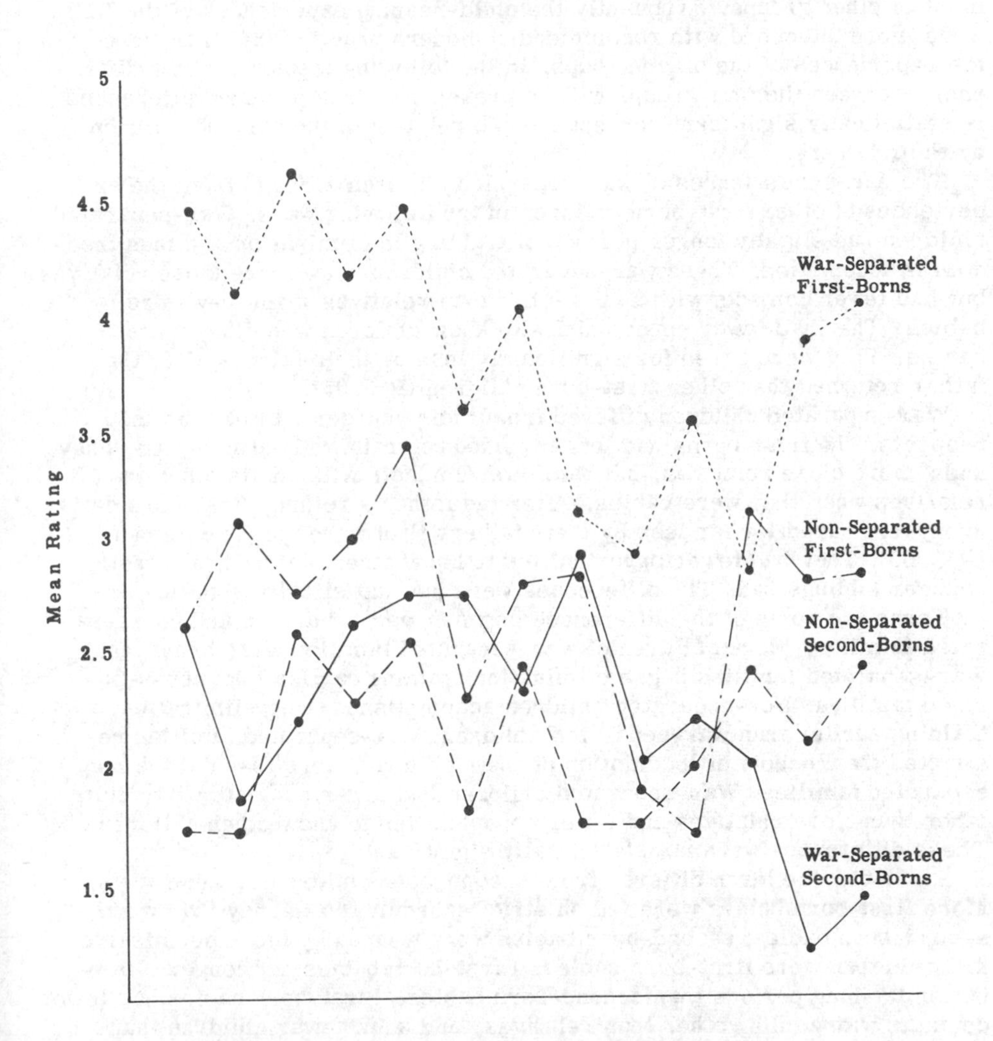

Figure 3. Profile for first- and second-born children in war-separated families and in non-separated families based on the mean ratings of behavior and interpersonal relations for each group.

Early Life Experiences

Although there were some differences between the various groups of children in their early life experiences, only two of these differences were statistically significant. However, in terms of the great differences in behavior which we discovered, the fact that few differences between the groups in early life experiences were found is very interesting. It cannot be said that one group was deprived or ill-treated in infancy in contrast to the treatment of other groups. Frequently the child-rearing experiences of the E1's were more in accord with recommended modern practice (84) than were the experiences of the other groups. In the following discussion, the differences between the four groups will be presented. None of these differences is statistically significant, except the two relating to the care of children by their fathers.

The early experiences of war-separated children differed from the experiences of other first-born children in the following ways. War-separated children had slightly longer periods of training in elimination and less freedom in locomotion. These war-separated children knew more close relatives but had fewer contacts with adults other than relatives when they were babies. They had fewer opportunities to know children when they were babies. They were cared for significantly less by their fathers after the father returned than other first-born children ($P < .05$).

War-separated children differed from their younger siblings in these respects. The first-borns had longer periods of training in elimination. They knew more close relatives, but had fewer contacts with adults other than relatives when they were babies. After the father's return, first-born children were cared for far less by their fathers than were the E2 children ($P < .05$). They had fewer opportunities to know other children than their younger siblings had. The differences were not statistically significant.

These are some of the differences between war-separated and non-separated families. More children of war-separated families were breast fed. War-separated families began elimination training earlier than non-separated families. Non-separated children accomplished their elimination training earlier than war-separated children. War-separated families restricted the freedom of locomotion of their children more than did the non-separated families. War-separated children had fewer contacts with adults other than close relatives and fewer opportunities to know other children. These differences were not statistically significant.

First-born children differed from second-born children in these ways. More first-born babies were fed on strict schedules in infancy than were second-born babies; second-born babies were weaned by more permissive methods than were first-born babies. First-born babies had longer elimination training periods than second-born babies. First-born babies had fewer contacts with adults, other than relatives, and knew fewer children than second-born babies. These differences were not statistically significant.

Behavior of Children

The behavior of war-separated children differed from the behavior of non-separated first-born children in several important respects. War-separated children had more serious problems connected with eating ($P < .02$), more serious problems connected with elimination ($P < .05$), more serious problems connected with sleeping ($P < .01$) and more serious problems connected with all three areas of organic needs combined than the non-separated first-born children ($P < .001$). They also manifested more fears of a serious nature ($P < .05$), had more tensions and comfort patterns ($P < .05$), and were less independent in eating and dressing ($P < .05$).

The behavior of war-separated first-borns differed from the behavior of their younger siblings in the following ways. They had more serious problems connected with eating ($P < .01$), elimination ($P < .001$), and sleeping ($P < .01$). In addition, they manifested more fears of a serious nature ($P < .01$), had more tensions and comfort patterns ($P < .01$), and were less independent in eating ($P < .05$).

The behavior of children in war-separated families differed from the behavior of children in non-separated families in two respects, both of them related to eating. Children in war-separated families had more serious problems connected with eating ($P < .01$) and were less independent in eating ($P < .05$).

The behavior of all first-born children also differed from the behavior of second-born children in the following ways. First-born children had more serious problems connected with eating ($P < .01$), elimination ($P < .001$), and sleeping ($P < .01$). First-born children also manifested more fears of a serious nature, and had more tensions and comfort patterns.

Children's Social Relations

War-separated first-borns differed from non-separated first-born children in their social relations. War-separated first-borns had poorer relations with children than did the non-separated first-born children ($P < .05$). They had fewer traits that annoyed their mothers (not significant) but more traits annoying to fathers. They were punished more often and more severely by their fathers ($P < .05$) and had poorer relations with their fathers ($P < .02$).

War-separated first-borns, also, differed from their younger siblings. They had more traits that annoyed their fathers ($P < .001$). They were punished more often and more severely by their fathers ($P < .01$). They had poorer relations with their fathers ($P < .001$). War-separated children had very poor relations with their fathers, while their younger siblings had extremely good relations with their fathers.

War-separated families differed from non-separated families in one interesting respect. In war-separated families, second-born children had far better relations with their fathers than did the first-born children. In the non-separated families, the opposite is true—first-born children had better relations with their fathers than second-born children. Second-born war-separated children had better relations with their fathers than did any other group.

These are the ways in which first-born children differed from second-born children. First-born children had more traits that annoyed their fathers than second-born children ($P < .001$). On the other hand, first-born children had better relations with their fathers than did the second-born children ($P < .001$).

The war-separated first-borns received less desirable mean ratings than did either their siblings or the non-separated first-born children in every area of behavior and relations except one (Figure 3). These children were less annoying to their mothers. Probably they were somewhat closer to their mothers because of the circumstance of their early lives. This one favorable item may be a symbol of the needed support these children have had which has brought them through the crises of father-reunion, the subsequent separation from loving relatives who meant so much to them in infancy, and finally the birth of a sibling after the father's return.

Conclusions

The mother-interview data substantiate in full measure the supposition that the first-born war-separated children were seen by their mothers as different from other children. The absence of the father during the child's first year of life and the circumstances surrounding his return, not only affected the child's behavior and social relations but, in addition, these influenced the mother. Her perceptions and attitudes toward her child took on a new dimension as she adjusted to her husband's return and his attitudes toward their child. Furthermore, as the father and child adjusted to one another, the mother was often caught in the middle. These war-separated mothers perceived and reported that all was not well between father and child. Not only did they recount that their first-born children had difficulties in relations with their fathers, but also they reported that they had more formidable problems in social relations with children and adults than did the other children. These mothers of the war-separated children described the early life experiences of their older children in much the same way as other mothers described their children's early life experiences. However, these first-borns were not described as behaving in the same way as other children. They had difficulties related to the areas of organic needs, to fears, tensions, comfort patterns, and to overdependence upon mothers.

The legion of problems which these war-separated children possess does not seem to be the inheritance of the period of the fathers' absence for they are described as having usual experiences and no more than normal problems during that period. Their allotment of difficulties seems to be the legacy of the fathers' return.

CHAPTER 8.
COMPARISON OF MOTHER AND FATHER ATTITUDES TOWARD WAR-SEPARATED CHILDREN

by Alberta Engvall

Description of this Study: Purpose and Methods

In Chapter 4, the attitudes of war-separated fathers toward their first-born children were analyzed by comparing these with the attitudes of non-separated fathers. In this substudy we view the attitudes of war-separated fathers from a different perspective, by comparing the attitudes of these fathers with those of their wives. We would expect systematic differences in these attitudes both because of the specific fact of war separation and also because our cultural situation induces general differences in the attitudes of mothers and fathers.

We expect attitudinal differences between all fathers and all mothers because (1) their parental roles are differently defined in our society— the social expectancy is that they will have different attitudes; (2) fathers and mothers have systematically different experiences with and responsibilities for their children, and their attitudes must be differently molded by these different experiences; and (3) fathers and mothers play different sex roles and acquire the attitudes deemed socially appropriate to members of their own sexes. Each of these factors, of course, operates upon the war-separated parents with whom our study is concerned.

In addition, however, the circumstance of war separation introduces other factors from which we would predict differences between war-separated parents' attitudes toward their first-borns. Typically war separation of couples meant that the women spent more than the usual time with their first-born children and thus developed exceptionally close relations with them. Living in less-than-complete families, the mothers derived much of their social status and social approval and consequently their own feelings of worth from their relations with their first-borns. Thus, war-separated mothers might be expected to be unusually identified with the welfare and success of their children. For their husbands, however, war separation meant lack of acquaintance with and responsibility for the child. For these men, return from war brought new stresses (discussed in Chapter 3), and important among these was adjustment to the intrusive, interfering, and demanding young strangers in their homes. Thus, in contrast to their wives, the war-separated fathers may be expected to be less than usually identified with their first-borns. The mothers may be expected to be well-informed and insightful about the behavior and idiosyncracies of their war-separated children, whereas the fathers might be expected to be relatively unaware of the details, complexities, and subtleties of their children's behavior except as they were directly affected by it.

In this substudy, we wished to compare certain attitudes of mothers and fathers in war-separated families toward their first-borns. We wish we could have made this substudy more conclusive by comparing differences between parental attitudes in war-separated families against a normative baseline of differences in parental attitudes in non-separated families. This was impossible because most of the non-separated mothers and the non-separated fathers interviewed in this project were from different families.

The Data

The basic data for this substudy are the interviews with the war-separated fathers (described in Chapter 2) and those with their wives (described in Chapter 6).

In the interpretation of the findings of this substudy, it must be remembered that there were systematic differences in the mother and father interviews. The father interviews were only slightly structured, whereas the mother interviews followed a fairly detailed interview schedule. Because of this, in the father interviews verbal participation by the interviewer was less frequent than in the mother interviews. The father interviews with the war-separated men were five hours in length; the mother interviews, two hours. Fathers and mothers were interviewed by different people, both women trained in interview techniques.

These differences between the mother and father interviews were due to the over-all plan of the project. However, they do contribute weaknesses to the analysis attempted by this substudy. The necessary disparities illustrate the difficulties encountered in designing research with human beings which will reveal a variety of information about them in such a manner that each element in that variety is uniformly explicated.

In the analysis of mother interviews (Chapter 7), summaries were made of the mothers' statements about various topics. These summaries involved considerable selection and condensation of the original interview material, though every effort was made to preserve the original quality and meaning.

The method used for organizing the material from the father interviews was to excerpt statements according to topic, and to group together all statements relevant to a given topic (see Chapter 4). In order that they should retain their meaning when lifted from context, these excerpts were sometimes altered in wording from the father's actual statements, but such alterations were minimal. The excerpts, therefore, were very close to the original statements made by the father.

In this substudy, it was found that the summaries of mother-interview data, since they were so brief, were useful only for the purpose for which they had been specifically prepared, i.e., to indicate the seriousness of the child's problems. For determining other variables, excerpts were made from the original mother-interview protocols, following the outline used for the father excerpts. Thus, excerpts were available for every parent interviewed in this project.

It was found to be impossible to disguise the sex of the parent being interviewed in the excerpts, so information about the sex of the parent was made uniformly explicit to the rater.

Quantification of the Data

Several rating scales were developed for comparing the parents' attitudes. Each of these scales had 5 points, with a rating of 1 representing the "good" end of the continuum. Each of these scales was developed a priori, and therefore the rater was instructed to use the verbal definitions of points along the scale as rough guideposts only, to be adjusted or revised in terms of the unique nature of the material being rated. Thus, a rating of 5 on one scale for one area of development is comparable to another rating of 5 on the same scale for a different area only in the sense that both represent the extremes of our group for these areas. Therefore, for example, it cannot be assumed that a parent who is rated with a 5 on the annoyance scale for his discussion of his child's dressing behavior is as annoyed as another parent who receives a 5 on the same scale for his discussion of his child's eating behavior. On the other hand, this difficulty is minimized by the fact that raters, though instructed to use all 5 points of a scale in rating each group of excerpts, were told that they should not try to assign ratings according to any predetermined distribution (e.g., normally).

The rating scales. Three scales were developed for this substudy, and one more was borrowed from another part of the research project. Each of these scales was used to test a general hunch about differences between war-separated fathers and their wives.

Scale I, seriousness of problem (Appendix 4), was developed originally to test the hypothesis that war-separated children were reported by their parents as having more severe developmental difficulties than non-separated children. It was used in rating father- and mother-interview data (Chapters 4 and 7). These ratings were used in this substudy to determine whether there were systematic differences between war-separated fathers and mothers in their reports of the seriousness of the problems of their first-borns.

Parental worry about the child's behavior was another variable we wished to investigate. We expected that the mothers, being more closely identified with their first-born children, would be more worried about their problems than would the fathers. Scale A (Appendix 7) was developed to quantify the degree of worry felt by the parents. Some parents consider their children's behavior to be normal or better, regardless of whether or not a specialist in child development might agree. For example, what a psychologist might see as "compulsive eating" could be interpreted by the parent as a "healthy appetite." This parent would receive a low rating on Scale A but a high rating on Scale I. Thus, Scale A attempts to isolate one element in the parent-child relation: the parent's own judgment of the normality or seriousness of his child's behavior. Such a judgment may be explicitly stated, or it may be implied by a parent's worried tone or general overconcern with an area of development.

Another parental attitude which seemed worth investigating was annoyance. We expected that the war-separated fathers would be more annoyed than their wives with their first-borns' behavior. Scale B (Appendix 7) was developed to quantify the degree of annoyance expressed by a parent about his child's behavior in a given area. Such irritation is, of course, also an element of the over-all matrix which Scale I measures.

Finally, we wished to evaluate the nature and relevance of the parents' understanding of their children's behavior. We expected that the war-separated mothers would show a higher quality of understanding than their husbands. For this evaluation, an "insight" scale, Scale C (Appendix 7), was developed. This scale attempts to quantify the extent to which a parent demonstrates understanding of his child's development in a given area. The quality of this understanding is judged by a psychologist who is acquainted with the child.

Methods of rating. Because we wanted to obtain the widest and most typical spread possible in our ratings, we decided to include excerpts from both war-separated and non-separated parents in our rating piles. This is the procedure also used in the analysis of the mother and father interviews in Chapters 4 and 7.

Another decision necessary before rating began was: should both fathers and mothers be rated simultaneously (i.e., in the same pile) or separately? If the parents were rated together, then a rating of 5 would indicate the most extreme kind of statement made by parents, regardless of sex. If they were rated separately, then a rating of 5 would indicate the most extreme kind of statement made by parents of that sex. It was decided that comparisons between fathers and mothers would be more meaningful if these parents had been rated by the same rater on the same scale at the same time. Therefore, the ratings on Scales A and B were made using this technique. Sixty-five parent excerpt sheets concerning a given topic were rated together on these scales. This rating pile included 19 war-separated and 19 non-separated fathers, and 17 war-separated and 10 non-separated mothers, intermixed randomly. Excerpts for several areas of behavior were rated by Rater W (Dr. Robert Wirt) who did not know which parents were war-separated and which were non-separated.

In using Scale I (seriousness of problem), a different technique was employed. This scale had been used for rating the summaries from both war-separated and non-separated mother interviews (Chapter 7). It had also been used separately for rating the excerpts from the war-separated and non-separated father interviews (Chapter 4). Both sets of ratings on Scale I were made by the same person (Laverne Johnson), who did not know which parents were war-separated and which were not. Thus, the mother and father ratings were made separately rather than simultaneously. Therefore, a rating of 5 on Scale 1 represents the most extreme kind of statement for parents of a given sex. Hence, differences between mothers' and fathers' ratings may be expected only insofar as the distributions of these ratings differed by sex of parent.

A further kind of rating pile was developed for the insight ratings (Scale C). Since these ratings could be made only by a person who knew all of the children being discussed, and since some of the children of the non-separated parents were not well-known to the rater, only war-separated children could be included in this rating pile. The rater (Dr. Edith Dowley) had known the war-separated children at nursery school or at Monday Club. The Scale C rating pile consisted of the excerpts from the 34 war-separated parents who constituted the 17 couples[1] who are the central subjects of this

---

1. The interviews of two war-separated fathers could not be used in this analysis because interview data with their wives were not available. Therefore, this chapter is based on analysis of 17 war-separated families.

substudy. In contrast with the other ratings, for which identities were disguised by numbers, the insight ratings were made with the rater's explicit knowledge of the identities of her subjects.

If a parent made no mention of an area, we assumed that, in that parent's eyes, that area was unimportant. That parent was given an "A" rating for that area. In the statistical treatment of our rating data, all "A"'s were entered as "low"'s in the median split; they were entered as 1's in computing means and medians.

Reliability of these scales. Reliability data on Scale I are presented in Chapters 4 and 7.

The reliability of Scales A and B was checked by obtaining the Pearson r between the ratings of W and E.[2] These r's ranged from .63 to .89 with a median of .75, which was considered satisfactory for use with the rather crude statistical devices which were employed in analyzing these data.

Since no one else in this project could be assumed to have knowledge about the children comparable with that of the rater on Scale C, no reliability check for the insight ratings was possible.

Statistical Inference

Since the ratings used in this study could not be assumed to be normally distributed, the usual small-sample statistical techniques were inappropriate for their analysis. Therefore, a nonparametric statistic for related groups was used. For analysis by this device, all ratings were considered as merely "low" or "high," depending upon whether they fell below or above the median of the group of ratings to which they belonged, i.e., the 34 ratings of the parents studied in this chapter. The 17 pairs of ratings (one pair for each war-separated couple) were then tabulated on a contingency table. The information necessary for testing the null hypothesis is entirely contained in cells A and D of the table, inasmuch as these cells contain the pairs which showed a between-parents divergence.

		Mothers	
		low	high
Fathers	high	A	B
	low	C	D

The significance of the split of A and D is determined by reference to the binomial expansion. This significance test determines: given the number A plus D, what is the probability of that number splitting in the way it does in this table or in an even more extreme way? The test may be either one-tailed or two-tailed. One-tailed tests, used whenever we had an advance hypothesis about the direction of the differences between parents, are here indicated by an asterisk.[3] Two-tailed tests were used whenever we had no advance hypothesis stating the expected direction of differences.

2. Ratings checked by Alberta Engvall.

3. These hypotheses are presented in Engvall (22a).

Organization of the Data

For purposes of exposition, we have grouped our data from topical excerpts around two general subjects: parents' attitudes toward their children's behavior and parents' attitudes toward parent-child relations. Included under children's behavior are the subtopics: eating, elimination, sleeping, dressing, tensions and comforts, relations with other children, and sibling relations. Included under parent-child relations are the subtopics: father-child relations, parent-child preferences, and parental insight into parent-child relations.

War-Separated Parents' Attitudes Toward Their First-Borns' Behavior

Eating

During their interviews most parents talked at some length about their children's eating behavior. The mother interviews averaged several pages of discussion of the child's eating history and present behavior, and most father interviews also contained considerable discussion of these topics. Parent excerpts regarding eating behavior were rated on four scales. Findings from these ratings are presented in Table 74.

It will be seen that both mothers and fathers described the war-separated first-borns as having serious eating problems: more than half of the parent excerpts received the maximum rating (of 5) on Scale I. Ten couples agreed roughly in their descriptions of their child's behavior (thus both receiving either high or low ratings), and for the seven who disagreed, there was no significant tendency for either fathers or mothers to be high while their spouses were low. As a group, mothers received slightly higher ratings for their descriptions than did their husbands as a group. (This is revealed by the two group means, differences between which are not tested statistically.)

Moreover, both mothers and fathers were worried about the eating behavior of their first-borns: they considered that behavior to be something of a problem. Only five couples diverged in degree of worry. Four of these were cases in which the father showed high worry and the mother low. This split for five cases is not significantly different from chance. As a group, fathers revealed more worry about their children's eating behavior than did mothers as a group.

Nine couples agreed roughly in their degree of annoyance with their children's eating behavior. Of the eight couples whose members were on opposite sides of the group median in degree of annoyance, seven were cases in which the fathers revealed high annoyance whereas their wives revealed low. Only one mother (Mrs. Harlow) had high annoyance as compared to her husband's low. A split as great or greater than this is significantly different from chance. Moreover, as a group the fathers showed considerably more annoyance than did their wives as a group.

The mothers showed incomparably more insight into their children's eating behavior than was shown by the fathers. This is revealed by the difference in the group means, but more significantly by the fact that of the 13 out of 17 couples who diverged in degree of insight, all were cases in which the mothers showed more-than-typical insight and the fathers showed little.

The reactions of the Wolfs are typical of those of the war-separated parents. Both of Dan's parents described severe eating problems (each receiving a rating of 5 on Scale I). Both were quite worried about Dan's eating, with Mr. Wolf (who was given a rating of 5 on Scale A) following the group trend for fathers to be somewhat more worried than mothers. (Mrs. Wolf was given a rating of 4 on the same scale.) Mr. Wolf showed much more annoyance than his wife (he received a rating of 5 on Scale B whereas she received a rating of 2), which was also typical for the war-separated couples. On insight, the Wolfs were not unusual in receiving ratings at opposite extremes: Mrs. Wolf was given a rating of 1 (considerable insight) whereas her husband was given a rating of 5 (no insight).

Table 74. War-Separated Parents' Attitudes Toward First-Borns' Eating Behavior

Rating Scale	Median-Split Contingency Table: Fathers	Mothers low	Mothers high	Significance of Differences in this Contingency Table	Measures of Central Tendency of Ratings (not tested for significance)
Seriousness of Problem (Scale I)	high	3	6	-	Median rating: 5 Mean, mothers: 4.2 Mean, fathers: 3.8
	low	4	4		
Parental Worry (Scale A)	high	4	5	-	Median rating: 3.5 Mean, mothers: 2.8 Mean, fathers: 3.4
	low	7	1		
Parental Annoyance (Scale B)	high	7	5	$P < .04$*	Median rating: 2.5 Mean, mothers: 2.2 Mean, fathers: 3.6
	low	4	1		
Parental Insight (Scale C)	high	13	2	$P < .0002$*	Median rating: 3 Mean, mothers: 2.0 Mean, fathers: 4.5
	low	2	0		

* One-tailed test.

Mrs. Wolf discussed her son's eating behavior by saying, "I was always worried about Dan's eating . . . He never did have much of an appetite, and we always had a feeding problem with him." She reported that Dan has always disliked eggs ("really, he almost gags on them"), and that after his brother was born Dan "refused to eat"—for three months he wanted nothing but milk and sweets. She reported, "The doctor told me I should let Dan decide what food he wanted, and if his choices were wholesome, let him try them out . . . I let him have whatever he wants. If I don't, he won't eat. If I fix something and he won't eat it, I don't insist. There's just no use." Mrs. Wolf's insightfulness is revealed in her ability to describe Dan's eating in terms of his own reactions to eating (rather than in terms of her reactions to his behavior exclusively) and by such statements as, "I nursed Dan for eight months . . . I think it's better for a baby if it is breast fed. I think it gives him more security and a feeling he's loved," and "I know now that you shouldn't force food on children. If they don't want it, just take it away and don't say anything. But I didn't know that when Dan was very young. I thought he had to have his egg every day."

Mr. Wolf described problems of similar seriousness to those discussed by his wife, but revealed rather different attitudes to them. He said, "As far as I can remember, Dan has always been a finicky eater . . . He got so bad there for awhile that he had to have a different fork for every different thing he had . . . Then he got so he wouldn't eat at all. So we stopped the in-between-meals stuff and he still wouldn't eat. So we had to start giving him those vitamin pills . . . We've tried everything." Dan's father complained, "Dan changes his mind so much. This I blame on my wife. He says he wants a soft-boiled egg; then he doesn't want it; he wants candy instead. He's getting better; I've squawked. All he was eating was candy." Mr. Wolf's lack of insight into Dan's eating behavior was particularly apparent in his discussion of attempts to improve that behavior: "He's always been a finicky eater, and I think my wife encourages that, too. Stuff like her giving Dan a piece of meat and saying, 'You don't have to eat that little fringe around the outside if you don't want to . . .' The most successful thing she tried was this bribery stuff, but I don't think that was so good. That way, everything the kid does he expects a reward for it."

Elimination

All of the war-separated parents discussed their first-borns' history and present status of elimination behavior, though few fathers gave the amount or detailed quality of information that was typically elicited from the mothers. Parent excerpts about elimination behavior were rated on four scales. The findings from these ratings are presented in Table 75.

Both the high means and the high median of ratings on Scale I indicate that these parents describe the elimination problems of their war-separated children as fairly serious. As a group, the mothers describe problems which are somewhat more serious than those described by the fathers, but the tendency for mothers to receive high ratings on this scale while their husbands receive low ones falls short of statistical significance.

Table 75. War-Separated Parents' Attitudes Toward First-Borns' Elimination Behavior

Rating Scale	Median-Split Contingency Table			Significance of Differences in this Contingency Table	Measures of Central Tendency of Ratings (not tested for significance)
		Mothers low	Mothers high		
Seriousness of Problem (Scale I)	Fathers high	1	6	—	Median rating: 4 Mean, mothers: 4.2 Mean, fathers: 3.0
	Fathers low	4	6		
Parental Worry (Scale A)	Fathers high	0	6	P < .04*	Median rating: 2.5 Mean, mothers: 2.8 Mean, fathers: 2.5
	Fathers low	6	5		
Parental Annoyance (Scale B)	Fathers high	3	3	—	Median rating: 1 Mean, mothers: 1.6 Mean, fathers: 1.9
	Fathers low	9	2		
Parental Insight (Scale C)	Fathers high	10	1	P < .02*	Median rating: 3 Mean, mothers: 2.6 Mean, fathers: 3.8
	Fathers low	4	2		

* One-tailed test.

Twelve of the war-separated couples agreed roughly in their degree of worry over their children's elimination problems. Of those five cases which diverged in worry, all were couples in which the mother's worry was rated above the median whereas the father's worry was rated below the median. This split for five cases is significantly different from chance. Notice, however, that the difference between fathers and mothers as groups is small, and that both groups show only moderate worry about this area of behavior.

Very little annoyance with their children's elimination behavior was revealed by these parents. This is indicated by the low median of the ratings and by the low group means. For those five couples who diverged in degree of annoyance, there was no important tendency for either husbands or wives to be consistently higher.

On the insight ratings, the mothers, both as a group and by couples, showed considerably more understanding of their first-born children than was shown by the fathers. Only 5 couples received roughly similar ratings. Of the 12 couples whose ratings diverged on opposite sides of the median, 10 were cases in which the mothers showed considerable insight (and hence were rated "low" on this scale) and the fathers showed little; two (the Harlows and the Snyders) were cases in which the reverse was true. This split for 12 cases is significantly different from chance.

Sleeping

All of the war-separated mothers, and all but one of the war-separated fathers (Mr. Ford) discussed their children's sleeping behavior. However, most of the fathers centered their discussion around sleep routines, only eight giving any mention to disturbances of sleep (nightmares, night fears, etc.).

Excerpts on this topic were rated on three scales. Scale I was used twice, however: once for rating statements concerning problems in sleep routines, and again separately for rating statements regarding sleep disturbances. Statements regarding these two subtopics were combined for ratings on Scales A and B. Results of these ratings are presented in Table 76.

In discussing sleep routines, although the fathers as a group tended to present disturbances in routines as being more serious than the mothers did, the large majority of couples agreed roughly in their descriptions of the seriousness of this problem. Of those couples who disagreed, there was no tendency for either mothers or fathers to be consistently higher.

For disturbances of sleep, the mothers presented a far more serious picture than did the fathers. Indeed, as is noted above, many of the fathers made no mention of this area. Eight couples agreed roughly in their description of the seriousness of problems in this area. Of the 9 who diverged, all were cases in which the mother received an above-the-median rating on Scale I, whereas the father's rating was below the median. This split is highly significant.

In degree of worry about sleeping problems (Scale A), there was no difference, either by groups or by couples, between the fathers and mothers. Both were fairly concerned about this area of behavior, as is suggested by the median rating of 3 for the 34 war-separated parents.

Both as a group and by couples, the fathers tended to be more annoyed than their wives were about their children's sleeping behavior. The tendency for couples to diverge in this way was not statistically significant, however.

Certainly the most dramatic finding in this area is the difference between fathers and mothers in their discussions of their children's nightmares and other sleep disturbances. For 7 of the 9 children whose fathers omitted this area in their interviews, their mothers described problems which were rated either 4 or 5 on Scale I. The other 2 were described by their mothers as having problems which merited a 3 rating on the same scale. It is remarkable that Mr. Soule, for example, should discuss Fran's sleeping behavior at considerable length without ever mentioning her sleep disturbances which his wife reported so vividly. Mrs. Soule reported that Fran "used

Table 76. War-Separated Parents' Attitudes Toward First-Borns' Sleeping Behavior

Rating Scale	Median-Split Contingency Table			Significance of Differences in this Contingency Table	Measures of Central Tendency of Ratings (not tested for significance)
		Mothers low	Mothers high		
Sleep Routines Seriousness of Problem (Scale I)	Fathers high	3	6	-	Median rating: 2 Mean, mothers: 2.2 Mean, fathers: 3.1
	Fathers low	6	2		
		Mothers low	Mothers high		
Disturbances of Sleep Seriousness of Problem (Scale I)	Fathers high	0	4	P <.004	Median rating: 3 Mean, mothers: 4.1 Mean, fathers: 2.1
	Fathers low	4	9		
		Mothers low	Mothers high		
Parental Worry (Scale A)	Fathers high	3	7	-	Median rating: 3 Mean, mothers: 2.6 Mean, fathers: 2.5
	Fathers low	5	2		
		Mothers low	Mothers high		
Parental Annoyance (Scale B)	Fathers high	7	3	-	Median rating: 1 Mean, mothers: 1.5 Mean, fathers: 2.8
	Fathers low	5	2		

to wake up early in the morning when it was barely light and complain that there were bugs in her bed and they were getting on her. It was strictly imaginary, but she would get very upset about them and I would have to go in and soothe her . . . she was afraid and would cry." Mr. Soule was so occupied in expressing his own worry and annoyance over Fran's problems in sleep routines (she insisted on an elaborate going-to-bed ritual which disturbed family routines and seemed to her father to serve mainly to keep his wife from him) that he gave no mention of this other area, whereas Mrs. Soule in her interview described both types of problem.

Dressing

If only because the topic of dressing was included in their interviewer's outline, all the mothers made some mention of their children's dressing behavior, though in some cases this mention was brief and perhaps perfunctory. On the other hand, of the 17 war-separated fathers considered in this analysis, only 10 made any mention of their children's dressing. Parent excerpts regarding dressing behavior were rated on three scales. The findings from these ratings are presented in Table 77.

It is apparent from the group means of Scale I ratings that the war-separated mothers described their first-borns as having rather serious dressing problems, whereas the fathers did not present this area of behavior as one of much seriousness. Moreover, the disagreement by couples is statistically significant. Of the 17 war-separated couples, 11 are cases in which the mother's description of the child's dressing behavior received an above-the-median rating for seriousness of problem, whereas the father's description was rated below the median. There is no couple for whom the reverse is true. This split for 11 cases cannot be attributed to chance.

In addition, the mothers were more worried than their husbands about their children's dressing behavior. Of the 10 couples who diverge on opposite sides of the median in their degree of worry, 9 are cases in which the mother demonstrated high worry and the father demonstrated low (the Wag-

Table 77. War-Separated Parents' Attitudes Toward First-Borns' Dressing Behavior

Rating Scale	Median-Split Contingency Table: Fathers	Mothers low	Mothers high	Significance of Differences in this Contingency Table	Measures of Central Tendency of Ratings (not tested for significance)
Seriousness of Problem (Scale I)	high	0	4	$P < .001$	Median rating: 3 Mean, mothers: 4.0 Mean, fathers: 1.9
	low	2	11		
Parental Worry (Scale A)	high	1	3	$P < .02$*	Median rating: 1 Mean, mothers: 2.6 Mean, fathers: 1.3
	low	4	9		
Parental Annoyance (Scale B)	high	2	2	-	Median rating: 1 Mean, mothers: 1.5 Mean, fathers: 1.6
	low	10	3		

* One-tailed test.

ners are the exception). This split for 10 cases is significantly different from chance. Notice, however, that the group means for both mothers and fathers are low; dressing behavior is not an area which causes either group any great worry.

Most couples agreed roughly in their degree of annoyance, usually revealing little or no annoyance about their children's dressing behavior. In the 5 cases in which spouses receive annoyance ratings on opposite sides of the median, there is no trend for either husbands or wives to be consistently higher. A marked general absence of annoyance with dressing behavior is indicated by the lowness of the group means as well as by the fact that the median rating is 1.

It is interesting to examine those 7 cases in which the fathers made no mention at all of the area of dressing behavior. Three of the wives of these men described their children's dressing behavior as serious enough to merit a rating of 5 on the seriousness of problem scale; 3 more received ratings of 4; the seventh's description was assigned a rating of 3. Thus, maternal reports indicated that all these children had moderate to severe problems in the area of dressing. It is remarkable that these 7 fathers, in five hours of interviews, gave no mention of dressing problems which were as extreme as those exemplified in the report by Mrs. Arnold: "Bruce (age four years, seven months) would let me dress him completely to this day if I wanted. Even now I have to encourage him to dress himself . . . If his going outside to play means that he has to dress himself, he'll be in the house until lunchtime."

Yet these fathers are only the extremes of a group who, as a whole, show relatively little interest or concern in their children's dressing behavior. This is one manifestation of the finding (reported in Chapter 7) that war-separated fathers take full advantage of the cultural tradition that assigns the responsibility of the child's routine care to the mother. An examination of the mother excerpts reveals that 14 of the 17 war-separated mothers made no mention of their husbands when discussing their children's dressing. Their discussion of dressing was entirely in terms of a mother-child relation. Three mothers did mention their husbands when discussing this area. One mother (Mrs. Holman) says, "We've tried to encourage Ray to do those things now that we finally realize that he seems a little overly dependent." Her use of "we" suggests that her husband shared her concern with Ray's dependence in dressing. Two mothers (Mrs. Statler and Mrs. Wolf) specifically mentioned their husbands' roles in their children's dressing: Mr. Statler was reported by his wife as repeatedly telling his son that he must learn how to tie his shoes; and Mr. Wolf was reported as having taught his son how to tie his shoes while Mrs. Wolf was in confinement with their third child. These are the only three war-separated cases in which the mothers gave any indication that the fathers participated in their first-borns' dressing routines. From this analysis we conclude that it is the mothers who experienced and, therefore, who reported and were concerned with their children's dependences and inadequacies in dressing.

Tensions and Comforts

Asked such questions as, "Did your child ever suck his fist, his thumb, or his fingers?"; "Did he ever rock his bed, blink his eyes, masturbate, or whine?"; "Does he ever bite his nails, or pull, twist, or pat his hair?"; and "Does he cry easily?" all of the mothers discussed at some length the topic of tensions and comforts. In the more permissively-structured interview situation, only 11 of the 17 war-separated fathers made any mention at all of this area of behavior. Parental statements concerning this area were rated on three scales. Findings from these are presented in Table 78.

As a group, the war-separated mothers described problems in this area which were rated as much more serious than those described by the fathers. All war-separated parents, however, described serious problems in this area: the median rating on Scale I is 4, and there was only one child (Betty Brown) whose parents both received ratings of less than 3. Of the 7 couples who diverged on opposite sides of the median in the ratings of their descriptions, all were cases in which the wife received a high rating and the husband a low one. This split for 7 cases is significantly different from chance.

No differences were revealed between the fathers and the mothers in their worry about their children's behavior.

Fathers as a group tended to be somewhat more annoyed at their children's behavior in this area than were mothers as a group. However, analysis by couples shows no tendency for either husbands or wives to be rated consistently higher. Moreover, their children's tensions and comforts did not evoke much annoyance from most of these parents: the median rating for all war-separated parents on the annoyance scale is 1.

Table 78. War-Separated Parents' Attitudes Toward First-Borns' Tensions and Comforts

Rating Scale	Median-Split Contingency Table			Significance of Differences in this Contingency Table	Measures of Central Tendency of Ratings (not tested for significance)
		Mothers low	Mothers high		
Seriousness of Problem (Scale I)	Fathers high	0	6	$P < .02$	Median rating: 4 Mean, mothers: 4.3 Mean, fathers: 2.8
	Fathers low	4	7		
Parental Worry (Scale A)	Fathers high	3	4	-	Median rating: 2 Mean, mothers: 2.4 Mean, fathers: 2.2
	Fathers low	7	3		
Parental Annoyance (Scale B)	Fathers high	3	4	-	Median rating: 1 Mean, mothers: 1.7 Mean, fathers: 2.3
	Fathers low	7	3		

The Marstons made statements typical of the war-separated parents' discussions of this area of behavior. Mr. Marston's only mention of tensions and comforts was: "Ken never sucked his fingers to speak of. He chewed his clothing a little bit in time of stress, or he would bite his lip." This description received a rating of 3 on Scale I. Mrs. Marston, on the other hand, described Ken's behavior as more extreme, therefore receiving a rating of 5 on the same scale. When asked what her son does when tired or upset, she replied, "He chews his clothes. Anything— buttons, zippers. Chews big holes in them." She said, "Ken has always put things in his mouth, but never sucked his hands. He chewed papers and all, but not his hands. He chews string— gets a whole mouthful of it." Moreover, "He's a terrible whiner . . . That's really increased in the last year." Asked whether he whined frequently or only when tired, Ken's mother replied briefly, "Always." As was typical of the war-separated couples, the Marstons did not diverge on worry or annoyance: both received ratings of 2 on worry and 1 on annoyance.

The couple who shared the greatest concern about their child's tensions and comforts was the Statlers. They both talked at considerable length about Allen's thumb-sucking; both discussions were given ratings of 5 on Scale I. Mr. Statler said, "Allen's thumb-sucking is persistent. His thumb has callouses on it. I think his mouth is malformed." Mrs. Statler said, "Allen sucked his thumb from the day he came home from the hospital . . . He has sort of large front teeth, and now we find out that's the reason."

Both of the Statlers reported that their son's thumb-sucking had been a topic of conflict between them. Mr. Statler said, "The reason for my wife's and my arguing over discipline was thumb-sucking. She had gone to two pediatricians. They said it wouldn't harm his teeth. I thought it would." Mrs. Statler concurred: "Allen's thumb causes a continual battle in our house. My husband doesn't like it at all . . . Allen always sucked his thumb and it was all right until my husband got home from the service, and then he didn't like it."

Perhaps even more significant, both parents reported considerable father-son conflict over thumb-sucking. When asked what effect father-separation had had on Allen, Mrs. Statler said, "Well, I suppose if his father had been home Allen's thumb would have been taken out of his mouth oftener . . . Allen's father doesn't like that habit, and so every time Allen puts his thumb in his mouth, he's told to take it out." Later in the interview, she commented, "I think it's too much for a little boy Allen's age to just never let go. I think sometimes Allen looks as if he's trying too hard to please, to do what he's supposed to do . . . I've always felt that maybe he's continued sucking his thumb so long because he's not quite up to things, isn't big enough to do all that my husband expects of him." Similarly, Mr. Statler reported conflict between himself and his son over this issue. "I tried to make him stop. I didn't like him to do it out in public. I didn't think it looked very good . . . I took it out of his mouth. I'd tell him to stop, slap his fingers. I'd never slap his face. He would sometimes stop, sometimes cry, sometimes look at his mother and put it back." On the basis of these and other statements not reported here, Mr. Statler was given a 5 rating on both worry and annoyance, and Mrs. Statler was rated 4 on worry and 3 on annoyance.

It is interesting to compare the statements of the wives of those men who did not mention this area of behavior with the statements of the wives whose husbands did. On Scale I, the means of the ratings of these two groups of war-separated mothers differ by 0.7, with the wives of those men who did discuss the area describing the more serious problems. On Scale A (worry), the wives of the men who mentioned this area of behavior receive ratings which average 0.9 higher than the ratings of the wives whose husbands do not mention this area. This suggests that in some families the first-borns' tensions and comforts are more of a topic of concern than in others, and that husbands and wives share to some extent their degree of concern.

Relations with Other Children

All of the mothers and all but one of the war-separated fathers (Mr. Mathews) made some mention of their children's social relations with their peers, and many of the parents discussed this topic at considerable length. The mothers revealed their attitudes toward this area in response to such questions as, "Does your child give evidences of sympathy to other children?" "Does he frequently play alone?" and "Which do you think he prefers as companions, children or adults?" The parent excerpts on this topic were rated on four scales. Findings from these ratings are presented in Table 79.

Eleven of the war-separated couples agreed roughly on their descriptions of the seriousness of their children's problems in social relations. Of those 6 who diverged, 5 are cases in which the father's description was more extreme than the mother's. This split, of course, is not statistically significant for so few cases. The group means also reveal the tendency for fathers to describe the social problems of their children as more severe.

In their worry over their children's social relations, again the tendency is for the war-separated parents to agree. Only 4 diverged in this attitude, and the group means reveal no important difference.

More than half of the war-separated parents diverged in their degree of annoyance with their children's social relations. The tendency for this divergence to be in the direction of fathers having high annoyance while their wives have low annoyance is not significant. The group means show the same tendency: fathers seem somewhat more annoyed than their wives about this area. Neither group of parents, however, reveals much annoyance when discussing this area: the median rating for all is 1.

In their insightfulness, in this area as in others, the mothers were rated superior to their husbands. Of the 11 couples who diverged in their insightfulness, 9 are cases in which the mother revealed considerable insight while her husband revealed little. The reverse is true for 2 couples: the Browns and the Osbornes. This split for 11 cases is significantly different from chance.

Although their ratings are more extreme than is usual for the war-separated couples, the Arnolds are typical of these couples in the similarity of their attitudes on all of the variables except insight and in their divergence on that variable. Both of his parents described Bruce as having serious developmental problems (ratings of 5) in his social relations. Mr. Arnold,

Table 79. War-Separated Parents' Attitudes Toward First-Borns' Relations with Other Children

Rating Scale	Median-Split Contingency Table			Significance of Differences in this Contingency Table	Measures of Central Tendency of Ratings (not tested for significance)
		Mothers low	Mothers high		
Seriousness of Problem (Scale I)	Fathers high	5	7	-	Median rating: 3 Mean, mothers: 2.6 Mean, fathers: 3.0
	Fathers low	4	1		
		Mothers low	Mothers high		
Parental Worry (Scale A)	Fathers high	2	6	-	Median rating: 2 Mean, mothers: 2.4 Mean, fathers: 2.6
	Fathers low	7	2		
		Mothers low	Mothers high		
Parental Annoyance (Scale B)	Fathers high	6	5	-	Median rating: 1 Mean, mothers: 1.8 Mean, fathers: 2.2
	Fathers low	3	3		
		Mothers low	Mothers high		
Parental Insight (Scale C)	Fathers high	9	3	$P < .04$*	Median rating: 3 Mean, mothers: 2.8 Mean, fathers: 3.9
	Fathers low	3	2		

* One-tailed test.

however, was somewhat more worried (rating 5) about these than his wife (rating 4) though both were disturbed. Both revealed moderate annoyance (ratings of 3). Mrs. Arnold is judged to have good insight (rating 2) whereas Mr. Arnold showed little understanding of his son's social relations (rating 4).

Mr. Arnold, who discussed this area at considerable length, described Bruce as a child who is quiet, unassertive, and hesitant to join his peers in playing. He said, "Bruce can fight— he knows how to fight— but I've never seen him do it. He can just be tormented. He certainly was the scapegoat in his group." Mr. Arnold was delighted that his son was currently becoming "quite different— quite noisy, even boisterous, maybe a little obnoxious." He says, "I like to see it. I'd rather have him more forceful than he was." Mrs. Arnold, though she used fewer examples than her husband and didn't dwell as heavily as he does on this aspect of their son's development, painted a similar picture of the boy's social behavior and showed similar attitudes toward it.

In understanding, however, the Arnolds revealed the real discrepancy which is typical between war-separated mothers and fathers. Mr. Arnold's attitude is summed up in such statements as: "Have you ever seen Bruce fight anybody? You never will. The fact remains, I've never seen him defend himself. He can be attacked . . . Someone will come up and swing on him and he won't fight back . . . He'll look at them and walk away. Where's the old drive? Where's the old self-preservation? Is he just going to be an organism to be molded any way anybody wants him to go?"

Contrast her husband's outburst with Mrs. Arnold's gentle statement: "Bruce is shy of children. He has a little social stigma . . . In playing with children, if they're strange, he automatically draws back. If he goes out and there's a group of children, he won't enter the play. He'll take a circuitous route around them, hoping that they'll call him over. But he takes the long way around, and then he'll come back and say, 'They won't play with me.' . . . He's very socially conscious, to the point of being quite hurt about it . . . He can't bring himself to go half-way over to join a group. He's hurt very easily that way, more easily that way than in physical contact. He's very sensitive socially, which I hate to see because I hate to see him leave himself open to hurt, and also I think as a rule you find those things in girls more than boys. But I've decided that maybe if he is that way, it's already instilled there. And if I can help him get the attitude that he's as good as anybody else, I really don't care. Then he might be happier if he matures that way and pretty soon begins to believe in himself."

Sibling Relations

Although the interpersonal relations between brothers and sisters were not intended to be a topic of the mother interviews, considerable incidental material about these relations was brought out in these interviews. This material was excerpted and compared with excerpts of the fathers' often-more-lengthy discussions of their children's sibling relations. Fourteen of the 17 war-separated couples considered in this substudy had more than one child but one mother was not interviewed about the second child, so data were complete for 13 couples. All of these 26 parents gave some mention of their children's relations with siblings. Excerpts concerning sibling relations were rated on two scales. Findings from these ratings are presented in Table 80.

Neither group of parents was very worried about their children's relations with siblings. However, just as was the case with their children's relations with their peers, the war-separated fathers show slightly more worry than their wives about these child-child relations. In the analysis by couples, this tendency falls far short of statistical significance.

In their interviews, these war-separated parents revealed very little annoyance at their children's sibling relations: the median rating was 1. The fathers reveal somewhat more annoyance than their wives in this as

Table 80. War-Separated Parents' Attitudes Toward First-Borns' Relations with Siblings

Rating Scale	Median-Split Contingency Table: Fathers	Mothers: low	Mothers: high	Significance of Differences in this Contingency Table	Measures of Central Tendency of Ratings (not tested for significance)
Parental Worry (Scale A)	high	4	4	-	Median rating: 2 Mean, mothers: 1.9 Mean, fathers: 2.4
	low	3	2		
Parental Annoyance (Scale B)	high	5	2	-	Median rating: 1 Mean, mothers: 1.8 Mean, fathers: 2.2
	low	4	2		

in other areas. Of the 7 couples who diverge on degree of annoyance at sibling relations, 5 are cases in which the fathers have high annoyance whereas the mothers have low. This split is, of course, not significantly different from chance.

Summary

Although we cannot be sure to what extent the disparities are due to differences in interview technique, it is apparent that the war-separated fathers tend to be interested in some areas of behavior, discussing these at length, and to ignore other areas. In contrast, their wives give more systematic and inclusive information. The fathers dwell on their first-borns' eating, elimination, sleep routines, and relations with siblings and other children, but frequently ignore dressing behavior, sleep disturbances, and tensions and comforts. Thus, in general they seem more concerned with aspects of their first-borns' behavior which intrude into those areas of family life for which our culture assigns to the father some responsibility. In those areas of behavior for which the father is assigned no responsibility (e.g., dressing) or which are not importantly interpersonal and culturally-ritualized (e.g., disturbances in sleep; tensions and comforts), the war-separated fathers show little or no interest, despite the fact that maternal reports indicate that their children have rather dramatic and severe problems in these areas.

Scale I was used to rate seven different areas of behavior. For their descriptions of all but two of the seven areas (the exceptions being eating behavior and relations with other children), the mothers as a group received ratings averaging higher than those received by the fathers as a group. The rather consistent trend for mothers to describe more serious problems is probably due to at least three factors: (1) the mothers are more familiar with their children's behavior (due to their greater association with the children) and can therefore report that behavior in more detail, thus revealing the real problems which these war-separated children have; (2) the interview technique for mothers elicited more detailed and systematic information from them than was volunteered by the fathers, thereby laying bare the real developmental problems which the first-borns have experienced; and (3) the rating piles for mothers, unlike those for fathers, contained excerpts concerning second-borns as well as first-borns. Since the second-borns seem to have fewer problems (according to the findings of Chapter 7), the presence in the rating piles of excerpts concerning them probably pushed upward the ratings of the first-borns.

Our rough statistical technique revealed significant differences between husbands and wives on Scale I ratings for only those areas about which the men displayed relatively little concern (as evidenced by the length and intensity of their discussions). That is, the war-separated mothers described much more serious problems than were indicated by their husbands in the areas of sleep disturbances, dressing, and tensions and comforts. For those behavioral areas about which the war-separated fathers do evidence concern, they report behavior which is roughly comparable in seriousness to that reported by their wives.

Scale A (parental worry) was used in rating each of the seven sets of excerpts about behavior. In discussing their first-borns' eating behavior and relations with other children, the war-separated fathers tend to be more worried than their wives (when compared by couples), but these differences do not even approach statistical significance. For the other five areas of behavior, if there were any differences between husbands and wives at all, it was the mothers who were more worried, although this difference was significant for only two areas of behavior: elimination and dressing. These findings confirm the finding in Chapter 4 that eating behavior and relations with other children are the primary behavioral areas with which fathers (whether war-separated or not) are concerned, and confirms our expectation that war-separated mothers would tend to be more worried about their children than their husbands are.

In annoyance (rated by Scale B), the war-separated fathers tended to be rated higher than their wives, although only in the area of eating behavior did this tendency reach statistical significance. There was no area about which the mothers showed more annoyance than their husbands.

We feel confident that the war-separated fathers were actually more irked with their first-borns' behavior than these Scale B ratings indicate. After having settled upon this method of attempting to quantify annoyance by rating the degree of annoyance in each separate topical excerpt, we realized the naiveté of expecting paternal annoyance to be revealed consistently in these excerpts. Annoyance toward one's child is sufficiently socially unacceptable that we should not expect expressions of it to permeate all of the statements of any except the most undercontrolled parents. The irritation which war-separated fathers felt toward their first-borns was expressed (in the interviews) summarily or in occasional outbursts, and not typically in consistent reiteration of annoyance with the introduction into the discussion of each new area of behavior.

The greatest differences between the war-separated couples were found in the insight (Scale C) ratings. This scale was used only for the materials on eating, elimination, and relations with other children, since only these excerpts were deemed of sufficient length and quality of coverage to justify ratings on insightfulness. For all three areas, a judge who knew the children found that the war-separated mothers had more insight into their first-borns' behavior than their husbands did. This difference between mothers and fathers was predicted from: (1) the mothers' more intimate association with the first-borns; (2) the greater social importance which success in the parental role has for women; (3) the current emphasis (in the educated groups within the middle class) upon maternal sophistication about child-rearing; and (4) the fact (asserted by both mothers and fathers, as reported later in this chapter) that in these war-separated families the mother-child bond is much stronger for first-borns than is the father-child bond.

Because of systematic differences in interview techniques and also because of our lack of a control group, it is impossible to draw any definite conclusions from these data. In general, it seems that war-separated fathers are concerned with only those areas of their first-borns' behavior which, because of the nature of our cultural directives to parents, require paternal attention. That is, the war-separated fathers conform to only the minimal requirements. For those areas with which they do show concern, these fathers describe behavior roughly comparable in seriousness to that described by their wives. In the other areas, their wives describe far more serious problems than they do. The war-separated fathers' rejection of their first-borns (demonstrated in Chapter 5) is suggested by their tendency to show somewhat less worry and somewhat more annoyance about these children's behavior than is shown by their wives, and by the fathers' inability to view this behavior with the degree of insight achieved by their wives.

War-Separated Parents' Attitudes Toward Parent-Child Relations

Father-Child Relations

Every parent interviewed discussed at some length the topic of the relation between the war-separated father and the child born during his absence. These discussions were excerpted under two general topics: father-child relations (including the father's feeling for the child and the child's attitude toward the father) and paternal discipline. Data from both of these sets of excerpts will be considered here.

The parents' statements concerning early paternal discipline were rated on the severity scale used in Chapter 3 (Appendix 3). The parents' statements concerning father-child relations were rated on Scale I (seriousness of problem). Findings from these two sets of ratings are presented in Table 81.

These data show that the war-separated parents described early paternal

Table 81. War Separated Parents' Attitudes
Toward Father-Child Relations

Topic and Rating Scale	Median-Split Contingency Table: Fathers	Mothers low	Mothers high	Significance of Differences in this Contingency Table	Measures of Central Tendency of Ratings (not tested for significance)
Father's Early Discipline (Severity Scale)	high	6	5	-	Median rating: 4 Mean, mothers: 3.6[a] Mean, fathers: 4.1
	low	5	1		
Problems in Father Relations (Scale I)	high	2	6	-	Median rating: 4 Mean, mothers: 3.9 Mean, fathers: 3.2
	low	4	5		

[a]. Excluding excerpts rated A.

discipline as rather severe (the median rating is 4), with the fathers presenting a somewhat more severe picture than their wives. Of those 7 couples who diverge on opposite sides of the median in their ratings on the severity scale, 6 are cases in which the fathers were rated high, their wives low. This split escapes statistical significance.

In discussing father-child relations, these war-separated parents again described rather serious problems (the median rating again being 4). The mothers' descriptions received somewhat higher ratings than the fathers' (perhaps because excerpts concerning father-child relations between fathers and second-borns were included in the rating pile for mothers). Of those 7 cases who diverged in their descriptions of problems in father-child relations, 5 were cases in which the mother's rating was above the median whereas her husband's was below. This split is, of course, not significantly different from chance.

Early paternal discipline. Of the 17 war-separated mothers whose interviews were analyzed in this substudy, 4 spoke so evasively or in such general terms when discussing their husbands' early disciplining that it was impossible to judge its severity with confidence. Those mothers were assigned ratings of "A." These ratings were entered as "low's" in the median split, but the 4 cases were not included in the group from which the mean maternal rating was computed. Of the remaining 13 couples from whom ratings could be made from both parents' interviews, only 2 (the Mathews and the Soules) received ratings differing more than one point. However, in every case of husband-wife difference except one (the Wycoffs), the husband described his own early discipline as more severe than that his wife attributed to him. In the 4 cases for whom comparison was impossible because of the inexplicitness of the mother's report, 2 of the husbands reported severe discipline (ratings of 5), 1 reported firm discipline (rating 3), and 1 reported mild discipline (rating 2). The distribution of these four ratings is roughly comparable to that of the other 13.

The Harlows are a war-separated couple who received identical ratings for their reports of mild early paternal discipline. Mrs. Harlow said, "Particularly during the first year after we returned to this country, Clarence's father was much too lenient." Mr. Harlow did not dwell on the topic of discipline in his own interview, but he did state, "I recall instances when I felt quite inept as a father, particularly in discipline . . . My wife was much more successful, and this bothered me . . . actually by temperament I tend toward the permissive." Mrs. Harlow concurred with this analysis: "He's a mild personality. I can't remember his ever spanking Clarence. It would just be entirely out of character for him to do that. He definitely registers disapproval." Both parents reported that their son resented maternal disciplinary measures, and Mr. Harlow even said that he thought the reason Clarence preferred his father was that Mrs. Harlow did the major part of the disciplining. (The reader may have noticed that the Harlows are frequently the exceptions in our findings about war-separated couples. Mr. Harlow was the man mentioned in Chapters 3 and 4 as being different from the other war-separated fathers because he retained his service-connected job after his reunion with his family and, therefore, participated little in family life. He is the only war-separated father who received a Scale I rating of 1 on father-child relations.)

The Osbornes are one of the couples who both reported severe paternal discipline. Mrs. Osborne said, "My husband has been pretty hard on George. He didn't know what to expect of a child when he came back, and he would just do anything that came to his head . . . he'd shake George or dangle him by his heels and let him flop upon his back on the bed from a distance—that would knock the breath out of him you know—and oh, cuff him in the head or do things that people don't generally do with children." When asked whether her husband had ever whipped George, she responded, "Well, he's spanked him, but I don't think he ever took a stick to him, though he might have." Mr. Osborne, though he avoided discussing the nature of his own disciplinary measures and concentrated rather on describing George's raging responses to them, revealed his methods in remarks like the following: "With George you have to hit hard enough to hurt his feelings or else do something else to insult his dignity . . . At home I tell him a couple of times, and then if he doesn't do it, I hit him . . . hit him a couple of times . . . If you tell him to eat something, he'll do everything under the sun. Finally you grab him and open his mouth and put it in and tell him 'Now keep it there!' " Both of the Osbornes dwelt on reports of George's tantrums in response to paternal punishment, and both mentioned the impression that punishment was effective with him because it "hurts his dignity."

The Soules were the couple who received the most divergent ratings for their reports of paternal discipline. In her interview, when Mrs. Soule was asked whether her husband ever spanked Fran very much, she responded, "No, I don't think he ever spanked her." The interviewer followed this response by questioning, "Even when he first came back from the war?" to which Mrs. Soule replied, "Oh, no." Asked whether Fran had ever been severely punished, Mrs. Soule responded by recalling an incident when she herself had punished her daughter, but made no mention of paternal punishment. At another point she told the interviewer that Fran had rejected her father when he returned. "My husband was terribly hurt (by the rejection). He never punished her or anything, but he felt hurt." Mr. Soule, on the other hand, reported that he "more or less took over the disciplining" of Fran after his return, and that this caused frequent clashes with his wife. He reported that he was "nervous," and Fran's behavior would annoy him. He would "fly up, shout at her, grab her, spank her . . . My wife's policy was to try to lead Fran rather than beat her, but I wasn't capable of any such finesse. I was trying a little more direct, physical approach."

Mrs. Snyder's comments on paternal discipline exemplify those maternal reports that were so general that they could not be rated. When asked whether Kate had ever been severely punished, she responded only with, "No; she's never really bad." She mentioned paternal discipline only when answering a question regarding the effects of father-separation: "I think he's definitely been a stranger to her, and the discipline and so forth. I think it wasn't until she was three years old that she really became 'pals' with her father." In contrast with his wife's evasiveness, Mr. Snyder had reported that "When Kate came to visit me at camp, I thought she was spoiled. I felt she needed disciplining and I spanked her several times." Following his return, "at naptime we often had difficulty. Kate would always fuss. I would spank her . . . I believed she should put her toys and clothes away neatly when she had finished with them. This I emphasized to the point of insistence, and resorted to spanking whenever Kate did not do as directed."

In summary, we may say that most of those mothers who discussed the issue in any specificity described their husbands' early discipline as being at about the same level of severity as the men themselves had reported. When they did differ with their husbands, all but one mother did so in the direction of minimizing the severity of paternal discipline. Four mothers were not sufficiently explicit in discussing this area to permit us to classify the severity of paternal discipline from their reports. Presumably their evasiveness reflected the same motivation which led many of the more explicit mothers to minimize their husbands' disciplinary severity.

Problems in father relations. Both groups of parents typically reported that father-child relations were a serious problem in their families. Only 1 of the war-separated parents (a father, Mr. Harlow) received a rating of 1 on Scale I for his discussion of father-child relations; 6 (4 fathers, 2 mothers) received ratings of 2; 10 (7 mothers, 3 fathers) received ratings of 5.

Although their ratings are slightly higher than average, the Wycoffs are typical in the relation between the ratings assigned to their reports: Mrs. Wycoff's description of father-child relations received a rating of 5 on Scale I; her husband's received a rating of 4.

Mr. Wycoff's intellectual convictions were important in his relations with Ann after he returned from the war: "Because of a book I had read,

I believed you spoiled babies by picking them up. I thought babies didn't need any attention until they were one year old. Fortunately my wife was of another opinion, and Ann got a lot of mothering . . . I had no strong feeling about Ann when I first got back; I remember feeling cold toward her. I didn't pick her up . . . I can recall feeding Ann when she was one year old and slapping her when she spewed food." His wife gave a similar report of Mr. Wycoff's early relation with their first-born: "My husband believed in a very rational approach toward children . . . When he came back, he didn't have the urge to just take Ann and cuddle her and play with her the way some fathers want to . . . After he returned, feeding problems began to develop. Ann didn't want to eat her vegetables. I didn't know exactly how to handle it, and so he tried to do it. He became angry and he'd slap her face. He would get her to open her mouth and then she'd spit at him and he'd slap her. It was terribly upsetting . . . If Ann would touch something she wasn't supposed to and he'd say no and then she'd touch it again, why he'd slap her hands. Well, there really wasn't too much slapping. But it indicated the approach he had . . . I think he would have had a very different feeling about her if he'd been there from the time she was born."

Both of Ann's parents agree that Mr. Wycoff's relations with her have improved over the years. Mr. Wycoff said, "I feel I've become increasinly warm. There has been a lot of change in my personality during the last three or four years. We cuddle and play games. I usually enjoy having her around. When she whines, I get angry. It annoys me when she wants my attention and I'm not ready to give it. It's kind of a tough situation." Mrs. Wycoff commented that her husband "really shudders now" when he thinks of his former relation with Ann, and said, "I think it isn't so much the philosophy that you have that influences the way you raise your children. I think it's the feelings you have about them. In the early years of Ann's life, I was pretty much mixed up and so was my husband, and it was bound to show on Ann. It's only been since we were working together better and being happier that we were able to relax more and to follow the permissive philosophy pretty well." Mr. Wycoff revealed his own continuing dissatisfaction with his relations with his daughter but also the optimism which his wife had expressed when he said, "I feel I am beginning to do a better job with Ann."

Parents' Descriptions of Parent-Child Preferences

Asked such questions as "Which child is easier for your husband to get along with?" and "Which child is easier for you to get along with?" the mothers usually revealed the patterns of preferences between war-separated first-born children and their parents. Although not asked such specific questions, the fathers tended spontaneously to discuss similar material. These expressions of preferences and judgments of the preferences of others in the family were tabulated and are summarized in Table 82.

As is reported in Chapter 4, no war-separated father feels closer to his first-born than to his second-born, and only two feel equally close to both children. The suggestion (in Chapter 4) that even those two cases are in doubt is supported by the fact that the wives of both of these men (Mrs.

Table 82. War-Separated Parents' Descriptions of Parent-Child Preferences

Fathers' Preferences	Father feels closer to:	Mother considers husband closer to:
First-born child	–	–
Second-born child	11	10
Equally close to both	2	3
Mothers' Preferences	**Mother feels closer to:**	**Father considers wife closer to:**
First-born child	7	3
Second-born child	4	–
Equally close to both	2	1
No information given	–	9
First-Born Children's Preferences	**Father considers first-born closer to:**	**Mother considers first-born closer to:**
Mother	15	8
Father	2	2
Equally close to both	–	2
No information given	–	5

Statler and Mrs. Holman) reported that their husbands are closer to their second-born children. Three other war-separated mothers asserted that their husbands are equally close to both children. In every war-separated family, however, at least one spouse reported that the father was closer to the second-born; no war-separated parent of either sex reported the father as being closer to the first-born; and in 8 of the 13 war-separated families having two children, both parents agreed that the father was closer to the second-born.

The Osbornes are typical of the war-separated parents in that both state that Mr. Osborne feels closer to Alvin, the second child, than he does to George. When asked which child was easier for her husband to get along with, Mrs. Osborne replied, "I think as a rule he gets along more with Alvin . . . he can't punish Alvin the way he can George. He has more sympathy for Alvin . . . My husband thought I really should be spanking Alvin and doing severe things to him because of his pants-wetting, but I wouldn't. So he said he was going to, but I notice he didn't get around to it very much . . . He hasn't been very hard on Alvin." Mr. Osborne said, "I have sometimes felt that George is more his mother's boy and Alvin is more mine, because Alvin is a rough and tumble kid . . . George is tight and skinny. He's different from Alvin; Alvin has a soft face, the kind you like to pinch."

Of the 13 mothers who had two children, 7 felt themselves to be closer to the first-born, 4 felt closer to the second-born, and 2 felt equally close to both. Combining these preferences with the fathers' preferences, we see that there were three war-separated first-borns (Rick Moore, Dan Wolf, and Alma Wagner) for whom neither parent felt a preference.

Very few war-separated fathers made any statement about which child their wives seemed to feel closer to. Those three who did were all fathers who themselves felt closer to their second-borns, and all claimed that their wives felt closer to their first-borns. In one case (the Wagners), this was in contradiction to the mother's own statement of her feelings. In addition, one father (Mr. Osborne) asserted that his wife felt equally close to each of her children, a judgment in which she separately concurred.

The Burgmans are typical of the war-separated parents in that Mrs. Burgman stated that she felt closer to Don than to Maria, whereas Mr. Burgman, though he stated that Don felt closer to his mother ("for most of the things in family life, Don prefers and seeks his mother"), made no mention of which child his wife might feel closer to. Mrs. Burgman said, "Don is easier for me to get along with because he can talk to me and understand things . . . I think he's more like I was when I was a child: more sensitive and more sympathetic."

All but two of the war-separated fathers judged that their first-born children felt closer to their wives than to them. Of those 12 mothers who made any statement on this issue, 8 agreed with their husbands that their first-borns felt closer to their mothers, 2 agreed with their husbands that their first-borns felt closer to their fathers, and 2 thought that their first-borns felt equally close to both parents.

Reflecting the usual pattern in war-separated families, both of the Irwins agreed that their daughter felt closer to Mrs. Irwin. Patricia's mother reported, "She is very affectionate, to me especially, and my mother." Asked if Patricia were affectionate to her father too, Mrs. Irwin replied, "To a certain degree, yes, but not the same." When asked whether Patricia would let her father do things for her after he returned from the war, Mrs. Irwin said, "No, she wanted me to do it. She's still that way. She doesn't want him to pour her milk or break her eggs or anything. She always brings things to me . . . She's better when I'm not there than when I am. When I go out in the evenings, she doesn't want me to go, of course, but then after I'm gone I guess it's all right." Mr. Irwin felt that "Patricia and my wife are close just like my wife is close to her own mother. As a husband I felt left out then, and as a father I feel left out now . . . It took Patricia a long time to get used to me. She was much more used to her mother and grandmother."

Most husbands and wives agreed in their reports of parent-child preferences. When omissions of information are not counted as disagreements, 11 of the 17 couples agree about the nature of parent-child preferences in their families. Of the remaining 6 cases, there is an outright contradiction in only one (Mrs. Wagner says that she feels closer to her second child whereas her husband believes she feels closer to Alma, the first); all of the other 5 disagreements are cases in which one parent claims that either he or his spouse feels equally about both children, whereas the other parent asserts that there actually is a preference.

Parental Insight into Parent-Child Relations

Parent-child relations was a central topic of all of the interviews, and one which each parent discussed at considerable length. On excerpts from these discussions, each parent was given three ratings on his insight into three parent-child relations: the disciplinary relation between father and first-born; his own relation with the first-born; and his spouse's relation with the first-born. Findings from these ratings are presented in Table 83.

The war-separated fathers showed far less insight into their own disciplinary relations with their first-borns than was shown by their wives. Of the ten couples who diverged in insight, all were cases in which the mother showed considerable insight whereas her husband showed little. This split is highly significant.

Although the mothers as a group tended to show more insight into their relations with their first-born children than the fathers showed about their own relations with the same children, the divergence by couples was not significantly different from chance. Self-child relations is thus the one topic rated (on Scale C) in this study in which the mothers did not show significantly greater insight than their husbands.

When rated on understanding of their spouses' relation with the first-born, the mothers showed considerably more insight than the fathers. That is, the mothers understood father-child relations better than the fathers understood mother-child relations. All of the 12 couples which diverged on this rating were cases in which the mother showed considerable insight

Table 83. War-Separated Parents' Insight into Parent-Child Relations

Topic Rated by Scale C	Median-Split Contingency Table: Fathers	Mothers low	Mothers high	Significance of Differences in this Contingency Table	Measures of Central Tendency of Ratings (not tested for significance)
Insight into Paternal Discipline	high	10	5	P < .001*	Median rating: 3 Mean, mothers: 2.6 Mean, fathers: 4.2
	low	2	0		
Insight into Self-Child Relations	high	7	4	–	Median rating: 3 Mean, mothers: 2.2 Mean, fathers: 3.2
	low	3	3		
Insight into Spouse-Child Relations	high	12	4	P < .0003*	Median rating: 4 Mean, mothers: 2.8 Mean, fathers: 4.3
	low	1	0		

*One-tailed test.

whereas her husband showed little. This split, of course, is highly significant.

In their understanding of the father-child disciplinary relation, the Statlers present the contrast typical of war-separated parents.

Mr. Statler regarded discipline as central in his relation with Allen; discussing his own return from the war, he said, "I was proud of everything about him except his discipline." But his complete lack of insight into this relation was demonstrated when, despite the fact that he discussed discipline more than he discussed any other topic (and more than it was discussed by any other father in this study), he said, "If we were on a farm, I wouldn't discipline Allen." After describing at some length his methods of control (spanking, isolation, grabbing Allen by the shirt and then shaking him, slapping his thumb when Allen was sucking it, etc.), Mr. Statler said, "Some children might be upset for months if they were treated the way I treat Allen, but he isn't that way at all. It doesn't bother him, except that he realizes he can't do what he's doing. That's the only way you can treat him." Because he showed so little understanding of his own motivation and of his son's reactions, Mr. Statler received a rating of 5 on Scale C.

Mr. Statler told the interviewer that he and his wife "almost separated over the fact that we didn't agree on how to raise children," and the unusual length of Mrs. Statler's discussion of discipline confirms her husband's assertion that this is a central issue and an unresolved one in the lives of the Statlers. She made this explicit when she said, "About the only trouble we have in our house comes when I think that what the children have done isn't too bad and my husband thinks it is." Her analysis of the father-child disciplinary relation was: "My husband is very strict with himself. He never exaggerates or anything like that. I have a tendency to think such things are unimportant. But my husband's training was a little different. He thinks that lying is just lying; there's no excuse for it ever . . . Allen doesn't get away with nearly as much as some children do. My husband will call him on everything . . . I think my husband has the tendency to hold the same standards for Allen that he holds for himself . . . He isn't as strict with our daughter. He thinks that a boy has to have more control over himself than a girl." Mrs. Statler echoed her husband's judgment when she said that "Allen usually thinks that he's wrong if his father tells him that he is," but she also commented that "I've always felt that maybe Allen has continued sucking his thumb so long because he's not quite up to things, isn't big enough to do all that my husband expects of him." For her ability to see the viewpoints of both father and son and to analyze the interaction of these, Mrs. Statler received an insight rating of 2.

The Arnolds are typical of the war-separated parents in the ratings they received on their respective degrees of insight into their own relations with their first-born (Mrs. Arnold received a 2, her husband received a 4) and into their spouse's relations with him (Mrs. Arnold's understanding of father-child relations was assigned a rating of 2; Mr. Arnold's understanding of mother-child relations was assigned a rating of 5).

Mrs. Arnold always had an intimate relation with her first-born. She had chosen his name "years before he was born," and she "wanted a little boy very much." When he was a tiny baby, she always rocked him to sleep. In reporting this, she commented, "they say that is bad for a child, but I did it for my own enjoyment." Mrs. Arnold's insight is revealed in her own sensitivity to this close relation. She observed that "Bruce's stuttering was worst when I was strictest, and when I would be patient it would let itself up. So I think to a big extent it's a reflection of my own tensions," and that "the fact that he's more easily given to tears is just a highsign for a little more patience, of which frankly I don't have too much."

Mr. Arnold was so preoccupied with his own reactions in his dealings with Bruce that he could not make such acute observations and inferences as his wife does. He discussed his postwar reunion with his family entirely in terms of his own reactions, with no mention of the child's behavior and responses: "When I first came home, I didn't feel I was playing the role of father. I only felt like a visitor or lover." After saying that he considers the younger child "my baby," Mr. Arnold characterizes his feelings toward his children by saying, "On the whole, I enjoy my children very much. I like them because they're my boys," again discussing the relation entirely from his own point of view. Throughout his interviews, Mr. Arnold never discussed Bruce's attitude toward his father; he could only see the obverse side of the father-child relationship. The closest he ever came to describing the relation from Bruce's point of view was to say, "Before we came to the Village, I didn't see Bruce often, and when I did see him he didn't pay much attention to me," and even this comment focuses on his own reactions rather than the child's.

In their understanding of the interpersonal relations between their first-born and his other parent, the Arnolds are even more typical. Mr. Arnold found it impossible to characterize Bruce's relation with his wife except in terms of his own reaction to that relation. Although he mentioned the mother-child relation several times in the course of his interviews, each time it is to make the same point: Mrs. Arnold is too absorbed in her mother role to be able to give sufficient time to her husband. He said, "I felt some resentment toward my wife's absorption in the baby when I returned from the war . . . I remember commenting, 'Now why is it, we two adults sit around here and let the infant take up all our time?' We used to watch him—admire him, I guess. We were very ardent fans; it was a little ridiculous." Beyond repeated expressions of concern over his wife's preoccupation with their children, Mr. Arnold did not discuss the mother-child relation.

Mrs. Arnold was more detailed in her discussion of her spouse's relationship with their first-born, and could see it somewhat apart from her own role in it. She asserted that father-separation had had little effect on Bruce, "because Bruce was never without a man who was head of the house. It wasn't as though I had him someplace where there were just women or just me, and it wasn't as though he was living with a grandfather who couldn't abide the children's noise or to whom he had to show deference. Actually, the whole house ran around Bruce." Discussing the period after Mr. Arnold's return, she said, "My husband had never been around a small child before, and I think he was somewhat frightened about it. But he wouldn't let anybody know, and he took care of Bruce in a very nonchalant way." Mrs. Arnold felt that currently her husband sympathized with their second son more than with Bruce, but "he's realized that too, and has tried to make an effort to equalize it."

Summary

In the typical war-separated family, both parents agree that the mother feels closer to their first-born child than to their second-born, and that, complementally, the first-born child feels closer to her than he feels to his father who was absent during the first period of his life and whose return created such a stressful period of family life. Both parents also agree that the father feels closer to the child who was born after his return. Husband and wife both report that the father's early discipline of the first-born was quite severe, and although the mother, presumably out of loyalty to her marriage partner, tends to minimize the severity of this discipline, it is the mother who shows greater insight into this disciplinary relationship. The parents concur that the relations between their first-born and his father are quite difficult. Both parents show only fair insight (median rating of 3) into their own relations with their first-born. Since this is the only area in which the mothers do not show significantly greater insight than the fathers, there is some suggestion that the five hours of interviews focused on father-child relations helped the fathers achieve greater understanding of this topic. In the typical war-separated family, however, the mother does show more insight into her spouse's relation with their first-born than he shows into her relation with that child.

General Summary and Interpretation

In Chapter 4, the attitudes of war-separated fathers toward their first-born children were compared with the attitudes of non-separated fathers toward their first-borns. In that substudy, the factor of fatherhood was kept constant, and war-separation was the factor which was studied for its effects. Necessarily, the two groups of fathers were discussing different children. In this chapter, the attitudes of the war-separated fathers toward their first-borns were compared with those of their wives toward the same children. This approach reveals the effects of war-separation from a different perspective. Since the children being discussed are the same for both groups (mothers and fathers), group differences cannot be attributed to the effects of different stimuli. On the other hand, since fathers and mothers, both in their parent roles and in their general sex and other social roles, are subjected to many differentiating experiences besides the experience of war-necessitated separation during the first year of their children's lives, all of the differences found in this chapter cannot confidently be ascribed to war-separation. The lack of an adequate control group precludes our distinguishing those husband-wife differences which resulted from war-separation and those differences which resulted from other disparities of experience and background.

War-separated husbands and wives both described their first-borns as having fairly severe developmental problems. The mothers presented their first-borns' problems as significantly more severe only in those areas about which the fathers revealed little interest.

The war-separated fathers tended to be more worried by their children's developmental problems than were non-separated fathers, but they tended to be less worried than their own wives. War-separated fathers tended to be more annoyed with their first-borns' behavior than were their wives, just as they were more annoyed than the non-separated fathers.

In every area rated except that of the parent's own relations with his first-born, the war-separated mothers showed significantly more insight into their children's behavior (as judged by a psychologist who knew the children) than was shown by the fathers. Presumably this difference is an effect of the exceptionally close mother-child bonds (which both parents report as existing in these families) as well as of the higher social expectancies leveled on mothers as compared with fathers.

The war-separated fathers reported much more severe discipline and much more difficulty between them and their first-born children than were reported by the non-separated fathers. Their wives do not disagree: they also report severe paternal discipline and problems in father-child relations. Their tendency to protect their husbands (by sometimes concealing or minimizing the severity of the disciplinary measures which the fathers themselves reported using) did not prevent their describing father-child relations of at least as much seriousness as those reported by the fathers themselves.

In general, the findings of this chapter confirm our belief that separations necessitated by war created an unusually close bond between the mothers left behind and their children born during the separation, but also induced difficulties between the fathers and the children after the latter returned from war, which difficulties enhanced the closeness of the mother-child bond and kept the father relatively distant from his first-born child.

PART III. OBSERVATION OF CHILDREN IN GROUP SITUATIONS

CHAPTER 9.
BEHAVIOR OF WAR-SEPARATED CHILDREN IN GROUP SITUATIONS

by Nancy Guy Stevenson, Leonard Ullman,
and Lois Meek Stolz

Description of the Study

Purpose

It was predicted in the original hypotheses presented in Chapter 1 that children whose fathers had been at war during the first year of the children's lives would behave differently from children whose fathers had not been separated from the family. This study was undertaken to determine whether there were differences in the behavior of the children in group situations such as nursery school, kindergarten, or primary grades.

The task of studying children in a group situation necessitated (a) the collection of observations, (b) the development of a method of analysis of these observations, (c) statistical comparison of the two groups of children, and (d) individual studies of war-separated and non-separated children.

The Use of Observational Records in Research

Throughout the history of psychological research with children, records of direct observation of children have been one of the most frequent techniques used for collecting data. Observation of behavior in group situations is a valuable source of information for the verification and supplementation of material obtained from interviews and experimental studies. Observations contain considerable information which can be acquired from no other source, including the range and type of activity, the quality of behavior, and the meaning of activity for the individual. The problem in the use of observational material has been to find a suitable method of analysis of the rich and often extensive information available.

Records with situation controlled. Following the early biographical records made by such workers as Preyer (64), Darwin (15), and Shinn (72), in the first 25 years of this century there was a trend toward making studies of children more scientific by presenting children with selected stimuli under controlled conditions. The method had its origin in psychological studies in animal laboratories. Children were studied in a controlled laboratory situation, with emphasis on observation of specific mental and motor responses.

Diary records. As psychologists began to be interested in social behavior, the conditions of the laboratory were no longer suitable for their studies. The aim was to see child behavior in natural, not contrived, situations. In response to the need for techniques for studying social behavior, Andrus (4) in 1928 developed a method known as the "diary" method. Under this method observers went into the classroom and recorded everything a child did during an entire morning.

Records with observer controlled. In order to make observations in natural situations more scientific and systematized, techniques of observation were developed around 1930 in which workers observed limited aspects of behavior in specific time periods according to well-defined directions. The requirement of reliability of the resulting observations, in terms of agreement between observers, was the guiding principle used in the construction of observer techniques. Such observations, using "time-sampling" or "repeated short sample" techniques, yielded reliable frequency counts of behavior traits. Olson (60) and Goodenough (35) at Minnesota and Thomas (80) at Columbia were largely responsible for work of this type.

These methods actually were as restrictive and atomistic as laboratory research. The selection of predetermined categories of behavior to be analyzed modified the picture of actual behavior as much as did the manipulation of the situation. Important aspects of behavior were obscured by artificial restraints of methodology (45).

Uncontrolled observations of specific behavior. Since these methods had been only slightly successful in increasing the understanding of human behavior, a new approach began to be made after the early 1930's. Research workers used the diary type of records, but had a particular purpose or emphasis in mind as they observed. The situations were natural, and the observers were ordinarily limited only to recording certain broad areas of behavior, such as social contacts with other children. Analysis was usually based on a frequency count of the behavior being studied, but items of behavior were judged in their context. Examples of such studies were those of Jersild and Markey on conflict behavior (44) and of Murphy on sympathy (58).

In summarizing the contributions of studies using uncontrolled observations, we see a methodological progression among them. In the Jersild and Markey study on conflict behavior, each act was judged according to its context, rather than by its inclusion in a predetermined category as had been done in the past, but observers used only objective terminology in describing the situations. In Murphy's study, observers were less restricted in the description of behavior, and the findings about sympathy were related to a variety of other behavior.

Methods of Observation in This Study

Observational technique. The observations used in this study were fluid, running accounts of the behavior of a child in the group situation. There were no controls on the observer either through time sampling or predetermined categories for checking. Each observer was asked to record as much of the behavior of the child as possible. A general outline was prepared to guide the observers to various areas of behavior considered significant in revealing personality (see Appendix 8). Sample records were discussed each week in seminar. Emphasis was placed upon the how of behavior and upon the subtle indications of feeling tone as seen in facial expression, tone of voice, muscular tension. Observers were advised to use adjectives, adverbs, and descriptive verbs in order to give a picture of the affect of behavior. They were encouraged to make comments at the end of each observation which might help in the interpretation of the meaning of the recorded behavior. Periodic summaries and interpretations of the behavior of the individual child were required (20a).

There is no doubt that the quality of the observations varied because of the difference among the various observers in perceptiveness, understanding of children, skill in recording, and insight in interpreting. However, the fact that on the average two observers recorded the behavior of each child helped to correct errors due to perceptual bias, lack of skill, or differences in interpretive insight. On the basis of our experience in this study, Stevenson (74) has made recommendations for observational techniques which would, perhaps, improve the quality of the observations.

Locale. The observations of children in this study were made in three different situations. Most of the observations were made in the Stanford Village Nursery School described in Chapter 2. The general philosophy of this school is child-centered. Its guidance permits children to reveal their feelings and develop new levels of adequacy in group situations. The older children were observed in the kindergarten, first grade, or second grade of a nearby public elementary school, and the kindergartens of two private schools.

The classrooms of these older children were more structured, with less freedom for spontaneous social interaction than the nursery school offers. We, therefore, organized a Monday Club for the older children. It met weekly for an hour and a quarter in the nursery school quarters and provided a child-centered, permissive environment for a variety of play activities. The total observations in nursery school and Monday Club for the war-separated group equal the observations in the nursery school for the non-separated group. Table 84 shows the percentage of observations in each of these situations.

Table 84. Locale of Observations

	Percentage of Observations	
	War-Separated	Non-Separated
Nursery school	46.0	64.7
Kindergarten	27.4	23.5
First and second grade	8.1	11.8
Monday Club	18.5	—

Observers. The observations were made by trained research workers and by students in child observation courses at Stanford. The latter were selected seniors or graduate students in psychology who had had at least one previous course which included training in observing children. There were an average of 2.6 observers per war-separated child and 1.4 workers per non-separated child. In addition there were supplementary single observations or observations cross-referenced from another child in most of the individual folders of observations.

Extent of observations. The total length of time covered by the observations varied among our subjects. Observations were begun as soon as a family was accepted in the father-child relations study, and were continued as long as the child was available. This meant that a child in a family that was accepted early was studied over a longer span of time than one in a family which came into the study later. In collecting observations of the war-separated children and most of the non-separated children, we required a minimum of 20 hours of observation and/or 50 single-spaced typewritten pages. After the method of analysis was developed, it was found that a well-trained observer could collect adequate data in less time.

Development of a Method of Analysis of Observations

The observations of a child in a group situation may be examined from two different points of view. First, they may be an objective check of what the child actually does— a descriptive record of the child's behavior in a relatively permissive situation. They offer a view of the child in action, of the person he is in a wide range of interpersonal experiences. Second, they may be considered as projective material. The group situation may be regarded as a relatively unstructured stimulus situation, from which each child is free to select those people and objects and play situations he wishes to use in whatever way he needs. A dynamic analysis of the particular people and situations a child typically seeks and the typical way in which he uses them should yield information regarding his basic needs and attitudes, by which the descriptive, objective material may be interpreted.

The conviction underlying our approach was that the examination of observations would yield most fruitful results if a child's behavior recorded in the observations was viewed as a projection of his personality as he explored, adjusted to, and utilized his life space. Behavior contained in observations in group situations becomes most meaningful, therefore, when studied in relation to the child's other behavior and to his life history. Any specific episode of behavior in an observational record can be understood best in the context of the situation and in relation to its idiomatic meaning for the individual child.

Problems involved. Our most difficult task was the development of a method for the analysis of the observational records which would preserve the integrity of the data for the individual child and also permit the use of statistical tools for comparison of war-separated and non-separated groups.

Often the data collected in observations have been treated either holistically or segmentally. The former approach preserves the dynamics of the child's behavior but is harder to quantify. The latter approach is amenable to statistical treatment, but at the cost of losing much of the uniqueness of the child. We have strived for a method which would be holistic and yet be amenable to quantification. Results from this method may be used for individual analysis, and also for group comparisons.

We also wished to avoid the pitfalls inherent in establishing a priori categories for analysis. We aimed to use all the material in the records as far as possible to determine the classifications for behavior analysis.

The method of analysis devised for this study with specific directions for its use will be found in Stevenson (74). Our discussion here gives only a general description.

Division of material into behavior units. In order to make use of all the important material contained in observational records, we had to develop a means of division of the records into objective, consistently defined units which could be classified and rated. The desire was to obtain units which were psychologically, rather than physically or temporally, determined. The unit selected was called a "behavior unit." It was defined as that portion of behavior which contains: (a) an event (external or internal activity) which is psychologically different from events preceding and following; and (b) the subject's behavior in relation to the event, which is psychologically different from preceding and subsequent behavior.

The psychological difference in events may result when the situation itself does not change but the behavior accompanying it does change; conversely, the psychological difference in behavior may consist of continued or unchanging behavior in the face of a changed situation. Thus, any change in the relation between events and the subject's behavior constitutes the beginning of a new behavior unit. By this definition of a behavior unit the continuity of behavior as seen in the records is preserved.

In dividing a record into behavior units, we looked for the elements of a behavior unit— an event, psychologically different from preceding or subsequent events, and the subject's related behavior, psychologically different from preceding or subsequent behavior. We listed the event in one column opposite the column in which the related behavior was reported. These columns were called the "situation" and the "behavior," respectively, and these determined the limits of each behavior unit. The "situation" column included a description of existing conditions and a statement of the event which began the behavior unit. The "behavior" column described the subject's behavior in relation to the existing situation and event. Listing the behavior in this way insured that it was considered in context with its accompanying environment. It permitted a later classification and rating of each unit which was based on all the information about the subject contained in the record.

Development of categories for variables. It was necessary to establish categories of behavior by which all the obtained units could be classified. These categories, herein called "variables," had to have a quantity of material to describe them in the observational records of all children, had to provide material that was especially significant in the understanding of the total personality of any child, and had to be comprehensive enough to include the important data found in the observations of all children. By consulting the records of many children, we found nine variables which accomplished these objectives. A complete definition of the variables will be found in Stevenson (74).

Six of the variables relate to the child's behavior with other children in the group. They may be described briefly as follows:

Social Participation: This variable includes all behavior units which show some level of activity on the part of the subject in relation to other children, in all situations where social intercourse is possible, where it is not discouraged by adult rules and prohibitions, and where some choice as to the degree of social participation is made by the subject.

Dominance: This variable includes all behavior units in which the subject shows some level of dominant or submissive behavior with another child in either a leadership or conflict situation.

Initiation of Agression: This variable includes all behavior units in which the subject makes some verbal or physical attack against a non-aggressing child, either within or outside of a conflict situation, in order to injure or punish the child, to control the other child, to arouse attention, or to vent feelings of force by impinging on the feelings of others.

Response to Aggression: This variable includes behavior units in which the subject is attacked by another child, either within or outside of a conflict situation, where the other child's purpose is to injure and punish, or to gain attention, to control the subject, or to vent feelings of force by impinging on the subject's feelings.

Friendliness: This variable includes those behavior units in which the subject expresses a desire to establish pleasant or unpleasant feeling in a relation with another child.

Sympathy: This variable includes behavior units in which the subject responds to another child who is in need or in distress or solicits help.

Three of the variables relate to the child's behavior with adults in the situation. They may be defined briefly as follows:

Child-Initiated Contacts with Adults: This variable includes behavior units wherein the subject initiates contacts with adults, shows interest in adults or makes an approach to adults.

Response to Adult-Initiated Contacts: This variable includes behavior units wherein an adult initiates contacts (other than adult imposition of authority), either directly with the subject or with his group.

Response to Adult Authority: This variable includes behavior units where an adult gives a command or direction to a group or individual, and where adult authority is being exercised indirectly through rules, routines, or generally accepted modes of behavior.

Development of levels within categories. Within the variables, different levels of behavior occurred. Definitions of the levels were empirically derived by studying all the units classified under each of the variables. Under six of the variables, five levels of behavior were found; under three, fewer than five levels seemed indicated. A definition of the sub-categories or levels is given in Stevenson (74). Examples from observational records of each level within each category will be found in Appendix 9. The levels may be described briefly as follows:

Social Participation:

1. Initiative: behavior in which a child makes a new contact or starts an interaction with a child or group where none previously existed.
2. Associative: behavior in which the child has sustained interaction with another child or group.
3. Parallel: behavior in which a child participates in the same activity as another child or group, but does not interact actively.
4. Onlooker: behavior in which a child watches the activity of another

child or group as an outsider without participating, or is with another child or group having unrelated activity.

5. Isolate: behavior in which a child plays alone although there is the possibility of choice of interacting on any of the above levels with another child or group.

Dominance:

1. Dominant: behavior in which the child forcefully directs another child, tries to control another child, and actively resists the dominance of another child.

2. Suitably Dominant: behavior in which a child makes suggestions expecting the co-operation of another child, and offers resistance to another child's dominance which is between equivocation and active resistance.

3. Noninvolved: behavior in which the child puts leadership on a situation-oriented basis or shows neither acquiescence nor resistance. The child's approach to a dominance-submission situation is a solution without status definition or involvement.

4. Acquiescent: behavior in which a child is ready to follow the lead of another child, but does not seek his leadership, and offers only slight resistance in a conflict situation.

5. Submissive: behavior in which a child eagerly follows another child's lead or demand, and offers no resistance in a conflict situation.

Initiation of Aggression:

1. Direct, Active: behavior in which the child aggresses against another child physically, with intent to hurt or punish.

2. Indirect, Active: behavior in which the child aggresses against another child by chasing, blocking, insulting verbally, or damaging that child's property with intent to annoy or punish.

3. Direct, Inactive: behavior in which the child's attack against another child is playful or with veiled intent, such as mock hitting, joking threats, teasing.

4. Indirect, Inactive: behavior in which the child tells on another or attacks another child to exclude him from his play.

5. Dependent, Mild: behavior in which the child expresses aggression against objects, asks other children to fight for him, talks about aggression, starts but does not go through with aggression, or joins aggression of others against another child.

Response to Aggression:

1. Resistant: behavior in which a child defends himself adequately, showing force which is at least equal to that of the attacker.

2. Mildly Resistant: behavior in which a child makes some attempt at resistance, such as name calling, chasing, but not in full measure and with some hesitation.

3. Indifferent: behavior in which a child responds to aggression by ignoring it, treating it playfully, or not considering it aggression.

4. Dependent, Indirect: behavior in which a child responds to aggression by making his needs known, but in which he hesitates and does not defend himself directly.

5. Nonresistant: behavior in which a child responds to aggression by

giving in to an aggressor, crying without making his needs known, or withdrawing without any resistance.

Friendliness:

1. Spontaneous, Uninhibited: behavior in which a child makes a free, warm expression of a desire to be pleasant and closely related to another child.

2. Restrained or Wishful: behavior in which a child expresses a pleasant feeling tone toward another child shyly, indirectly, with hesitation, or without a follow-through.

3. Indifferent: behavior in which a child is indifferent to another child's affective overture and/or is indifferent to possible relations with another child.

4. Discouraging: behavior in which a child is unfriendly toward another child without trying to alienate him, showing such behavior as excluding another child from play, criticizing him, and/or leaving play at the entrance of a new child.

5. Hostile: behavior in which a child wishes to punish and/or alienate another child and overtly makes his hostile feelings known.

Sympathy:

1. Sympathetic: behavior in which a child is interested and thoughtful of other children, recognizes their needs, and/or spontaneously gives them help.

2. Non-Sympathetic: behavior in which a child shows no interest in or kindness to a child who is in distress and/or laughs or teases a child in distress.

Child-Initiated Contacts with Adults:

1. Positive: behavior in which a child shows friendly interest in adults, starts conversations, shows off, and/or smiles.

2. Dependent: behavior in which a child appeals to an adult for help, reassurance, and permission, and/or stays near an adult when afraid of other children.

3. Demanding or Controlling: behavior in which the child's primary object is to control rather than to gain something for himself.

4. Negative: behavior in which a child is unpleasant or indifferent when a pleasant adult contact is easily possible.

Response to Adult-Initiated Contacts:

1. Positive: behavior in which a child responds pleasantly to an adult initiation by smiling or by being attentive in groups, or accepts willingly adult suggestions.

2. Indifferent: behavior in which a child responds to adult initiation without interest or enthusiasm, or in a way which is not indicated by the adult but which is not negative.

3. Negative: behavior in which a child refuses to co-operate and/or resists adult suggestions and/or makes unfavorable comments to an adult initiation.

Response to Adult Authority:

1. Dependent or Compulsive: behavior in which a child obeys direct and indirect adult dicta with compulsive and fearful rapidity.

2. Obedient: behavior in which a child obeys adults from a sense of co-operation or convenience rather than a wish to conform.

3. Indifferent: behavior in which a child shows indifference to the influence of adult authority and delays response seemingly without obedience or disobedience in mind.

4. Disobedient: behavior in which a child covertly tries to outwit and indirectly disobey adult authority.

5. Defiant: behavior in which a child openly disobeys adult directions and shows himself conscious and resentful of adult authority.

Application of the Method of Analysis

Procedure for analyzing observations. Before analysis of the observational records of any child was begun, the entire series of records for the subject was read. This was done to gain some knowledge of the child, so that the analysis would be more accurate. After the records were read, they were divided into behavior units, according to the method described previously. In Appendix 9 we have included a sample observation divided into behavior units.

After the behavior units had been obtained, each unit was classified under one or more of the nine variables selected. Each judgment was made on the basis of the meaning of the behavior for the individual child. The subject's motivation, insofar as it could be determined, was the basis for the classification of a unit.

Following the classification of units into variables, all the units in each variable were rated according to the levels listed within the variable. As in the judgment of what variables a behavior unit represented, the desire was to rate the unit according to the meaning it had for the particular child. The entire context of the unit as well as the child's personality, as it was known to the rater from reading the observations, were considered in rating any behavior unit according to its level within the variable.

Number of behavior units. The number of behavior units used in the analysis varied from 231 to 1,054. The first four cases analyzed had 657, 668, 883, and 1,054 behavior units respectively. A test was made of one case comparing the results of analysis of 500 behavior units with the results of analysis of 600 behavior units. In terms of percentages of units in each variable, based on the total behavior units or on subtotals, and in terms of percentages of units in each level of each total variable, differences between the two analyses were extremely small. The average difference between the two analyses in percentage points was 1.8. We assumed that as statistically accurate a picture of the child was obtained from the use of 500 as of 600 behavior units.

Only four cases had fewer than 500 behavior units. In those protocols which had either fewer or more than 500 behavior units, all scores were prorated to a base of 500 behavior units. If a child had 400 behavior units, for instance, in his protocol, each score in the 39 levels was multiplied by 1.25. Protocols were prorated and allowed in this sample only if they were judged to have given a fair and adequate picture of the child in the group situation.

After the initial four cases had been analyzed, in the war-separated group the first 500 units in a protocol were used. In the non-separated cases analysis was begun at the matched age and continued consecutively for 500 behavior units.

Reliability of the Method of Analysis

The method developed includes three processes which may be tested for reliability: the division of the observational records into behavior units; the classification of each behavior unit into one or more categories; and the rating of the unit within each category. The reliability was checked for each of these three steps two times.[1] The analysis of S (N. Stevenson) was compared first with the analysis of R (J. Ryder) and second with the analysis of U (L. Ullmann).

Reliability of the division of the protocol into behavior units was determined by the method of complete agreement. The major source of error between S and R was in either worker's classifying together two of the other worker's units; between S and U error lay in the placement of transitions from one unit to another. Errors of this type do not affect the score of an individual child since by the method elements may be rated exactly the same by two raters even though organized within different behavior units. Here the primary source of reliabili ty lies in the categorization classification and level ratings.

The reliability of the process of categorization was checked between S and R on the basis of their agreement of judgments whether each of 154 behavior units was or was not present in each of the nine variables. Agreement ranged from 86 percent to 99 percent, but a high agreement would have been expected by chance.

The categorization check between S and U was one of complete agreement, all nine categories being used at once. This was done to reduce the effect of chance agreement possible in the previous method. There was 80 percent complete agreement between S and U on 360 categorizations.

Once a unit of behavior has been put into a category, it must be rated. S had selected the variable friendliness as that variable which was most difficult for her to rate. S and R found a contingency correlation of greater than .95 between their ratings on this scale. S and U were working with a protocol which had only 11 units in the category and, therefore, too few to use contingency correlation. A product moment correlation yielded a .90 correlation in spite of the severe attenuation involved. No rating between the two disagreed more than one scale point.

In the light of these results, we considered that the method was reliable enough to be used in our study.

Summary and Evaluation of Method of Analysis

Advantages of the method. It was found possible to develop a method of analyzing observations which could be used both for statistical evaluations of group differences and for developing holistically a picture of a child's behavior in a group situation.

The method divides data into units of behavior that may be classified and rated for statistical analysis. The units provide a basis for analyzing various aspects of a child's behavior in relation to his whole pattern of behavior.

---

1. Complete analysis of the reliability will be found in Stevenson (74) and Ullmann (82).

An accurate and somewhat penetrating analysis of the records was possible by the flexible criteria for rating units which permitted the grouping together of behavior which was psychologically equivalent though behaviorally dissimilar from one child to another.

The method was found to categorize, without straining definitions, most of the behavior in our protocols; it was, we believe, inclusive. This is an asset because it is possible to interpret any one aspect of behavior in relation to the whole. The importance of this is well illustrated in the individual profile analysis presented in the case study of Ned Ford (Chapter 14).

Suggested improvements. In developing the method, we have come to feel that we have but taken the first step. Improvements which can and should be made are:

1. Certain aspects of behavior which were included in the descriptive case studies made by Stevenson (74) and used in Chapter 14 could not be analyzed statistically by our method. Further work will be needed so that such areas as evidences of tension, locomotor behavior, and language can be included in the statistical analysis.

2. Further analysis should be made of the levels within the categories. Several of our level boxes might very well be scales in themselves, so that we could quantify differences in such aspects of behavior as sympathy, solitary play, or covert disobedience. In some categories, such as child initiation of contacts with adults and adult initiation of contacts with child, additional levels suggested by Stevenson (74) would help in further differentiation of behavior.

3. Intensity of feeling associated with types of behavior should be more directly taken into account by the system. This is especially true of the scales for aggression, dominance, friendliness, and child initiation to adults. Aggression which is mild in spirit should be quantified, just as we have quantified aggression which is mild in activity. For instance, name calling through clenched teeth should be differentiated from name calling which is louder but less hostile.

4. We have found a number of patterns which we feel to be particularly revealing and worth further work. Such patterns are: above-average initiation and below-average association in social participation as revealing non-acceptance of other children; below-average frequency of aggressive acts combined with above-average frequency of aggressive acts with unfriendly connotations as revealing repressed hostility; and above-average frequencies in both compulsive obedience and defiance of adult authority as indicative of conflict as to acceptance of adult authority. The possibility of profitable investigation of such patterns is further discussed in Ullmann (82).

5. Our method of classification into categories was empirical rather than a priori. Now that the first step has been accomplished, a reordering of levels along more theoretical lines seems feasible, especially if it is done with data from a cluster analysis of categorization and level rating.

6. The observations we used were not made with this particular form of analysis in mind. This eliminated the tendency of observer to describe children to fit our method. In the 34 protocols we can assume randomized observer biases. It would probably help to train observers in the psycho-

logical meaning of the behavior units in order that records consistently would include a description of changes in the environment as well as in the child's behavior.

Description of the Subjects

There were 34 children in this study. The 17 experimental children were first-borns whose fathers (discussed in Part I) were at war during at least the first year of their lives, the 17 control children were first-borns whose fathers had not been separated from the family. The children were from families of the same socioeconomic class and were similar in age and sex. There were 11 boys and 6 girls in each group.

Table 85. Age and IQ of Children

	War-Separated		Non-Separated	
	Range	Average	Range	Average
Age 1st observation (mos.)	39- 84	58.6	40- 93	57.3
Age last observation (mos.)	51- 88	64.4	41- 94	59.6
IQ	93-138	120	100-156	123

As can be seen in Table 85 the war-separated and non-separated groups had about the same average age at the beginning of the observations but the war-separated group was 4.8 months older at the last observation. This was due to the fact that the observations of the non-separated group were somewhat more concentrated in time than those of the war-separated group. Comparison of IQ's was limited to 13 non-separated children. The IQ's of the two groups were quite similar but the range was greater in the non-separated group due to one child's high score. More complete data about the children are given in Appendix 1.

Comparison of War-Separated and Non-Separated Groups

Purpose of the Comparison of Groups

The purpose of this study was to determine the differences in behavior of the war-separated and non-separated children. We set ourselves the task of finding in what specific types of behavior there were differences, how great these differences were, and in what aspects of behavior the two groups were similar.

This information was of value in a number of ways: in defining differences of child behavior in group situations which were correlated with father absence and/or presence; in supplementing the picture of the children obtained from parent interviews and projective data; and finally, in the study of individual cases. We expected that the war-separated children would appear more maladjusted than the non-separated children; that the war-separated children would have more needs which were suppressed or in conflict than the non-separated children because of the extra stress of the adjustment to the returning fathers. As a result of this we expected that the war-separated group would be less able to establish and maintain warm interpersonal contacts with other children and adults, since needs outside the situation would enter into their behavior and distort it. Their behavior would to a greater extent be determined not by the objective situation, but by individual needs, and these being greater, greater distortion of perception would cause greater maladjustment. Another way of saying this is that the added stress of the adjustment to the returning father would cause a distortion of perception which would make the learning of healthy and effective modes of social approach more difficult. This difficulty we expected to be reflected in the war-separated children by more dominant, aggressive, and unfriendly behavior with other children. With adults, we expected the war-separated children to be more tense, role-structuring, and negative.

Method of Group Comparison

The two groups were compared on the basis of the mean number of behavior units in each category and in each level of behavior. The number of behavior units for each was adjusted to a basic total of 500. The significance of the difference between the means was determined by the small sample technique for testing the difference between uncorrelated means (54).

Differences Between the Groups in General Categories of Behavior

There were no differences between the means of the groups significant at the .05 level in the frequency of behavior of children in any of the nine major categories. This fact is important because it indicates that differences between the means of the two groups in specific levels are not due to an over-all difference of the frequencies of the two groups in respect to the category.

From Table 86 below it can be seen that the means of the two groups do not differ significantly in the average number of times the children acted in any of the nine areas. The major finding in this analysis is that the large segments of behavior we have investigated are part of the social repertoire

Table 86. Differences Between Groups in Frequencies of Behavior in Categories

Category	Mean		t	Significance
	War-Separated	Non-Separated		
Social participation	329.9	334.9	.13	–
Dominance	55.6	55.2	.01	–
Initiation of aggression	25.6	27.9	.12	–
Response to aggression	20.0	8.8	1.64	–
Friendliness	46.3	41.1	.19	–
Sympathy	9.8	7.4	.07	–
Initiation to adults	111.6	113.6	.03	–
Response to adult initiation	67.3	79.9	.51	–
Response to adult authority	53.1	35.4	.90	–

and life of all children, and frequency of behavior in them seems to be a normal aspect of the child's social life, while specific types of expression may, and do, differ significantly within these areas.

Social Participation

This category includes all units of behavior in which a child shows some level of social participation with other children, where such behavior is not discouraged by adult rules. Table 87 shows the frequencies of the two groups with respect to this category. In this table and those that follow we have indicated our predictions regarding the differences between the war-separated and non-separated groups. These are discussed in detail by Ullmann (82).

Table 87. Difference Between the Groups in Social Participation

Level	Mean		t	Predicted	Significance
	War-Separated	Non-Separated			
All Social Participation	329.9	334.9	.13		—
1. Initiative	74.8	33.1	4.34	a	$P < .001$
2. Associative	79.3	136.0	3.95	a	$P < .001$
3. Parallel	74.5	58.4	1.75		—
4. Onlooker	47.2	41.0	1.19	a	—
5. Isolate	54.1	66.4	.41	b	—
4 & 5. Out-groups	101.3	107.4	.27	b	—

a. Prediction accepted.
b. Prediction rejected.

Category as a whole. The two groups are similar in the average number of times they behave in social participation. While the war-separated group has approximately equal frequencies in the initiative, associative, and parallel levels, the non-separated children behave predominantly in an associative manner.

Levels of behavior. The war-separated group's average frequency of initiating social contacts is significantly greater than that of the non-separated group, while the non-separated group's frequency of associative contacts is significantly greater than that of the war-separated group. The war-separated are more frequently "fringers," parallel participants, and onlookers, while the non-separated somewhat more frequently play alone, although these differences are not statistically significant. The two groups are similar in their frequency in the out-group combination of levels, but the war-separated are more frequently onlookers, the non-separated more frequently isolates.

Dominance

This category includes units of behavior in which a child shows some kind of dominant or submissive behavior with another child. Table 88 shows the frequencies of the two groups with respect to behavior in this area.

Table 88. Difference Between the Groups in Dominance

Level	Mean: War-Separated	Mean: Non-Separated	t	Predicted	Significance
All Dominance	55.6	55.2	.01	a	—
1. Dominant	27.2	14.9	2.67		P<.02
2. Suitably dominant	9.6	13.5	1.39		—
3. Noninvolved	5.6	5.9	.17		—
4. Acquiescent	7.4	13.0	2.67		P<.02
5. Submissive	5.8	7.9	1.50		—
1 & 5. Extreme	33.0	22.8	1.82	a	P<.05
2 & 4. Syncretic	17.0	26.5	1.98	a	P<.05

a. Prediction accepted.

Category as a whole. The two groups are practically equal in their frequency in dominance-submission relations with other children. Half the war-separated group's behavior in this category is of the dominant kind, while the non-separated group is similar in its frequency of dominant, suitably dominant, and acquiescent behavior.

Levels of behavior. The war-separated group is dominant significantly more frequently than the non-separated group. The non-separated group is acquiescent significantly more frequently than the war-separated group. The combination of suitably dominant and acquiescent behavior we have called "syncretic behavior," on the suggestion of Dr. Luckert of Munich. This behavior is of a nonextreme, give-and-take kind. The non-separated group behaves in this way more frequently than the war-separated group. The war-separated group is extremely dominant or submissive significantly more frequently, but this difference is due to a preponderant frequency of dominant behavior, the non-separated group having a greater (but not significantly greater) frequency in submissive behavior.

Initiation of Aggression

This category includes all units of behavior in which a child makes a verbal or physical attack against another, nonaggressing child. Table 89 shows the frequencies of the two groups with respect to this category.

Category as a whole. The two groups are similar in the frequency with which they initiate aggression. The war-separated group's most frequent forms of initiating aggression are indirect: indirect active and direct inactive, while the most frequent forms of initiating aggression for the non-separated group are indirect active and mild.

Levels of behavior. The non-separated group aggresses mildly significantly more frequently than the war-separated group. Other differences

Table 89. Difference Between the Two Groups in Initiation of Aggression

Level	Mean		t	Predicted	Significance
	War-Separated	Non-Separated			
All Initiation of Aggression	25.6	27.9	.12		—
1. Direct, active	2.1	4.1	1.50	b	—
2. Indirect, active	8.7	7.6	.48		—
3. Direct, inactive	8.8	5.5	1.21	b	—
4. Indirect, inactive	2.5	1.8	.88		—
5. Dependent, mild	3.5	8.9	2.52	b	$P < .02$
Hostile aggression	4.5	1.7	1.87	a	$P < .05$

a. Prediction accepted.
b. Prediction rejected.

between average frequencies in the levels are not statistically significant: the war-separated are slightly more frequent in indirect active, direct inactive, and indirect inactive forms on initiating aggression. The non-separated are slightly more frequent in direct active initiation of aggression.

To investigate further the affect related to overt aggression we counted all the behavior units which were rated as aggressive and also rated as unfriendly (4 and 5) in the friendliness category. On the basis of this analysis we conclude that the war-separated group has more units of aggression which have an unfriendly connotation than the non-separated group. This difference is statistically significant (see hostile aggression in Table 89).

Response to Aggression

This category includes those units of behavior in which a child is aggressed against by another child. Table 90 shows the frequencies of the two groups with respect to behavior in this area.

Table 90. Differences Between the Two Groups in Response to Aggression

Level	Mean		t	Predicted	Significance
	War-Separated	Non-Separated			
All Response to Aggression	20.0	8.8	1.64		—
1. Resistant	2.6	1.9	.78		—
2. Mildly resistant	3.6	1.1	3.13		$P < .01$
3. Indifferent	3.2	2.1	1.31	b	—
4. Dependent, indirect	5.4	2.2	3.56		$P < .01$
5. Nonresistant	5.2	1.5	4.07	a	$P < .001$

a. Prediction accepted.
b. Prediction rejected.

Category as a whole. The difference between the two groups in the frequency with which they are aggressed against, although not statistically significant, does suggest that the war-separated children are more often the target for aggressions than the non-separated. Differences in the way the two groups handle aggression may explain why. The war-separated group has a greater frequency than the non-separated group in all levels, and its most typical response to aggression is nonresistant and dependent, indirect resistant.

Levels of behavior. The more passive the type of response to aggression, the more frequently do the war-separated children adopt that response. There are no significant differences between the two groups in the frequency with which their response is resistant or indifferent. However, the difference between the groups becomes increasingly great as the response to aggression gets milder: the mean of the war-separated group is significantly larger in mildly resistant, indirectly resistant, and, finally, nonresistant behavior.

Friendliness

This category includes behavior units in which a child expresses a wish to establish pleasant or unpleasant relations with another child. Table 91 shows the frequencies of the two groups with respect to behavior in this category.

Category as a whole. The two groups are similar in the frequency with which they express affect in their interpersonal relations. The most frequent response for both groups is found in the levels of spontaneous and restrained friendliness which include about 75 percent of all acts in the category friendliness in both groups.

Levels of behavior. The war-separated group is hostile toward other children significantly more often than the non-separated group, while the non-separated group is more often (not statistically significant) discouraging of friendship. The war-separated group is spontaneously friendly, re-

Table 91. Differences Between the Groups in Friendliness

Level	Mean		t	Predicted	Significance
	War-Separated	Non-Separated			
All Friendliness	46.3	41.1	.19	b	—
1. Spontaneous	13.7	12.6	.32	b	—
2. Restrained	18.4	16.9	.33		—
3. Indifferent	4.9	3.2	.89		—
4. Discouraging	4.9	6.5	1.00		—
5. Hostile	4.4	1.9	1.79	a	$P < .05$
4 & 5. Negative	9.3	8.4	.37	a	—

a. Prediction accepted.
b. Prediction rejected.

strained, and indifferent more frequently than the non-separated group, but these differences are not statistically significant. Because the war-separated group is more frequently hostile and the non-separated group more discouraging in expressions of unfriendliness, the frequency difference between the groups at the combination of levels we call negative is not statistically significant.

Sympathy

This category includes behavior units in which the subject shows some response to a child who is in need of help. Table 92 shows the frequencies of the two groups with respect to behavior in this area.

Table 92. Differences Between the Groups in Sympathy

Level	Mean		t	Predicted	Significance
	War-Separated	Non-Separated			
All Sympathy	9.8	7.4	.07		—
1. Sympathetic	6.9	4.3	1.63		—
2. Unsympathetic	2.9	3.1	.20		—

Category as a whole. The two groups are statistically similar in the frequency with which they respond to situations which evoke sympathy or lack of sympathy.

Levels of behavior. While no level differences between the two groups in this category were significant, the war-separated group was more sympathetic than the non-separated on our scale and the non-separated children showed a lack of sympathy more frequently. For both groups, sympathetic behavior was more common than unsympathetic behavior, and this was especially true of the war-separated.

Child-Initiated Contacts to Adults

This category includes acts in which a child shows an interest in adults or initiates a contact with adults. Table 93 shows the frequencies of the two groups with respect to behavior in this area.

Category as a whole. The two groups are almost equal in the frequency with which they initiate contacts with adults. The preponderant approach of both groups is a positive one.

Levels of behavior. The war-separated children initiate contacts with adults in a dependent fashion more frequently than the non-separated, who initiate contacts in a negative manner more frequently than the war-separated. These two differences between the means of the groups are statistically significant. The non-separated are more positive than the war-separated; the war-separated are more demanding; but neither of these differences is statistically significant. The war-separated are more frequently dependent and demanding while the non-separated are more frequently negative. The difference between the two groups in nonpositive initiations to adults is in the predicted direction, but not significantly so.

Table 93. Differences Between the Two Groups in Child-Initiated Contacts to Adults

Level	Mean		t	Predicted	Significance
	War-Separated	Non-Separated			
All CI contacts	111.6	113.6	.03		—
1. Positive	71.1	81.2	.73	a	—
2. Dependent	27.7	16.1	2.78	a	P<.01
3. Demanding	10.2	7.9	.62	a	—
4. Negative	2.6	8.4	4.43	b	P<.001
2, 3, & 4. Non-positive	41.1	32.4	1.02	a	—

a. Prediction accepted.
b. Prediction rejected.

Response to Adult-Initiated Contacts

This category includes behavior in which an adult initiates with a child a contact other than the imposition of adult authority. Table 94 shows the frequencies of the two groups with respect to behavior in this area.

Category as a whole. The two groups are statistically similar in the frequency with which they respond to adult-initiated contacts. The preponderant response for both groups is a positive one. For the war-separated children, the positive responses represent a higher percentage of their total responses in this category than they do for the non-separated.

Levels of behavior. The non-separated group is indifferent in response to adult-initiated contacts more often than the war-separated group, and this difference is statistically significant. The two groups are similar in the other two levels.

Response to Adult Authority

This category includes behavior in which a child responds to either the

Table 94. Differences in the Two Groups in Response to Adult-Initiated Contacts

Level	Mean		t	Predicted	Significance
	War-Separated	Non-Separated			
All Responses to AI	67.3	79.9	.51		—
1. Positive	49.1	51.0	.15		—
2. Indifferent	11.4	21.8	2.77	a	P<.005
3. Negative	6.8	7.1	.12	b	—

a. Prediction accepted.
b. Prediction rejected.

direct or indirect direction of an adult. Table 95 shows the frequencies of the two groups with respect to this category.

Category as a whole. Although the difference is not statistically significant, the war-separated group responds to adult authority more frequently than the non-separated group. The war-separated group responds to adult authority dependently and obediently, with equivalent frequencies, while the non-separated group's most frequent response is of the co-operatively obedient manner.

Table 95. Differences Between the Groups in Response to Adult Authority

Level	Mean		t	Predicted	Significance
	War-Separated	Non-Separated			
All Responses to AA	53.1	35.4	.90		—
1. Dependent	13.6	5.6	2.50		$P<.03$
2. Obedient	13.4	16.9	.67		—
3. Indifferent	10.1	7.5	.60		—
4. Disobedient	6.5	3.9	1.28	a	—
5. Defiant	9.5	1.9	1.70	a	$P<.05$
4 & 5. Negative	16.0	5.8	2.12	a	$P<.02$

a. Prediction accepted.

Levels of behavior. The war-separated group responds to adults significantly more frequently with dependent or what might be termed compulsive obedience and defiance. The war-separated group is somewhat, but not significantly, more frequent in disobedient behavior. When defiance and disobedience are combined into a measure of negative response to adult authority, the difference is significant. The non-separated are somewhat more frequent than the war-separated in co-operatively obedient responses, while the war-separated group is more frequent in making responses of a nature indifferent to adult authority and of a covertly disobedient nature, although these three differences are not statistically significant. It is interesting to note that within the non-separated group, disobedience is more frequent than defiance, but that within the war-separated group, the opposite is true.

Other Comparisons of Group Differences

Analysis of the performance of individuals on traits where there was a significant difference. Figure 4 is a picture for each child in our sample of his behavior in respect to the 18 levels or combination of levels in which there was a significant statistical difference between the two groups. An "X" is placed in the child's square for a given level if the child's frequency was above the average of the 34 children in a trait where the war-separated group's average was greater than that of the non-separated group, or if the child's frequency was below the mean frequency of our 34 children where

	SP	SP	D	D	IA	RA	RA	RA	F	CA	CA	AC	AA	AA	AA	D	D	F	Sum
Level:	1	2	1	4	5	2	4	5	5	2	4	2	1	5	4&5	1&5	2&4	1	
War-Separated																			
Mary	x	x	x		x		x	x		x	x	x		x	x	x		x	13
Kate				x		x	x			x	x	x	x		x		x		9
Joe	x		x				x	x	x	x	x	x	x	x	x	x	x	x	14
Rick	x		x	x	x				x		x	x	x	x	x	x	x	x	13
Ann		x	x	x			x	x	x	x		x				x	x	x	11
Dan		x	x	x		x		x	x	x				x	x	x	x	x	12
Allen	x	x		x	x	x	x	x	x	x	x	x	x	x	x		x	x	16
Ray	x		x	x						x	x	x	x			x			8
Bruce	x	x	x	x	x	x	x			x	x					x	x		11
Ken	x	x	x	x		x	x		x	x		x		x		x	x		12
Don	x	x		x	x			x		x	x	x	x			x	x		11
Ned	x	x	x		x	x	x	x			x	x	x			x			11
Patricia	x	x					x			x	x	x	x						7
George	x	x		x	x	x		x	x	x	x	x	x				x		12
Fran			x			x	x				x	x	x			x			7
Alma		x		x		x	x	x	x		x		x		x		x		10
Clarence	x	x	x	x	x	x		x			x	x	x			x	x		12
Non-Separated																			
Ella					x						x		x	x			x		5
Lisbet													x		x				2
Hugh	x	x	x	x	x													x	6
Leonard				x							x		x						3
Cathy		x			x					x	x						x		5
Waldo							x		x						x			x	4
Roger			x						x		x		x			x		x	6
Luke				x					x								x		3
Philip		x	x	x			x			x						x			6
Duncan			x			x					x	x				x			5
Art			x													x			2
Arnold				x		x				x									3
Carrie		x		x			x						x					x	5
Si						x					x	x				x			4
Amelia				x	x		x					x					x		5
Flo		x		x	x					x		x					x		6
Louis				x	x		x	x	x			x					x		7

Figure 4. Children in both groups who behaved like the war-separated group in levels characteristic of the war-separated group. This figure lists the levels which are circled in Figure 5, i.e., those where a statistically significant difference was found between the war-separated and non-separated group. A cross (x) indicates that the child behaved like the war-separated group in the specific level or combinations of levels indicated.

the average of the non-separated group was greater than that of the war-separated group. For example, on S. P. 1, initiating social participation, the war-separated group's mean frequency was greater than that of the non-separated. Mary Bryan's frequency was above the average frequency of our 34 children in this level, so she is given an "X" under S. P. 1. In S. P. 2, associative social participation, the war-separated group's mean frequency was less than that of the non-separated group. Mary's frequency in this level was below the mean of the 34 children. Therefore, she received an "X." An "X" means that on this level a child behaved in the way the war-separated group did. From an inspection of Figure 4 it can be seen that in no specific behavior were all the war-separated children acting the way the war-separated group did; and in every specific behavior characteristic of the war-separated group, some non-separated children acted the way the war-separated group did. In short, no specific behavior is typical of the war-separated group to the extent of completely differentiating all non-separated and war-separated children.

On the right hand margin the reader will find the total number of "X's" the child has. This is a rough measure of how much like the war-separated group the child behaved. It can be seen that there is only one overlap between the two ranges of totals, that of Patricia and Fran with Louis (each of whose total is 7). This is a demonstration that specific behaviors which in themselves do not differentiate, when combined may make a pattern which comes close to differentiating the two groups.

Summary and Integration of the Differences and Similarities Between War-Separated and Non-Separated Groups of Children

The similarities and differences in social behavior in group situations of the war-separated and non-separated groups of children have been analyzed in nine major areas or categories of behavior. Frequency of behavior in broad areas of social interaction such as initiation of aggression or dominance does not differ between our two groups, but types of behavior within these areas do differ significantly. We believe that the pattern of behavior is more meaningful than any specific set of differences. This section attempts to summarize the specific similarities and differences between the groups and present them in the pattern of behavior in which they are found. We have endeavored to abstract the meaning of this pattern as it relates to the child's adjustment to parents, teachers, and other children.

To provide a visual aid in grasping the patterns of behavior we have developed the charts in Figure 5. These charts are in standard scores with the mean of the non-separated group as a Z or standard score of 50. The war-separated group's scores are shown as deviations from the non-separated group's mean, put into standard scores on the basis of the standard deviation of the non-separated group's scores. Each standard deviation equals 10.

Behavior in relation to children. The non-separated group of children more often makes associative contacts with other children than the war-separated group. In contrast, the war-separated children more often initiate overtures and more often are onlookers and fringers. Both groups spend more time-space with other children than with adults, but the non-separated children seem to be more socially acceptable to other children than the war-separated group.

The war-separated children more frequently assume extreme dominant roles than the non-separated. The non-separated, on the other hand, are more frequent than the war-separated in all other forms of dominance-submission behavior, especially syncretic behavior of the give-and-take type of limited dominance and acquiescence.

The non-separated children more frequently initiate aggression than the war-separated children, and the war-separated are more frequently aggressed against than the non-separated. The war-separated group far more frequently combines a demonstration of unfriendliness with aggressive be-

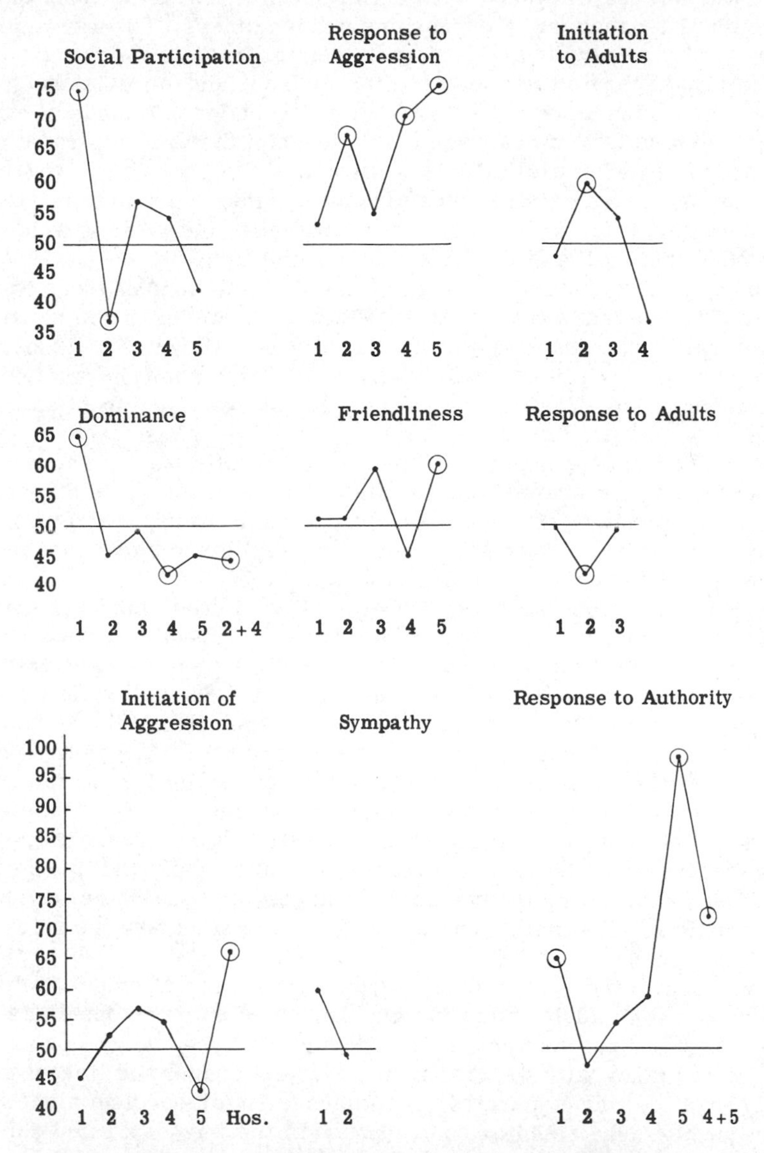

Figure 5. Means of war-separated and non-separated groups in 9 categories of behavior. A score of 50 represents the non-separated group's mean. The war-separated group's mean scores are plotted as Z scores in relation to the non-separated group's mean. The circles indicate levels of behavior in which the difference between the two groups was found to be statistically significant.

havior. The war-separated children handle aggression against themselves poorly, far more frequently showing panic and being submissive to aggression.

The two groups are about equal in the frequency with which they express friendliness, but the war-separated children differ markedly from the non-separated in their manner of expressing unfriendliness. The war-separated more frequently are overt and hostile in their expressions of unfriendliness, while the non-separated are more often indirect and mild in their expressions of unfriendliness. The non-separated children's mode of expressing unfriendliness is to discourage a relationship; the war-separated children's mode is to wish explicitly to destroy it.

The war-separated children more frequently than the non-separated display behavior which we have called sympathetic, behavior in which a child is disturbed by the difficulties of other children.

The comparative picture of the child-to-child relations of these two groups of children indicates that the non-separated children are more socially successful than the war-separated children. They are in association with other children while the war-separated children are fringers trying to get into the group. The war-separated group takes a dominant approach while the non-separated group is more syncretic in its approach to status problems. The war-separated aggress less frequently but with more hostility than the non-separated, and express unfriendliness more directly than the non-separated. The non-separated seem to handle aggression more naturally than the war-separated, being less hostile and more capable of defending themselves.

Behavior in relation to adults. The two groups initiate contacts with adults in equal amount, and they are similar in the frequency with which they are positive in their overtures. The war-separated group is relatively more often dependent and/or demanding in their overtures, while the non-separated are relatively more frequently negative in their initiations of contacts to adults. The non-separated seem more natural in their relations with adults, while the war-separated group seems to need to structure their roles in relationships with adults to a greater degree.

Adults initiate contacts with the non-separated relatively more frequently. The war-separated children are relatively less frequently indifferent to adults. They seem to see the contact as charged, and again are less natural in their relations with adults, and in more need to structure the roles in the relation.

The war-separated group is more dependent upon and compulsively obedient in response to adult authority, but they are also more openly defiant of adult authority than the non-separated children. The two groups are similar in the frequency with which they are obedient and/or indifferent to adult authority, and the war-separated group is covertly disobedient somewhat more frequently. The seeming contradiction of the war-separated children being more frequent in both dependent and defiant responses to adult authority suggests that they have a conflict as to how to respond to adult authority.

The comparative pictures of the two groups in their relations with adults indicates that the non-separated seem to have fewer conflicts and behave more naturally than the war-separated, whose behavior shows conflicts and a need to define their relations with adults by a greater amount of structuring of the roles in the child-to-adult relation.

Interpretation of the Differences Between the Groups

The non-separated group of children is better able to establish and maintain associations with other children than the children of the war-separated group. On a behavioral level this can be explained in their greater frequency of syncretic modes of approach and their smaller frequency of acts of an extreme dominant nature. The ability to give and take, democratically, which the non-separated group shows to a greater extent than the war-separated group, seems to be essential for the maintenance of associative contacts over a long period of time. It may also reflect the freedom of the non-separated, as contrasted with the war-separated, from psychological needs which are outside of the present situation. That is, the extreme dominance of the war-separated group may be both an assertion of suppressed individuality and also a habit learned as a necessity in their dealings with parents and siblings at home.

Aggression seems to be a normal part of a young child's repertoire of social behavior, but our two groups handle aggression differently. The war-separated group aggresses less frequently than the non-separated group, but more often aggresses with unfriendly intent. They are aggressed against more frequently than the non-separated children; they are more submissive to it and show more panic when faced with aggression. These facts seem to point out that the war-separated group has a greater amount of hostility and a greater fear of aggression than the non-separated. This would suggest that the war-separated have been suppressed in their expression of aggression, either by others, or because they fear the social isolation involved in expressions of hostility. Aggression is an area of conflict for them, and the conflicts which lower their amount of initiation of aggression also cause them to respond to aggression against themselves ineffectually, and, therefore, cause still greater aggression against them. Hostility and conflict over aggression are both present in the war-separated group to a greater extent than the non-separated group, and we suspect that these attitudes may have been developed because of the suppression at home of impulses of which aggression is but one.

The two groups of children are about equal in the frequency and the modes of expressing friendliness, but the war-separated group is more overtly unfriendly while the non-separated group is more controlled and discouraging in their expression of unfriendliness. By its very nature, the unfriendliness of the war-separated cuts off associations with children. This unfriendliness is similar to the aggression and unfriendliness which is more frequent in the war-separated than the non-separated. There seems to be a core of hate built by suppression and distrust in the war-separated group from which their dominance, aggression, and unfriendliness arise. These factors are interrelated, and we have looked for their etiology in the parents the child brought to school with him. In school these behaviors combine to cause the child to function inefficiently in associations with children, and this failure may cause secondary reinforcement of the asocial pattern.

The non-separated children behave more naturally with adults than the war-separated children. They are more positive and negative, while the war-separated tend to be more dependent and demanding. In other words, the non-separated express themselves more overtly, while the war-separated resort more to role-structuring and definitions of the situations which put a barrier between themselves and the adults. The adults in the nursery school are permissive, and, in a good sense, something special. The non-separated children make a freer, broader, more personal use of this opportunity. The war-separated children may have felt that any negative behavior might change these adults, and, therefore, cause a loss of valued relationships with permissive adults. In either case, the war-separated children, as in their behavior in child-to-child relationships, carried needs from another situation into the new situations. This view is confirmed in the behavior of the two groups in their response to adult initiations, for the non-separated were more frequently seen accepting the adult with indifference, rather than positively or negatively.

In responding to adult authority the war-separated group shows a conflict in its behavior. More frequently than the non-separated group, the war-separated children are both defiant and compulsive in their response to adult authority. They are somewhat less obedient and somewhat more covertly disobedient. They show both an overrespect for authority and a dislike which causes them to defy it. It is as if the overemphasis of the returned fathers on discipline and their poor methods of enforcing discipline had led to overreaction to authority both in obedience and disobedience. Perhaps some of the war-separated children's defiance in the nursery school was because they felt that they could dare to express their needs with these permissive teachers, but the conflict and fear were certainly present.

Individual Studies of Children

The method used in the group analysis can also be adopted for study of individual children. Individual case analyses add several dimensions to the group analysis. The study of an individual illustrates with a real child the meaning of high and/or low frequencies in the various categories and levels of behavior. In addition, an individual case study shows the importance of patterns of behavior, especially of the integrated picture, rather than the segmented kind made necessary by our statistical techniques. Finally, it shows by example some of the intrinsic, sometimes idiosyncratic, differences between the two groups, illustrating how the children whose fathers returned after the war responded to the added stress in their environment.

Individual analyses have been made by using standard scores. The non-separated group, as representatives of the normal population, is used as the basis. In all cases, the average of the non-separated group is 50 and the standard deviation of the non-separated group's scores is used in arriving at the scores of individual children, each sigma being 10 points on the scale.

In the study of Ned Ford presented in Chapter 14, analysis of Ned as seen in kindergarten and Monday Club is included. This analysis is based upon the data of the present investigation. The scores of Ned in all categories and levels of social behavior are shown in standard scores (or Z scores) in diagram. The idiosyncratic meaning of these scores is revealed through direct quotations from the original observation records.

Several other case analyses were prepared by this method but limitations of space in this monograph precluded their publication.

PART IV. CHILDREN IN PROJECTIVE PLAY SITUATIONS

CHAPTER 10. CHILDREN AS REVEALED IN PROJECTIVE PLAY SITUATIONS

by Margaret Siler Faust

General Purpose of the Studies

There were two general aims which led to the series of studies to be presented in this section. In the first place, we wished to investigate the child's concept of his father and his responses to him. We wanted the child to tell us about his relations with his father and how he felt about these relations. Our research project was based on hypotheses concerning the difficulties which might arise between father and child after the father's return from war (see Chapter 1). We needed to secure data directly from the child about these relations. Such data would be the counterpart to the data which the father had given in personal interviews. Some aspects of this relation might have been obtained by direct observations of interactions between father and child; but the problems involved in such an approach seemed too great to overcome in a research project of this sort.

In the second place, we were interested in exploring the covert feelings of the child. We wanted to probe more deeply into basic aspects of personality than we had been able to do through observations of the children in group situations. Especially we wished to study hostility and anxiety in situations involving a father figure. If war-separation and subsequent return of the father were disturbing to the children, then we might expect to find among the war-separated group greater evidence of hostility and anxiety manifested through aggression and other types of disorganized behavior.

As the studies progressed, we became interested in studying, as a peripheral area, the degree of the child's conformity to the father's standards. The study of conformity developed on the basis of the assumption that in a projective situation the degree to which a child's resolutions conform to the expectancies of a father will be an indication of the child's covert acceptance of the father. This does not imply that conformity in real life is necessarily indicative of desirable father-child relations. Rather, our assumption is that a child who conforms unwillingly in real life, will refuse to conform, will express aggression or reveal anxiety, or will show some combination of such behavior in the freedom of the projective situation. The child who does have a desirable relation with his father will be able to resolve the problem of a conflict projective situation in line with parental expectancies, and without emotional stress.

Methods of Investigation

In order to secure data for this part of the investigation, the children were studied by means of projective play situations. The studies were designed to investigate children's affective responses in semistructured situations. The primary concern was to determine what the child exposes of his own private world in responding to these structured situations. The attempt was to bring into overt form some of the emotional feelings which the children were experiencing internally, and perhaps could not even put into words. We were aware of the fact that the research worker was in direct contact with the child during the play situations, and thus the immediate interpersonal relation during the session entered into the total impression which the child left with the experimenter.

Projective Techniques

The essential feature of a projective technique is that it presents unstructured or semistructured stimuli, and evokes responses from the subject which are, in various ways, "expressive of his private world and personality process" (26, p. 42). Each individual organizes the ambiguous stimuli of a projective situation in his own way. Lawrence Frank (26, p. 47) said: "The personality process involves a selective awareness of all situations, as patterned by the prior experience of the individual . . . so that he sees, hears, and otherwise perceives what has become relevant and meaningful to him and ignores or rejects all else."

Many writers have discussed the limitations of projective techniques as research tools. Seaton (71, p. 153) points out that among the problems in interpreting projective protocols has been "the separation of elements or themes that mirror the subject's own overt experiences and the life he sees around him from those that represent projections in the original Freudian sense, and from fantasy produced by the subject as a means of vicarious satisfaction."

While fully aware of the limitations of projective techniques, the research group has felt that projective material provides valuable information which cannot be gained in other ways. At the present time projective techniques seem to be the best method of investigating with young children the quality of interpersonal relations and the covert aspects of personality which, to a large extent, determine behavior.

Techniques Used

The problems studied by means of the techniques described in the following chapters stemmed from the hypotheses concerning father-child relations of war-born children which were formulated as the research began. These hypotheses have been described in Chapter 1 of this monograph.

Since there were no direct methods available for measuring the quality of the father-child relation, it was necessary to utilize indirect methods to obtain such information. Thus, situations were arranged in which a child might reveal informational data which could be quantified and subsequently used to evaluate the less overt father-child relation in which we were interested. In recent decades many projective techniques have been devised—some of them more carefully standardized than others. However, none of these techniques was designed specifically to study children's feelings about their relations with their fathers. Therefore, it became necessary to devise new techniques or to adapt existing methods to suit our purposes and special problems.

Two new techniques were devised specifically for this father-child relations study. One of them consisted of a series of story completions, and the other was a series of dramatic play completions presenting unfinished family situations involving the father. Both techniques were designed to elicit material about the father-child relation by presenting unresolved family situations which the child was to complete.

The degree of the child's conformity to the father's standards was studied in relation to the modes of children's resolutions of certain conflict stories, first in the story completion technique and later in the dramatic play completions. Anxiety was studied through manifestations in the story completions, and indirectly both through evasions in the dramatic play completions and from inhibitions in the experiments designed to elicit aggression.

In investigating aggression several techniques were used with minor adaptations from their original form. These included doll play with miniature life toys, Stone's balloon technique (78) and Lerner's blocking technique (47, pp. 187-210). The play with balloons was the only projective technique used which was not focused directly upon the area of father-child relations. It was hoped that in this experimental session the child might reveal the depth of his general feelings of hostility. Since these feelings stem from the frustrations, emotional privations, and insecurities experienced in interpersonal situations, they may be related to the father-child relation in an indirect way.

All of the studies were short-term; the number of experimental sessions comprising the various studies ranged from one to four. Therefore, the material which was collected differed greatly from the content of long-term therapy interviews. These short-term play interviews were deliberately structured to tap specific areas; certain demands were made upon the subjects; the limited time restricted the depth of investigation. These were the compromises necessary to meet the exigencies of research.

Assumptions in Interpretation of Projective Material

In interpreting the projective material we have made several assumptions which must be kept in mind. It is assumed that:

1. Behavior in short-term, focused play situations provides reliable material from which inferences concerning personality variables may be made.

2. Each individual will respond in a manner which is consistent with the characteristics of his own personality, even though the possible patterns of responses are limited by the structuring and focusing of the situations.

3. The children have had a certain communality of past experience with cultural patterns which provides a basis for comparison, because the elements of the projective situations are familiar to the children in the study and have a common meaning for all of them. Their idiomatic responses are merely variants of this shared, fundamental meaning.

Collection of Data

The Experimental Room

These individual play sessions were conducted in the experimental room of the Stanford Village Nursery School. This room was constructed for the specific purpose of studying children in individual situations. The experimental room is in the same building as the nursery school, but it is not adjacent to the large room or to the yard where the children play during the hours of nursery school and Monday Club. Completely soundproofed throughout, the 8 × 12 foot room is carpeted from wall to wall. There are two entrances to the room: the one most generally used enters from out-of-doors, the other from an adjoining office.

The room contains a fluorescent ceiling light, an inconspicuous heater in the corner, one opaque window, and four unadorned walls. The furnishings of the room are kept at a minimum, including only such equipment as is necessary for each experimental situation. Suspended from the ceiling, above the child's line of vision, are two undisguised microphones. Both microphones lead to an adjoining observation room where one is connected to a loudspeaker and the other is connected through an amplifier to an electrical recorder. In the wall which separates the experimental room from the observation room is a one-way vision mirror which is 28-1/2 inches high and 64 inches wide. From the observation room the observer can see and hear plainly the interplay of the child and the experimenter.

Recording the Data

In all the experimental sessions a trained observer behind the one-way vision mirror recorded manually the behavior of the child, while the verbal responses were recorded electrically by means of the Audograph. Later, the verbal material from the Audograph was transcribed into typewritten protocols and integrated with the observations of expressive behavior. For purposes of clarity and uniformity, the verbal behavior was typed on the left side of the page opposite the concurrent observed behavior which was typed on the right.

Analysis of Data

The analysis of the data from each of the studies in this section has stressed statistical comparisons between the group of children whose fathers went to war and the group of children whose fathers were not separated. Although primarily statistical, each study has contributed to our understanding of the qualitative differences between the groups as well as the individual differences among the children within the groups. The qualitative and quantitative analyses of each study were accomplished independently of the other studies in the project. Each study has presented sample descriptions of a few children to illustrate some of the individual variations in each study. Space did not permit the inclusion of all the individual analyses.

One of the advantages of group research is that each study supplements the data collected in the other studies. In this way, the understanding of individuals and groups of individuals is extended and enriched. As a final step in the research project we have attempted to assemble and integrate the data of individual families and to analyze patterns of adjustment within these families. The case of Ned Ford and his family has been included in this monograph (Chapter 14).

CHAPTER 11.
AGGRESSION WITH BALLOONS, BLOCKING, AND DOLL PLAY

by Joyce Marian Ryder

Description of the Study

Purposes

General purpose. In the nursery school, where there were enrolled a number of the children of the families in the father-child relations study, it was noted that in some cases children who had been separated from their fathers during their first year seemed to show an unusual amount of aggression. This study was carried out in order to investigate further the hypotheses that arose from these somewhat casual observations.

Relation of study to the whole project. The area of feelings variously designated as hostility, aggressiveness, and the impulse to destroy seemed an important enough aspect of personality to warrant investigation in the children whom we were studying. A child's total life adjustment, his relations with parents and others may be much affected by his aggressive feelings and behavior; and, conversely, these relations may be the antecedents to a child's aggressiveness.

Assumptions and Hypotheses

The nature of aggression, its source and dynamic principles is not a matter of certain knowledge. Some believe the deeper roots of aggression lie in instinct, some believe it to be a product of the individual's culture and others hypothesize a combination of the two. In this study it was assumed that aggressive impulses are a result of frustration (19; 31, p. 134; 56). Individuals may differ not only in what situations are frustrating but also in their degree of response to frustration, but no assumption was made as to whether these are inherited differences or environmentally caused. While no one-to-one ratio of frustration to aggression was expected from individuals, it was assumed that, in general, children who had experienced more frustration would have more aggressive impulses than children who had experienced less frustration. Insecurity was regarded as an important type of frustration which might lead to aggressive feelings.

The concept that the feelings of aggression within the organism form a dynamic unity was accepted (19; 78, p. 150). That is, a child's feeling of hostility toward his father was not regarded as a separate entity from his hostility toward another person or thing but as a part of the same emotional whole. The aggressive feeling within the child, resulting from any number of different frustrations, might express itself directly or indirectly upon the frustrating agents, or be displaced to other objects, or be repressed. Repressed aggression would not be dissipated until expressed in one form or another. Any expression of aggressive feelings would lessen the intensity of the whole. It was assumed that a child who was inhibiting the expression of aggressive feelings would give evidence of his inner conflict by tense musculature, anxiety, lack of spontaneity, blocked aggressive movements, or similar signs.

In this discussion, the term "hostility" is used to indicate person-directed aggression, and "destruction" to indicate object-directed aggression. "Aggression" is the more general term referring to the dynamic whole (78, p. 147).

From observations in the nursery school several hypotheses were evolved. The primary hypothesis was that the children who were separated from their fathers during their first year of life might have more aggressive feelings than children not separated. Such aggressiveness might be related to the insecurity and larger number of frustrations encountered in their lives because of upset home conditions caused by the father's absence, and to the difficulties encountered in establishing a relation with the father after his return.

It was further hypothesized that, in most cases, the war-separated children may have repressed much of their hostile feeling and may reveal such inhibition by tense movements and other signs. The war-separated children may exhibit more overt aggression in situations permissive of such behavior than children who have not been separated from their fathers.

Additional hypotheses were that the war-separated children may show more aggression toward the father than the other group shows; that the war-separated children may show more aggression toward the father than toward the mother and this difference will be larger than any difference in response to the father and mother shown by children whose families have not been separated.

These hypotheses were investigated experimentally through studying aggression elicited from children in a series of projective-play situations.

Experimental Procedures

Methods available. Experimenters studying aggressiveness in young children by projective techniques frequently have presented the child with dolls representing family members and observed his play with them (5; 8; 18; 69; 70).

L. Joseph Stone developed a technique for studying destructive tendencies and for differentiating gradations of attitudes by presenting the child with a large number of balloons which could be played with or broken. The purpose of the experiment is to provide a situation in which the child can project his destructive or aggressive impulses. He is provided with a large number of breakable objects and given a graded series of opportunities to break them (78, pp. 134-35).

Eugene Lerner developed a series of "blocking" games in order to study the child's reactions to a variety of simple primary frustrations such as collisions, intrusions, and prohibitions. The experimenter and child both take active parts in the game, sometimes switching their play roles so as to provide an opportunity for the child to have an inverse authority relation with the experimenter, in order to see how complementary his response is in comparison with his response in a more usual power field of the adult-child relation. Since the adult is involved in the play-fantasy and does not intrude upon it from an outer level of "reality," the responses tend to remain symbolic on the level of dramatic play fantasies. Lerner uses this blocking technique chiefly to investigate the child's style of ego-demarcation (47, pp. 187-210).

Description of method used. In the study which is being reported here each child had four individual play sessions with the experimenter. In the first play session the child played with balloons; in the second and third he played a series of "blocking" games with the experimenter. In the fourth play session he played with family dolls and household furniture.

The balloon experiment. The technique used in this part of the study followed that of L. Joseph Stone as closely as possible (78, p. 135). The experimental room was arranged with ten balloons scattered about the floor (see Figure 6). The experimenter sat at one side on a small chair. The experimenter invited the child to play with the balloons and carried on whatever conversation seemed appropriate to keeping an easy, friendly relation with the child. After asking such questions as, "Have you played with balloons before? Is it fun to play with them?" the experimenter would say, "Would you like to break one? You may if you want to." If the child responded to this invitation, or whenever the first balloon was broken, he was asked, "Is it fun to break balloons? Would you like to break more balloons? You may if you want to." If the child did not break one, after a few minutes he was again encouraged to do so, and later the experimenter would offer to break one herself. If a fourth invitation to break balloons did not bring that response from the child, the experimenter would "accidentally" break one unless she thought that this might be frightening to the child. Once the child had started breaking balloons, he was occasionally encouraged to break more, and was reassured by the experimenter. She tried to maintain the child's interest in the balloons but entered the play only if he indicated that he wished her to do so. The session ended when all the balloons were broken, or shortly after the experimental procedure was completed if no balloons were broken, or when the child tired of playing with the balloons.

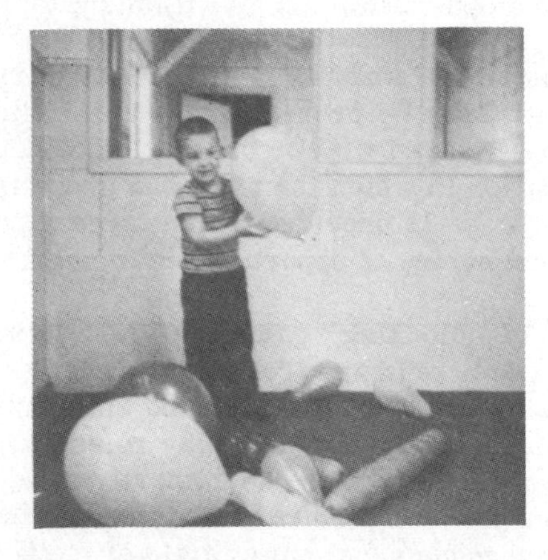

Figure 6. The Balloon Experiment.

Blocking experiment. The "blocking" games used in the study were adapted from Eugene Lerner's "Blocking Technique Number 2" (47). Of the nine play units described by Lerner, seven were selected for this study.

In the games as described by Lerner, the play is between the child and the experimenter. For this study, the adult role was identified as "daddy" in one play session and "mommy" in the other play session.

The materials used were four twelve-inch wooden nursery school blocks, two six-inch blocks which could be hooked together to form a train, and dolls to represent the father or mother and to represent either a boy or a girl, depending on the sex of the child. The games were played on a low table with the child and experimenter sitting across from each other in child-sized chairs.

Each of the seven play units was played three times. In each case the term "boy" or "girl" was used to agree with the sex of the child. The description of the play units which follows gives the form used for a boy subject in situations relating to the father.

Play unit 1: Long blocks are laid out to form a track; at each end a small block "car" is placed. The experimenter says, "This is the boy's car, and this is the daddy's car. The boy's car comes from there, and the daddy's car comes from here. Let's meet in the middle. How can the daddy's car pass? How can the daddy pass?" (see Figure 7).

Figure 7. Play-Unit 1 of the Blocking Experiment. "How shall the daddy's car pass?"

Play unit 2: The two cars are hooked together and placed at the end of the track toward the child. The experimenter holds the father doll at her end of the track. "Now this is the boy's train. I come with the daddy, and you come with the boy's train. Let's meet in the middle. And the daddy stops the boy's train. What happens? What shall happen?" (see Figure 8).

Play unit 3: "Now you come with the boy's train and the daddy is waiting beside the track and wants to get on the boy's train. May the daddy get on?"

Play unit 4: The long blocks form an "L" shaped track. The block "cars" are placed at each end. "This is the boy's car, and this is the daddy's car. You come from there, and the daddy comes from here. Who will crash? What happens?"

Play unit 5: The experimenter pushes the blocks toward the child saying,

"Now you build a house." When it is built, "It's the boy's house. And the daddy comes and wants to come in. May the daddy come in?" "The daddy does come in. What happens?"

Figure 8. Play-Unit 2 of the Blocking Experiment.
". . . and the mommy stops the boy's train. What happens?"

Play unit 6: "Now I'll build a house." The experimenter builds a house with the blocks. She gives the boy doll to the child. "It's the daddy's house and it's a house where the boy must not touch anything. The boy comes and asks if he may touch anything. All right? What does the daddy say? What happens?" If the boy does touch things, "But it is a house where the boy must not touch anything. What happens?" (see Figure 9).

Figure 9. Play-Unit 6 of the Blocking Experiment. "This is the daddy's house, and it is a house where the boy must not touch anything. The boy comes and asks if he may touch things."

Play unit 7: "Now you build a house. It's the boy's house where the daddy must not touch anything, and the daddy comes and says, 'May I touch things?' What does the boy say?" "The daddy does touch things. What happens?"

The child was allowed a brief period of free play with the dolls and blocks after the play units were completed.

Doll-play experiment. The dolls were made simply and crudely out of yellow plastic clay held together with pipe-cleaners. The dolls representing adults were about seven inches tall. The children were about five inches tall. In each case, the family consisted of father, mother, and children, duplicating the members of the child's own family. The furniture described in Chapter 13 was used. A red peg "gun" was included in the equipment.

The situation was left as free as possible for the child. The experimenter sat to the left of the child. As soon as both were seated and the experimenter had the child's attention, she said, pointing to each object in turn, "Here is a family, the father, the mother, boy, and girl. And here are their beds. This is the toilet and the basin, and table and chairs. Here is a stove, a refrigerator, and a couch. And this is the gun." "You may play with them however you like" (see Figure 10).

Figure 10. Materials arranged for the Doll-Play Experiment.

During the play session the experimenter was an interested and friendly onlooker. She did not enter the play unless the child invited her to do so. She talked with him as he played to encourage him to verbalize the dramatic play he was carrying on with the dolls. The child was permitted to destroy the dolls, and the experimenter remade them or helped him to remake them if he desired. She tried to reassure him verbally if he seemed to feel guilty about aggressive behavior, e.g., "Yes, the daddy comes apart. They come apart easily, don't they? They're just made out of clay." If the child's attention wandered from the dolls, the experimenter brought him back by asking, "What do they do now?" or "Is the daddy still asleep?" or similar questions. The play session ended when the child seemed to be through playing with the dolls.

Rationale of the method. To investigate the hypotheses which had been made about aggression in the children being studied, material and procedures were selected which were thought likely to elicit aggressive responses, so that a large enough sample of aggression might be obtained for making intra- and inter-individual comparisons. It seemed advisable to have a series of play sessions since the experience of other experimenters has shown that a child is likely to show more aggressive behavior in the second play session than the first and that the amount of such behavior tends to increase as he feels more familiar with the situation (63). The child's four play sessions with the experimenter were spaced one to three weeks apart.

It was thought that the results of a variety of projective techniques might be more clearly indicative of the child's aggressive impulses than any one technique, since children might vary in the type of situation in which they would feel most free to reveal their underlying feelings. The three techniques selected represent three different approaches to the child's aggressive feelings. The first play session, with balloons, and the last, with dolls, are relatively unstructured play situations in which the child can express any hostile impulses which he brings with him. The blocking games are more structured and may show the child's response to an immediate frustration as well as give an opportunity for expressing aggression carried over from other experiences. The three techniques, balloons, blocking, and doll play, give progressively more direct outlets for the child's feelings of hostility.

Stone found that the child's attitude and action toward the balloons seemed to approximate very closely the degree and nature of his aggressions toward other children. This sort of observation gives justification to using the child's response to breakable objects in a permissive situation as an index to his feelings of hostility.

In light of the frustration-aggression hypothesis, it seemed that the response to Lerner's blocking games involving simple frustrations might be indicative of the child's aggressive feelings. The relatively structured blocking situations lend themselves to more precise scoring of the overt aggression shown than do the other two techniques.

In the games as described by Lerner, the play is between the child and the experimenter, the hypothesis being that the child's responses to the experimenter's part in the games will reveal his usual attitudes toward any adult or person of authority (47). For the father-child relations study it seemed desirable to investigate the possibility that the child might respond in a different way to his father than to his mother or to symbolic representations of them. Each child played the series of blocking games twice. In one session the trains and doll manipulated by the experimenter were referred to as "the daddy's" and "the daddy," and in the other play session the trains and doll manipulated by the experimenter were referred to as "the mommy's" and "the mommy." It was hoped that the week or more which elapsed between the two play sessions would serve to minimize any carry-over effect by which the child would tend to respond to the second series in the same way he responded to the first. In order that the effect of playing with one parent before the other might not affect the total results, half of the war-separated children and the non-separated children played with the father first and the other half of each group played with the mother first.

Play with family dolls and miniature household furniture has been widely used as a method for studying the personality of young children. Despert noted aggressive reactions as the most striking single item in doll play (18). It was added to the other projective techniques in this study with the hope that the child's use of the dolls might reveal more of the quality and direction of his hostile feelings than either of the other techniques employed. Since the crude plastic clay dolls were not objects of value and could easily be remade, it was thought that the child would feel free to destroy them if he so desired. It was thought that these dolls might be more acceptable to the six- and seven-year-old boys than more realistic dolls. The requirements for the furniture were that it should be only realistic enough to stimulate dramatic play and simple enough that the child would not spend much time in exploring the material before he began to play. The "gun" was included to encourage aggressive behavior. While the situation, in terms of procedure, was left as free as possible, the materials were planned in such a way as to invite, or at least not discourage, hostile or destructive behavior.

Procedures for conducting the study. The experimental room described in Chapter 10 was used for the play sessions.

In the play session, the role of the experimenter was that of friendly, interested onlooker and, occasionally, participant. If the child's out-of-field conversation was related to aggression or destruction, she was particularly careful not to impose moral ideas, simply reflecting what he had said, or answering in a noncommittal way.

An observer watched the play sessions through a one-way vision window. During the balloons session she made as complete a record as possible of all that the child did and said. In the later sessions verbalizations were electrically recorded on a disc while she recorded the child's behavior. The observer was instructed to note: the child's manner of approaching the materials; what he did with the materials in response to the situations posed by the experimenter; amount of activity and changes in tempo; type of posture; freedom or restraint in movement; tenseness of muscles; nervous mannerisms or tics; changes and emotional quality of facial expression; any indications of emotion, feeling tone, or mood. Acts of hostility and destructiveness were to be recorded in detail.

Ratings of Covert Aggression

It seemed advisable to reduce to numerical form the variety of responses which different children might give to the projective techniques employed in order that the two groups might be more readily compared on the strength of their aggressive impulses. The overt aggressive behavior shown by children in these situations is affected by two opposing forces within the personality of the child which are of particular interest in this study. They are described by Stone (78, pp. 141-42) as: the strength of the impulse to destroy and the strength of the restraints against destruction (mainly fear, moral inhibitions, interiorized adult prohibitions, and fondness for the objects).

For measuring these factors, two scales were devised: one dealing with the strength of aggressive feelings, the other with the strength of inhibitions against aggressive behavior. The flaws inherent in the use of rating scales were recognized. The richness and variety of a child's response during a play session cannot be reduced easily or accurately to one or two numbers. Rarely can a child be placed on such a scale with assurance that the scoring is correct. However, the rating scales were used, since some indication of the degree of underlying feelings of aggression seemed more important for the purposes of this study than the more easily obtained measurement of overt aggression.

Scale of strength of aggressive feelings. This scale was developed to deal with the dynamics of aggression within the individual rather than with the overt aggressive behavior. It attempts to measure those aggressive feelings which are a more or less continuing aspect of the individual's personality. It is concerned with the individual's responses to specific situations only insofar as these are indicative of the quality and force of the underlying structure of feelings. The scale contains 7 points, ranging from no covert aggressive feelings to avid or violent aggressive feelings. The rating scale will be found in Appendix 11.

Check list and scale of strength of inhibitions. While it seemed desirable to have a descriptive scale for strength of inhibitions against aggressive behavior similar to the scale for strength of aggressive feelings, the task of devising such a scale was not attempted since the indications of restraint of aggressive impulses take such a wide variety of forms. Instead, a check list of various overt indications of inhibition or repression was used in connection with a simple linear scale.

The check list includes 13 items such as withdrawal from activity, moralistic verbalizations, tense or restrained movements, indirect hostility; 5 items under guilty behavior; and a third category of fear in the situation. The items listed are not mutually exclusive; many are overlapping. A child may demonstrate behavior in any number of the categories. The work of Levy (48, 49, 50) and the work of Stone (78, pp. 140-48) were drawn upon in compiling the list.

The linear scale has 5 steps, from excessive inhibition to practically no inhibition. In scoring the child on the scale of strength of inhibitions against aggressive behavior, the rater is to take into consideration the items on the check list and the total pattern of inhibitions. The scale may be checked anywhere along the line, on or between the points. The check list of overt indications of inhibition and the rating scale are in Appendices 12 and 12a.

Measurement of Overt Aggression

The relation of overt aggression to covert aggression is a complex one. Overt aggression may be an immediate response to a situation or it may arise from deep, underlying feelings of aggression or both. A child with strong aggressive impulses may have equally strong inhibitions which may prevent the expression of aggression even in an unusually permissive situation such as projective methods provide. Overt aggression can be more exactly and objectively measured than feelings of aggression. Some measure of overt aggression was used with each of the play techniques.

Balloons. For the balloon play, overt aggression was measured by the number of balloons broken by the child directly, or indirectly through requesting the experimenter to break them. In addition, each child was rated on a scale for destructiveness with balloons. The 6 points of the scale go from relaxed and playful approach to violent attack. The scale is in Appendix 13.

Blocking. For each of the blocking play units the child's response was scored on a 5-point scale, ranging from nonaggression to aggression. These points were comparable for each of the seven play units insofar as possible. The points of the scale are designated as acquiescence, compromise, impasse, assertiveness, and aggressiveness. The scale is in Appendix 14.

Doll play. The overt aggression in the doll play was measured by the ratio of the number of aggressive acts to the number of minutes in the play session. An aggressive act was defined in accordance with Sears' usage, as one having the intent to injure, punish, destroy, or generally disparage and depreciate (70). Describing a doll character as having an aggressive-hostile nature, attitude, or mood was considered an aggressive act. The dolls, equipment, experimenter, or room might be involved in the aggression. An aggressive act was considered as one unit until some relevant change in person or method of expressing aggression was noted, or until a definite break in the sequence of aggression occurred. Group aggressive action was recorded as a single unit. Verbal aggression was scored as a unit unless it was accompanied by behavioral aggression.

Description of Subjects

The experimental group included 13 first-born children who were separated from their fathers until they were a year old or more. The control group included 13 first-born children who had not been separated from their fathers for any extended period. They were matched to the experimental group by age and sex. The age range was from four years, four months to seven years, two months, for the war-separated group; and from four years, two months to seven years, five months, for the non-separated group. The mean age for the war-separated group was five years, four months; for the non-separated group it was five years, six months. In each group nine of the children were boys and four were girls.

The IQ scores for the war-separated group ranged from 93 to 138, with a mean of 118. For the non-separated group, the scores ranged from 96 to 158 with a mean of 123. A descriptive list of the children will be found in Appendix 1.

At the beginning of the experimental play sessions the children varied in their degree of familiarity with the situation. So as to make it possible to ascertain whether this difference was affecting the responses to the play sessions, a scale of familiarity with the situation was devised and each child rated on it. There was no difference between the two groups in ratings on familiarity with the situation.

Description of Data Collected

Qualitative. The qualitative data collected about each child were four protocols of projective-play sessions, one in which the child played with balloons, two in which the child played ''blocking games'' with the experimenter, one in which the child played with a family of dolls. The protocol for the play with the balloons was a running account of everything the child did and said, recorded by an observer at the time of the play session. For the other three play sessions the protocol was a running account of the child's behavior written by an observer, combined with verbalizations from the electrically recorded disc. The two records were combined in the protocol.

Quantitative. The quantitative data collected for each child were a series of scores on his aggressive feelings, his inhibition of aggressiveness, and his overt aggressiveness. In each of the four play sessions the experimenter and the observer independently rated the child on the scale of strength of aggressive feelings. These ratings for each play session were combined later into one rating by the experimenter, taking into consideration the total protocol as well as the two original scores. The experimenter and observer independently marked a check list of signs of inhibition of aggression and rated the child on a scale of strength of inhibitions of aggressive behavior. The same procedure as above was followed in giving each child a combined final rating on inhibition for each play session.

Some measure of overt aggression was made for each of the projective techniques employed. In the balloon experiment, the number of balloons broken and the point in the procedure where breaking first occurred were noted and a rating was made on destructiveness. In the blocking experiments, for each of the three repetitions of the seven play units, the child's response was scored on a 5-point scale of overt aggression. Where necessary, these scores were revised at the end of the total experiment so that similar responses would be marked consistently from child to child. The mean was taken of the scores of the three repetitions of each play unit, and then a mean for the seven play units in each blocking session. During the doll-play experiment, the observer noted each aggressive act and noted the time at five minute intervals. The overt aggression score for each child in his play with the dolls was expressed as the ratio of aggressive acts per ten minute period of time.

Reliability of Ratings on Scales

The Pearson r was computed, to give an indication of the amount of agreement between the ratings given each child independently by the experimenter and by the observer on the various scales used in each play session.

On the scale of strength of aggressive feelings for the first two play sessions the ratings of the experimenter and the observer correlated .67 and .77. In the last two sessions the agreement decreased to .46 and .38. On the scale of strength of inhibitions there was the same trend. The coefficient of reliability was best for the first session (.58) and grew progressively smaller in each session to a low of .10 in the final session. It may be that the ratings in the later sessions were done more hastily and as a result less accurately. The results showed that it was possible for the experimenter and observer to arrive independently at similar ratings, but they also showed that continued care must be used in the rating in order for them to remain accurate. The final ratings used in the analysis were probably more accurate than the reliability scores would indicate, since the total protocol for each play session was taken into consideration as well as the original ratings of the experimenter and observer. That the coefficient of reliability was larger for the scale of strength of aggressive feelings than for the scale of strength of inhibitions against aggression is probably a reflection of the scales themselves (68).

Aggression with Balloons

Comparison of the War-Separated and Non-Separated Groups

Strength of aggressive feelings. The mean rating for the war-separated group on the 7-point scale on strength of aggressive feelings in the balloon experiment was 5. The mean for the non-separated group was 3.3. The ratings were converted into standard scores and the t technique used for testing the significance of the difference. The group scores were different at the $P < .01$ level. The four children given ratings of 6 and 7 on the scale (most aggressive) were all in the war-separated group. The three children given ratings of 1 and 2 (least aggressive) were in the non-separated group[1] (see Table 96).

Since 9 of the 13 children in each group were boys, it was possible to analyze the data for boys separately, but not for the girls. The means for the boys were 5.3 for the war-separated group and 3.1 for the non-separated group; P for this difference was $< .004$.

Strength of inhibitions against aggression. The mean for the war-separated group on the 5-point scale for strength of inhibitions against aggression was 3.5. The mean for the non-separated group was 3. When converted into standard scores and tested for significance by the t technique, no significant difference was found between these means (see Table 96).

Destructiveness with balloons. The mean for the war-separated group on the 7-point scale of destructiveness with balloons was 3.9, and for the non-separated group, 2.8. When converted to standard scores and tested

Table 96. Comparison of Responses to the Balloon Experiment Made by War-Separated and Non-Separated Groups

	Mean Score		t	P
	War-Separated	Non-Separated		
Aggressive feelings (1-7)	5	3.3	3.72	<.01
Inhibition (1-5)	3.5	3	.79	—
Destructiveness with balloons (1-7)	3.9	2.8	2.12	<.05
Number balloons broken (0-10)	4.3	3.6	.41	—
Breaking point (1-6)	3	3	.00	—
Breaking score (0-18)	8.5	7	.54	—

1. For each comparison the four children with extreme scores at either end of the scale (most or least aggressive; most or least inhibited) are designated according to their group (war-separated or non-separated). When several children received the same score, two, three, or five children may be cited instead of four.

by the t technique, these scores were significantly different ($P < .05$) (Table 96).

Number of balloons broken. Of the ten balloons, the mean number broken by the war-separated group was 4.3; by the non-separated group, 3.6. The frequency distributions of the number of balloons broken were similar for the two groups. In both the frequency curve was high at each end and low in the middle; that is, most of the children either broke all the balloons or none of the balloons. Of the eight children who broke no balloons, three were war-separated children and five were non-separated children. Of the six who broke all the balloons, four were war-separated and two were non-separated children.

Point in procedure of first breaking balloons. The mean point in the procedure of first breaking balloons for the war-separated group was 3 and for the non-separated group, 3. These figures include only those children who broke one or more balloons: ten war-separated and eight non-separated children.

Breaking score. The breaking score is a combination of the point in procedure of first breaking balloons and the number of balloons broken. The number of balloons broken intentionally by the child and by the experimenter at the child's request were added to the inverted number of the point in the procedure where breaking first occurred. The later in the procedure the first breaking occurs and the more balloons broken, the higher was the score. The scores ranged from 0 to 18. The mean for the war-separated group was 8.5; for the non-separated group, 7.0. The difference between these was not statistically significant (Table 96).

Relations Among Some of the Measures of Inhibitions

It was possible that the child's familiarity with the experimenter and the experimental room might have affected the degree of inhibition of his behavior. The correlation coefficient was found for the ratings on the scale of strength of inhibitions against aggression and the child's degree of familiarity with the situation (see p. 221). The correlation was -.28. Apparently the factor of familiarity with the experimental situation had little effect on the child's inhibitions in balloon play as measured by the scale.

Since it had been hypothesized that the point in the graded series of opportunities for breaking balloons where the child first broke a balloon would be indicative of the amount of inhibition against destructiveness, the correlation coefficient for the point in the procedure of first breaking and the child's rating on the scale of strength of inhibitions against aggression was computed. The r was .05, which gives no indication of a relation between the two sets of scores.

The correlation between the child's rating on the scale of strength of inhibitions against aggression and his breaking score was -.11, which gives no indication of a relation between the two sets of scores.

Discussion of Findings in Balloon Experiment

The children who were separated from their fathers during the first year of life seemed to have stronger feelings of aggression as measured in the balloon experiment than the children who had not been separated from their fathers ($P < .01$). The $P < .004$ which was obtained when the scores of the boys alone were compared also seemed to indicate a real difference between the two groups.

In overt aggression, the larger number of balloons broken by the war-separated group may indicate a trend toward more overt aggression in that group, but such an interpretation can only be stated tentatively. The differences in the scores on the scale of destructiveness with balloons showed the war-separated group to be more aggressive, the differences reaching a .05 level of probability.

The results of the balloon experiment gave no indication of a difference in strength of inhibition against aggressiveness in the two groups, either as measured by the scale or in the point in the procedure where the child first broke balloons.

Aggression in Blocking Games

Comparison of the War-Separated and Non-Separated Groups

Strength of aggressive feelings. The mean for the war-separated group on the 7-point scale of strength of aggressive feelings was 4.6 for the first blocking session and 4.8 for the second blocking session. The mean for the non-separated group was 3.6 in each blocking session. The ratings were converted into standard scores and the difference tested for significance by the t technique. For the first blocking session, the differences were significant at the $P < .09$ level. For the second blocking session, the differences were significant at the $P < .06$ level (see Table 97).

In the first blocking session, of the five children rated most aggressive (scores of 6 and 7), four were in the war-separated group and one was in the non-separated group; of the five children rated least aggressive (scores of 1 and 2), one was in the war-separated group and four were in the non-separated group. In the second blocking session, of the five children rated most aggressive, four were in the war-separated group and one was in the non-separated group; the four children rated least aggressive were in the non-separated group. When the boys were compared, the differences were significant at the $P < .06$ level for the first blocking session, and at the $P < .04$ level for the second session. The means for the war-separated boys in the two sessions were 4.7 and 5.1; for the non-separated boys, the means were 3.2 and 3.6.

Strength of inhibitions against aggression. The mean for the war-separated group on the 5-point scale of strength of inhibitions against aggression was 3.2 for the first blocking session and 3.1 for the second. The means for the non-separated group were 2.7 and 2.5. The difference between the two groups in the first blocking session was not significant; in the second blocking session it was significant at the .07 level of probability (Table 97).

Overt aggression in the two sessions. The mean was taken of the overt aggression scores on the 5-point overt aggression scale for the three repetitions of each play unit, and then a mean for the six play units in each blocking session.[2] The mean of the means for each play session for the war-separated group was 3.2 for the first blocking session and 3.6 for the second blocking session. For the non-separated group the means were 3.1 in both sessions. The difference in the first blocking session was not significant. The difference for the second blocking session was significant at the .06 level of probability (Table 97).

In the first blocking session, of the four children with the smallest amount of overt aggression, two were in the war-separated group and two were in the non-separated group; of the four with the largest amount of overt aggression, two were in the war-separated group and two were in the non-separated group. In the second play session, the four children with the smallest amount of overt aggression were in the non-separated group, and of the three with the most overtly aggressive responses, two were in the war-separated group and one in the non-separated group.

The mean of the overt aggression scores for the war-separated boys in the first blocking session was 3.2 and for the non-separated boys was 3.0; this difference is not statistically significant. The mean for the war-separated boys in the second blocking session was 3.6 and for the non-separated boys, 3.0. The difference was not statistically significant.

When the six play units were considered separately, in the first play session the war-separated group was more aggressive in play units one, two, three, and five. The non-separated group was more aggressive in play units six and seven. None of the differences was statistically significant. In the second play session, the war-separated group was more aggressive in play units one, five, six, and seven. The non-separated group was more aggressive in play units two and three. The differences found in play units one and five were significant at the .06 level. In play unit seven, the difference was significant at the .1 level. The difference in play unit six was not significant (Table 97).

Table 97. Comparison of Responses in the First and Second Blocking Sessions

	First Session				Second Session			
	Mean		t	P	Mean		t	P
	War-Separated	Non-Separated	t	P	War-Separated	Non-Separated		
Aggressive feelings (1-7)	4.6	3.6	1.9	<.09	4.8	3.6	2.1	<.06
Inhibitions (1-5)	3.2	2.7	1.1	—	3.1	2.5	2.0	<.07
Overt aggression:								
Mean score (1-5)	3.2	3.1	.3	—	3.6	3.1	2.1	<.06
Play unit 1	2.3	2.0	.8	—	2.4	1.8	2.1	<.06
Play unit 2	3.5	3.3	.3	—	3.5	3.6	-.1	—
Play unit 3	2.3	2.2	.7	—	2.7	3.1	-.4	—
Play unit 5	3.1	2.8	.6	—	4.0	2.8	2.1	<.06
Play unit 6	3.7	4.1	-1.1	—	4.5	3.9	.2	—
Play unit 7	4.0	4.3	-.8	—	4.5	3.7	1.8	<.10

2. One play unit (number D) could not be rated because of difficulty in judging the child's response.

Overt aggression in response to father and mother. In the blocking session with the father doll, the war-separated group had a mean score of 3.3; the non-separated group, 3.1. Of the four children who showed the most aggressiveness, three were in the war-separated group and one was in the non-separated group. Of the four who showed the least aggressiveness, one was in the war-separated group and three were in the non-separated group. The mean score for the war-separated boys in response to the father doll sessions was 3.7. For the non-separated boys, it was 3.0. The difference was not statistically significant (Table 98).

For the blocking sessions with the mother doll, the war-separated group's mean response on overt aggression was 3.5. The mean for the non-separated group was 3.2. The difference was not statistically significant. Of the three children who showed the most aggressiveness, two were in the war-separated group and one was in the non-separated group. Of the four who showed the least aggressiveness, one was in the war-separated group and three were in the non-separated group. The mean score for the war-separated boys in response to the mother doll session was 3.9. For the non-separated boys it was 3.1. The difference between the two groups was not statistically significant.

Table 98. Comparison of Overtly Aggressive Responses to the Father Situations and the Mother Situations in the Blocking Experiments

	Father Responses	Mother Responses	Difference (F-M)
War-Separated (mean) :an)	3.3	3.5	-.2
Non-Separated (mean) :an)	3.1	3.2	-.1
t	1.1	.8	.1
P	—	—	—
War-Separated boys (mean)	3.7	3.9	-.2
Non-Separated boys (mean)	3.0	3.1	-.1
t	1.2	.8	1.48
P	—	—	—

Discussion of Findings in Blocking Games

In both sessions of the blocking games, the children who were separated from their fathers during the first year of life were rated as having stronger aggressive feelings than the children who were not separated from their fathers. The levels of probability for the significance of the differences between the two groups (<.09 and <.06) were not sufficient to be interpreted as positive evidence of a difference. When the boys alone were compared, the differences are somewhat more significant (P<.06 and <.04).

The war-separated children were rated as having only slightly stronger inhibitions of aggression than the non-separated children in the first blocking session, but in the second session the difference approached significance, reaching a probability level of <.07.

In the first blocking session, the difference between the two groups in overt aggression was negligible. In the second blocking session the non-separated group continued to show the same amount of overt aggression while the war-separated group became more aggressive. The P of <.06 for the difference in the last blocking session may be taken as at least suggestive of a real difference between the two groups. Overt aggression and signs of inhibitions of aggression both increased among the war-separated children in the second session, whereas we expected that the relation between these two scores would be an inverse one.

In both play sessions, play unit one (The two cars meet in the middle. "How shall the daddy's car pass?") distinguished best between the two groups of children on the overt aggression scale. In both groups the most predominant response was a compromise solution, e.g., the two cars both edge over and pass, or one car goes over the other one. In the first blocking session a few of the war-separated children withdrew their cars, but in the second session none of them did. Several of the non-separated children withdrew their cars in both sessions.

Play unit five (The child builds a house for the boy. "May the daddy come in?") was next in distinguishing between the two groups. In both groups, the responses were distributed fairly well along the scale with few responses scored 3 or "impasse." The number of aggressive responses remained constant for the non-separated group but increased considerably for the war-separated group from the first to the second blocking session.

In play units six and seven (the houses where the boy or daddy may not touch anything) the non-separated group had more aggressive responses in the first session and the war-separated group had more aggressive responses in the second play session. Since the results were so variable, play units six and seven cannot be regarded as an adequate index of the child's aggressiveness. The responses were predominantly aggressive in both groups.

The difference in response to play units two and three (the daddy stopping the boy's train and waiting to get on the boy's train) was slight in both play sessions. In the first session the war-separated group's responses were slightly more aggressive and in the second session the non-separated group's responses were slightly more aggressive. These play units added little to the comparison.

The expected difference in response to the father and the mother was not found. In both groups there was only a negligible difference in the direction of being more aggressive toward the mother than toward the father. While the difference in the amount of aggressiveness shown in the two groups was greater when only the boys were compared, the difference in father and mother responses for the boys alone was no different than for the group as a whole.

Aggression in Doll Play

Comparison of the War-Separated and Non-Separated Groups

Strength of aggressive feelings. The mean for the war-separated group on the 7-point scale of strength of aggressive feelings in the doll-play experiment was 5. The mean for the non-separated group was 3.9. When the ratings were converted into standard scores and the t technique used for testing the significance of this difference, the P was <.05. The two children given the most aggressive ratings were in the war-separated group. When the boys only were compared, the mean for the war-separated group was 5.1 and for the non-separated group, 3.6, with the P for this difference being <.04.(Table 99).

Strength of inhibitions of aggression. The mean for the war-separated group on the 7-point scale of strength of inhibitions of aggression was 3.1. For the non-separated group, the mean was 2.8. No statistically significant difference was found.

Overt aggression. The mean number of aggressive acts per ten-minute period of time for the war-separated group was 8.3; the mean for the non-separated group was 7.7. The mean number of aggressive acts per ten minutes for the war-separated boys was 9.0; for the non-separated boys it was 7.5. The differences were not shown to be significant when tested by the t technique (Table 99).

The mean number of aggressive acts during the play session was 19.0 for the war-separated group and 14.4 for the non-separated group. For the boys the means were 18.7 and 15.7. The differences were not significant although t was larger for this comparison than for the number of aggressive acts per ten minutes.

Table 99. Comparison of Responses in the Doll-Play Experiment

	Mean Score		t	P
	War-Separated	Non-Separated		
Strength of aggressive feelings (1-7)	5	3.9	2.1	<.05
Strength of inhibition against aggression (1-5)	3.1	2.8	1.0	—
Aggressive acts per ten minutes	8.3	7.7	.3	—
Total number of aggressive acts	19.0	14.4	1.2	—

Discussion of Findings in Doll Play

In the doll-play experiment the children who were separated from their fathers during their first year were rated as having more feelings of aggression than children who had not experienced such separation (P <.05). There was a slightly larger difference between the scores of the two groups of boys than between the scores for the groups as a whole.

The war-separated children were rated as having slightly stronger inhibitions of aggression than the non-separated group, but the difference was not statistically significant. In overt aggression, the war-separated children averaged only .6 more aggressive acts per ten-minute period of time than the non-separated group. In the total number of aggressive acts for the play session, the trend toward greater aggressiveness in the war-separated children was closer to being statistically significant. The latter comparison was not valid since in a few cases the play sessions had to be ended before the child chose to leave, because of time limitations. Perhaps a more accurate measure of overt aggression would be the number of aggressive incidents as compared to the total number of incidents in the doll play. This would eliminate from the scoring the factors of differences in tempo of play and differences in amount of tangential activity. None of these schemes of measuring overt aggression makes any distinction between a violently aggressive act and a mildly aggressive act and therefore none measures the amount of overt aggression precisely.

Integration and Interpretation of Findings

Strength of Aggressive Feelings

The mean rating on the scale of strength of aggressive feelings was consistently higher for the children who had been separated from their fathers during their first year than for the children who had not been separated for any extended period. While the probability level for the significance of the differences in each play session was not high enough to draw any positive conclusions about the difference between the two groups, the consistency of the ratings over the four play sessions made it seem likely that a real difference existed between the two groups in strength of aggressive feelings as measured by the scale. It seemed unlikely that the rating given a child in one play session could have affected the rating given him in the next play session, since, with the large number of play sessions, the experimenter and observer soon found it impossible to remember what the child had done in the previous sessions. When the ratings of the four play sessions were combined, the significance of the difference reached a probability level of $< .01$ (Table 100).

Strength of Inhibitions Against Aggression

The difference in the ratings on strength of inhibitions against aggression was small for each play session, approaching significance only in the third play session. The difference in the combined ratings was close to a $< .1$ level of probability. What difference existed was consistently in the direction of showing the war-separated children to have the stronger inhibitions of aggression. While there may be a trend in this direction, no statistically significant difference was found.

Overt Aggression

With the use of different techniques the overt aggression had to be measured in different ways; scores were not directly comparable from one session to the next. In each session, the war-separated group was more aggressive than the non-separated group. On the destructiveness scale with balloons the difference reached a probability of $< .05$. In the second blocking

Table 100. Comparison of the Findings in the Four Experimental Play Sessions

	I	II	III	IV	Combined Ratings
Strength of aggressive feelings (means)					
War-Separated	5.0	4.6	4.8	5.0	4.9
Non-Separated	3.3	3.6	3.6	3.9	3.6
P	$<.01$	$<.09$	$<.06$	$<.05$	$<.01$
W-S boys	5.3	4.7	5.1	5.1	
N-S boys	3.1	3.2	3.6	3.6	
P	$<.004$	$<.06$	$<.04$	$<.04$	
Strength of inhibitions of aggression (means)					
War-Separated	3.5	3.2	3.1	3.1	3.2
Non-Separated	3.0	2.7	2.5	2.8	2.8
P	—	—	$<.07$	—	—
Overt aggression (means)					
War-Separated	3.9	3.2	3.6	8.3	
Non-Separated	2.8	3.1	3.1	7.7	
P	$<.05$	—	$<.06$	—	
W-S boys		3.2	3.6	9.0	
N-S boys		3.0	3.0	7.5	
P		—	—	—	

session the differences approached a statistical significance, with a probability level of $<.06$ (Table 100).

Comparison of the Boys from the Two Groups

A number of comparisons on aggressiveness were made between the two groups of nine boys. A similar comparison was not made for the girls since the sample of four girls in each group was too small for the differences to be particularly meaningful. The difference between the boys was consistently larger and more significant than for the whole group in both overt and covert aggressiveness. The difference between the two groups of boys in strength of aggressive feelings reached a level statistically significant in the balloon experiment, with $P < .004$ (Table 100).

Rank Order of War-Separated and Non-Separated Children

The rank order of the 26 children was obtained from the totals of their standard scores for the four play sessions on the scale of strength of aggressive feelings and on the scale of strength of inhibitions against aggression.

The five children rated most aggressive were in the war-separated group.

In the group of the children who were rated above the group median in aggressive feelings (those ranking from 1 to 13), only four children were in the non-separated group. Only four of the war-separated group rank among the lower half of the children in strength of aggressive feelings. The lowest ranking of the war-separated children, Ann, does not appear to be there by virtue of her life's having been unaffected by her father's absence and return. Her responses in the play sessions indicate that her solution to the many problems created by the disruption of family life has been submissive withdrawal from conflict situations, regression, and withdrawal into herself. In the rank order of inhibitions of aggression, a group of six war-separated children are clustered at the top, but there is no similar segregation of non-separated children at the other extreme of lack of inhibitions.

Responses of Individual Children

In order to give a more adequate picture of the quality of the children's responses in the play sessions than can be obtained through the statistical comparison of the scores of the two groups, we endeavored to bring together the data for each individual from the three experimental situations and to show the pattern of behavior which emerged. In most cases the total pattern seemed to have a consistent meaning for the child, the whole configuration revealing something of his unique personality. Summaries of the play sessions for two war-separated children and one non-separated child are given here.[3] While each of these was selected as exemplifying some of the behavior patterns of his group, each child's responses to the experimental situation, as to his life situation, were unique.

Dan Wolf—4 years, 7 months; War-Separated Child

Dan's behavior was unpredictable. He had to be brought to some of the play sessions by indirect approaches; he would say "No" when invited and then demand to play the games when it was too late. In the play sessions, he went from extremes of rather negative insistence upon nonaggression to avid, uncontrollable aggressiveness.

In the play session with balloons, Dan started with a very limited field of activity, kneeling on the floor and playing only with the balloons he could reach. Gradually he extended his field to include the whole room. As he batted the balloons about the room, he seemed exceedingly stiff, particularly in the hands and arms. His movements were puppetlike. His elbows were straight, his hands stretched out and tense. His face was solemn, masklike, or slightly frowning; only occasionally did a shade of a smile appear. He asked if the balloons were new, and when told that they were, said he would break only old ones. When urged to break a balloon, he snapped, "I said 'no'!" His only attempt to break a balloon was in placing one on the radiator which he had turned on. When the experimenter broke a balloon, he paced up and down facing the wall, silent and tense. He ended the session in a narrow field again, kneeling on the floor concentrating upon tying balloons together. He was more relaxed than at first and did not want to leave.

---

3. The summaries for all cases can be found in Ryder (68).

At his request, Dan had a second period of balloon play with the experimenter. He played more aggressively with the balloons than before and made several thrusts toward breaking them but did not carry the action through. He asked the experimenter to break each one in turn while he stood outside the door and smiled, looking the other way. He broke none himself. After he returned to the nursery school, he broke a window.

Dan showed considerable aggressiveness toward the father doll in the first blocking session. His play was more relaxed than with the balloons, but his behavior was still rather tense and inhibited. A tightness about the mouth was noted at times. In the middle of the session he knocked the table over against the experimenter apparently to knock over the house she was building. He continued pushing the table forcefully and would not stop. He was excited and almost panicky in his intentness over what he was doing. He turned the table upside down and took all the legs off by unscrewing the bolts by which they were attached. Then he screwed them on with the experimenter's help. They finished the games under the table since he would not play on top. His destructiveness heightened throughout the experiment and ended in his throwing the father and boy dolls against the far wall and all the blocks after them.

A month later, Dan was quite violently aggressive in response to the blocking games with the mother, but his aggression was under better control. He entered the room stiff-legged with an apprehensive look and remained rather tense and anxious throughout the session. He was able to stop at the limits the experimenter set for him (e.g., he was not to tear the fuzz off the rug). He threw the mother doll across the room several times and put her on the radiator and turned the steam on.

In the doll-play session six weeks later, the behavior seemed relaxed for Dan. He smiled. His play with the dolls and furniture was not in conventional fashion; he turned the furniture over and made it into boats. He did not seem very involved with the dolls. Most of his aggressive behavior occurred after he left the dolls and played with other objects in the room such as the fuzz on the rug, rubbing it against the experimenter. He turned the table over and removed the legs and replaced them again, but this time it was in a more mechanical way without the extremely aggressive overtones that had accompanied the action in the first blocking session. Although he still showed much aggression, it was not the wild, uncontrollable aggressiveness he had displayed earlier.

The play sessions with Dan were spread over an unusually long period, and it may be that the changes in his response to the play materials were a reflection of the changes within Dan during that period. Dan seems to have been a child with avid aggressive feelings which, when released from the powerful inhibitions with which he held them in, were expressed violently against not only the materials provided but the experimenter and other objects in the room as well. When not being aggressive, he revealed something of his underlying feelings by his extreme tenseness of musculature, his masklike expression, his interest in but sharp denial of aggressiveness. He revealed guilt feelings after aggressive action by looking away from the experimenter, by heightened tension, and by making reparations for the damage—e.g., putting the table back together.

Dan's aggression scores are given in Table 101. His rank order among the 26 children for strength of aggressive feelings in the four sessions is 1, or most aggressive. In strength of inhibitions of aggression his rank order among the 26 children is 2 (1 being most inhibited). He also ranks second in inhibitions among the 13 children in the war-separated group.

Table 101. Aggression Scores of Dan Wolf

	Balloons	Blocking		Doll Play
		Father	Mother	
Scale of strength of aggressive feelings	7	7	7	7
Scale of strength of inhibition of aggression	5	4	4	3.5
Overt aggression	0 broken	3.7	4.7	7.3 acts/10 minutes
Destructiveness scale	2			

Fran Soule— 5 years, 10 months; War-Separated Child

Fran was an extremely inhibited child whose feelings of hostility were not expressed until the later play sessions. Her early ratings on the scale of aggressive feelings were probably too low.

In the balloon play session, Fran's face was serious, almost sad. Occasionally her mouth would draw up tightly for an instant, relax, draw up, and then relax again. While using her right hand, her left hand was usually bent at the wrist and held rather stiffly. Her gait was slow, using stiff, short steps. Her tempo of activity was slow, controlled. One pattern of activity which she repeated several times, usually following the experimenter's suggestion of breaking the balloons, was piling the long balloons in the corner and the other balloons around them. It was as if she were trying to arrange the situation so that she would have complete control over it. Sometimes she arranged the balloons in a line. She would roll the big balloons back and forth gently, one under each hand, and rhythmically, as if concerned with her own private world. Her play with the balloons was industrious but not free or joyful. She manipulated them where she could be sure that they would stay under her control. She paid little attention to the experimenter.

In the first blocking session, using the mother doll, Fran's responses were almost entirely nonaggressive. Her mouth had a tense, quivering smile or was pursed up tightly. The muscles in her hands were tense. She nervously shuffled her feet under the table as she played. She spoke little, seeming to be afraid or unwilling to present any endings to the play units. In the final free-play period she played a repetitive game of the girl running away and hiding from the mother, and the mother hunting and finally finding the girl.

In the second blocking session, using the father doll, Fran seemed to be more at ease and to enjoy herself more than before. She was freer in her responses, but there were still distinct signs of tension: twitching about the mouth, tight hand muscles, stiff and angular finger positions, rocking in her chair. Her responses started with compromise and compliance but increased in tempo and aggressiveness (throwing the father doll from the house) to a real climax in which she seemed emotionally involved as she ran wildly around and around the room saying that the girl and the father were sailing in boats. The theme of the father-child fantasy was repeatedly some form of establishing distance between them. She did not let him on her train. She locked him up. She pushed him out of the house. She put him on one side of the room and the girl on the other. However, they were together briefly in the sail-boat play and ended the session taking sun baths together.

In the doll-play session, Fran again showed signs of tension and seemed extremely involved in the play. She did not verbalize what she was doing until late in the session. Toward the father, she showed an affectionate relation, almost a baby-father relation. The emotional direction of her play seemed to be chiefly related to the baby. At first she isolated it, putting it under the table or under the stove. Then she showed more hostility toward it by dropping it on the floor. Her play reached a climax of excitement in which she crawled and ran about the room as in the blocking session. Fran hid the baby in the experimenter's hands, and then she pointed the gun as if to shoot the baby but said that she had shot the experimenter. She repeated the hiding of the baby in the experimenter's hands, "Then I look through the window. I see her. I pick her up and I shoot her. And she's dead. And I'm so tired I go back in the water and go to sleep." Her mounting activity level slowed down and she crawled slowly about the room. Afterwards the baby was revived, "Poor baby wants her mama." There were elements in her play which indicated that, in addition to feeling hostile toward the baby, she might want to *be* the baby, e.g., crawling about the room, having the girl and baby trade beds early in the session.

Fran had an interesting pattern of progression in identification in her play in which she first moved the dolls about in dramatic fantasy, apparently identifying with the girl doll, until the identification became so strong that she carried out the actions herself, carrying the girl doll with her and, finally, leaving the doll behind. After initial inhibition, her aggression tended to be revealed in emotional episodes which reached a climax of tempo and hostility and then receded into more constructive play. Aggression toward the other dolls was frequently followed by aggression toward the girl doll.

From Fran's responses to the play sessions one can make some tentative assumptions about her inner feelings in relation to her family. Fran's fantasy of the girl hiding and being found by the mother may indicate a desire to be somehow "found" by her mother, not literally, but in the sense of regaining a feeling of closeness with her mother which she, quite possibly, may have lost with the return of her father and later the arrival of her baby sister. Fran seemed to have deeply repressed feelings of hostility toward the baby. It was only after many preliminaries and shunted-off attacks that she was able to pretend to shoot the baby doll. After expressing her hostility toward the baby, she went on to express what may have been affection or concern for it, or possibly a restitution for her guilt feelings when she had the baby revived and returned to the mother. She revealed ambivalent feelings toward her father. Her fantasies of separating the girl and father were occasionally interspersed with scenes in which the girl and father sailed away together or were placed in the same bed. The conflicts between her desires and reality and between her impulses and her standards of behavior probably lie behind the tension which is noted in her behavior.

Fran's aggression scores are given in Table 102. Her rank order among the 26 children for strength of aggressive feelings in the four sessions is 5 (1 being the most aggressive). Her rank is 5 among the 13 children in the war-separated group. In strength of inhibitions of aggression, her rank order among the 26 children is 1, or most inhibited.

Table 102. Aggression Scores of Fran Soule

	Balloons	Blocking		Doll Play
		Mother	Father	
Scale of strength of aggressive feelings	4	5	5	7
Scale of strength of inhibition of aggression	4	5	4	4
Overt aggression	1 broken	2.9	3.1	8.2 acts/10 minutes
Destructiveness scale	2			

Leonard King— 7 years, 5 months; Non-Separated Child

Leonard entered the games quietly and co-operatively. His initial idea seemed to be to conform to the experimenter's instructions. He may have been slightly disturbed by her lack of directions to him, but as the sessions progressed he seemed able to drop that attitude and accept the situation as a permissive one.

Leonard presented a masculine pattern of activities in the balloon play session. He pretended that the balloons were punching bags and kicking balls. The room seemed too small for his large muscle activities. He was awkward, tripped over the balloons and had difficulty in maneuvering through them on the floor. His expression was mostly serious. He played with great energy, but it was not relaxed enjoyment. He seemed to be striving very hard to do the right thing and conformed quite precisely to the experimenter's suggestions. He broke the balloons by jumping from one to the other with vigorous movements.

In the first blocking session, using the father doll, Leonard initiated much constructive play in the elaboration of his responses to the play units. The father played with the "kids." In the play unit in which the boy was not to touch anything in the father's house, the boy did touch things, and, with a sorrowful expression, Leonard had the father spank him. It seemed that he felt that it was absolutely necessary that the punishment be meted out even though he felt unhappy about it. Toward the end of the session, he seemed though he felt unhappy about it. Toward the end of the session, he seemed to be really emotionally involved in the play, to be identifying himself closely with the boy doll. He stopped talking and acted out the events with the dolls. There was much hiding by the boy and chasing by the father. The interpretation may be suggested that Leonard felt somewhat pressed by adult requirements and was showing his desire for escape in running and hiding in the fantasy. He responded with some aggressiveness toward the father; he seemed to be really revealing his feelings in the father-son area, both positive and negative. The aggressiveness he showed was probably the total of what he felt.

In response to many of the play units in the second blocking session, he repeated a fantasy which included only the events which punctuate the day: bedtime, breakfast, lunch, and dinner. He hit the mother doll when she touched things in the boy's house, was more aggressive toward her than he had been toward the father. By the third session Leonard seemed to have lost his concern over doing what the experimenter considered proper. He seemed emotionally involved in his responses which developed into a dramatic episode with a definite conclusion, "That's all."

In the play session with the dolls, he continued to punctuate his fantasy day with eating and sleeping. It seemed to be a technique for keeping him from revealing his inner feelings although he revealed more as the session progressed. He seemed to lack freedom in his play but was not noticeably tense. His play seemed inhibited and was lacking in imagination. He showed a small amount of mild aggressiveness.

Leonard seemed to be a child who, in his effort to conform to the demands of society, had inhibited not only the expression of negative emotions such as aggression but the more imaginative and creative side of his personality as well.

Table 103. Aggression Scores of Leonard King

	Balloons	Blocking		Doll Play
		Father	Mother	
Scale of strength of aggressive feelings	3	2	2	3
Scale of strength of inhibition of aggression	2	3	2	3
Overt aggression	10 broken	2.0	2.1	6.2 acts/10 minutes
Destructiveness scale	3			

Leonard's aggression scores are given in Table 103. His rank order among the 26 children is 24 (1 is most aggressive). His rank is 11 among the 13 children in the non-separated group. In strength of inhibitions of aggression, his rank order among the 26 children is 19 (1 being the most inhibited). His rank is 9 in the non-separated group.

Patterns of Aggressive Behavior

Each of the children in this study has had a unique life experience. Each life included greater or lesser amounts of frustration, and each has experienced different results in his experimentation with various solutions to conflict situations. Yet all have come up against a somewhat similar culture and have experienced frustration at its hands. All must have aggressive feelings at times, but the strength of their aggressive feelings varies as does the degree and form in which aggression can be expressed.

On scrutinizing the responses of the individual children to the play materials used in this study, we find a number of patterns of behavior in the manner of expressing and inhibiting aggressive behavior. The expression of aggression was almost always complicated by the child's initial inhibition of such behavior and by his feelings of guilt in connection with it.

While each child's responses to the play sessions were unique, there were recurrent patterns of behavior which can be used as cues in distinguishing between the children with greater or lesser strength of aggressive feelings.

Children without moral restraints. According to the concept of aggression presented here, if a child had not learned that aggression was undesirable behavior, he could act aggressively without tension or other sign of guilt feelings; he would simply respond with a direct aggressive attack it he were frustrated and no substitute activity were offered. Such a pattern of behavior did not occur in any of the children studied, and probably would be impossible among children in our culture. All learn, in greater or lesser degree, that aggression is not good behavior.

Slight aggressive feelings. In children with slight aggressive feelings, overt aggression seldom appeared except in response to frustration and was not out of proportion to the situation. The child would simply do what was necessary to remove the block to his goal. There probably are no children completely devoid of hostile feelings toward their parents. Even the least aggressive of the children in this study, such as Ben, revealed some aggression in their play beyond what could be directly attributed to the frustration of the situation. These least aggressive children may identify strongly with their parents and have interiorized a definite code of right and wrong after the patterns of their parents. In accordance with the strength of this inner code, the amount of guilt which they apprently feel over aggression will vary. Since the aggressive behavior would be slight, the guilt feelings never would appear to be great. Tenseness in muscles and facial expression and an anxious attitude are frequently symptoms of inhibition of aggression and were usually not present in the behavior patterns of children with only slight underlying feelings of aggression.

In general, the children with slight aggressive feelings were relaxed and free in their play. They had many creative ideas to bring to the materials, showed initiative and imagination in their responses. They made free use of the space and of the materials. They carried on fantasies with the materials in which some small amount of aggression usually appeared. The boy might hit the daddy or be spanked for doing something bad, but the aggression generally stayed fairly close to the reality level and was outbalanced by the more positive, constructive aspects of the play. If, in their fantasy, they were revealing their concept of life, then aggression fit in as a natural part of it. Aggression was not a problem in their lives and they did not give it particular emphasis. They were the children who might say, matter-of-factly, "What for?" when asked if they would like to break a balloon; yet they were not adamantly opposed to breaking the balloons when assured it was permissible, and it seemed to be a part of the game.

Strong aggressive feelings. The children with strong underlying feelings of aggression varied widely in their responses, but within the variations are some configurations of responses which are helpful in distinguishing them from children with weaker feelings af aggression. The degree of inhibition of aggression, either from the child's own moral prohibitions or from fear of punishment, in its relation to the strength of the aggressive feelings seems to determine how much aggression will appear on an overt level.

Easiest to recognize among the children with strong aggressive feelings are those who have only slight inhibitions against aggression in a permissive situation such as the experimental play sessions. The aggressiveness in the responses of these children was far out of proportion to the situation. Each play situation merely served as an introduction to aggressive episodes. The aggression in such a child is indirectly expressed or is displaced aggression; the original object of the hostile feelings is most often the child's parents, but he may or may not be directly aggressive toward them. However, in a play situation where he does not feel inhibited, he redirects the aggression toward the object which most closely resembles the original object, in the later play sessions, to the parent dolls. It is aggression which has been repressed and carried over from earlier life experiences and is released in overt behavior when the situation permits it.

The patterns of behavior of the children whose impulses to aggression were overlaid with inhibitions were different. Overt aggression is dependent upon the comparative strength of the two factors— strength of the impulse toward aggression and strength of inhibition against aggression. Some of the children studied had strong aggressive feelings but exhibited little or no overt aggression, particularly in the early play sessions. Still it was possible to infer their underlying feelings from their behavior. These children, of whom George Osborne, a war-separated child, is a good example, characteristically had tense, tight musculature. Their movements seemed awkward, stiff, or jerky. The facial expression was frequently tense, particularly around the mouth. They often had nervous mannerisms, such as picking at fingers, pursing lips, pulling at clothes. While some configuration of these types of behavior was always present in children in whom powerful aggressive impulses were strongly inhibited, these signs were not sufficient to mark a child as having strong underlying feelings of aggression, since similar behavior may be due to conflict within the child not involving hostility or may be due to the child's general unfamiliarity and anxiety about the experimental situation. Confirmation was found in other signs of inhibition of aggression. One of these seems to be the use of a limited space, as by the child who kneels in one place on the floor in his play with the balloons. Another sign is a lack of imagination in the use of the play materials, as in the child who does not carry on a fantasy with the dolls or whose fantasy is limited to the stereotyped routines of eating and sleeping. Perhaps one of the best clues is apparent interest in aggressiveness, even though the child does not behave aggressively himself, as in the child who talks about aggression. An example is seen in the repeated remark of

Dan, a war-separated child, that he would break only old balloons and these were new balloons. A strong or emotional refusal or denial of destructiveness or aggressiveness seemed also to be indicative of underlying feelings of aggression. Sometimes these children would start to do something aggressive and then stop before the action was carried out. Frequently these children escaped from the idea of destructiveness or hostility, if it were introduced by the experimenter or brought up in the course of their own play, by suddenly shifting the subject of the conversation, by ignoring the experimenter's questions, by leaving the play materials or the room. These children could not be casual about aggressiveness; it was an area of behavior which they surrounded with anxiety.

Guilt feelings as a clue to aggression. When overt aggression was displayed, the amount of accompanying guilt feelings was an indirect clue to the child's degree of inhibition of aggressive impulses. A child who gives evidence of strong guilt feelings in connection with aggression probably would not behave aggressively unless his impulses in that direction were strong. If he feels guilty about the expression of aggression, it is probable that he will often keep aggressive feelings repressed. There is no one-to-one relation here, since the picture is complicated by the fact that guilt feelings are a result of the child's own moral code, and families and children differ in the amount of emphasis which they place upon "good" and "bad" or "right" and "wrong." Like inhibition of aggression, guilt cannot be directly seen in the behavior but must be inferred from the child's pattern of behavior. Heightened muscular tension or other signs of anxiety during aggression seemed to be indicative of guilt feelings. One of the most frequent ways of showing guilt feelings was in relieving the guilt by self-punishment. If the child had behaved aggressively toward the parent dolls, he then would reciprocate and behave aggressively toward the boy doll. Another way of relieving the guilt feelings was in making reparations. The child would restore to order the miniature furniture he had thrown about the room or make something out of the clay dolls he had smashed or think up some use for the broken pieces of balloons. Sometimes he would try to conceal what he had done, placing the smashed doll under a piece of furniture or piling the broken balloons in a corner of the room. Occasionally he would try to verbally justify or excuse his action.

Changes in expression of aggression. In children in whom aggressive behavior was initially inhibited, aggression was usually increasingly expressed on an overt level as the sessions progressed. In children in whom the underlying aggressive feelings were strong, when aggression was expressed, it tended to appear tentatively at first and then increase in tempo and intensity to a climax of emotional release. At this point some of the children who had been expressing their aggression through the dolls shifted the agent of aggression from the surrogate-self to the real self and seemed to have a tremendous burst of energy, jumping from table to floor or running or crawling about the room. Such a child appeared to be completely involved in acting out his impulses. Afterwards he would seem more relaxed and often showed more creative ideas in his play than before. With other children, before the expression of overt aggression had quite reached an emotional climax, the aggression was halted and there would be a brief quiescence of activity. It was as if the child had suddenly become self-conscious about his aggressiveness, remembered that it was "bad," and was unable to go on.

Aggressive behavior not only increased in intensity during the sessions but also in directness. For example, a child whose feelings of hostility were chiefly directed toward his mother, but who did not dare express these feelings, might first pretend to shoot the gun at "bears," then he might shoot the experimenter, and, after awhile, he might take a passing shot at the father; in the meantime, he would be likely to have aimed the gun at the mother doll a few times and turned it away again. Finally, he would shoot the mother, and probably follow it by shooting the boy.

These patterns of behavior were noted among both the war-separated and the non-separated children, but responses indicative of strong aggressive feelings were more frequent among the children whose fathers had been away. Responses indicative of a sharp sense of morality, of a clear distinction between good and bad, of identifying with the cultural patterns of acceptable behavior, were more typical of the children whose fathers had been present throughout their lives.

General Conclusions

Conclusions in Relation to the Initial Hypotheses

Aggressive feelings. The primary hypothesis was that the children who were separated from their fathers during the first year of life might have stronger aggressive feelings than children not separated from their fathers for any extended period. The war-separated children were rated as having stronger aggressive feelings than the non-separated group in each of the four play sessions. The combined ratings reached statistical significance.

From the findings one may say that the war-separated group of children tend to have stronger aggressive feelings than the group of children whose fathers have been present. The difference between the two groups of boys is consistently larger and more significant than for the whole group. The findings here are certainly not conclusive, but they suggest a further hypothesis that the father's absence with its accompanying disruptions of family relationships may have a different effect upon the boys than upon the girls in regard to increasing aggressiveness.

While this difference in strength of aggressive feelings which has been noted may be true of the two groups, it does not hold for all of the individuals within the group, nor could it be expected to do so. In every child's life, the process of growing up and meeting social demands involves numerous frustrations which may result in aggressive feelings. The father's absence and return is only one more thing which may contribute to the total load of frustrations to which the child must develop an adjustive pattern. The general feeling of insecurity in a home where the father is away in the service, moving to grandparents' homes and moving away again, the lack of understanding for the child on the part of a father who has not watched his development, may all have been factors operating in greater or lesser degree in each of the families of the war-separated group. That these, or other factors contingent on the father's absence, did, in many cases, increase the amount of frustration and consequent feelings of aggression in the child to a degree noticeably beyond the strength of aggressive feelings in children whose fathers were not away, is indicated by this study. In considering the results, it must be borne in mind that there may be individuals in either group who have had unusually insecure or frustrating life experiences from causes outside the realm of this study.

Inhibitions of aggression. It was hypothesized that, in most cases, the war-separated children might have repressed much of their hostile feelings and might reveal such inhibitions by tense movements and other signs. While the war-separated group was rated, in each play session, as having slightly stronger inhibitions, the differences did not reach statistical significance. It would appear that in a few cases the father's absence and return, with its consequent effects upon the child's life, may have contributed toward developing a child in whom aggression is repressed and in whom rather extreme forms of tension, inhibited movements, and lack of initiative can be noted. This study does not indicate any general trend in that direction.

It is evident that the scheme devised in this study for judging and rating inhibitions of aggression was not satisfactory. An examination of the patterns of behavior displayed by the children in relation to the expression and inhibition of aggression indicated that muscular tension tends to increase with the overt expression of aggression. Tension and some of the other signs used for judging inhibition of aggression are apparently indicative of some inner conflict. It may be the conflict between the child's desire to be aggressive and his fear of punishment if he acts out his impulse, or it may be the conflict between the child's behavior when he is behaving aggressively and his concept of what is acceptable, or it may be due to some other inner conflict. It is difficult to distinguish between the signs of inhibition of aggression and the signs of feelings of guilt for aggressive action. Because of this lack of clarity as to what behavior is indicative of inhibition of aggression, the ratings could not be very precise.

Overt aggression. It was hypothesized that the war-separated children might exhibit more overt aggression in situations permissive of such behavior than children who have not been separated from their fathers. In each of the four experimental play sessions the war-separated children were slightly more aggressive than the children who had not been separated. The differences between the two groups reached statistical significance in destructiveness with balloons ($P < .05$) and in the second blocking session. The other measures did not show differences that reached statistical significance, but the differences were in the same direction. The findings of the study indicate that there may be a slight trend toward children who were separated from their fathers during the first year of life being more overtly aggressive in a permissive situation than children who were not separated from their fathers. Overt aggression in its endless variety of forms of expression is not easily reduced to a simple quantitative measurement; the measurements used in this study were, admittedly, crude ones. The scoring did not weight the quality of an overt act of aggression. A slight spank of the father doll counted equally with a hard, vicious pounding or a shot in the head. Had these qualitative differences been taken into account, the differences between the two groups might have been larger.

Father aggression. It was hypothesized that the war-separated children might show more hostility toward the father than the other group of children. It was also thought that the war-separated children might show more hostility toward the father than toward the mother and that this difference might be larger than the difference in response to the father and mother shown by the children whose families have not been separated. The findings of the blocking sessions show that the war-separated children were only slightly more aggressive to the father than the non-separated group. The difference was not statistically significant. Both groups were more aggressive to the mother than to the father and the difference was larger among the children in the war-separated families than in the other group. The differences were not statistically significant. The hypotheses regarding a difference between the responses to the father and the mother were not supported by the data from the blocking play sessions.

Interpretive Summary

The findings of this study indicate that first-born children who were separated from their fathers for the first year of life tend to have stronger underlying feelings of aggression than first-born children who have not been separated from their fathers. The significance of this in the lives of the war-separated children is not that they will behave more aggressively. Although their aggressive impulses may sometimes lead to aggressive behavior, the findings of this study indicate that they have, in general, learned to control their hostile impulses and exhibit little more of it on an overt level than the children whose lives have been more normal. Rather, it is that they may need to devote so much of their energy to holding in their aggressive impulses and guilt feelings that they may be handicapped on the positive side of their emotional lives. They may not have enough inner freedom to be creative.

CHAPTER 12.
FATHER-CHILD RELATIONS IN STORY COMPLETIONS

by Margaret Siler Faust

Description of the Story-Completion Study

Relation of This Study to the Total Project

A consideration of such hypothetical material as that presented in Chapter 1 concerning the "model" of a family from which the father was separated during the war suggested that one major proposition which warranted careful investigation was: that, other things being equal, a child who had never been separated from his father would have a closer relation with his father than would a child who had been separated for a period of time from his father early in life. This proposition became the central focus of the present substudy. It would not be expected that all non-separated children and their fathers would have a better relation than would all war-separated children and their fathers. Such factors as the characteristics of the mother and the father as well as all of the child's life experiences determine the way in which a child responds to his father. It is not within the realm of this study to investigate all the factors which might affect father-child relations. Yet, on the whole, testing the major proposition of this study would seem reasonable if a large group of war-separated and a group of non-separated children were used in the comparison.

From the major proposition several hypotheses were derived. These hypotheses were stated in terms of the differences expected of war-separated children as compared with non-separated children, because of the emotional distance between father and child which seemed to characterize the group separated from the father during the war. The hypothesized differences follow:

1. That the war-separated child and his father would not share experiences as fully as would a non-separated child and his father.
2. That the war-separated child would resent his younger sibling more than would a non-separated child.
3. That the war-separated child would not feel as free to admit his misdeeds to his father as would a non-separated child.
4. That the war-separated child would feel more resentment in his acceptance of his father's demands than would a non-separated child.
5. That expression of impulses against the father would be more disturbing to a war-separated child than to a non-separated child.
6. That the war-separated child would be less likely to trust the father in a threatening situation than would a non-separated child.

In the present study these six hypotheses were tested. They will be referred to as the story hypotheses. Two additional hypotheses were concerned with the responses of the children in the story situation. These hypotheses, also, were related to the original proposition that the non-separated children would have a closer relation with their fathers than would war-separated children have with their fathers. One hypothesis was that the war-separated child would be less likely to accept his father's standards than would a non-separated child. Another hypothesis was that the war-separated child would be more anxious in his response to a situation which presented a child in conflict with the father. These two hypotheses seemed to warrant careful analysis.

Description of the Technique

Story completion as a research tool. In an earlier substudy of our project, certain hypotheses of the father-relations study were tested by Halnan (37). She used a projective technique in which the beginning of a story was told by the experimenter and dramatized by acting the story with dolls. The children were then asked to complete the stories in this dramatic way. The doll-play technique was successful in studying the behavior of preschool children. However, some of the older children, particularly the school-age boys, seemed to think the dolls were "babyish." It was felt that a presentation in which the uncompleted stories were read from an illustrated book would be more appealing to the older children of the study. The children would be expected, then, merely to tell the ending of the story, without manipulating dolls. With this in mind, the present technique was designed.

Story completion seemed an especially appropriate technique to use in studying certain of the hypotheses of the father-relations study. By using this technique, the area under investigation could be limited to a fairly specific topic. Therefore the investigation of the child's personality could be focused on specific aspects of the father-child relation. Because the stories could be structured around a given theme, the individual solutions offered for any story might be compared on a prescribed variable. The technique also allows the subject to select important elements of the story and to create an ending for the story in terms of the elements which are important for him.

In using story completion as a technique, several assumptions must be made in interpreting the projective material. These assumptions are:

1. That the unique way in which a child completes a story has meaning to him as an individual.

2. That there is a functional relation between a child's response to the stories and his behavior in the outside world.

3. That important information about a child's relation with his father can be gained from the child's responses to all of the stories.

4. That the responses of different children to the same story may be compared, for they are measuring the same aspect of the relation.

Relation of stories to hypotheses. The six story hypotheses listed in the first section of this chapter were to be tested by the story-completion method. Each hypothesis stemmed from the major proposition that the relation between a war-separated child and his father would be more emotionally distant than would the relation between a non-separated child and his father. Therefore the six stories, taken as a whole, should give some indication of the emotional distance between the father and the child. One uncompleted story was written specifically to test each one of the six hypotheses about the father-child relation. That is, the uncompleted stories were structured in such a way that each story would elicit material relevant to a particular story hypothesis. It was expected that the war-separated children, as a group, would respond differently to the stories than would the non-separated children.

The relation between the stories and the hypotheses is presented below. Only a resume of each story is given here. The six stories are presented in their complete form in Appendix 15.

Story I was designed to test the hypothesis that the war-separated child and his father would not share experiences as fully as would a non-separated child and his father. Sharing experiences, in this sense, could mean doing things together, or it could mean merely telling each other about one's own experiences. This story was designed in such a way that the child might reveal whether or not he and his father shared experiences by doing things together.

Theme of Story I: On the day that the family has planned to take a trip, the baby suddenly gets sick. The mother says that she must stay home with the baby, and that she cannot go on the trip. The child asks the daddy if just the two of them might go anyway.

It was expected that the non-separated children would be more likely to complete the story in such a way that the child would go on the trip with the father. The war-separated children, because of their more distant relation, would be expected to respond that the child would have to stay home with the mommy and baby and couldn't go on the trip with the daddy.

Story II was designed to test the hypothesis that the war-separated child would resent his younger sibling more than would the non-separated child. In families where the parent's preference is for the second-born child, the first-born child would find it necessary to stand up for his own rights.

Theme of Story II: A child and younger brother (or sister) are riding on their bikes when they crash, breaking the front wheel of both bikes. The children ask their daddy to fix the bikes. The daddy says that he has but one wheel, and thus he can only fix one of the bikes today. Both children ask that their bike be fixed first.

The non-separated children, as a group, would be expected to let the baby have his bike fixed first. Because the war-separated children feel less secure in their family relations, they would be expected to stand up for their own rights by having the older child's bike fixed first.

Story III was designed to test the hypothesis that the war-separated child would not feel as free to admit his misdeeds to his father as would a non-separated child. A child who is fearful of the father would be less inclined to confess his wrongdoings to the father.

Theme of Story III: A child is playing in his room with his daddy's watch, although he knows he is not to play with his daddy's things. The child drops the watch and it breaks. His parents do not hear the watch drop, and the child wonders what he should do.

It would be expected that the war-separated children through fear of the father, would be more likely to hide from the father, or in some way to destroy the evidence of the broken watch. The non-separated children, as a group, would be more likely to tell the father that the watch had been broken.

Story IV was designed to test the hypothesis that the war-separated child would feel more resentment in his acceptance of his father's demands than would the non-separated child. By resentment is meant that the child would defy the father's demands or that the child would accept the demands with reluctance and after some rebelling.

Theme of Story IV: A child has left his toys all over the living room and now he wants to go outside to play. His daddy comes and asks him to pick up his toys before he goes outside to play.

Because of the non-separated child's greater acceptance of the father, the non-separated children would be expected to consider the father's demand a reasonable request. Therefore they would be expected to conform to the demand more willingly than would the war-separated children.

Story V was designed to test the hypothesis that expression of impulses against the father would be more anxiety-producing for the war-separated than for the non-separated child. The child who fears his impulses and is trying to repress them would be very disturbed by any expression of his impulses. Expression of feelings against the father would be particularly disturbing.

Theme of Story V: The father has asked the child to fly his toy airplane outside, but the child continues to play quietly with it in the house. Quite accidentally, the airplane flies through the air and hits the daddy in the head.

It would be expected that defying the father and then hurting him would be disturbing to all children. However, the war-separated children might tend to overlook the accidental nature of the flight of the airplane, and to interpret it in terms of their own hostility toward the father. Therefore, the war-separated children would be expected to feel more guilty than the non-separated children, and to evade the issue at hand.

Story VI was designed to test the hypothesis that the war-separated child would be less likely to trust the father in a threatening situation than would the non-separated child. The child who has little confidence in the father would not trust him in a dangerous situation.

Theme of Story VI: A child and his daddy are taking a walk when they come to a very high wall. The child climbs to the top of the wall and the daddy calls to him to jump. The daddy appears to be very far below the child, and the child does not know whether to jump to his daddy or to walk down the stairs.

Because the war-separated child would be less likely to trust the father, he would not be expected to jump from the high wall to his father. His fear that the father might not catch him forces the war-separated child to walk down the stairs. The non-separated children, on the other hand, would be expected to jump to the father.

The stories presented. An attempt was made to keep the stories as unstructured as possible within the limits of testing a specific hypothesis. That is, it was necessary to structure each story to the extent that the completion of the story would produce, from each child, material which was relevant to a specific hypothesis. Before the stories were used as an experimental tool, they were pretested on five children who were not used as subjects in this experiment. After the pretesting, some of the stories were altered so as to meet certain criteria more exactly. To be considered acceptable, it was necessary for each story to:

1. Be realistic, concrete, within the realm of the child's past or quite possible future experience.
2. Be dramatic enough to get the child involved.
3. Be simple enough for the child to understand.
4. Present a conflict situation which the child would resolve, and could resolve either by action on the part of the father or of the child.
5. Be structured enough to set the conflict, yet unstructured enough to allow idiosyncratic solutions.
6. Be of such a nature as to elicit responses from which could be inferred information about the quality of the father-child relation.

Two comparable sets of stories were devised, and each set was bound in a separate book. One set of stories concerned a girl and her father, and these stories were read to the girls. The other book of stories concerned a boy and his father, and this book was read to the boys. The stories in the two books were identical, except for the use of the word "she" instead of "he," and "hers" instead of "his" in the girls' book. The sex of the baby in Story II was changed to correspond to the sex of the subject's own sibling. Both books contained illustrations which were appropriate to the stories and to the sex of the child involved in the stories. The pictures were drawn so as to give no clue to the feelings or emotions of the characters. The six experimental stories which have been described were introduced by a preliminary story which was also included in the book. The preliminary story, however, was not related to any experimental hypothesis. It merely served to acquaint the child with the method of completing stories.

General procedure for conducting the study. The experiment was conducted in the experimental room at the Stanford Village Nursery School. The experimenter and child sat next to each other at the child-sized table so that they were facing the one-way vision mirror.

Each child, individually, was brought from his home to the experimental room by the experimenter. In many cases the child had never seen the experimenter before the time appointed for the story session. Most children came eagerly to the nursery school, and talked quite freely about things which were of interest to them. However, some children seemed apprehensive about departing for the nursery school with a strange adult. Therefore, the trip to the nursery school was important because it provided the experimenter an opportunity to establish rapport with the child and to become accepted as a friendly adult. Although the child was told he would play some interesting games, he was never told in advance exactly what would be expected.

Once in the experimental room, the child and the experimenter conversed freely until the child seemed ready to accept the instructions. Often the child would ask about the book on the table, and this gave the experimenter an opportunity to introduce the test to the child. The instructions were not memorized and repeated verbatim, although the content was much the same for all subjects. The instructions were presented in a way appropriate to the child's age and varied somewhat in wording from child to child. However, the instructions were essentially this:

"This book has some stories about a little girl (boy). These stories are new, and they're a little different. They don't have any endings. I don't know what happens in the end of the stories. So I want you to tell me what you think happens. You can have the stories end any way you want. O.K.? I'll read the first story, and you tell me how you think it should end."

Each story was read by the experimenter, regardless of whether the child could read (see Figure 11). Any comments during the story were accepted and the experimenter continued to read. Often when the story was over, the child would spontaneously offer an ending. If an ending were volunteered, it was accepted and the child was encouraged to elaborate fully. If an ending were not volunteered, the experimenter would ask direct questions, such as "What do you think would happen?" until the child responded in some way (see Figure 12). If the child's responses were ambiguous, the

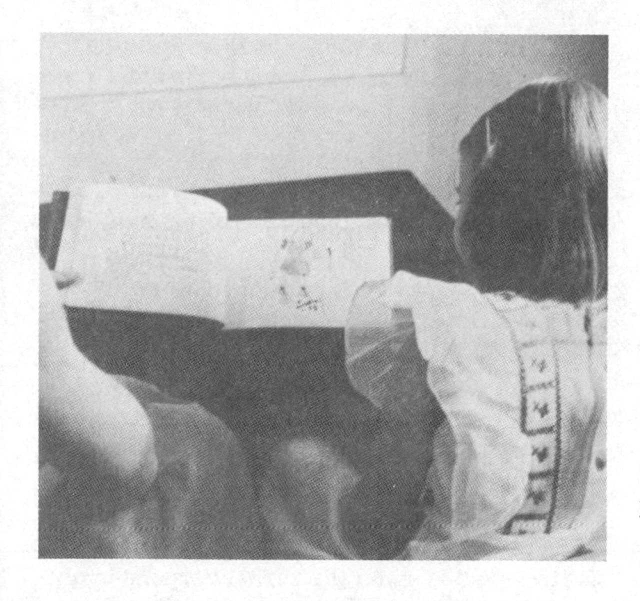

Figure 11. The Story-completion situation.

experimenter asked the child a further question. The child was encouraged to elaborate as long as he seemed interested. After his story was finished, the child was praised and encouraged to complete the next story. When the session was over, the child was allowed to hear any of the stories again if he asked for them. If the experimenter thought the child would enjoy it, the child was invited to hear an "ordinary" children's story in the nursery school before returning home.

Description of Subjects

The subjects of this investigation were 40 children of preschool and early elementary school age. Twenty first-born children whose fathers had been absent during the first year of the child's life comprised the experimental group. Matched with this group for age and sex were 20 control children, who had never been separated from their fathers for an extended period of time. Each group was made up of 11 boys and 8 girls. The age range of the war-separated children was from four years, seven months to eight years, nine months, while the non-separated children ranged in age from four years, three months to eight years, four months. In none of the matched pairs did the age difference between the war-separated and non-separated children exceed five months. The average difference in age between paired subjects was 2.7 months (see Appendix 1). Most of these subjects were included in other of the father-relations studies, while a few of the children

Figure 12. Experimenter and child as seen from the observation room in the story-completion situation.

participated only in this substudy. However, it is felt that no important selective factors were operative which would make this sample significantly different from those of the other studies.

Description of Data Collected

Recording child behavior. During each session the verbal responses of both the child and the experimenter were recorded by an Audograph. A trained observer, hidden behind the one-way vision mirror,[1] wrote a running account of the child's behavior. The instructions to the observer are in Appendix 16.

Rating child behavior. As soon as possible after the story session had ended, the experimenter and the observer rated the subject[2] on two different variables. One variable was the degree of anxiety which the child showed in response to the stories. The other variable was the amount of involvement

---

1. See Figure 12. This is approximately the way the session looked from the observer's booth.

2. In most cases the observer and the experimenter knew which subject was a non-separated and which was a war-separated child. Two war-separated children, Albert and Fran, were not rated, because they were tested by a different experimenter.

the child expressed during the stories as well as in his completion of the stories. These two variables were scaled so that they could be rated on a 5-point scale. In addition to rating on these two variables, both the experimenter and the observer checked, on a check list, the signs or clues upon which these ratings were made. The check list and rating scales of anxiety and involvement are included in Appendix 17. The instructions for rating anxiety and those for rating involvement were given to the experimenter and observer, together with the rating scales and the check lists. The instructions for rating anxiety are in Appendix 18. The directions for rating involvement are similar to those for rating anxiety, and they may be found in Faust (24a).

A rating of 1 on the anxiety scale indicates a low degree of anxiety, whereas a rating of 5 indicates a high degree of anxiety. Similarly, on the involvement scale a rating of 1 indicates a low degree of involvement whereas a rating of 5 indicates a high degree of involvement.

Combined protocols of verbal and behavioral data. The protocol for each child consisted of the Audograph record of verbal behavior co-ordinated with the observer's record of behavioral data. Four sample protocols may be found in Faust (24a).

Analysis of Children's Responses to the Stories

Degree of Involvement

The ratings of involvement were investigated to determine whether or not the children were involved in the story to the extent that interpretations could be made on the basis of their responses. It was also necessary to determine whether the children of both the war-separated group and the non-separated group were involved in the stories to the same extent.

The average rating of involvement for all children, regardless of group, is 3.94. No child received a rating of less than 3 on the involvement scale. The reliability between the experimenter and the observer on the involvement ratings is .57. The disagreements between the two raters are not particularly important since all ratings were 3 or above. Since each child was rated as being interested and involved in the stories, his responses may be accepted as a basis for further investigation. When the experimenter's ratings of the non-separated group were compared with the experimenter's ratings of the war-separated group, there was no significant difference between the two groups with respect to degree of involvement.

Anxiety Manifested

Degree of anxiety: ratings made immediately after the session. The experimenter's ratings of anxiety made immediately after the session correlated .94 with the observer's ratings.[3] The war-separated boys and girls

---

[3]. The analysis of variance presented in Table 104 shows that the war-separated and non-separated groups are from two distinct populations. Therefore the correlation of .94 is higher than one would expect from rat-

were compared with the non-separated boys and girls on the basis of these ratings of anxiety. The analysis of variance technique was used in testing the differences among the four groups of children (see Table 104).

Table 104. Analysis of Variance of Anxiety Rated at Session

	df	s^2	F	P
Sex	1	2.53	1.77	—
Group	1	16.53	11.55	$<.004$
Interaction	1	.3	.21	—
Within	28	1.43	—	—

The children of the war-separated group, as a whole, were given anxiety ratings which were significantly higher than those of the non-separated group. The difference is significant beyond the .01 level of probability. The anxiety ratings of the boys and girls were not significantly different from each other.

Degree of anxiety: ratings made from behavioral records. There was some doubt that the written observations of the children's behavior would be precise enough to be used as a basis for studying the degree of anxiety which the children showed in response to the stories. Certainly, at the time of the story session, the observer and the experimenter were able to see different degrees of anxiety in the war-separated and the non-separated groups as a whole, as seen in Table 104. Yet it seemed possible that when the child's overt responses were written in an observation that the finer gradations of "anxious" behavior might be lost. In comparing the check list of anxiety for the non-separated children against the check list records for the war-separated children, it was found that children in both groups manifested "escape-type" behavior and "nervous mannerisms." In both groups there were children who became quite disturbed during the father-child conflicts in the stories. A more sensitive technique than a mere "counting" of anxiety indicators was needed. Therefore, a method was devised whereby the war-separated and non-separated children could be compared on the observational material in the form in which it was recorded.

A 5-point rating scale was devised which was to be used in studying the behavioral signs of anxiety which were recorded in the observations. A rater who was not familiar with the observational material rated the anonymous behavioral data of each protocol. Only Stories III, IV, and V were considered, because they seemed to be the most disturbing stories for all the children.

Several factors were considered important in rating anxiety from the written records. One factor was whether the child enjoyed the build-up of

---

ings of a normal population or from ratings of a homogenous group of children. It is the diversity with which the war-separated and non-separated children are rated that tends to produce this high correlation.

the story, or whether this build-up merely served to make him uncomfortably anxious. Another important factor was the tension which the child exhibited at the climax of the story. The third factor was the degree to which the child's anxiety was absolved when he had completed the story.

The rating scale assigned values from 1 to 5 to certain observations, depending upon a combination of all these factors in the three stories. The criteria for each point on the rating scale are in Appendix 19.

The war-separated boys and girls were compared with the non-separated boys and girls on the basis of these ratings. Using the analysis of variance technique, it was found that the war-separated groups were significantly ($P < .001$) more "anxious" than the non-separated groups (see Table 105). When both groups of girls were compared with both groups of boys, it was found that the boys received significantly ($P < .05$) higher ratings than did the girls (see Table 105).

Table 105. Analysis of Variance of Anxiety Based on Observations

	df	s^2	F	P
Sex	1	7.03	6.28	$< .05$
Group	1	19.53	17.44	$< .001$
Interaction	1	.77	.69	—
Within	28	1.12	—	—

Investigation of Hypotheses of Father-Child Relations

From the typewritten protocols, the verbal responses of all subjects were investigated relative to the six story hypotheses mentioned in the first section of this substudy. Criteria were made by which any response to a given story was assigned a plus or minus value. If a child responded to the story in a way which was deemed characteristic of a war-separated child, he was given a minus rating for that response. The minus was assigned regardless of whether he was actually a war-separated or a non-separated child. If, on the other hand, a child gave a response which seemed characteristic of a non-separated child, according to the criteria, that response was given a plus value.

The responses to the stories which were expected of the war-separated children, and thus given minus values, were these:

1. In Story I the child does not go on the trip with the daddy.
2. In Story II the older child demands his bike be fixed first.
3. In Story III the child does not tell the father that the watch has been broken.
4. In Story IV the child does not willingly clean up the room when the father requests it.

5. In Story V the child is punished and he evades the conflict of having hit the father with the airplane.

6. In Story VI the child does not jump from the wall to the daddy; or if he does jump, he is not caught by the daddy.

The subjects' responses were scored for each of the six stories, according to the above criteria. After each individual's scores were summed algebraically, this score was added to a constant of 7 in order to make all the scores of positive value. Therefore, the lower a child's score, the more similar to a war-separated child he would be, according to the hypotheses. This total score for each individual gives, in fact, a measure of the original proposition stated in the first section: that a child who has never been separated from his father would have a closer relation with his father than would a child who had been separated from his father early in life.

Table 106. Analysis of Variance of Scores of Father-Child Relations

	df	s^2	F	P
Sex	1	46.7	11.9	$< .01$
Group	1	6.2	1.6	—
Interaction	1	34.0	8.4	$< .01$
Within	32	3.9	—	—

When the total scores for each group were tested by means of analysis of variance (see Table 106), it was found that the scores of the boys differed significantly ($P < .01$) from the scores of the girls. On the other hand the war-separated group, as a whole, did not differ significantly from the non-separated group, as a whole. Yet this group difference, or more exactly, lack of group difference, must be re-evaluated when the significant interaction ($P < .01$) between group and sex is considered. When the means are considered (see Table 107) it is clear that this interaction arises from the diversity of the means of the war-separated boys and the war-separated girls. The means for the non-separated boys and the non-separated girls are similar and fall in between the means of the war-separated boys and the war-separated girls. The interaction indicates that the war-separated boys are more like war-separated children were expected to be than are the non-separated groups, while the war-separated girls are more like non-separated children were expected to be. This tendency for "oppositeness" among the war-separated boys and the war-separated girls is significant at a P level of $< .01$.

It can be seen, then, why the over-all difference between the groups is not significant when the two groups of boys and the two groups of girls are combined. It is the compensatory difference between the scores of the war-separated boys and the war-separated girls which obliterates the group difference. Since the non-separated boys and girls received about the same scores, it is the averaging of the discrepant scores of the war-separated boys and the war-separated girls which makes the group differences insignificant.

Table 107. Mean Scores of Father-Child Relations

	War-Separated	Non-Separated	Mean
Boys	4.32	5.44	4.89
Girls	8.44	5.77	7.11
Mean	6.39	5.61	

Degree of Conformity

It was felt that Stories III, IV, and V, unlike the other stories, all presented a stressful situation which put the child in conflict with the father. However, in Stories III, IV, and V, the child had a chance to minimize the conflict with the father by conforming to his demands or expectations, rather than by acting out his own fear of the conflict situation. The facility with which the child subject can create an "acceptable" solution to the story indicates to some extent the degree to which he has integrated his father's standards and values into his own behavior. The child who does not consider the father as a "just" and "fair" person may have difficulty in completing the stories in a way which is acceptable to the child in the story. A child whose wishes are at odds with his father's may become so disturbed by the story conflict that he is unable to face the problem. This disturbance may be indicated by the subject's responding irrelevantly, or by his refusing to complete the stories at all.

The subject's resolution of the father-child conflicts in these stories was used as a measure of the child's conformity to society's demands, as represented by the father. A 5-point scale of "conformity" was devised which would apply to all three of these stories. This general scale assigns values from one to five to certain responses depending upon the degree of conformity to the father's standards which the responses show. The ratings are assigned so that 1 indicates high and 5, low conformity. The scale is in Appendix 20.

Corresponding to these general ratings, specific criteria for rating the responses to each of the three stories were devised. Thus a response rated 3 for one story would be comparable to a response rated 3 for a different story. In Appendix 21 are listed the specific criteria for each rating of Story III, Story IV, and Story V with a sample response for each rating.

After each child's responses to all three stories had been rated, a complex analysis of variance was used in testing the significance between three variables: the groups (war-separated vs. non-separated), sex (boys vs. girls), and the stories (Stories III, IV, and V). Table 108 presents the variance estimates, their degrees of freedom, the "F" ratios, and their probability levels for the analysis of variance design based on these ratings.

In the analysis of variance test, the triple interaction between groups, sex, and stories was found to be significant ($P < .001$). The fact that the triple interaction is significant indicates that all of the variables interdetermined the ratings which a child received; the responses of the individuals varied from group to group depending upon the sex of the subject and the particular story in question. However, since this study does not expect to generalize to other stories and to all possible conditions, the significance of the triple interaction is not crucial to this investigation.

Table 108. Analysis of Variance of Ratings of Conformity

	df	s^2	F	P
Main Effects				
Stories	2	6.04	6.36	<.004
Sex	1	.58	.61	—
Group	1	14.81	15.59	<.001
Double Interactions				
Stories × Group	2	.61	.64	—
Stories × Sex	2	.15	.15	—
Group × Sex	1	16.43	17.29	<.001
Triple Interaction	2	8.19	8.52	<.001
Between Individuals	32	.46	—	—
Individuals × Stories	64	1.19	—	—
Error (a)	96	.95	—	—

a. This error term is the average of the between individuals and the individuals × stories error terms. This error term was used to test the other effects.

When the interaction between stories and groups is tested, no significant relation is found between the group to which a child belongs and the patterning of responses to the three stories. Similarly, when the interaction between stories and sex was tested, there was found no significant relation between the sex of the child and the patterning of responses to the three stories. However, the three stories were found to be significantly different from each other beyond the .01 level of significance. Since the interactions involving stories are not significant, but the main test for stories is significant, it means that both groups and both sexes tended to respond to the stories in a consistent way. That is, all groups had a similar pattern of responses to the three stories. Therefore, each story consistently elicited different aspects of the father-child relation.

The interaction between group and sex is significant at the .001 level. This indicates that the responses of the war-separated boys differ from the responses of the war-separated girls in quite another manner than the responses of the boys and the girls in the non-separated group differ from each other. This relation between the four groups can be seen clearly when the mean ratings for the three stories are studied.

From Table 109 it can be seen that the war-separated boys show the least conformity,[4] while the war-separated girls show the most conformity

4. The lower the numerical rating, the greater the conformity to father's standards.

to father's standards. The non-separated boys and girls fall between these two extremes. The significant interaction indicates that while the non-separated boys and girls do not differ in their responses to the stories, the war-separated boys and girls respond in diametrically opposite manners. When the differences between these two means are tested using a t test,[5] the non-separated boys and girls are found to respond similarly. The war-separated boys respond in a manner significantly ($P < .01$) less conforming than

Table 109. Mean Scores of Conformity

Boys		Girls	
War-Separated	Non-Separated	Non-Separated	War-Separated
3.85	2.92	2.96	2.33

do the non-separated, while the war-separated girls respond in a way which is significantly more conforming than the non-separated. The main test of sex is significant at a P level of .001. However, the main contribution to this statistical sex difference is made by the discrepant scores of the war-separated boys and the war-separated girls. Since the scores of the non-separated boys and the scores of the non-separated girls are not significantly different from each other, it is the scores of the war-separated girls which tend to increase the conformity totals for the two groups of girls. Contrariwise, it is the war-separated boys who account for the low degree of conformity in the combined group of boys.

When the main test between the war-separated group, as a whole, and the non-separated group, as a whole, is made, there is no significant difference between the two groups. The factors producing this lack of difference between the groups become evident when the interaction between group and sex is considered (see Table 110).

Table 110. Mean Scores of Conformity

	War-Separated Group	Non-Separated Group
Boys	3.85	2.92
Girls	2.33	2.96
Mean	3.09	2.94

It is the intermediate position of the two non-separated groups and the compensatory diversity of the two war-separated groups which render the over-all group comparisons insignificant. The important relation demonstrated in this discussion of the analysis of variance of conformity ratings is this: that there is probably no difference between the responses of "normal" boys and "normal" girls, because such children show an intermediate conformity to the father's standards on the basis of this scale. On

5. The error term in the analysis of variance design was used as the variance estimate in the t test.

the other hand, the war-separated boys, in general, complete the stories in a manner which is at odds with the father's standards, while the war-separated girls tend to complete the stories with extreme conformity to the father's standards.

Discussion and Interpretation

Degree of Involvement

When the war-separated children were compared with the non-separated children on the basis of involvement ratings, it was found that both groups of children were involved in the stories to the same degree. Children in both groups evidenced extreme interest in the stories and seemed to identify with the child who was depicted in the stories. The children's remarks and comments during the story session indicated that they felt the father-conflict situations in the stories to be quite "real." There can be little doubt that both the war-separated and non-separated children became ego-involved in the stories as well as in their own completions of the stories.

"Emotional Distance" of the War-Separated Children

When the verbal responses to the stories were accepted as a measure of emotional distance, it was found that the boys who had been separated from their fathers had a more distant relation with their fathers than did any other group of children. The war-separated girls, on the other hand, responded to the stories in such a way that they appeared to have an excellent relation with their fathers. Characteristically, the war-separated boys ended the stories by ignoring the father's demands, by defying the father, or by having the child in the stories be punished severely for misdeeds, Further, the war-separated boys tended to circumvent the father and to ignore the father-child conflict presented in the story. Rarely did a war-separated boy depict in his story ending a warm, sympathetic, understanding father.

The responses of the war-separated girls, however, depicted a girl who conformed to the father's demands, confessed her wrong-doings to the father, and allowed the baby priority because "he was littler." The war-separated girls consistently overresponded on the side of conventionality. The fact that the war-separated girls depicted such a perfectly intimate relation with the father suggests some distortion of reality in terms of the girls' own needs or wishes. Extreme morality and selflessness may help to reduce conflicts with the father in real life situations. However, it would seem that in a situation as unstructured as this one, that the moral controls of these war-separated girls would allow the expression of more assertive and negative feelings than could be tolerated in the home. Yet, perhaps even in a play situation with an adult, they still felt it necessary to be moralistic and valuative in order to be acceptable.

"Conformity" of the War-Separated Groups

Before evaluating these differences in emotional distance of father and child, let us consider the similar group differences which obtained in the ratings of conformity. Typically, the war-separated boys ended the stories in a way which indicated that the father's demands and the boy's own wishes were irreconcilable. This incompatibility of the father's demands and the boy's wishes was indicated clearly in the numerous irrelevant responses, as well as in the failure to consider the father's demands when completing the stories. The war-separated girls, on the other hand, responded in quite a different manner. It was characteristic of the war-separated girls to portray a girl who knew how to please the father by behaving according to conventional standards. The father-child conflicts were resolved by acting in conformity with a father's expectations for a "good little girl." It is difficult to determine whether or not a child who consistently gives conforming endings to the stories has really accepted and integrated the expectancies of her parents in these areas which the stories are designed to test. The response could be related to fantasy of a wish-fulfilling nature, or it could be a superficial response in terms of what the child has learned is desirable behavior. Nevertheless, it can be said that the war-separated girls had these responses "on tap" and were able to produce them from their repertoire, which was not the usual case for the war-separated boys.

"Emotional Distance" and "Conformity" of the Non-Separated Groups

It has already been noted that the responses of the non-separated boys and girls were similar to each other with respect to conformity and emotional distance. Neither group tended to respond in a manner that indicated extreme defiance nor extreme conformity. As a whole, the non-separated group responded to the conflict situations by recognizing and reconciling the discrepancies between the child's wishes and the father's demands.

Relation of Sex to Conformity and Emotional Distance

The overresponse of the war-separated girls in terms of conventionality indicates that these girls have a distant relation with their fathers. Their extreme need to gain acceptance and approval from the father seems to show that they have not been satisfied in their relations with him. Overconformity represents as great a disturbance as do the more overt problem behaviors, such as aggression and defiance. Overconformity is a problem because it represents a real need for affection and approval which has not been satisfied. Expressing their own feelings is so unacceptable to these war-separated girls that they must deny their feelings to be accepted at all. When the need for conformity is so great, the child's behavior necessarily lacks spontaneity. Thus the responses of the war-separated girls tend to indicate that these girls really do have a distant relation with their fathers.

The question arises: why are the responses of the boys so different from those of the girls in this war-separated group? One conjecture immediately suggests itself. The war-separated girls responded on a fantasy level, and the completions of their stories represent their wish for a close relation with their fathers. However, if the war-separated girls responded on a fantasy level, what then of the war-separated boys? One might speculate that the fantasy of the war-separated boys consists of their wish to defy the father, something they would not dare to do in reality. The story conflicts presented an opportunity for the war-separated boys to express their feelings toward the father by defying him. Yet, their expressed defiance sometimes resulted in punishment on the part of the father. This punishment could not be termed "wish-fulfilling"—unless possibly it served to reduce the guilt associated with defying the father.

It might be conjectured further that the non-separated child, who has had a "normal" relation with his father, has accepted the father as an individual, and thus is better able to deal with the father-child conflicts realistically. These are merely speculations, because there is no evidence from this study to support either the hypothesis that the responses were wish-fulfilling or that they were realistic solutions to the story conflicts.

The results of this study seem to agree with those of Seaton (71) who reports that the responses to uncompleted stories are distorted by factors other than direct projection. Seaton found that the girls, more than the boys, tended to select story endings which would be considered "acceptable." Distortion in terms of conventional norms operated more strongly in determining the responses of girls than in determining the responses of the boys. In the present study this sex-difference of "conventional" responses was outstanding between the war-separated girls and the war-separated boys.

Father's Role in Relation to Boys and Girls

It seems reasonable to suppose that the absence and return of the father would affect boys and girls differently. Upon his return from war when not accepted by the child, the father might respond differently to a daughter than to a son. However, the analyses in Chapters 3, 4, and 5 of the father interview data and in Chapter 7 of the mother interview data do not show differences of the fathers in their attitudes toward or relations with first-born boys contrasted with first-born girls.

Cultural Roles as an Explanation.

The diverse cultural roles which these boys and girls are learning at this developmental level may be a possible explanation. During this period the girls are being urged to act like "girls," to be sweet, to be responsive, to be accepting and nonaggressive. Such behavior is encouraged and rewarded, even by a father with whom the girl has a distant relation. The boys, on the other hand, are expected to be "boys" and act like "boys." In their peer relations, boys must "stand up for their rights and be aggressive in leadership" and are urged to do this by their fathers. Yet when the boy is assertive in his personal relations with his father, his behavior is unacceptable to his father. Such "boyish" behavior only antagonizes the father. The boy consequently may reject the father and his standards, and may even give up trying to please him.

In a war-separated family, it may be more difficult for a boy to accept his own sex-role than it is for a girl to accept her role. The close relation which the girl has established with her mother early in life provides a good basis for later identifying with the mother. Her object choice is clear, and her feminine role becomes established. The acceptance of her feminine role is not prohibited to such a great extent by a distant relation with her father. The girl can gain acceptance from the father by conforming and by being a "good little girl," and thus her feminine orientation is reinforced. The girl learns to "overlay" her real feelings about the father with socially acceptable feminine modes of response. Although the girl's feelings become "culturally overlaid," the initial feelings are still present. One might speculate that the girl's distant relation with her father would reappear as an important factor during adolescence. It might be expected that the girl's basic rejection of her father might hinder the establishment of genuine heterosexual relations during this later period of development. The heterosexual adjustment of the war-separated girls during adolescence would provide an interesting follow-up study.

On the other hand, the boy's relation with his father is crucial to the boy's acceptance of the masculine role. When the father returns, the boy's emotional attachment is to his mother. Yet the culture demands that he become a masculine person. "All theorists seem agreed that both identification and object choice depend upon a positive, affectional relationship between the individuals concerned" (57, p. 606). If the child cannot accept the father or, conversely, if the father cannot accept his son, the boy is frustrated in his attempt to conform to society's demands that he become a masculine person. The boy's confusion over his own sex-role may result in a continued emotional identification with his mother, and possibly only a behavioral identification with the father. The boy may attempt to be a "he-man" like his father, but the emotional identification with the father may still be absent. Unlike the girl, the boy cannot gain acceptance from the father by extreme conformity and by being affectionate, for these are not part of the cultural definition of masculinity. A poor relation with the father may be more disturbing to a boy than to a girl at this developmental level.

Individual Differences in Story Completion

The preceding discussions have necessarily been in terms of group differences. Above, the groups have been characterized as a whole without regard for the variability within each group. Certainly there were individual differences in the responses which the children gave to the stories. If these idiomatic ways of responding could be properly analyzed, greater insight into the behavior of each child could be obtained. It is recognized that much of the meaningful data is disregarded when only group comparisons are made.

Each of the war-separated children has "adjusted" to the father's intervention in a way which combines unique elements with certain common elements. The responses of these war-separated children to the stories represent, in a way, the uniqueness as well as the similarity with which the children have related to an absent father.

However, one case seems particularly worthy of mention in this respect. It would be quite misleading to think of Patricia (war-separated) as responding to the stories by conformity and by striving to gain the father's approval by "being good," as was the tendency of the war-separated girls. Consistently Patricia responded to the father-conflict situations by evasion or defiance— a type of response which was quite characteristic of the war-separated boys in this study. Her "adjustment," then, is not one of cultural overlay of her real feelings toward the father. Factors in her unique life experiences have made Patricia quite different from the general pattern which the other war-separated girls tend to represent.

Anxiety of War-Separated Boys and Girls

In this study two measures of anxiety were used. The ratings immediately following the session, as well as the ratings of anxiety from the written behavioral records, showed that the father-conflict stories evoked more "anxious" behavior from the children who had been separated from their fathers than from the children who had not been separated from their fathers. Further, the boys showed slightly more anxiety in relation to the stories than did the girls.

In considering the differences between war-separated and non-separated children's responses to the stories, a formulation of anxiety must be presented. In discussing Karen Horney's view of anxiety, May (55, p. 140) states:

> "Neurotic anxiety and helplessness are not the result of a realistic view of inadequacy of power, but arise out of an inner conflict between dependency and hostility, and what is felt as the source of danger is primarily the anticipated hostility of others."

In further discussing this relation between anxiety and hostility, May says that resentment is directed toward the person who has caused the initial anxiety. Hostility mounts in proportion to the dependence the child feels toward the object. Because of the child's fear of alienating the person upon whom he is dependent, the child may begin to repress his hostile feelings.

This formulation of anxiety aids in understanding why the war-separated children are more anxious than are the non-separated children in their response to the father-conflicts in the stories. Further, this formulation of anxiety, as well as the preceding discussion of the identification process, provides an explanation for the greater anxiety among the boys than among the girls.

It has already been noted that the returning father necessarily "intrudes" upon an established mother-child relation. The resentment of the war-born child is directed toward the father because the father has precipitated the child's initial anxiety of being displaced in the family. This initial anxiety is an undifferentiated fear of loss of security. When the father remains in the family picture, the child channels his hostility and directs it toward the object which threatens his security. A daughter, similarly, may resent the father's intervention in the family, but the girl's later identifications are with the mother. The girl's relation with her mother may be continued even though the girl may not have successfully related to her father. The boy, however, not only resents the father, but he is also dependent upon the father. In order to accept a masculine role a boy has to identify with a father whom he rejects. The boy's hostility toward the father mounts in proportion to his dependence upon him. Therefore the boy's status with his father is ambivalent, for he is both dependent upon and hostile toward the father. It is because of the boy's greater dependence upon the father that the boys shows more anxiety in father-conflicts than does the girl.

Because of the war-separated child's fear of the father, he anticipates counterhostility on the part of the father. With the child's primitive perception of his environment he feels that "if I am hostile toward my father, he may displace me from the family altogether." Thus any conflicts with the father are very threatening to these children. In the story session, the anxiety evidenced in relation to the father-conflicts was greater for these war-separated children, who had established only tenuous relations with their fathers.

Summary

The purpose of the study was to determine the effect of the father's absence and return upon the child's relation with his father in later years. Several hypotheses about such war-separated children were proposed and tested.

The subjects of this investigation were 40 children who live, or have lived in the Stanford Veteran's Village. The experimental group was of 20 first-born children whose fathers had been in the armed services during the first year or more of the child's life. There were 9 girls and 11 boys in this group. They ranged in age from four years, seven months to eight years, nine months. The remaining 20 children comprised the control group. None of these children had been separated from their fathers. These control children were matched for age and sex with the experimental children. The average difference between pairs of matched subjects was 2.7 months.

Story completion was used as a technique in studying these children. Six stories about a child and his father were read to each child individually. The child was asked to complete each story. The stories were each designed to test a hypothesis about relations of the war-separated children and their fathers. During the session an Audograph recorded the verbal responses, while a hidden observer recorded the child's behavior. After the session the experimenter and the observer rated each child on a 5-point scale of anxiety and a 5-point scale of involvement, on the basis of the child's response to the stories. The reliability between the observer and the experimenter for the anxiety ratings was .94 while the reliability for the involvement rating was .57. Since all of the ratings of involvement were 3 or above, this discrepancy is not considered important for this study.

Both the war-separated and non-separated groups showed a very high degree of involvement and interest in the stories. When the war-separated boys and girls were compared with the non-separated boys and girls on the basis of the anxiety ratings made immediately after the session, it was found that the war-separated children, as a group, evidenced more anxiety in relation to the stories than did the non-separated group. The ratings of the boys and the girls did not differ significantly from each other. When the four groups of children were later compared on the basis of anxiety rated from the anonymous observational material of three of the conflict stories, it was found that the war-separated children were more anxious than were the non-separated children.

The verbal responses to the stories were rated on a 5-point scale designed to analyze the degree of conformity to father's standards. It was found that the war-separated boys showed the least conformity to the father's standards, whereas the war-separated girls showed the most conformity. There was no over-all group difference between war-separated and non-separated children, because of the differential way in which the war-separated boys and girls responded. The non-separated girls showed the same degree of conformity to the father's standards as did the non-separated boys.

When the initial hypotheses about father-child relations were investigated, the responses of the war-separated boys confirmed the hypothesis that "experimentals" would have an emotionally distant relation with their fathers. However, the war-separated girls responded in a way which was not deemed characteristic of "experimentals."

The evidence of the study seems to justify the conclusion that the father's absence and return to the family had a different effect upon the boys than upon the girls. In an effort to systematize the findings, an explanation was offered in terms of the differing process of identification for girls and boys. A good father relation seems more crucial to boys at this developmental level. The boy's hostility toward the father and the father's lack of acceptance of his son may result in an incomplete masculine identification on the part of the developing son. The definition of the girl's feminine role, however, is consistent with the girl's emotional identification with her mother, and thus her appropriate sex-role is more readily accepted. An explanation was offered in terms of "cultural overlay" which the girls learn as a part of their sex-appropriate pattern.

CHAPTER 13.
FATHER-CHILD RELATIONS AS REVEALED BY DRAMATIC-PLAY COMPLETIONS

by Laverne C. Johnson, D. Bob Gowin, and Lois Meek Stolz

Description of Study

Purpose

The purpose of the studies presented in this chapter was to gain insight into the child's relations with his family and his father in particular through a series of structured and unstructured play interviews with miniature life toys. We hoped to obtain, through adding new information to supplement the data revealed by the other media, a more complete picture of the child and his family relations.

As Chapter 10 states, the various projective techniques, of which doll play is one, are often used to study what has been called the "deeper," "hidden," "repressed," "unconscious," or "inner" life of the individual. Thus, this study takes its place in the over-all project by studying at a dynamic level the family relations as inferred from the child's behavior in the doll-play situation.

The general and guiding assumption of this project and therefore of this particular study was the expectation that there would be a significantly different quality about the father-child relation in those families where the father had been absent from the home because of war service. We expected these children to differ from those where the father had not been absent in how they responded to punishment, in the way they showed affection, and in the manner in which they referred to their mother or father. All of this was investigated through the child's presentations in his doll play. No attempt was made to see if the child behaved in a similar way in his home when confronted with these problematic situations. For validation, then, our study must be related to the larger context of the other researches in this monograph (see Ned Ford and His Family, Chapter 14).

Methods for the Collection of Data

Doll play has long been used as a substitute for more verbal methods in the study of children, especially in the treatment of emotional problems. As Erikson (23) states:

> "To play it out is the most natural autotherapeutic measure childhood affords. Whatever other role play may have in the child's development, and I do not think these are well known, the child also uses it to make up for defeats, suffering, and frustrations, especially those resulting from a technically and culturally limited use of language."

However, the use of doll play as a research tool is of more recent origin and poses many problems which cannot be discussed adequately here. The central problem in planning this study was whether to choose the completely free and unstructured type of play interview, or the more structured play with definite situations presented. In addition, decision had to be made regarding whether the doll-play material should be of high or low realism value and what type of doll figures would afford the best stimulus. These problems were faced and resolved by Halnan (37), who conducted the exploratory study.

Structured dramatic play. The more structured type of play in response to uncompleted dramatic doll play was chosen for two reasons. First, the fathers in interviews (reported in Chapter 3) had indicated certain areas of relations in which they had problems and about which they showed concern. Frequently mentioned problems were those related to discipline and punishment; permissiveness and lenience vs. firmness; the establishment of affectionate relations between the father and child after the father's return to his home; and the relative strength of attachment of the child to father, mother, and grandparents with whom the child lived during the father's absence. Therefore, doll-play situations were devised to explore the child's own feelings about these areas. Second, the structured stories presented to each child in both groups gave a comparable basis for exploring differences.

Play materials. Utilizing Robinson's (67) findings that children identified somewhat more readily with a doll family if it duplicated their own family constellation, dolls were provided which duplicated the child's own immediate family. In the dramatic situations utilized to investigate the feeling the child displayed toward his grandparents, dolls representing the grandparents were included in addition to the central family constellation.

Figure 13. The doll furniture arranged as presented to the children in the dramatic-play completions.

Because the interactions between the doll-family members which the child depicted in his play were to be of primary importance in the analysis of the data, dolls were used which were fairly realistic, easily manipulated, and sturdily constructed (see Figure 13). Phillips (62) found that with doll-play materials of "high realism" value there was relatively more exploratory and less organizational behavior than with material of "low realism" value. In accordance with this and also to accentuate the doll-family member interaction, the doll furniture was constructed with "low realism" value (see Figure 14).

Figure 14. The central doll family and grandparent dolls used in the dramatic-play completions.

Experimental procedure. The experimental procedure consisted of presenting to the child 16 doll-play situations and encouraging him to complete these situations, expressed through the media of manipulative activity with the play materials and verbal activity. (The stories which present the dramatic situations for completion will be found in Appendix 22.) Preceding and following the structured situations each child was given a period of free play with the materials. The initial free play allowed opportunity for exploration of materials and situation. The closing free-play periods mitigated to some extent the disadvantages arising from the fact that the subjects in their play behavior might be restricted because of the structured nature of the main session.

Two doll-play sessions were held. The first was devoted to the initial free-play period and to dramatic play related to the central family constellation. The second session included dramatic play related to the grandparents and a closing free-play period. The two short periods decreased the tendency to fatigue or satiation.

Each child was brought to the experimental room by the experimenter, and after the free-play session the experimenter said: "Now we're going to do something else with the dolls and furniture that I think you will like. You see, here's the family— the mommy, the daddy, the little boy, and the little baby. And here is the house where they live. Here's the living room with the davenport, the table, the chairs, and bench. Here's the stove and refrigerator and sink in the kitchen. Here's the bathroom with the toilet and washstand. And here's the bed."

After naming family and furniture, the experimenter structured the situation. "Now I'm going to tell you some stories about what happens to the family. I will start the story and you show me what happens. You can move the dolls around and you can tell me what happens." The situations for the first session were then presented. The experimenter was permissive and only entered into the situation, after presenting the situation, to ask questions, mainly for clarification, or to give support and encouragement.

The second session with each subject took place within 48 hours after the first session and was conducted similarly to the first. In this session the free-play period followed the presentation of structured dramatic situations.[1]

Subjects

In the exploratory study, there were 5 boys and 5 girls in both the war-separated and non-separated groups. The chronological age range for the war-separated children was from 49 to 80 months, with an average of 61 months. The age range of the non-separated children was from 51 to 89 months, with an average of 62.5 months.

In the main study the sample was increased to 34 children. One of the war-separated and 4 of the non-separated subjects in the exploratory study were dropped because they did not fully meet the criteria for experimental and control subjects. The experimental group consisted of 6 girls and 11 boys, ranging in age from 49 to 88 months. The average age for this group was 64 months. The control group consisted of 6 girls and 11 boys ranging in age from 51 to 92 months, with an average age of 65 months. (See Appendix 1 for a list of these children.)

Description of Data Collected

The 34 protocols for analysis consist of the verbal and behavioral responses of the children to the 16 dramatic-play completion stories. The data were recorded by an observer behind a one-way vision mirror and with an electric recording machine, as described in Chapter 10.

The role of the observer, who was seated in the observation room next to the one-way mirror, was to record in as detailed a form as possible the activity of the child as he interacted with the play materials. The observer's record of activity included the actual content of the play behavior, with particular reference to the content of the completions; the affect associated with the thematic sequence depicted by the child; signs of tension and anxiety revealed through facial expression or motor behavior; and the manner in which the child handled the play materials. The verbal content was briefly noted in order to provide cues which would make it possible to integrate the verbal records obtained on the recording machine with the observer's record. The two sets of records then were integrated into a single protocol so that there was available a complete record of the child's behavior in the experimental session.

Two persons acted as experimenters during the course of the study. Both were trained in the specific techniques to be used; in addition they had had previous intensive training in methods of observing young children's play

---

1. For a more detailed description of the experimental procedure see Halnan (37).

activities. Experimenter A collected data on 9 war-separated and 6 non-separated subjects; Experimenter B collected data on 8 war-separated and 11 non-separated subjects.

Methods Used in Analysis of Data

Treatment of doll-play material has been mostly qualitative, in keeping with its therapeutic setting. However, with its introduction into research quantification became necessary. In this study, five types of analyses of the same data were attempted, four of them with the use of statistics. These ranged from a more atomistic and quantitative counting of behavior elements to a more holistic and qualitative rating of the father-child relations using the complete protocol. The first analysis, made in the exploratory study, consisted of dividing the story told into father-related elements, counting them, and comparing the two groups. The second type of analysis was essentially that used in the exploratory study, with improvements in definition of elements and changes in classification of elements. These differences will be clarified and amplified later. The third analysis was done by rating the father-relation the child presented in each story and then comparing the two groups. The fourth analysis consisted of rating the father-relation from a summary of all the play material the child presented and then comparing the two groups of children. In addition, in the exploratory study a qualitative analysis of each child was made comparing the matched pairs of war-separated and non-separated children, without the use of statistical tools.

The Exploratory Study

Analysis of Data

In the exploratory study conducted by Halnan (37), two levels of analysis were made. The first level was primarily an analysis of the completions to the dramatic-play situations in terms of units or logical subdivisions within the completions. The second level was a more qualitative and dynamic approach to the data.

Categorical division of the story-endings. As a basis for dividing the completions into parts which would be manageable and empirically clear for analysis, an attempt was made to use episodes. An episode was defined either as a sequential part within the completions involving a related series of interactions between doll-family members or the related actions by one doll involving a single thematic sequence. This form of classification was unsuccessful for two reasons. Not only was it impossible to get agreement on what constituted an episode, but an episode was too long and complicated to enable a categorization scheme to be developed.

The completions were therefore divided into smaller units which we have called elements. An element consisted of a single specific action by a doll-family member or a single specific thought expressed by the child as he played with the materials. An element was delineated from another element by a change of activity, or of thought. In a sequence in which a causal factor appeared, or a reason was given for a particular act or thought, this causal factor, if specifically stated as a cause, was considered a part of the particular element to which the act or thought belonged. It was then scored as one element rather than two. If several doll-family members engaged in a single activity, the several actions were scored as separate elements.

An example of the division of a story-completion into its elements is given here for explanatory purposes. Manipulative activity is given in parentheses. Verbalizations are recorded as quotations. A subject's responses to dramatic-play situation 1 (father shaving, boy comes in) included the following elements: (1) "He wanted to shave." (2) "Father gives him a razor," (3) "and lets him shave." (4) (Subject moves blond boy to father) "The other little boy wants to shave." (5) (Subject moves brunette boy to blond boy.) (6) "Father doesn't let him." (7) "Doesn't have enough shaving cream."

The total number of elements in each protocol was obtained through adding the number of elements in each of the 15 story-endings. The percentage of agreement on the classification of elements by the two raters on seven protocols was 91. (The raters were H. Halnan and L. M. Stolz.)

Classification into father elements. The next step in the categorical analysis of the protocols consisted of selecting from among the total elements in each completion those elements which involved the father doll. The criteria for classifying an element as a father element were as follows: (1) a pantomimed action by father doll; (2) a statement by the subject which dealt with an action or thought of the father doll, even though not directly pantomimed; (3) a pantomimed action by any doll-family member which was directed toward the father doll or involved a form of interaction between the family member and the father doll; (4) a response to a question by the experimenter which expressed clear doubt as to the action of the father doll. The number of father elements in each protocol was obtained by adding the number of father elements in each completion.

The father elements were then classified into three groups: positive and negative (as described on page 273), and neutral. In order to determine whether there was significant difference between the two groups with respect to positive, negative, and neutral father elements, the t technique for differences between correlated means was applied.

Dynamic approach to the dramatic-play completions. The second level of analysis in the exploratory study was a qualitative comparison of the feelings toward the father figure of the matched war-separated and non-separated subjects. Since certain of the dramatic-play situations tended to elicit responses which revealed clearly the attitudes toward the father doll, while others proved to be less revealing with respect to the father-child relation, it was decided to compare the matched subjects on the completions or responses to several chosen dramatic-play situations. Inspection of the protocol revealed that 8 of the 16 situations tended to elicit responses which pertained to the father-child relation in particular. These were dramatic-play situations 4, 5, 6, 7, 8, 12, 13, and 15. (See Appendix 22 for these dramatic-play completions.)

A brief account of the contents in these 8 dramatic-play situations was obtained by first summarizing the child's completions, then describing briefly the thematic sequences within the completions and the responses of one doll-family member to another. From these completion summaries, a fairly direct comparison between the matched subjects could be made.

Findings of Exploratory Study

The total number of elements in the completions of the ten war-separated subjects was less than the number in the completions of the ten non-separated subjects. However, the father elements constituted 31.3 percent of the total elements of the war-separated group and 31.7 percent of the total elements of the non-separated group. There was a rho correlation of .82 between the total number of elements and the number of father elements.

When the completions were classified into positive, negative, and neutral father elements, the war-separated subjects' completions tended to have slightly more negative father elements and slightly fewer positive father elements than the non-separated subjects'. The differences between the two groups were not statistically significant, however, in spite of the general trends.

Qualitative analysis of the selected completions and other pertinent data revealed that the war-separated subjects depicted more negative or ambivalent feelings in their perceptions of the father-child relation than did the non-separated subjects. There were seven war-separated children who appeared to have basically negative perceptions of the father, three who depicted ambivalent relations. In contrast, seven of the non-separated subjects depicted a relation which appeared to be basically positive, one appeared to have a basically negative relation, one basically ambivalent, and one so disturbed that the father-child relation could not be understood. No statistical comparison was made of these findings.

Conclusions from exploratory study. It was felt that this dramatic doll-play technique provides a means of studying the father-child relation depicted by the child as he interacts with doll-family materials. Both verbal and manipulative activity may be analyzed in terms of the ways in which the child reveals his feelings and attitudes toward the father.

Upon the basis of the above findings, we increased the size of the sample and devised new and more refined methods for analysis.

Content Analysis of Father-Related Responses

On the basis of the general conclusions from the exploratory study, the investigation was continued with certain changes.[2] The sample was revised and extended to 17 war-separated and 17 non-separated children, as described on page 268. Certain situations were eliminated from the analysis because the exploratory study showed that they had not revealed material concerning the father-child relations.[3] Changes were made in the method of analysis, as we shall show.

Method of Analysis

Categorization into story elements. The technique for dividing comple-

---

2. For a complete report of the content analysis study see Johnson (46a).

3. Dramatic situations 3, 4, and 14; 9 unless some direct reference had been made to the father. See Appendix 22 for these dramatic-play completions.

tions into elements as defined in the exploratory study was retained. This type of approach, while clearly atomistic, has statistical advantages. By this method it was not only possible to deal with all parts of the study in comparable fashion, but it was also possible to arrive at group means for the various categories in relation to which each child would assume a certain position.

Classifying the responses into father-related elements. In the exploratory study, Halnan found a rho correlation of .82 between the total number of elements and the father elements, indicating that the two were closely related. Consequently, only elements relating to the father were used in this analysis. As the dramatic-play situations were designed to bring the father-child relation into sharp focus, it might not be too far afield to suggest that the subject's behavior is never entirely free of father influence. In all probability the influence of the father-child relations on the solution of the stories becomes more intense as the session continues, due to the cumulative effect.

General criteria for father elements included all criteria used in the exploratory study. In line with the supposition that the father influence was probably present in all the completions, these general criteria were extended to include: (1) any response to a question by the examiner when the question refers to father-related activity; (2) a response where there is a choice situation involving the father doll and other doll-family members, even though the father is not the object of the choice; (3) verbalizations or pantomimed activity which are comparisons of the father doll with other doll-family members; (4) doll-family member responses to father-doll behavior or any direct result of the father's behavior; (5) doll-family member responses to father behavior which are efforts to justify, make restitution, or explain their behavior, or an attempt to explain the father's behavior; (6) first responses to dramatic-play situations; (7) action which places any doll-family member next to father, or father alongside another doll-family member.

In the actual classification of the completions into father elements, the rater was first to decide if the responses were father related. If so, he was then to divide the responses into elements according to the instructions for dividing completions into elements. The rater was thus required to make two judgments: (1) is the response father related? (2) how should it be divided into elements?

Reliability of classification of story endings into father elements. To determine the reliability, two raters (L. C. Johnson and L. M. Stolz) independently classified 16 of the 34 protocols (8 non-separated and 8 war-separated children). The percentage agreement was computed by the formula: 2 × number of agreement of A and B divided by total of A plus total of B, where A and B are the raters. The range of agreement was from 80.9 to 90.1 percent. The average agreement for the 16 protocols was 87.1 percent. Since the percentage agreement between the two raters was fairly constant in the last 5 protocols, it was felt that this would also be true if all 34 were classified. Therefore, the percentage agreement was considered acceptable.

Classifying father elements into categories. The father elements were then classified into negative, positive, evasive, and routine categories. A residual category, called "other elements," was included for those elements which could not be scored in one of the four mentioned.

As it was obvious that the scorer could not adequately classify an element when the element was considered by itself, the context in which the element appeared was important in deciding into which category the element should be placed. That is, the separate elements in an episode were scored in relation to the total meaning of the sentence or episode. Elements concerning manipulations of the father doll were also classified in relation to the contexts in which they appeared.

Content revealing negative behavior. In general, negative behavior was defined as those father-related elements having the intent to injure, punish, destroy, or generally depreciate. If a doll-family member, or the subject, was described as having an aggressive, hostile manner, attitude or mood, such descriptions were recorded as negative. Refusal to comply with a request or ignoring a request was scored as negative. When the father was not the object of a direct choice situation, it was to be scored as a negative element.

The negative category was then subdivided into types. This was done in an effort to see if there was one predominant type of negative behavior in the separate groups or in the groups combined.

Each negative element was also scored as to the instigator of the behavior and the recipient of the action if either were specified; that is, whether the behavior was by the father and directed toward the subject or by the subject and directed toward the father.

It was initially planned also to classify the negative elements as to the situations causing the negative behavior, e.g., commands, child misbehavior, response to previous negative behavior, and other situations. This was discarded after it was found that in many cases there were no clear or obvious reasons for the negative behavior. Also, negative behavior in one completion might be related to behavior that happened two or three stories back and thus difficult to classify as to cause. Due to this lack of clarity as to cause and the subjectiveness of the classifications, the reliability was low and the plan was dropped.

Content revealing positive behavior. In general, a positive behavior element was defined as subject or doll-family member behavior denoting praise, reward, affection, friendliness toward other doll-family members, or enjoyment of other doll-family member's company. Offers to aid or play with another doll-family member were also positive elements. Sympathetic responses and positive responses to father behavior were scored as positive. Placing the father doll beside another doll-family member, and placing a doll-family member beside father were scored as positive.

As in the case of the negative elements, the positive category was divided into types of positive behavior and tabulated as to the instigator of the behavior and the receiver of the action if one was specified.

Content revealing evasive or inhibited behavior. Elements were classified as evasive or inhibited in which the doll-family member or subject attempts to avoid responding to the situation either through refusal to answer, requests to leave, or completions that remove the subject or doll-family member from the original threatening situation. Responses that implied a lack of knowledge, e.g., "I don't know," "You tell me," "I can't say," etc., were scored as evasive when it was felt that their intent was to avoid responding to the situation. In contrast to the negative and positive elements, the evasive elements were scored only for subject or subject doll-family member. Classification of these elements as to types of evasion contributed no significant information.

Content revealing routine behavior. The elements were called routine where there were dramatizations of doll-family members or by the subject himself which simulated habitual routine actions and experiences that could ordinarily be expected (on the basis of stereotypes of home and family life) to be performed in an analogous actual situation. Stereotyped doll or subject actions and experiences were felt to be like photographic reproductions of commonly appropriate, "proper," nonindividualistic behavior, e.g., polite greetings, sitting down to dinner, sitting down, listening to radio, going to bed, using toilet properly, cooking dinner, going to school, studying, shaving.

When routine family behavior was used in a negative, positive, or evasive fashion, it was scored under one of these categories and not as a routine family behavior element. This of course reduced the number of elements in this category and also made comparison with other studies, which did not place this restriction on the routine behavior, impossible as far as routine elements were concerned.

All the elements that could not be classified as positive, negative, evasive, or routine were scored under the residual (all other elements) category. These consisted mainly of uncompleted sentences and ambiguous remarks by the subject.

Reliability for classification of father-related elements into categories. Reliability was secured by having two raters (L.C. Johnson and C. Nakamura) score 18 protocols— 9 non-separated and 9 war-separated children— independently. A rho correlation coefficient was computed for the negative, positive, evasive, and routine categories. The reliability coefficient for the negative category was .97; for the positive, .98; for evasive, .92; and for the routine, .84. Since there were more elements placed in the negative and positive categories and since they were more clearly differentiated than the other two, it is logical that they should have the highest reliability figures. These figures indicate that the technique used to score the protocols was reliable enough to use with confidence.

Statistical treatment of the data. Since the total number of elements differed for the two groups, the first step was to convert the elements in each category for each subject into percentage scores of his total. Thus, each breakdown remains relative to the total performance of the individual. However, the disadvantages and assumptions entailed in the use of relative indices should be kept in mind. The assumption is made that the obtained proportions are unbiased estimates of a child's fantasies (responses) under the described conditions, and that if the child had produced a greater number of fantasies under these conditions, the obtained percentages would remain the same. It is impossible to check this assumption, but due to the varying scores there was no alternative but to use the percentages as absolute scores. In the comparison of groups for statistical significance, the small-sample technique for matched groups was used (54).

Statement of Hypotheses

If we assume that the relation between the father and child will be more difficult in those families where the father was absent from the home because of duty in the armed services, we would expect more negative elements in the war-separated group than in the non-separated group.

Conversely, because the non-separated families were not subjected to the conflicts and problems resulting from the father's absence as well as the readjustment of the family pattern upon his return, we would assume that the father-child relation in the non-separated group would be less difficult. We would, therefore, expect more positive elements in the non-separated group than in the war-separated.

As evasive or inhibited behavior is a technique often used to avoid anxiety-provoking stimuli, in light of the clinical findings related to the anxiety resulting from hostile feelings toward a parent, we would hypothesize that the play situations would be more threatening to the war-separated group. We would therefore expect more evasive elements in the war-separated than in the non-separated group.

A child whose home and parental relations are friendly will be less threatened by the situations presented in the stories and therefore freer to reproduce and play out routine family behavior patterns; we would thus expect the percentage of routine family behavior to be higher in the non-separated group than in the war-separated.

A child who is not threatened in a situation will respond more freely and more creatively; we would therefore expect the total number of elements in the non-separated group to be higher than in the war-separated.

In addition to these five hypotheses we made seven other comparisons. A check was made to see:

1. If the boys were more negative than the girls, as found in other studies.
2. Whether girls had more positive elements than boys.
3. Whether there was any difference between boys and girls in regard to evasive elements.
4. Whether there was a sex difference in frequency of routine elements.
5. Whether there was a difference in the number of negative and positive elements given by the boys when groups were combined.
6. Whether the girls gave more positive than negative elements (both groups combined).
7. Whether both war-separated and non-separated groups combined had more negative than positive elements.

It was felt that even though there might be no significant difference between the groups by the standard statistical procedures, if the two groups were combined and ranked as to percentage of negative and positive elements, there would be more non-separated children in the top ten when ranked as to percentage of positive elements and more war-separated children in the top ten when ranked as to percentage of negative elements.

Results of the Content Analysis

Regarding hypotheses. From the results reported in Table 111, it is clearly evident that the predictions were not substantiated. With the exception of the mean scores for the total number of elements, all mean scores reported in Table 111 are percentage scores.

Table 111. Comparison of Responses to the Story Situations Made by War-Separated and Non-Separated Groups

Elements	Mean Score		Mean Difference	$s_{\bar{D}}$	t	P
	War-Separated	Non-Separated				
Total Number	84.8	127.5	42.7	20.0	2.14	<.05
% negative	34.1	37.1	3.0	7.0	.43	—
% positive	31.1	27.2	3.9	6.5	.60	—
% evasive	10.5	11.8	1.3	2.6	.49	—
% routine	16.8	17.6	.8	4.0	.20	—

The comparison as to the total number of elements reaches a probability level that indicates a trend for the non-separated children to be more verbose than their matched war-separated children. This supports preliminary findings in the exploratory study. However, the significance of this is not known since the hypothesis used to predict this was not substantiated. Nine of the 17 non-separated children had more negative elements than their matched war-separated children. Eleven of the 17 war-separated children had more positive elements than their matched non-separated children. The two groups were almost balanced with respect to evasive and routine elements.

When the girls were compared separately, 5 of the 6 war-separated girls had more negative elements than their non-separated counterparts. The meaning of this is not immediately clear. It may be a function of the sample. Eight of the 11 non-separated boys had more negative elements than their war-separated counterparts. Eight of the war-separated boys had more positive elements than their non-separated counterparts, but only 3 of the 6 war-separated girls had more positive elements than their non-separated counterparts.

Other comparisons. The findings in regard to possible sex difference in relation to negative, positive, evasive, and routine elements are presented in Table 112.

Table 112. Responses to Story-Situations Made by Boys and by Girls Separately (Groups Combined)

Elements	Mean Score		Difference Between Means	s_{D_M}	t	P
	Girls	Boys				
% negative	28.3	39.6	11.3	21.5	1.53	—
% positive	35.5	25.7	9.8	6.3	1.56	—
% evasive	11.8	10.8	1.0	3.4	.29	—
% routine	18.0	16.8	1.2	3.5	.34	—

The findings in Table 112 indicate that for this sample there is no difference between boys and girls with respect to the percentage of negative, positive, evasive, or routine elements.

The results of the comparison in regard to the percentage of negative and positive elements made by boys and by girls separately and when all 34 subjects are combined are given in Table 113.

Table 113. Combined Negative and Positive Responses to Story-Situations Made by Boys and by Girls Separately (Groups Combined)

	Mean Percent Score		Mean Percent			
	Negative	Positive	Difference	$s_{\bar{D}}$	t	P
Boys	39.6	25.7	13.9	6.9	2.01	$<.05$
Girls	28.3	35.5	7.2	8.8	.82	-
Boys and girls	35.6	29.1	6.5	5.8	1.12	-

As in the other results, there is no statistically significant difference between the scores compared. The results do indicate that the boys tend to have more negative elements than positive. This, however, can only be regarded as a trend.

Examination of the frequency of the various types of negative, positive, evasive, and routine behavior elements showed no striking difference between the two groups. The data were not treated statistically due to the failure to find any significant differences in the major categories.

When the two groups were combined and ranked from the highest to lowest in regard to percent of negative, positive, evasive, and routine elements, the expected larger number of war-separated children among the topmost negative and the larger number of non-separated children among the topmost positive subjects were not found. The two groups were equally mixed as to rank in regard to evasive and routine percentages.

Rating of Father-Child Relations

At the time that the content analysis of the father-related responses was being done, another approach along more holistic lines was undertaken.[4] The same 34 protocols were studied. From Halnan's (37) dynamic approach to the completions in the exploratory study came some of the most suggestive results. Although no statistical comparison was made, Halnan found that 7 of the 10 war-separated children showed negative or ambivalent perceptions of the father, while 7 of the 10 non-separated children depicted a basically positive relation.

The method of summarizing thematic sequences and comparing matched children used in the exploratory study was not retained because the results were not subject to statistical treatment, and it was thought that a holistic

---

4. For the complete report of the rating study, see Gowin (35a).

rating of feelings and attitudes specifically would be more appropriate to the problem and to the kind of material presented. Consequently, a rating scale was prepared in an attempt to rate the quality of the relation between father and child as presented in the dramatic play.

In a dramatic-play situation we assume that the child feels free to present his father in any light, since to the child it is only a "play" situation and does not concern his real father. However, we assume that the child does identify with the father doll enough to present how he feels about, if not how he acts toward, his own father. If we assume that the problems posed by the completions are sufficiently structured to present a situation in which the child is never free of the influence of the father, then the quality of feeling toward what was presented could be interpreted as related to the father.

Method of Analysis

The plan of the rating scale. The rating scale as finally developed has 8 categories, ranging from +4 to -4. The categories are meant to be descriptions or characterizations of various levels along a continuum from the most positive to the most negative.

The extremes of the continuum used for rating are not extremes of actual father-child relations, but only extremes found in this study of dramatic-play materials. The +4 score is a rating of the most positive father-child relation that occurred in the 34 protocols and not what might be considered the "best possible" father-child relation. Neither is the -4 the "worst possible" relation.

The scale has a zero category in which were placed all responses that could not be rated on the continuum. In many cases there was no way to tell or to infer the meaning of a response. Into the zero category went those types of evasive responses which seemed to be associated with other factors than the psychological situation of the father and the child. Such responses could be attributed to lack of rapport with the examiner or lack of acceptance of the play period, to fatigue or satiation, or to lack of acceptance of this general type of "game." The zero category was also used in dramatic-play situations 12, 13, and 14, which are primarily situations with grandparents, if the father was excluded. The reason for this rating was that no mention of the father did not mean rejection of the father by the child (and thus require a negative rating), but rather a sort of neutral omission.

Each step on the rating scale was defined in three ways. First, there was the "A" level, the most abstract, which provided an interpretive statement of the quality of the presented father-child relation in general. Second, the "B" level contained a group of specific statements, each of which applied to a specific part of the father-child relation such as affection or discipline. The third, or "C" level, was composed of very brief examples extracted from the protocols. It was thought that this method of definition would best guide the rater in his subjective judgments. The rating scale is presented in Appendix 23.

Reliability of ratings. To test the reliability of ratings on the father-child relations scale as devised, the protocols were, after preliminary training, evaluated independently by two raters (D. B. Gowin and C. Nakamura). At the time of the rating, the raters did not know whether the protocol belonged to the war-separated or non-separated group.

On the 34 cases the two raters achieved point-by-point agreement in more than 63 percent of the ratings; that is, where one rater scored a +2, the other rater also scored a +2. Agreement expected by chance would be 11.07 percent. Plus-or-minus one point (including perfect agreement) was achieved on 88.5 percent of the ratings, the chance expectancy being 30.75 percent. Agreement of not more than plus-or-minus two points was achieved on 97.4 percent of the ratings and greater variance occurred only in less than 3 percent of the cases.

The total score was added up for each child, the non-separated group was ranked by total scores and a rho correlation between raters was computed. This correlation was .96. For the war-separated group the rho correlation was .92. Considering these figures, we are confident that the two raters were using the scale in the same manner.

Computation of scores. After the check on reliability was completed, every particular completion where disagreement was obvious was discussed by the raters and a conference score was reached. In the calculations of the significance of the difference of the two groups, the conference score was used. It was thought that this procedure would preserve the integrity of the data. At the time of the rating, the raters did not know whether the protocol belonged to the war-separated or non-separated group.

Each separate completion was given a score so that each child received 15 scores. An attempt was made to see if these scores arranged themselves into any meaningful patterns, but none was found. Graphs of the frequency of ratings for each dramatic-play situation and for each child were drawn up, but there was no detectable difference between war-separated and non-separated groups.

In order to apply statistics to the results of the ratings, each child's total score was computed. Each individual child was given a total score by each rater, based on the summation of the scores on the 15 separate stories. These totals were then added to get the combined total score. Because of the high correlation between raters, it was thought that this combined total score gave a better spread and, thus, greater sensitivity to possible differences. The pluses and minuses were added up algebraically to get a total figure. One can see that the psychological meaning may easily be lost in averaging, a problem faced in applying quantitative symbols to qualitative judgments.

Statistical treatment of the data. The same statistic was applied here as in the treatment of the father-related elements. In the comparison of groups for statistical significance, the small-sample technique for matched groups was used (54).

Statement of Hypotheses

The experimental hypothesis is that there will be a difference in the father-child relation between children whose fathers were absent and children whose fathers were present during the first year of the life of the first-born child.

We expect this difference to manifest itself in the quality of the expression of fantasy that the child shows in the dramatic-play situation. We hypothesize that the father-child relation will be more difficult in those families where the father was absent, and that this difficulty will be expressed as a more negative relation on our scale.

In addition, it was thought that if all the subjects were put in a rank order with the most positive score at the top, then the non-separated children would be clustered among the top ten and the war-separated children would be clustered among the bottom ten.

Results of the Rating of Father-Child Relations

Table 114 indicates that the central hypothesis was not proven. In our experiment, the t value was .97. A t of 2.1 is needed to reject the null hypothesis at a .05 level of significance, and 3.96 at the .001 level. Ten of the 17 war-separated group had a more positive score than their non-separated counterparts and 7 had more negative scores. Five of the war-separated girls were more negative than their non-separated counterparts, and one girl was more positive. Nine of the war-separated boys, however, were more positive than their non-separated counterparts, and two boys were more negative.

If we separate the subjects according to sex and compare rank orderings from positive to negative, we see the following: 5 of the 6 war-separated girls are below the median rank of 6, whereas 4 of the 6 non-separated girls are above the median rank of 6. A trend of this sort was expected. The trend among the boys, though, is just the opposite, with the non-separated boys more negative, as 8 of the 11 are below the median rank of 11. Among the war-separated boys, 8 out of the 11 are above the median rank of 11 and 3 are below it.

Table 114. Comparison of War-Separated and Non-Separated Groups, Using Combined Total Score

Sex	Number WS.	Number NS.	Mean WS.	Mean NS.	Mean Difference	s	t	P
Boys and girls	17	17	-5.7	-15.7	10.0	10.3	.97	-
Boys	11	11	-7.5	-26.5	19.0	14.9	1.28	-
Girls	6	6	-2.66	4.0	6.66	11.9	.56	-

Table 114 also gives a breakdown of war-separated and non-separated groups on the basis of sex. This table illustrates that the non-separated girls, with a mean of +4.0, and the non-separated boys, with a mean of -26.5, are at opposite ends of the continuum. When these scores are averaged to get a mean for the whole non-separated group, it can be seen that these differences between boys and girls will tend to counteract each other and consequently cause the non-separated groups mean to approximate more closely the mean of the war-separated group.

It should be pointed out that these comparisons between boys and girls are made on a sample that contains just about twice as many boys as girls (11 to 6). The idea of finding sex differences was not a part of the original hypothesis. Any interpretation post hoc must be limited by the initial intentions of the experiment.

When all the subjects were placed in a rank order with the most positive score as the highest rank, 6 non-separated and 4 war-separated children were found in the top ten. The distribution in the bottom ten was exactly the same— 6 non-separated and 4 war-separated children.

Conclusions of this experiment. The central hypothesis was not substantiated and we must require than a strict interpretation be given to the results: With the dramatic-play technique here used for gathering data, with the method of analysis here attempted, we were unable to find any differences between the non-separated and war-separated groups. The original suggestive results of the exploratory study were therefore not substantiated.

Summary and Conclusions

The findings of the two analyses of the data from the dramatic-play completions presented in this chapter agree that there is no difference between the war-separated and non-separated children. The results do not support the general findings of the exploratory study and are at odds with the original hypothesis. If this were a single study, we would be inclined to believe that our original hypothesis was incorrect. Since this study is a part of a larger project investigating the same hypothesis and using the same population, a comparison of our findings with the findings of others is possible and helps in our search for explanations of these negative findings.

The findings of other studies in the project, without exception, supported the original hypothesis. This suggests that the explanation for the finding of this study lies either in the experimental technique of obtaining data, in the method of analysis, in the control sample, or in some combination of these factors. Our search for causes led us to explore four possibilities.

First, we may have tapped an area which differed from the areas tapped in the other four projective situations and may have explored an area in which the two groups of children actually are alike. We have carefully analyzed the situations presented in these dramatic-play stories and they seem to us to relate very definitely to the same general areas studied by M.S. Faust (Chapter 12) and to be somewhat allied to those studied by Ryder (Chapter 11). We would certainly expect similar group trends, though not identical individual responses to these various situations. We would expect children who have difficulties in relation to their fathers in general to have deeper feelings of hostility as measured by Ryder. We would expect a child who is disturbed by the situation of breaking his father's watch in the story completions to be disturbed by spilling ink on his father's books in the dramatic-play situations. Since the groups did behave differently, there must be some other reason.

Second, we examined our methods of analysis. It seemed possible that neither of the methods really tapped the basic father relation as the nonstatistical analysis in the exploratory study had done. The analysis by behavior units was perhaps too atomistic. The score in the father-child relations scale, made by the summation of ratings by two raters on 15 stories representing different aspects of the relation, may have canceled out the meaning. To test the possibility of inadequacies of these methods we tried two other approaches.

The first approach was an attempt to obtain a more holistic evaluation of the protocols. Each child's response to the 15 stories was summarized in a paragraph of approximately 200 words. These summaries were made by one person and checked in conference by another. These workers (L. C. Johnson and D. B. Gowin) knew the protocols well, but did not know the children. The summaries were then rated on a 5-point linear scale of father-child relations extending from good father-child relations to poor father-child relations. The ratings were made by two independent raters (E. Chance and W. L. Faust) who did not know the protocols. Analysis of these ratings showed no significant differences between the war-separated and non-separated groups. This holistic method did not support the general hypothesis of the project.

To investigate further why the findings from this projective technique differed from the findings from the story-completion technique, we developed a series of rating scales on conformity, patterned after the scales used in analyzing the story completions. We selected dramatic-play situations 4 (spilling milk on the kitchen floor), 7 (spilling ink on father's books), 8 (refusing to eat supper), and 9 (not wanting to go to bed). These situations represented stressful situations somewhat comparable to three stories in the story completions which dealt respectively with breaking the father's watch (Story 3), with picking up toys (Story 4), and with accidentally hitting the father (Story 5).

A new rater (R. Wirt), who had never seen the protocols before, rated these stories on the scales of conformity of the child's behavior to the father's expectancies. Again there was no difference between the groups.[1] This analysis confirmed the findings of the two analyses already reported.

Third, we looked at our original protocols critically. We found that there were some situations in which Experimenter B had seemed to change her technique. The change was either in giving further stimulus to continue after the child seemed to have completed his story or in not setting any limits for termination of the play. In other words, Experimenter B, through the quality of her own action, had stimulated and encouraged behavior not related to the theme of the story.

On the basis of this impression we drew up specific directions and two workers independently examined the protocols indicating the dramatic-play situations and the place in the completions where the experimenter seemed to have changed her technique.[2] Four dramatic-play situations were then examined carefully for each of the 34 children. These were the same situations used in the previous analysis (4, 7, 8, 10). Out of the 136 dramatic-play completions examined, 27 were found which the two workers agreed showed a change in experimental technique. These included 6 dramatic-

---

1. This analysis of conformity was made by M. S. Faust, L. M. Stolz, and W. L. Faust.

2. This analysis was made by L. M. Stolz and M. S. Faust.

play completions in the protocols of two war-separated boys and 21 dramatic-play completions in the protocols of ten non-separated children (nine boys, one girl). These children were all of the children examined in the last two months of the study and three others examined earlier.

Although we studied only four of the dramatic-play completions to verify our impression regarding the change in Experimenter B's technique, cursory inspection indicates that this change permeated the total protocols of these 12 children. We are inclined, therefore, to believe that a change in the technique of Experimenter B, which consistently occurred during the final two months of the study, may have influenced the data. The changed interaction between experimenter and subject influenced the response of the subject. Our findings were therefore definitely affected, since of the 17 non-separated children, 10 seemed to have been influenced by the change in interaction. Only one of the non-separated boys who was examined by Experimenter B seemed to have been subjected to the same situation presented to the rest of our sample.

Fourth, there is the possibility that the non-separated sample for this substudy differed from the non-separated samples in our other studies. There were 4 non-separated children out of 17 in the dramatic-play completions who were not in the control group of the story completions. None of these was a child whose protocols showed evidences of change in experimental technique. The 10 non-separated children whose protocols did show change in technique in the dramatic play were all in the control group of the story completions.

We are led to conclude, therefore, that the situations in which we collected data were not comparable for war-separated and non-separated groups as evidenced in the interaction between experimenter and subject. Consequently, the findings from our analyses can have no implications regarding the general hypothesis of this study. They can only serve to emphasize the importance of the experimenter-subject interaction as a variable in research utilizing projective methods.

PART V. SUMMARY AND INTERPRETATION OF STUDY

CHAPTER 14.
NED FORD AND HIS FAMILY

Purpose of this Case Study

Our purpose in presenting this case study of one family is to demonstrate the interrelations of the data we have collected and analyzed.[1] We wish, also, to illustrate the idiosyncratic nature of interpersonal relations and consequent personality manifestations. The statistical analyses of data presented in the previous chapters show that there are significant differences between war-separated and non-separated fathers in certain aspects of their relations with their first-borns and in some aspects of the behavior and personality characteristics of their children. In the analysis of the Ford family we have used this general statistical data as a background for highlighting the stresses and subsequent adjustments which war-separation brought to one family.

The Ford family was selected from our 19 war-separated families because ratings and scores of both father and first-born were not extreme in all the characteristics which had proven to be significantly different for the war-separated group. In some respects Ned was like the non-separated group of children; in some measures the father does not represent the group of war-separated fathers. We believed that an analysis of such a family which was not completely "typical" would be more representative than a more consistently extreme family.

We have disguised identifying data concerning this family but without jeopardizing the important factors in the dynamics of the father-child relation.

The case study is organized into six sections. The first section, Background, deals with the history of the Ford family before our investigation began. The data in this section were obtained from the father and mother interviews; data from Mrs. Ford are indicated, otherwise the data are from Mr. Ford.

The second section discusses the areas of stress to which the family had to adjust upon the father's return from the war. The data in this section are taken primarily from the father interviews, with supplementary material from the mother interviews. The group analysis of these topics is in Chapter 3.

The third section discusses the patterns of adjustment made by Ned and his father to the stresses of postwar family life. The data are from the mother and father interviews. The group analyses of father data are in Chapters 4 and 5; of mother data, in Chapter 7.

The fourth section attempts to give further insight into Ned's pattern of adjustment by a picture of Ned as he functions with his peers and with adults

---

1. Material was contributed for this case analysis by Edith Dowley, Erika Chance, Nancy Guy Stevenson, Leonard Ullman, Joyce Ryder, Margaret S. Faust, Laverne Johnson, and D. B. Gowin.

in group situations. The data are from observations of Ned in social situations. The group analysis of data on children in social situations is in Chapter 9.

The fifth section presents what we know of Ned's private world as revealed in projective-play situations. The analyses of group differences in projective-play situations are in Chapters 11, 12, and 13.

The final section is a summary and interpretation of the effect of father relations on Ned Ford.

Background

From Mr. Ford's account, both he and his wife were small town people from Ohio who had lived all their lives in the same general community until the war. Mr. Ford was one of the four men in the study whose father's occupation was on the professional level. His was a puritanical family, with strict prohibitions against smoking, drinking, dancing, and just as strict encouragement for proper behavior that would be a credit to the father in his community. Mr. Ford felt that he had fewer restrictions since he was the youngest, but learned what not to do through witnessing the severe punishment his brothers received. His father was a strong authoritarian figure to be admired and feared and, perhaps, to be hated. Mr. Ford had assumed a passive role toward the authority of his father but he had conflicting emotions about it.

War Experience

When World War II began, Mr. Ford was attending college, like most of the men in this study. He was drafted into military service when he was 20 years old and a junior in college. He had not minded being drafted since most of his friends had already gone into the services. Indeed, he had seriously considered enlisting six months earlier but his father had persuaded him that he should finish college if he could. The draft settled the argument in his favor— and gave him the chance to do what he was eager to do.

His experience in the service was similar to that of most of the men in this study. He spent approximately a year in training in three different states. Opportunity came about this time for him to enter Officer's Candidate School. "I found it probably the most disturbing influence that I had all the time I was in service." Here he had some difficulties in his relations with his superiors— men who knew less than he did— which brought rather drastic penalties and delayed his graduation several months. Another year was spent in several camps in the West. Finally, three years after he entered the services, he left for overseas. He was in one major operation in Europe. Later, he became part of the occupation troops for five or six months. He was overseas 14 months, in the armed services almost four years; a war service above the average of the men in the study.

Mr. Ford was not too happy about his military service experience. He felt that the hierarchial system kept him from using his real abilities. He had not wanted to go into a technical field like heavy equipment maintenance but felt his abilities might better have been used in personnel or teaching work. He felt "pretty young all the way through" for the responsibilities he was given. He felt "swallowed up, as a number rather than being an individual." But in spite of real difficulties, at times he feels he made the adjustment better than many. As he talked about these experiences in great length and detail, he bowed his head, clasped and unclasped his hands; his face was sad and distressed.

Mr. Ford talked about four effects that the war had on him. He felt that he developed a good deal of maturity during the time he was in service, primarily because he was so young when he entered. He felt his strong moral character made it possible for him to have a wide variety of experiences and come out with a good deal of moral character. It made him more tolerant— "maybe not internally but externally." The second effect was that he lost a lot of self-confidence during this period. "The particular attributes that I thought most desirable, in the service were not particularly desirable. For example, a tolerant attitude towards inferiors as far as rank was concerned." But while he regrets this, he says, "It was probably a good thing that I did lose some of it, I don't know. I do find myself, occasionally, feeling pretty inadequate." Third, Mr. Ford thinks he has tended to become less outgoing as a person than he was before. During the war he learned "to keep my feelings as much to myself as possible, which I don't think is a particularly good thing." But, again, he is ambivalent as he says, "It perhaps made me develop a closer shell than I had previously. I don't know whether that's good or bad." He thinks that this characteristic is closely related to his lack of self-confidence. A fourth effect was that "occasionally I have feelings against those who are in authority over me . . . if a person is in a position to tell me what to do, he has at least one strike against him if not two." Mr. Ford doesn't think this is a good attitude really, and he is not sure whether it is completely the result of his military experiences. He, perhaps, remembers his early feelings toward his dominating father.

Marriage

The war hurried up the marriage of the Fords. The couple had known each other since high school days. Their families were close because of community interests. The couple was allowed a good deal of freedom because of this, and Mr. Ford thought it was "perhaps too much freedom for our own good." After Mr. Ford went to college, he began to feel somewhat more sophisticated than this small-town girl who had not been away from home. They had their ups and downs, with each trying out relations with others. But their interest in each other continued and finally, after he had been in the service about a year and a half, Mr. Ford bought an engagement ring and they became formally engaged. A few months after this, an unexpected assignment brought him near home and he wangled a few days leave. When he arrived, he found everything arranged for his wedding the next morning. He was decidedly shocked. He wasn't ready for marriage. He felt too young at 22 years, too uncertain; he was "rather leery of the whole thing." Both he and his wife were below the average age at marriage of couples in our study.

After marriage their life was very similar to the lives of most of our war-separated group. Mrs. Ford joined her husband at camp and they had a small apartment off the post. Soon, however, he received orders which he thought meant overseas duty, so his wife went home. This was a false alarm, however, so in six months his wife joined him again for several months. Altogether, she traveled about 20,000 miles in order to be with her husband before he left for overseas.

The baby was conceived very soon after they were married, earlier than any baby in our study except one. Like most of the other wives, Mrs. Ford was living near a training center at the time. They hadn't planned the baby (like six other families) and Mr. Ford was ambivalent in his feelings. The fact he was going overseas complicated matters, but, on the other hand, "she would have something to do at home which she would enjoy." "There was the worry that I might not come back which would have made it difficult—." Mrs. Ford was ambivalent too. She said that she was "very pleased" but she was also frightened. Her "main worry was having an abnormal baby," one who "might be missing a hand or have a scar on his face." Otherwise, she "was very glad to have the baby." The couple was together for about six months of the pregnancy. Mrs. Ford "was never ill at all, never."

Birth of Ned

About three months before the baby was born, Mrs. Ford went home to her own family. Her baby was born while she lived in the maternal home, as were 12 others in our study. Her memory of the birth was definitely unpleasant. Her labor lasted 17 hours and her time in pain seemed very long. She was under an anesthetic during the delivery, which was a difficult one. Mrs. Ford was "quite a while recovering from it." It hurt her for "quite some time." She also got "milk fever" which kept her in bed for about two weeks following Ned's birth. Mr. Ford feels that his wife was quite apprehensive about the whole thing, that the difficult birth exhausted her, and that her postpartum illness made the experience seem anything but pleasant.

Mr. Ford, at camp, had not been apprehensive at all and he doesn't know why, except that his wife had a good doctor in whom he had confidence. He heard about Ned's birth by telephone from his mother-in-law. "That was just about all there was to it. Rather an undramatic occasion."

Mrs. Ford was not surprised when her baby was a boy. She "had planned on it being a boy" and was very pleased that it was. Mr. Ford seemed unconcerned.

Two weeks later Mr. Ford received overseas orders and en route to embarkation he stopped at home. His wife had just got out of bed and was still having difficulty feeding the baby. The father said, "He didn't particularly seem like my child too much. He wasn't the best-looking child you ever saw to begin with . . . So during that time I didn't feel attached to the youngster at all, as far as personal attachment was concerned."

Ned's Development During Father's Absence

The Fords were married only 13 months when Mr. Ford left for overseas, 2 months more than the median of our group. Mr. Ford was overseas 16 months, somewhat less than the average 23.4 months. During that time his wife and son lived with her family, as did most of our war-separated group. Besides Mrs. Ford's parents, there was her sister whose husband was overseas. Her sister's son had been born a few months earlier than Ned. Mrs. Ford sometimes made trips with Ned to visit Mr. Ford's family in a town not far away.

Feeding and weaning. Ned's mother reported that she planned to breast feed him and did so for three months, with supplementary bottle feedings after the first six weeks. She discontinued the nursing because "he was too hungry all the time" and she didn't have enough milk for him. He seemed "very happy" with the bottle. She held him in her arms for feeding at first and later— around four or five months— used a bottle holder. Ned was fed on a "demand schedule," and "fed when he was hungry." At first, it was about every hour and his mother "just couldn't keep him on a schedule until he was on three meals a day."

At eight months of age he was weaned very suddenly from the bottle to the cup all in one day. He was on a trip with his mother and en route the bottle had spoiled so his mother gave him milk from a cup and he "just took right to the cup," so she didn't bother with the bottles any more. He never cried for a bottle and although he drank a little less milk after that, he showed no ill effects from the weaning.

Elimination. Mrs. Ford reported beginning training Ned for bowel control at about six months. She put him on a toilet once a day at first and more frequently later. She would spank him sometimes if he soiled his diapers. His mother feels he was easy to train for defecation, and by 16 months, when his father returned, he was pretty reliable and would tell her his needs.

Sleeping. Ned has always been a sound sleeper; from two months on he slept through the night.

Motor behavior and activity. Ned was not an active baby. His mother said, "He was unusually quiet and would be still and watch things." It was never difficult to bathe him or change his diapers. Mrs. Ford never had to worry about his activity, but rather about his inactivity. "He'd rather sit."

Mrs. Ford does not remember much about his sitting or standing alone for the first time, but remembers that he never got out of his crib by himself. "He never did, never did," she said. He enjoyed his playpen very much and spent hours at a time in a small one until he learned to walk, and in a larger one after that. He walked at 10 months and at 16 months could go up and down stairs. He was a cautious child always, as his mother remembers. Mrs. Ford early taught him not to touch things by slapping his hands and this has made him a very careful child.

Experiences with people. Ned's experiences with people while his father was away were similar to those of other war-separated children. Mrs. Ford says she never left Ned for more than a day during his first year of life and took him visiting and shopping with her often. His aunt and two grandmothers often helped his mother in caring for him. "It was never just his mommy." Ned's maternal grandafther was busy during the day and Ned, unlike most of the other war-separated babies, had little contact with his grandfather.

Language. His mother said she sang and talked to Ned "continually" as a little baby and went to him "mostly" when he cried. He was a very responsive baby and seemed to understand his mother when she talked to him. "Yes, even from the moment he was home from the hospital it seemed he would look at me, and he just seemed to respond to every move, and he's still that way."

His first words were "da-da," "kitty," "mama," "water," and "by-by"; he was saying them at 11 months. He talked in sentences by 18 months or so. She feels she may have pushed his language development "so that he would keep up with his cousin who was six months older, and he not only kept up, in fact, he was ahead of him in lots of ways."

Comfort patterns. "Ned never sucked his thumb or fingers or ever put things in his mouth like many children." If he was fussy as a baby, his mother often gave him "a cooky to satisfy him, but it was never the thing to do when he cried. He was very content most of the time and he didn't need extra things."

He seldom cried as a baby and was not a whiner. He did chew all along the edge of his crib when he was cutting his teeth.

Methods of disclipine. Mrs. Ford was a fairly strict parent from the start. Although she fed this child "when he was hungry," she did not apply the self-regulation philosophy to his weaning, to toilet training, or to sleeping. She used spanking in teaching bowel and bladder control and to teach him not to touch things.

Contact with Father Overseas

While Ned was developing rapidly, his mother, like other war-separated wives, tried to keep his father informed of all the important changes. Mr. Ford said, "She made a point to be sure to take a series of pictures every month. . . The boy changed considerably . . . he became a rather attractive boy, but, of course, even so it was a rather remote thing, rather than a personal thing. I don't know, it's sort of like being proud of, oh, one's clothes or something, yet you can say, 'That's mine.' "

Stress Areas on the Father's Return from War

During the 16 months of separation both husband and wife were adjusting to new experiences: his wife to the warm, protective, interpersonal relations of a mother with her dependent first-born; Mr. Ford to the harsh realities of modern warfare. He was seeing sudden death while she nourished life. He was in a man's world of stark danger, gnawing fatigue, and inflexible discipline; she was among women and young babies, training and educating but loving at the same time. At the end of the period of separation, Mr. Ford had to learn to live in a new world. His adjustments were in the areas typical of the war-separated group: to vocation, to wife, and to first-born child.

Vocational Adjustment

Mr. Ford was one of the six war-separated and four non-separated men of whom returning to college was expected after the war. Even before Mr.

Ford was off his terminal leave, he was back in school and in a semester had completed his work for the AB degree. He had some difficulty in deciding what to do next, what he wanted to be, where he should go for training. He also had to figure out how to support his family. He came from a family of lawyers for many generations; three of his brothers were already in the field. Finally, after advice from several sources and much consideration, he followed the family pattern and joined his brothers at Stanford. He said, "Sometimes I feel that I've kind of been tag-along in some educational respects."

Like the war-separated group, these decisions and adjustments caused him considerable anxiety. "I feel I lost a lot of self-confidence in the armed services and when I first came to Stanford it was a pretty dismal situation as far as my own feelings of adequacy were concerned."

Adjustments with Wife

Mr. Ford was among the two-thirds of war-separated men for whom it was relatively easy to re-establish relations of intimacy with his wife when he returned. "We had no difficulty whatever." He was one of the 16 men who had not been involved in extramarital relations during the war though "there were many opportunities for sexual relations with girls if one wanted to take them." He felt that the men who did take advantage of these opportunities became more frustrated than they were before because of their guilt feelings. He said, "I don't mean to say that it isn't a strain to be away from one's wife for a long period of time; it certainly is— but I don't know whether it's only sexual relations that make the tension. I would tend to think it's a lot of factors, rather than just sex alone. And the vague loneliness that occurs by being away from people at certain times, away from people that you would care to have deep friendships with . . . It was the separation, not the war, that caused the anxiety."

Wife and child. Mr. Ford did not feel that his son came between him and his wife but he did feel that Ned interfered somewhat in their relations. He said, "I felt that Ned interfered with my wife and me doing things together, that we might have done." He felt, like 14 of the war-separated group, that there was a close bond between his wife and Ned which somehow left him on the outside.

The main disagreements which Mr. and Mrs. Ford had on his return were in regard to his method of disciplining Ned. Like most of the war-separated group, their differences in child-rearing practices were extreme. Mrs. Ford had been strict in her discipline of Ned but according to her husband she considered that he was "much too harsh, too severe all the way down the line in dealing with Ned." They had several arguments and many unpleasant moments about this. Mr. Ford said, "My wife thought what I was doing was all right, Ned was my son and he should behave as I wanted him to, but she felt I was much too severe. She felt I should make allowance for the fact Ned had had no men around."

The mother and Ned slept in the same room together, as did 15 of the war-separated group, and one of Mr. Ford's first difficulties with Ned occurred because of this (see p. 291).

The in-laws. Mr. Ford, like the majority of the war-separated group, lived with his in-laws for about a month when he first returned. He was one of the six men who had known his wife's family well before he went overseas, as a single man dating and courting the younger daughter and as a new husband on a brief visit before he went away. He felt the maternal grandmother and Ned were very close and that she spoiled Ned. The grandfather was not much of a factor in Ned's life as he spent long hours away from home. His wife's mother, as well as his own mother, was critical of the way Mr. Ford disciplined Ned when he came home.

Early Relations with First-Born

Mr. Ford returned from overseas when Ned was 16 months old, two months younger than the average war-separated child at the time of the father's reunion.

Father's readiness. He felt very impersonal about this son of his. "I didn't feel that I didn't want the child or anything like that, any time. It was just one of those things. I hadn't had personal contact with him very much, so there wasn't a close bond between us." Mr. Ford was one of the six fathers given a rating of 4 on the scale of the father's readiness to accept his child; only three men were more rejecting.

Child's acceptance of father. For Ned, the arrival of his father was rather bewildering. He would look at his father's photograph and call it daddy, but wouldn't look at his father and call him daddy. He held himself aloof from his father. Ned was one of the seven children who was rated most rejecting of his father. His father was disturbed about this. He said, "Ned is much more his mother's child— that was a very common feeling I had at first and still is. Now I expect it; then I wasn't ready for the situation I found."

Father's attitude toward child's behavior. In this family the father did not take long to make up his mind about his baby's behavior. Mr. Ford was rated as one of the ten fathers who was extremely disapproving and critical of his child on his return from war. He describes this episode immediately after his return: "It was interesting, the very first day that I got back, the very first morning; and this goes to show you what a nice start we had . . . When we awoke the very first morning after I'd been there— he and his mother slept in the same room— and he raised up in his crib and saw a strange man in bed with his mother and howled like nobody's business. Well, he howled for a little while and I finally got up and gave him a swat on his several pads of diapers and told him to lay down and not make so much noise. Well, he laid down and didn't make any noise, that was for sure; and strange enough, he's never made any noise waking up in the morning since. But we tangled just that early, the very first day after I got back."

The father clashed with his 16-months-old boy in regard to many areas of behavior. He thought he was "spoiled" and that he could play on his mother's and grandmother's sympathies very easily to get what he wanted. He cited instances of bad behavior at mealtimes. He said, "I don't know why that is, but very often I tended to feel that Ned was getting away with a lot more than he should get away with."

Father's early discipline. As Mr. Ford told so dramatically above, like most of the war-separated group he assumed his role as father immediately by disciplining his son. He said, "I tended to step in whenever I felt he was getting away with a lot." He was rated among the 11 fathers using the most severe discipline. He slapped, spanked hard, isolated. Mr. Ford described his early discipline of Ned in this way:

> "I spanked him. I spanked him. Once or twice— maybe even more than that— I spanked him very hard, much harder than I should have. For a while it was rather a common occurrence that he got a spanking. Then we'd have quite a breathing spell, and then we'd go through another round of it, with another breathing spell, and so forth."

This became a delicate subject between him and his wife as well as his wife's family and his own family. He was one of 13 men who had extreme ratings both on discipline and on disagreements with his wife. In retrospect, Mr. Ford feels that he was much too severe himself but, here, too, he is ambivalent and wonders whether Ned would be as good a boy now if he hadn't been as severe with him then. He feels that some of the authoritarian ideas he developed during the service may have influenced his "initial combats with Ned" and his "demand for unquestioning obedience."

Mr. Ford was among the 8 men who had extreme negative ratings on both father's readiness to accept child and on discipline; among the 9 who had extreme negative ratings on both child's acceptance of father and discipline; and among the 13 whose ratings on both discipline and attitude toward the child were extremely negative.

Child's immediate response to father's discipline. Ned's shyness soon turned to fear. "He was afraid more than anything else." When his father would go after him, he would run to his mother. He was rated among the five children in both groups who were most rejecting of their fathers in the early years. In this, he was like other war-separated children.

Mrs. Ford felt that Ned's fear of his father was due to the fact he hadn't known men. Her husband quoted her as saying, "Well, what do you expect with three women in the house?" She felt that a great big rough-voiced male in the house was something new to Ned and that her husband should make allowances for it.

In describing the early relations between Ned and his father, Mrs. Ford said, "Ned's father never knew a baby or a child well until he met Ned at 16 months. Ned's habits were pretty well set by then and daddy's coming home didn't change that." She added that Ned's father had been "commanding people and he insisted that Ned obey him. 'Ned's my son and what I say goes' was his attitude." Ned avoided him and took all his difficulties to his mother. He just wouldn't accept his father and "it was pitiful." Mrs. Ford felt that his father's return was very hard on Ned and it was especially hard because Mr. Ford did not understand the situation and tried to solve it by military ways of commanding and demanding.

Patterns of Adjustment to Stress

When we began our study of this family, almost four years had elapsed since Mr. Ford had returned home. He had been attending school all this time except for nine months when he did some field work in connection with his graduate training.

Ned was five years, five months old when we completed the interviews with his father; five years, eight months old at the time of the interview with his mother. Both parents talked about Ned's development during the four previous years, both discussed the father's attitude toward him. We have integrated the data from these two sources in the following discussion.

Ned's Development

Eating. Ned was one of two children in the war-separated group whose mother reported no serious problems in eating. It is surprising that Ned has no food problems since his father early began disciplining him for being messy and playing at the table. Some of his first "battles" with Ned were over table manners and he is still strict and critical about his behavior at the table. His father's discussion of Ned's eating behavior was rated 4 on seriousness.

But Ned seems to have been able to keep his good appetite and enjoyment of food in spite of this. We get a glimpse of the strong controls this child has built up when his mother says, "He won't touch candy when it is around the house, he won't even ask for it except rarely, but if we offer it to him, he always takes as many as he can get."

Elimination. When his father returned from the war, Ned at 16 months of age had accomplished bowel control and training for control of urination was just beginning. This was somewhat later for beginning bladder training than the average of the war-separated group. By about 26 months he was trained for day and night, about a year younger for bed dryness than the average child in both groups.

For a period of several months around two years of age, Ned rebelled. Mrs. Ford said, "He just wouldn't go when I wanted him to," but he soon acquiesced and there were no problems after two-and-a-half years. The parents did not use punishment in teaching Ned bladder control as the mother had done in bowel training.

Sleeping. In sleeping habits, Ned is unusually good, his mother reports. Despite the fact that for eight months after the father's return Ned slept in the bedroom with his parents because they had no other place for him, he was very pleased when at two years he got his own room and bunk bed in place of his crib. He was never afraid or reluctant to sleep alone.

Even when Ned was sleeping in the room with his parents he never voluntarily crawled into bed with his parents. It will be remembered that it was Ned's protest about his father being in the bedroom that brought Ned the first spanking from his father. His father said that after that incident he never made any fuss again.

In spite of the fact that Ned conforms in every way to the parents' desired behavior in sleeping, Ned's mother reports that his sleep is sometimes disturbed by nightmares. Like other war-separated children, his cumulated anxieties find outlet in the phantasies of his dreams and he wakes up crying.

Activity. The mother's strict training of Ned not to touch things in the early years bore fruit. He continued to be a passive child after his father returned. His interests led him to puzzles, the phonograph, and books—all quiet, isolated activities of which Mr. Ford approves.

But lately there has been a change in Ned. His mother mentions that "he is getting better now and is more active," but his father notes these changes with genuine disapproval. He says that Ned "sometimes gets off on an emotional jag with one of his friends and becomes boisterous . . . he acts silly, makes odd sounds, sometimes profane." He will run out of the house and let the door slam, which is particularly irritating to his father. Mr. Ford has disciplined Ned for this, at times he thinks it is curtailed, but then it breaks out again.

Tensions, fears, and comfort patterns. Ned has never developed any form of oral comfort pattern. His mother felt he didn't need it because he was content most of the time.

But like other war-separated children, he does show evidences of fear and anxiety. According to Mrs. Ford he was always terrifically afraid of all types of masks until the Hallowe'en when he was five years old and he had his own. When he was 18 months, two dogs knocked him down and dogs have been "the biggest fear of his entire growing up and to this day he doesn't want anything to do with them." He was rated among the children having the most serious fears.

Mrs. Ford reports that he cries easily now when his feelings are hurt. But he is most tense when he is being disciplined. "When he's called on the carpet, he plays with his shirt in the front and twists it around his fingers." Mr. Ford, too, feels that when he criticizes his son, there is an immediate reaction, "Ned is subdued—probably more than he ought to be." Ned's fear of his father that was shown in the early months in running away, now seems evidenced in tension and overcontrol. Mr. Ford thinks Ned may be afraid he'll get hurt and, therefore, shies away from physical contact with other children, just as Mr. Ford, himself, did when a boy. Ned was among the children with the most extreme rating on tension.

Affection and sympathy. Mr. Ford feels Ned has a loveable attitude toward everyone. He is generous and tolerant of others, is gentle with the younger kids, and likes to show people that he likes them. His father is very happy that Ned has these traits.

Mrs. Ford says that at times Ned is very affectionate and at other times he just says, "Aw, go on." He likes affection when he gets in bed and as he gets older he seems to need it more. But Ned likes affection only from his mother. He doesn't like it from his father. His father tries to kiss him now and then and Ned doesn't want that. This bothers his father but he says, "I prefer that Ned have affection for his mother rather than for me." Mrs. Ford says Ned is shy about showing affection to his playmates, too. It is only recently that she has ever seen him put his arm around even his best friend.

Both parents feel that Ned is sympathetic. He seems to be aware of the feelings of others. He especially identifies with children in distress and with his mother when she is upset.

Relations with other children. Like other war-separated children, Ned's parents felt he had problems in his associations with his peers. According to his mother, he is not friendly or outgoing outside of the home. Up until recently he preferred to play alone. He seems to have changed since he went to kindergarten and Monday Club. "Now he prefers to be with children and amazingly enough, he's getting so he prefers boys and boys his own age . . . When he first came to the Village (at four-and-one-half years), he preferred the smaller children and girls."

Mr. Ford is concerned about Ned's relations with children. He says Ned withdraws from children and children reject him; his behavior is friendly but sex-inappropriate. He says Ned had "a terrible time when he first played with other children who were competitive." He was three years old before he played with anyone except his own cousin. He says, "It is a common occurrence at kindergarten for him to get his feelings hurt, to weep all over the place . . . He can't handle conflict situations, even though he has the physical ability to do so." Mr. Ford feels he gets along beautifully except in conflict situations and that he keeps friends, once they are made, for a long time. These traits, Mr. Ford admires.

Relations with sibling. Ned shows affection to his ten-months-old sister but this may be to get attention from his parents and may represent his conformity to the accepted pattern of loving one's baby sister. Ned has never been hostile to her. Mr. Ford feels Ned is not receiving the attention he used to get for he has to share it with his sister now. He says they do go out of their way and make a conscious effort to give him attention. However, he believes Ned's recent noisy and unruly behavior which annoys his father exceedingly is definitely related to his feelings of jealousy for his sister. His father's description of Ned's relations with his sister received a rating of 4 on seriousness of problem and father's annoyance.

Relations of Ned and His Father

Ned, like the other war-separated children, is distant from his father. He received the most extreme negative rating on father-child relations on both the data from mother and father interviews. Ned won't accept affection from his father. Mr. Ford says, "When Ned needs sympathy, he doesn't come to me; he doesn't expect much from me. He comes to me with his intellectual problems, for he thinks I am a walking encyclopedia, but not with problems he's tied up with." Mr. Ford adds, "My major trouble is that I don't understand Ned as well as I should. I think this was because I was away when he was young. I am intolerant of some of his problems." Mrs. Ford feels that the relation between Ned and his father is better now; she thinks "the reticence is still more on his father's part than on Ned's."

Father's criticism of Ned. Ned's father, like the war-separated group, was critical of Ned's behavior in eating and in his relations with other children but his main criticisms related to his reponse to authority. Mr. Ford seems somewhat ambivalent about his son's personality. He admires his even temper, his good nature, the fact that he seldom gets angry. "If things do not go the way he wants, he doesn't make much fuss about it. Sort of accepts it as a matter of course and does something else." His father takes pride in the fact that Ned is sympathetic toward other children, is aware of their feelings, doesn't like to hurt their feelings, and is gentle with younger children. He says, "Even at a young age, Ned would be the one to give up a toy he was playing with and go get another toy and offer it to the other person to get his own toy back." But the father believes that "with this loveable attitude toward everyone, Ned will have a tough time adjusting to the competitive, dog-eat-dog society that he meets with boys and girls." He doesn't know whether he should try to get Ned to "stand up for his rights, to become a little stinker about his own things, or let it go along as it is." The father feels that there are "too few people who have the inner feelings that Ned has," but questions "whether it is the right thing, just because he has them, to make him a little bit unadjusted to the group."

Mr. Ford would like to see Ned more aggressive. In his lack of aggression and fear of physical combat, Mr. Ford feels Ned is like he was when a child. Ned's father wonders if the things he has done to Ned have made him less aggressive than he would have been, even as he may wonder if his own father made him like Ned when a child.

His father likes the fact that Ned is usually quiet, playing by himself with puzzles or phonograph, but he becomes critical when Ned is boisterous or silly with one of his friends. Mr. Ford thinks Ned has a good sense of humor and that he learns quickly and eagerly. But, again, he adds that Ned may not be brilliant as his father isn't.

Most of all, the father admires Ned's strong moral sense, the fact that he does what he knows is right. If this trait is a result of the father's strict discipline in the early years, then the father feels it probably was justified. This strong moral sense is one of the traits Mr. Ford admires in himself. In general, his father feels Ned is too sensitive, unhappy, too much of a sissy, and too noisy and inconsiderate.

Relation with mother. Mr. Ford feels that the relation of Ned to his mother has interfered in his own relations with Ned. Like the other war-separated children, Ned is close to his mother. Ned goes to his mother when he is in trouble and he identifies with her when she is in trouble. He shows affection only to her. She considers him a very pleasant and enjoyable child who will do what she wants him to do. This close bond exists even though she has been strict in her training, and has pushed him steadily to attain standards beyond his years.

Father's attitude toward first and second child. The Fords were one of 16 war-separated families who had a second child. Lucille was born about three years after the father's return, when Ned was about four-and-a-half years old. She was about ten months old at the time of the interviews. Mrs. Ford said that her husband feels distinctly different toward Ned and toward Lucille. Mr. Ford says, "I tend to be much more sympathetic with Lucille than I am with Ned. I don't know whether I show it but I feel that way . . . each thing that she does that's new is an accomplishment whereas with Ned, each new thing he does, why, that's what he should have done . . . I tend to enjoy my relationship with Lucille already, more with her than I do with Ned . . . I'm more sympathetic towards her than I am with Ned in the same situation." In this difference of feeling toward his second-born, Mr. Ford was like other war-separated fathers. Both he and his wife felt this was due to Mr. Ford's not seeing Ned when he was a baby and not watching him develop.

Discipline of father. Mr. Ford has been anxious to make his boy a good boy: obedient, trustworthy, and with a high moral character. To do this, he has not hesitated to use discipline which was strict and even severe at times. He relied heavily on spanking and isolation formerly (rating 5), but now he uses these somewhat less and "most of his punishment now is in the form of reprimand" (rating 4). Ned has to stay in the house now (isolation from children) rather than in his room (isolation from family), as formerly.

He is punished mainly for disobedience, for his father "still demands immediate obedience and gets it." Recently he has been spanked for not telling the truth, for evading. "Ned has never been allowed to jump up and down on the couch, or run around the furniture in the house. As soon as he does anything destructive, he's cautioned, and that usually curtails his activities."

Mr. Ford's methods of discipline do not differ as much from his wife's as many of the parents in the war-separated families differed, for Mrs. Ford was a fairly strict parent from the start. She puts great stress on conformity and obeying. When he was four years old, after she punished Ned severely for running away from her, she "told his daddy about it and his daddy spanked him severely again. That is probably the worst spanking he ever had, but he hasn't run away since."

Mr. Ford seems somewhat ambivalent regarding the success of his disciplining of Ned. On the one hand, he says, "A year ago there was never any bickering and now I have to speak two or three times." Then he says, "When I criticize Ned, there is an immediate reaction. He is subdued—more than he probably ought to be. He associates me with his conscience." Mr. Ford indicates that he feels his severe discipline has put a barrier between him and his son. But he thinks Ned is a good boy now either because of or in spite of the trouble in the early days. If it's "because of," then the father is glad he was severe, but he rather thinks it is "in spite of."

Father's perception of self and Ned. The underlying structure of Mr. Ford's relations with Ned can be seen through an analysis of the relation of Mr. Ford's perception of himself to his perception of his first-born.

As one might expect from his account of his own childhood (a history in which he describes a puritanical family, an authoritarian father, and his own tendency to submit and conform), 60.6 percent of Mr. Ford's self-descriptive statements fall into categories in which he has a passive role. His conflict with authority figures, his feelings of inadequacy, his tendency to "keep himself to himself," and what he calls his "external tolerance of others" are reflected in the high percentage of statements which fall into the negative passive group of categories (43.2 percent).

There are two further indications that Mr. Ford is greatly disturbed and confused in his self-perception where situations might demand active outgoing responses: he sees himself about equally positively active and negatively active in relation to others (22.1 percent and 19.8 percent of the self-descriptive statements fall into these groups, respectively). The largest single trait score for self-perception is for the category of retreating and withdrawing. Thus, whenever the situation demands control and mastery, he appears to be ambivalent in his feeling tone toward others and seems to resolve his insecurity by adopting one of the roles in the negative passive categories. Most frequently he retreats from the situation; alternately he resists it passively and complains about it. These negative passive roles carry neither cultural approval nor are they supported by approval of family figures important to him. Thus, Mr. Ford is unable to establish a sense of ego-identity, and as he says, "feels swallowed up as an individual."

His feelings of conflict and inadequacy are evident in the content of his material and in his high self-rejection score (Z, 81). He is ambivalent about evaluating himself on 11 of the 20 trait categories describing self-perception (inconsistency Z score, 67). Nine of these conflict-laden roles are directed against people and describe him in hostile roles.

In his perception of Ned, Mr. Ford's own conflicts appear to play a large part. He has a high child-rejection score (Z, 67) and this is based to a large extent on phobic projection; that is, Mr. Ford tends to reject Ned outright whenever he perceives him engaged in one of the negative relations about which he himself has so much conflict. He tends to emphasize these traits and, thus, the trait-correspondence score which measures the degree of similarity between self-perception and child-perception is here used almost entirely for phobic projection. Mr. Ford may well derive some gratification from perceiving his child disapprovingly as retreating, resentful, passively resisting, and complaining. It is possible that this man sought refuge in the role of disciplinarian and that the perception of Ned as predominantly a passive, resistive person gives him opportunity for combining release of hostility and a sense of mastery. He may derive gratification from punishing which may seem to him an appropriate function for the head of the family.

Summary of Patterns of Adjustment as Revealed in Parent Interviews

The picture we get of Ned from interviews with his father and mother is different in one respect from that of the other war-separated children. By the time he is five-and-a-half years old, he has no problems in eating or elimination. Ned has kept his good appetite and learned control of bowels and bladder in spite of the fact that his parents have made demands beyond his developmental level and have used strict discipline in relation to both oral and anal habits.

In the activity-rest area he has learned the controls his parents desired, too, but there is evidence here of the cost to his developing personality. Ned is a quiet, passive child whose interests have been channeled into quiet, intellectual activities. He has learned to be careful of things at the expense of spontaneous and creative activity with them. Ned plays the same passive role in his relations with people. He is kind and generous and sympathetic; but he has difficulty in showing affection or accepting demonstrations of affection from other children, his father, or even his mother.

His long hours of sleep and rest seem comforting to Ned but his dreams reflect the anxieties of his waking hours. In this, he is like other war-separated children. Ned's high level of anxiety is especially revealed in conflict situations with his peers and in authority situations with his father. Ned's conflicts here seem complex. It may be that his early specific fear of his father and his continuing fear of punishment have been transformed into a generalized anxiety concerning his own impulses and especially those impulses which relate to physical conflict.

As is typical in the war-separated group of children, Ned is close to his mother and emotionally distant from his father. His mother accepts him as a person but his father is ambivalent in his feelings. He is one of the men most critical of his first-born child's behavior and personality. Of Ned's behavior his criticism is mainly leveled at lack of immediate obedience. He is critical, on the one hand, of sex-appropriate noisy, boyish behavior and, on the other hand, sex-inappropriate fear of physical combat. He is alternately praising and condemning of Ned's passive, friendly personality.

Mr. Ford is ambivalent in his perception of himself, is rejecting of Ned, and rejects in him the characteristics about which he is ambivalent in himself.

Ned in Social Situations

We hoped to gain further insight into Ned's pattern of adjustment through direct observations of Ned in kindergarten and Monday Club, to discover how Ned functions in social situations with his peers and adults.

We observed Ned for two months, beginning when he was five years, two months of age. He had been enrolled in kindergarten in Suburban Public School for about six months. This kindergarten group was composed primarily of children from Stanford Village. Every Monday afternoon he attended Monday Club, an informal play group organized for children in this research study, which included many of the children in Ned's kindergarten group. The observations were distributed: 72 percent at kindergarten, 28 percent at Monday Club.

Figures 15a, 15b, 15c, and 15d present Ned's standard scores in the various categories which are discussed below in relation to the average of the non-separated group and the average of the war-separated group of children.

General Description of Ned

Ned is a good-looking, tall, broad-shouldered, healthy boy. His crew-cut hair is appropriately boyish. His dark eyes are soft and appealing.

Activity. He is almost constantly moving about. When he is not engaged in activity such as running or climbing, much of his energy is consumed in nervous, random body movement. Ned shows better than average skill in gross motor activities and can compete successfully with other children here. In manipulatory performance, he is not so outstanding, although his skill is usually adequate to accomplish the tasks at hand. He generally avoids painting, clay, and other fine motor tasks.

Language. Ned usually speaks in a loud voice, wanting to be heard. He depends heavily upon language in attention getting, in social participation, and in maintaining a feeling of control over his environment.

A strikingly important use of language for Ned is nonsense syllables, rhyming, sing-song chants, and other word play. Sometimes he makes up whole nonsense sentences like the following: "I knew a boy named Buzzy, and you know what? He buzzes around my head." "High-ho, big fat toe." There seems to be an element of conscious humor as well as unconscious enjoyment in these utterances. Often he repeats what other children or adults have said, laughing at the sound. Ned rhymes his own and other children's names, such as, "Ward, board," "Stevie is a pleavie," "Ned, head." He spells out words in a chant, such as b-u-s, c-a-r. He sings nonsense syllables, often beginning with the letter "d," such as "dee, dlee, dlee," "do, doe, doe," "sting, da, bohhh," or he shouts out pleasant sounds like, "whee! whee!" "rrrr, rrr!" This means of calling attention to himself is relatively successful for Ned; children laugh and adults smile at his improvisations.

Tension. Ned has more than an average amount of tension compared with other war-separated children. Ned's feet, legs, or body are often moving, his hands twisting or rubbing. He often frowns in worry or with the effort of carrying out an activity. In moments of fear, Ned's body becomes stiff and his facial expression tense. Nearly three-fourths of the tension manifestations occur in group situations, where Ned is with other children in some adult-supervised activity. The times when Ned shows greatest tension in interaction with other children are during conflict situations, when Ned's face sometimes becomes suffused with color or becomes tense and constricted.

The highest number of tension manifestations are connected with facial tension or finger sucking and mouth play; nearly as many, with general body or hand movement. Finger sucking, mouth play, and general body movement seem to represent a diffuse anxiety, and occur during many of Ned's seemingly unoccupied moments. The tight, constricted facial expression occurs mainly in frightening situations with other children and during adult criticism.

Another evidence of tension is seen in Ned's need to clean up after his play and to keep everything in neat order. He is upset if he or other children do not do what is expected. This unusual meticulousness seems to indicate an inner anxiety which Ned seeks to relieve by keeping careful control over the tangible effects of his activities.

Relations with Other Children

Social participation. Ned was observed in social activity with children more than the average non-separated child. This observation is in contrast to his parents' reports that he is somewhat withdrawing. The quality of his participation was similar in pattern to the war-separated group of children (see Figure 15a).

His desire to mingle actively with children is reflected in his high score in initiating contacts and in parallel play. His initiation of social participation is relatively high and follows two rather distinct patterns. Ned often makes exaggerated head or hand movements accompanied by the use of nonsense language in an effort to attract attention. He "clowns" for the other children, and laughs with them at his own antics. This method of calling attention to himself is quite successful, for Ned nearly always gets a laugh. Quite often Ned calls directly for attention, saying, "Look at me, look at me," or "Who wants to push me, who wants to push me?" He also tries to suggest ideas for play, but he does so with so little self-assurance and conviction that he is almost always ignored. Ned rarely follows up his own suggestions when they are ignored by other children, hence stands even less chance of having his ideas accepted. At the parallel play level, Ned is above both group means and this is the most frequent type of play for him. He is typically a "joiner," and characteristically plays alongside of other children. When children are climbing, he climbs; when they are playing games, he plays along beside them.

Ned achieves associative play with other children but far less often than the average of the non-separated children. Children will accept him though they do not look to him for leadership; he was observed in active, exuberant play outdoors or maintaining a lively conversation indoors.

Though Ned is acutely aware of other children most of the time they are present, watching them or smiling at them, he can sometimes become so absorbed in an activity that he forgets to watch them or clown for them. Level four, in which he is about at the average, represents this kind of independent, individual concentration while Ned is within a group of children. Often this happens when Ned is behind in completing a class project.

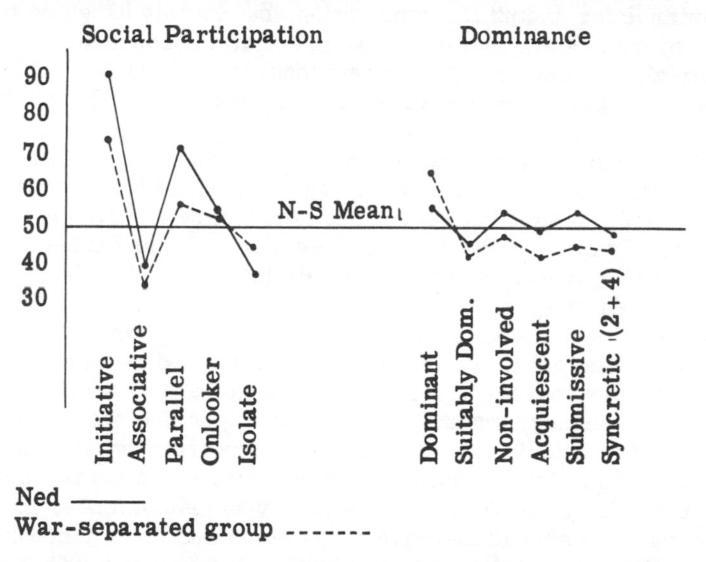

Figure 15a. Standard scores of Ned in relation to the mean of the non-separated group of children. The war-separated group mean is shown in Z score values to the non-separated group.

Ned is alone relatively rarely. When he is, his activity seems rather aimless. He will flit from an activity with other children to a brief try at the swing or teeter-totter by himself and then return to the activity. He seems to dash from one activity to another unless concentrating on a defined class project.

Most of Ned's social participation is flighty and somehow tentative. He has considerable vitality, but it is seldom constructively channeled. His "silly" antics and loud chanting of nonsense syllables are amusing to the other children, but Ned has little in the way of constructive, creative ideas to offer them. Ned substitutes clowning for leadership. He calls himself "the funny man." He laughs at any joke, even without knowing the joke or when it is on himself. His antics as "joker," however, are always within the bounds of adult authority. Actually, his comedy seems to represent an attempt to attract attention without breaking away from prescribed patterns of behavior, since it involves no friction with other children and bears no risk of punishment from adults.

Dominance. In situations with children which call for some form of dominance or submission, Ned behaves very much like the average of the non-separated children, showing a balance of dominant, syncretic, and submissive behavior. He follows the pattern of the war-separated group but is relatively less dominant and slightly more submissive (see Figure 15a).

Ned attempts to be dominant but many of his direct attempts fail. He demands that the other child "come here," but does not carry through when he does not come. He has conflicts over play materials or space. When Ned's play materials are contested, he often kicks or hits, or does whatever is necessary to maintain possession. Less often he responds with insufficient resistance for ending the competition, but merely hangs on to the equipment. All of such dominance-submission situations concerning conflicts over play materials or space are full of emotional impact for Ned. During the contest his face tightens or turns red, and he looks generally upset. For example:

"They ask for rides (in Ned's wagon) and Ned allows Fran to sit behind him. One child grabs at the handle of the wagon, and Ned hangs on tightly, frowning and looking weepy, but refusing to let go. The children give up and push Ned and Fran . . . By the slide Wert comes up and tries to take the wagon. Ned yells crossly and hangs on. He hits at Wert and turns a bright red. Just then Mrs. X. calls to Wert to leave Ned alone. All the children leave Ned and he stands, one knee in the wagon, his body bowed, and his hands covering his face, crying. He tries to swallow his sobs, half stands, and bends over again . . . Suddenly a large gang of boys, who have been plotting in the corner, make a dash for the wagon and begin to push it backwards. Ned is astonished and hesitates, then cries out angrily and hits at the boys, who dodge his blows. He turns purple and screws up his face, crying and yelling. He looks at Mrs. X., who just watches, then he kicks at the boys. In a second they tire of the sport and leave him for a minute, but quickly they all descend upon him again. He yells, 'Quit it, quit it,' striking out at them, his face still tense and frowning. The boys leave and he puts his hands over his face again. After a second he wipes his eyes and sits silently in his wagon" (5 years, 2 months).

Ned seems to be in a state of flux concerning his behavior in dominance-submission situations. Half the time he resists in the conflict or attempts leadership. Half the time he compromises, accepts the leadership of others, or is nonresistant. The times he does react with dominance are often accompanied by obvious signs of distress. Ned seems to want to be accepted so much that any conflict in status relations brings unhappiness.

Initiation of aggression. Again, we find Ned following a pattern similar to other war-separated children except that he has no acts of direct, active aggression and, therefore, none that can be termed hostile. Although he initiates aggression as often as the average non-separated child, the quality is idiomatic (see Figure 15b).

Ned's indirect active aggression includes his aggressive attempts to use play equipment which other children are using, or his threats of aggression against other children. Several times Ned took the wagon, an object highly coveted, from another child, or prevented another child from using the record player or puzzles when he himself wanted to use them. It is interesting, in view of Ned's distress in competitive situations with other children, that he himself aggressively initiated these conflict situations as often as the average non-separated child. Apparently, in contradiction to what his father thinks, Ned is not afraid of physical combat, since he does use physical attack when he wants something. It would seem that Ned's distress may be concerned with a conviction that conflicts are wrong. He sometimes attacks forcefully because he must, but he obviously does not enjoy or approve his own or others' use of force.

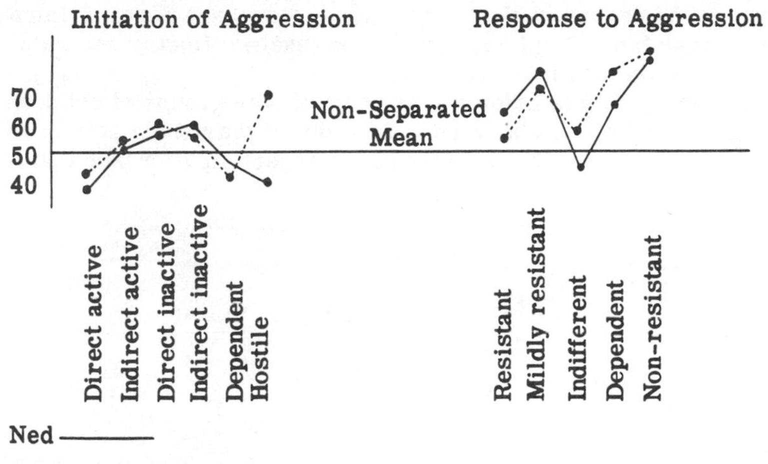

Figure 15b. Standard scores of Ned in relation to the mean of the non-separated group of children. The war-separated group mean is shown in Z score values to the non-separated group.

The direct inactive aggression which represents Ned's playful poking or teasing is above the non-separated children's average, similar to the war-separated group. The units in levels four and five consist of Ned's frequent criticism of other children's work and of telling the teacher when another child is doing something wrong.

Response to aggression. Relatively, Ned is aggressed against much more often than he aggresses. This corroborates Mr. Ford's feeling about Ned. In his response to the aggression of other children, Ned seems again to be a typical war-separated child. He is involved in such episodes about as often as the war-separated group but twice as often as the non-separated (see Figure 15b).

During the time when Ned responds with full resistance, he shows obvious signs of distress. His face turns red, and he sometimes cries after he has defended himself and the attackers have gone away.

Like most of the children in both groups, Ned can rarely respond with indifference to another child's aggression. Equally as often as Ned resists actively, he shows only partial resistance, or cries and seeks an adult's help, or offers no resistance. In this he is similar to the war-separated group who show such behavior much more often than the non-separated group.

It seems clear that Ned's emotional reaction to aggression is due to a conviction that aggression is wrong, rather than to fear of physical combat itself. He can defend himself adequately, but at the same time he is distressed, almost ashamed at doing something he really ought not to do.

There is evidence that Ned seeks the teacher's help when children aggress against him but that the teacher is trying to teach Ned to fight his own battles. However, she comes to his aid when he is really overwhelmed by the children. The teacher's acceptance of Ned's defense of himself seems to influence the degree of Ned's aggressive response. Several times during his active resistance, he looks toward the teacher; finding her watching and saying nothing, he continues to fight.

Friendliness. Ned is below the average of both groups of children in the number of times he was observed in friendly or unfriendly acts in spite of the fact that he was more than average in social participation (see Figure 15c).

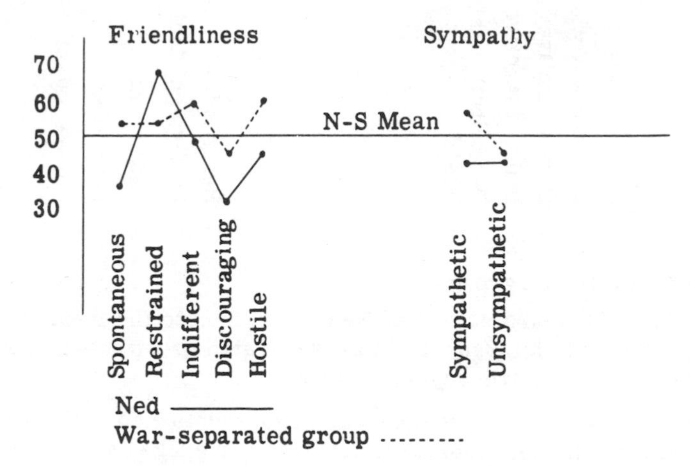

Figure 15c. Standard scores of Ned in relation to the mean of the non-separated group of children. The war-separated group mean is shown in Z score values to the non-separated group.

He is below both groups in spontaneous, uninhibited expressions of friendliness, but is extremely high in restrained or wishful attempts at friendship. He visibly enjoys pleasant interaction with other children, often laughing and smiling with them, which supports the impressions of Mr. Ford. His playful clowning and loud laughter suggest enjoyment of close relations with other children, although he infrequently expresses friendliness directly toward another child. Occasionally, he holds another child's hand or smiles warmly at a particular child. He was never observed discouraging a child's friendly advances and only once being hostile.

The absence of unfriendly feeling toward other children, together with the rather low level of initiation of aggression, suggest either that Ned feels generally positive toward other children, or that he has negative feelings toward other children which he suppresses. Actually, there is much evidence that Ned strongly likes other children and wants them to like him. He does not show pleasure at any time when he does attack other children, even with the approval of his teacher. He is deeply hurt by other children's unpleasantness toward him, crying silently for several minutes or spending long periods in unhappy solitude.

Sympathy. Ned expresses less sympathy or lack of sympathy than the average of either group of children (Figure 15c). It looks as if Ned is too insecure in his relations with other children to offer them sympathy and help. Ned's adjustment in social relations with other children at a "clowning," artificial level indicates that he does not identify with them on a realistic level. Disguising his own unhappiness, he does not perceive or acknowledge distress in others. These observations do not agree with Mr. Ford's feeling that Ned is a very sympathetic child. It looks as if in social situations Ned is too much concerned with his own problems to be free to identify with others in distress.

Behavior with Adults

Ned had relatively few contacts with the teacher in the kindergarten or the adult leaders in Monday Club, fewer than any other child in the war-separated group.

Initiation of contacts with adults. Ned initiates contacts with adults only slightly more than half as often as the non-separated children. This is indicative of the way Ned uses his time-life space in kindergarten and Monday Club. He is more "interested" in children than adults (see Figure 15d).

Most of the contacts Ned initiates with adults are positive but they occur relatively much less often than the average of either group. Except for Ned's announcements about his or other children's progress or his bids for approval on a project, Ned's overtures consist mainly of passive watching of an adult or smiling at an adult from a distance. Sometimes his staring at adults is with a very serious, almost scrutinizing expression. He rarely volunteers personal, intimate information or asks personal questions of adults. While he is not shy about volunteering comments to adults in class, he avoids personal interaction on any but a "progress report" basis. His overtures to adults are in the nature of seeking approval rather than of relating to them on an affective basis. Being good, behaving in a grown-up way, is apparently the way Ned knows best to please and satisfy adults.

Ned made very few overtures of a dependent nature to adults, but his Z score in relation to the control group is similar to his score on positive overtures. His dependent overtures were usually appeals for help in defending himself from other children. Apparently, it is threatening to his highly developed conscience to defend himself without support from adults. It is interesting that Ned rarely goes to an adult for help in a project. Instead, he watches and copies from other children. It seems that Ned has to rely on adult help in matters that touch his strong moral sense; but in his work he prefers not to expose his possible inadequacy to the adult, and, therefore, stays away.

Ned never was observed making demands on any adult and only once was observed making a negative overture. This negative overture was really more in the nature of showing off to an adult whom he liked. In these levels he is far below the non-separated group.

It seems that Ned has no faith in his own ability to deal with adults and, therefore, has set up a barrier of other activities to keep him from situations which he feels he cannot handle.

Response to adult-initiated contacts. Adults initiate contacts with Ned only 56 percent as often as the average of the non-separated group. Such contacts depend on the teacher's perception of a child's need or the child's desire to participate in teacher-led groups. This very low percentage probably indicates, again, Ned's preference for children over adults and his avoidance of situations that court adult contacts. His scores are similar in pattern to the war-separated group but below in frequency (see Figure 15d).

Nearly all Ned's responses to adult-initiated contacts are positive. He gives close attention to games, stories, and other adult-led discussions, and often participates in the discussion when he can. He is enthusiastic and co-operative and extremely responsive to adult suggestions. In group situations with adults presiding, Ned shows considerable evidence of internal tension. It seems that in the effort of responding adequately in competition with other children, Ned tries "too hard." The following illustrates his typical behavior during an adult-led activity:

"Mrs. X. shows pictures. Ned looks carefully, his mouth open and his body wiggling. He names the baby animals as she shows them. During this time he pulls at the top of his jeans, wiggles, half grins for a second, fiddles with his shoe, pulls at his shoe string, starts to pick his nose, returns to his shoe string, and wiggles some more" (5 years, 2 months).

Ned is rarely indifferent to adults when he is approached and only once was observed responding negatively.

Response to adult authority. In spite of the fact that Ned has relatively few contacts with adults, he has more responses to authority than the average of the non-separated children. This indicates that Ned is conscious of adult authority in a large part of his behavior (see Figure 15d).

One of the most outstanding aspects of Ned's behavior is his unusually high score in what we have called compulsive obedience (level 1). He runs to carry out adult instructions; he anxiously reports infractions of the rules; he becomes upset when other children do not follow directions; and he is exceedingly fearful when he, himself, has inadvertently opposed adult authority. The following example illustrates Ned's extreme tension in regard to adult authority:

"He starts to open his milk and it spills all over the table, chair, and floor. Ned stiffens and stands frozen, his face scared and tense. He looks at Mrs. X., who reprimands him and tells him to get the sponge. Still stiff and frightened he runs for the sponge and quickly begins to wipe the floor. He works hard, grunting with the effort. The sponge won't pick up all the milk, so he runs back to rinse it at the sink and runs back, wiping with large swipes. His face is tight, and he keeps glancing at Mrs. X., then works faster. She ignores him. He breathes hard and moves fast, hopping. He smears the milk around but finally clears an area about six by four feet. Then he crawls under the table and works hard. He runs to rinse his sponge. Several boys at the sink comment and tease. He looks at them but says nothing and runs back. He moves the table to get a puddle under one leg. By now he works more slowly, deliberately, and thoroughly. His face is still worried and tense. Mrs. X. calls over to him in a quiet, gentle voice to say that next time he shouldn't open his milk before sitting down. He stops to listen, frowning and unhappy. Again, he rinses his sponge. He wipes the chair seat and then dabs at the pool on the table. Then he rinses the sponge and puts it away, returning to his seat to drink the remaining milk. He is still tense, his body rigid, his glances at Mrs. X. still wary" (5 years, 2 months).

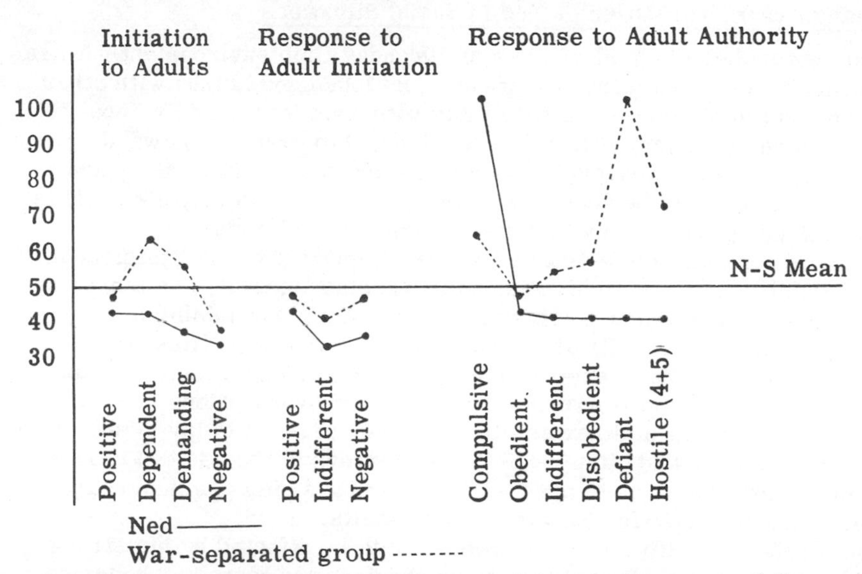

Figure 15d. Standard scores of Ned in relation to the mean of the non-separated group of children. The war-separated group mean is shown in Z score values to the non-separated group.

Ned's high score in compulsive obedience is highlighted by his low scores in other levels. He has no defiant responses, in great contrast to the high score of the war-separated group. This seems to indicate that Ned has incorporated to a very great extent the rules of adults. This incorporation of adult expectations and inhibitions may explain his relatively nondominant, unaggressive, and unaffective behavior with children. Although he prefers to be with children, he takes adult standards and expectations with him, and this causes him to be bland and inefficient in child-to-child relations.

The fear of punishment for misdemeanors like the above also colors much of his behavior with other children. It has been mentioned that Ned reports other children's infractions of the rules to adults, and tries to correct their behavior when it doesn't correspond to adult directions.

Ned also threatens other children with telling the teacher on them, and curbs his activities and tries to curb theirs in accordance with his ideas of adult prohibitions. The following observation illustrates Ned's attitude:

"Mrs. X. says it's cleanup time, but since thay have worked so hard with blocks, they can stay. Ned seems to be the only child that hears her, because Eric and Adam begin to dump the blocks in the box. Ned grabs their arms and yells violently, 'Leave these blocks! You don't have to clean them up.' The boys ignore him and Ned pushes at them, turning red and yelling wildly, 'Don't clean up! We don't clean up! You didn't listen! We don't have to!' Mrs. X. tells Eric and Adam that Ned is right. Ned watches them walk away, then calls after them accusingly, 'You didn't listen, did you?' " (5 years, 3 months).

Summary and Interpretation of Ned in Social Situations

Ned approaches the kindergarten and Monday Club environment with enthusiasm and a vast eagerness to please. He jokes and laughs with other children and tries to get along with them with good humor and without friction. He is ready to accept their leadership and to curb his outward aggression. He courts adult approval, being well-behaved, dutiful, neat, and responsible. He tries to be accepted by children on a clowning, show-off level without offending adults or violating his strong moral code.

There is considerable evidence that Ned is making this adjustment with effort, and that underneath his zeal he is worried, fearful, and tense. He can be friendly in a muted, indirect way, but seems too inhibited to show his friendliness openly. His attention span is short and he flies from one activity to another. He is easily upset in conflict and aggressive situations with other children. He is exceptionally neat and overcautious about cleaning up. He is critical of other children's work, is quick to lay blame on them for their mistakes, and often reports their errors to the adult in charge. He anxiously competes with children— with other boys, for dominance and peer status, and with girls, for the approval of adults.

Ned's relations with other children seem to be affected by his strong moral code. He holds himself rigidly to obedience to rules and becomes anxious if others transgress. Conflicts and aggression are sins that he avoids; if he finds himself involved, he is anxious and guilty and unhappy. In his strong desire for friendly relations, he resorts to silly clowning.

Ned avoids adults but his contacts with them are usually positive. He seeks their approval, he answers questions, and pays close attention. But he is extremely tense in adult-led situations. He is compulsively obedient and seems terrified when he does something adults will disapprove. Even small accidents or the disobedience of other children give him great concern. Ned also seems to be dependent upon the rewards for "good" behavior, for instead of doing the minimum to conform, a good part of Ned's energy is devoted to the service of adult authority. The fear of punishment and/or rejection prevents him from becoming friends with adults, for he must always demonstrate co-operation, obedience, punctuality, and progress, and be on guard against mistakes. His fear of adults also conditions his behavior with children, forcing him to compete with them for adult approval. Indirectly, it prevents him from developing a constructive, self-confident, totally realistic role in social participation with children.

Ned in Projective-Play Situations

In an effort to learn something of Ned's private world we observed him in several projective-play situations. These included a series of three situations designed to study his level of aggressive feelings, a series of story completions, and a series of dramatic-play completions designed to study his concept of and attitude toward his father.

Balloons, Blocking, Doll Play

Ned was five years, three months old at the time of the individual play sessions which were organized to study levels of aggressive feelings.

Balloon experiment. He played with the balloons with vigorous enjoyment, running and crawling about the room, kicking the balloons and then bouncing them from his head, telling the experimenter about his play and referring to the balloons occasionally as footballs and hats. He said he did not want to break one, and when he broke one accidentally, his fist clenched and he laughed uneasily, looking to the experimenter for reassurance. Later, he said he would break them all, sat on one, but too gently for it to break and then continued playing with them. After the experimenter broke one, he said he did not want to break any but immediately broke two small ones. During the rest of the session he repeated several times to the experimenter, "Don't pop any." He ended the session making letters with the balloons. Ned broke three balloons. His rating on the 7-point scale for strength of aggressive feelings was 5; on inhibitions of aggression, 4; overt aggression, 3.

Blocking games. During the first series of blocking games, in which he played with the father doll, Ned seemed rather tense. He was quite ingenious in his solutions to the various play units, tending to assert the boy's rights without denying the father's rights. Aggression was displayed in a cautious way. When the father came into the boy's house, Ned began playing train, using the wall of the house as a track. The father doll, who was leaning against the wall, was knocked down in each of the repetitions of the game. Whether or not the knocking down was intentional could not be determined easily, but since it was repeated three times, one might assume that it expressed aggression. It was aggressiveness revealed in such an apparently accidental way that Ned could pretend, even to himself, that no hostile intent was involved. In the next play unit, the boy touched things in the father's house, and the father spanked the boy. When the father touched things in the boy's house, the boy sent the father home— he had built a house for the father, too— until the third repetition when he spanked the father rather hard. He finished the session with original dramatic play, a fantasy episode which is, perhaps, revealing of ambivalent feelings toward his father. He had the boy and father sailing together on a block "boat" and then the father was killed. Next he built a bridge and put the boy and father on it and then pushed both into the water. After this, he piled the blocks neatly, put the dolls on top, and left. His ratings on this session were 3 for aggressive feelings, 2 for inhibition, and 2.8 for overt aggression.

In the second blocking session, when the boy touched things in the mother's house, the mother sent the boy out, locked the door, and called the police who shot him. He was punished for his misdeeds but not at the hands of the mother as in the same situation with the father doll. When the mother touched things in the boy's house, he kicked her clear out of the house. Once again, he ended the session with a revealing dramatic fantasy in which he definitely identified himself as the boy doll. The boy, "Ned," threw everything on the floor, "even the mommy's glasses." The mother woke up the father who was sleeping, although there was actually no father doll, and the father spanked the boy. Ned's play indicates that he conceives of the father as the one who punishes; the mother may see that the justice is done, but she is not the punishing agent. As in the first session, he left the materials in neat order. His ratings in this session were 4 for aggressive feelings, 2 for inhibition, and 2.9 for overt aggression.

Doll play. In the doll play, Ned immediately began actively carrying out his ideas. He put the dolls through the routines of eating and sleeping and had the family move. The only aggression which he showed was quite indirect. Twice during the session he "shot" the gun, but at nothing in particular. He knocked down a pile of furniture, and he handled the baby girl a bit roughly. He ended the session with the dolls and furniture arranged in a circle about the father doll. His ratings for this session were 3 for aggressive feelings, 2 for inhibition, and 4.4 for overt aggression.

Summary and interpretation. Ned's responses were usually constructive and often showed ingenuity and originality, but it appeared that he would have liked to have been more aggressive than he allowed himself to be. Inhibition of aggressive impulses may have contributed to the tenseness which was consistently noted, particularly in his facial expression, but it did not inhibit his rather vigorous approach to the play materials. Overt aggression appeared only in rather tentative, indirect ways accompanied by some signs of anxiety and then dissolved into more creative play. His responses revealed ambivalent impulses; apparently he could see both constructive and destructive possibilities in the play materials and was impelled in both directions, but the constructive impulses usually remained dominant.

Ned's rank among the 26 children for strength of aggressive feelings in the four sessions is 19 (1 being the most aggressive). His rank is 12 among the 13 children in the war-separated group. In strength of inhibitions of aggression, his rank order among the 26 children is 21 (1 being the most inhibited). His rank is 11 in the war-separated group.

These experimental play sessions reveal Ned as a child with an abundance of creative ideas which he can carry into action. This differs from the picture we gain through the parent interviews or observations in social situations. He is revealed also as a child who has aggressive impulses which he carries out only hesitatingly and often indirectly. He is frequently serious and tense, particularly when the play verges on being aggressive. He seems anxious about aggressiveness, and in his fantasies, the boy is punished for each aggressive act. This picture agrees with other data about Ned. It seems that Ned has incorporated his parents' prohibitions to such an extent that he is his own parent, inhibiting and punishing himself. It may be that the emotions underlying much of Ned's behavior are anxiety and hostility resulting from suppression of his basic impulses to activity.

Dramatic-Play Completions

Ned was five years, three months when he had the sessions with the dramatic-play completions. He was serious throughout both sessions, only occasionally smiling or grinning at the experimenter. In the preliminary play, he actively went through family routines with the dolls, going to bed, getting up, eating breakfast, and sending the daddy off to school. He talked freely and seemed at ease.

In his completion of the dramatic plays, Ned perceives the father as a punishing person (spanks in dramatic plays 2, 7, and would spank in 5 if he knew about the boy's previous misdeeds).

The father is not perceived as helpful either when the truck breaks (play 6), when the boy hurts himself (play 13), when he wants a story read (play 15), or when he needs a playmate (play 2).

Ned seems somewhat afraid of his father. In dramatic play 5 he shows he is still worrying about the boy's spilling the milk in the preceding story because the father would have spanked the boy had he known. Although Ned makes the boy defy the daddy about eating his supper by spilling food on his father's books (play 8), he doesn't dare to face the result of his behavior. When pressed, he finally presents a somewhat mild admonition by the father but shows by his evasive techniques that he feels the response would have been much more strict. Evasion of describing the father's behavior increases in dramatic plays 9, 10, 11, and in 12. He persistently refuses to say what the father would do when the boy wouldn't eat at grandpa's, but finally has the little boy give in and eat his supper. Ned is serious and business-like, and evasive in threatening situations with the father. He is not free to express hostility to the father except in indirect ways (plays 7, 8, and possibly 1, when he has the family eat breakfast without him).

In contrast, Ned's relations with his mother seem much less threatening. He dares to disobey her flagrantly and openly. He can joke about mother, saying, "drop dead" with a sly grin and some enjoyment. She is perceived as helpful (play 13) though certainly not indulgent (play 15). He sits in the mother's chair when father punishes him (play 2).

During the final free-play session, a father doll dressed in a military uniform was added to the dolls. Ned was excited and grinned enthusiastically. He made up this story: "The daddy's in the uniform and he just came back from the war. (Long silence. Inspects uniform and fingers doll. Sighs.) And— he came at grandmother's house. He sits down in the chair, just sits there and talks. And he doesn't want to do, he just doesn't want to. (Sits back in chair and looks at experimenter blankly.)"

In the ratings on the father-child relations scale, Ned had a total score of -23, the most negative score of any war-separated child except one.

Story Completions

At the time of the father-child relations story session, Ned was five years, six months old. The story completion technique seemed a very appropriate technique to use with Ned, for he thoroughly enjoyed the story session, and yet his behavior and responses revealed much about the quality of his relations with his father.

When the session began, Ned appeared confident, eager, and pleased. The relation with the experimenter seemed important to him, for he continually looked to the experimenter for a cue before responding. Of the boys, he was one of the most dependent upon approval from the experimenter.

Anxiety. During each story Ned became quite tense and he showed signs of extreme anxiety during the father-child conflicts. He wiggled and squirmed, his whole body tense. Yet, at the end of each story he would suddenly stop all "nervous mannerisms" and assume an outwardly calm and passive attitude. It was as if he quickly gathered himself together before responding to the next story. Immediately after the session, Ned was rated 3, or as showing moderate anxiety. He was given a rating of 5, or extreme anxiety, from the observation.

Story content. Ned responded as we expected the war-separated children to do in each of the six stories. Ned realized the conflict in the stories and faced the conflict. The general pattern of solutions was to defy the father and to expect a spanking from the father. In the watch story, the boy hides the pieces in the wastebasket, the father finds out and then spanks the boy. In Story IV, when the father asks the boy to pick up his toys, the boy "just played outside." The father threatens to spank, but the boy continues to play. In Story VI, when the father calls to the boy on top of the wall to jump or walk down the stairs, the boy "didn't make up his mind and he didn't hurry up." He just played around.

This gives us a different picture of Ned than we gained from any other source. Here are signs that Ned is putting up much resistance to accepting his father and his demands. His desire to resist the father seems strong and impelling. The father-child relation, as revealed by this method, seems distant and hostile. It should be pointed out that this play session took place three months after other data on Ned were collected.

Summary and Interpretation of Ned's Responses in Projective Play

Ned's ratings on feelings of aggression and inhibition were about average or below in comparison with the non-separated group of children in all situations except the balloons. Here he was like the war-separated group. In the blocking and doll play which involved interpersonal relations, Ned was not rated high in hostile feelings or evidences of inhibition.

In the story completions he evidenced extreme anxiety and was above the average of both groups in lack of conformity to the father's demands in two out of three situations. Ned was more conforming than the average of the war-separated boys, but less than the average for the war-separated group which was influenced by the overconformity of four of the five girls.

Aggression. Ned's aggressive feelings as revealed in these situations are of a low order. One might be tempted to conclude that Ned is a passive child not only physically as his mother describes, but also emotionally, with little feelings of antagonism or hostility toward people. He displayed his most aggressive feelings with balloons and this becomes more significant when we remember that his mother said he was so careful with objects. He showed mild aggression in the blocking games and in the doll play but in very cautious ways, accompanied by signs of anxiety and followed by self-punishment. In the dramatic play he showed some aggression but this seemed to block responses to later stories so that compared to the other children there was relatively little.

Anxiety. The key to understanding Ned's aggressive feelings probably lies in his high level of anxiety. This shows clearly in his ratings in the story completions. Ned also evidenced anxiety in the blocking and doll play whenever he "dared" to be aggressive. In the dramatic-play situations, Ned showed anxiety following misdeeds of the boy doll or when confronted with a threatening situation involving the boy doll and father doll.

Father-child relations. Ned seems to perceive his father primarily as a punishing person. One might almost judge that he can only see his father in an authority role for in situations when Ned has needs for companionship, services, comfort, or reassurance, he seeks elsewhere, depends on himself, or goes without. Ned seems afraid of his father and in conflict about his own feelings toward him. In situations involving the threat of punishment by the father, he evidences extreme anxiety. In dramatic-play situations, although he expressed a little aggression toward the father, his primary response was evasion; but three months later he mustered up courage to defy the father in several of the story-completion sequences.

Ned's relation with his father is in contrast to his relation with his mother who seems much less threatening to him even though she is perceived as an authoritarian person. He dares to aggress against her and to make a joke of her punishment. He can rely upon her for help.

Summary and Interpretation of the Effect of Father Relations on Ned Ford

Ned Ford and his family illustrate how the stress occasioned by war separation and subsequent reunion affected the interpersonal relations of one father and his first-born.

The family fits the model of the war-separated group. Marriage was precipitated by and occurred during the war, early married life was spent around camps, the first child was conceived under these conditions without planning, the wife returned to her family while the husband was overseas, the baby was born in the maternal grandparents' house, and the child was over a year old when the father returned from war. Ned's early life experiences in his grandparents' home were similar in most respects to other war-separated babies, including the close relation to his mother and the curtailment of his activities in exploration and manipulation. In two respects his situation differed: there was another baby in the grandparents' home to share honors, and his mother was somewhat more strict in her methods of training.

The return of the father to his wife and unknown son brought with it the stress that most war-separated men experienced: in vocational adjustments, in re-establishing relations with his wife, in living with his in-laws, and in relations with his 16-month-old baby. In building anew his life with his wife he had only one difficulty— their disagreements in relation to his methods of dealing with their son.

Mr. Ford felt inadequate and anxious in assuming these roles. His war experiences had made him conscious of some of his own personality characteristics: his conflict with authority figures, his intolerance of others, his tendency to keep to himself. He had come out of the war with a deep feeling of inadequacy which was evidenced in his high self-rejection score— a characteristic of the war-separated group.

In some ways it seems as if Mr. Ford, like other war-separated men, used his first-born as a scapegoat for his general feelings of inadequacy in assuming the role of head of the family. This reaction to the role requirements occurred because he had had no experience with young children and did not realize either the needs of the child or the effect which his own behavior would have upon him. In a way it was peculiarly difficult for a young man who had finally proven to himself and to others that he could organize and direct men to be faced with insubordination from a 16-month-old child. Ned became the testing ground for his strength. He used strict disciplinary methods of immediate obedience and severe punishment; methods recently experienced in the armed services and reminiscent of his own childhood family; methods closely related to his feelings of inadequacy and, thus, indirectly perhaps, to his feelings of hostility.

The effect on Ned was to build into his already passive personality a deep feeling of anxiety which permeated his interpersonal relations with parents, with playmates, with teachers. He feared his father who became the authority figure and who later became "his conscience." Ned at five years was a "good" boy, good not only because of the vague fear of punishment that he always carried with him but also because he wanted to be good and was anxious about his own impulses.

Ned's passive, anxious personality brings him certain rewards at home but with his peers keeps him from making a straightforward relation. He has incorporated so well the prohibitions against natural, spontaneous play behavior that he lacks techniques for making his way in the rough-and-tumble give and take of the playground. It is here that he shows his anxiety about physical aggression and his feelings of guilt when he becomes involved in conflicts. He can seldom identify with his peers for his "strong moral character" keeps him conscious of adult rules and regulations, makes him anxious if they are transgressed, and forces him to reprove and tattle on other children.

Ned shows his anxiety with teachers by avoiding them, by being compulsively obedient, and by showing great concern when they disapprove of him.

The early experiences of Ned with his father have inhibited Ned in expressing or receiving friendliness and affection from anyone except his mother. He seems to yearn for friendship with children and for attention from teachers but he cannot receive them easily. Even with his mother, he cannot accept love freely.

At five years of age Ned perceives his father primarily and almost exclusively as a punishing person. He shows extreme anxiety in both actual and fantasy situations involving threat of punishment by his father. He avoids contact with his father and can tolerate no affectionate relations. Ned has not dared to aggress against his father and what hostility he feels lies buried deep within him. Even in fantasy play his mild aggression usually brings anxiety and self-punishment. It is only recently that even in such indirect ways can he dare to defy his father.

Mr. Ford's feelings for his five-year-old son show ambivalence. There is no evidence of warmth or genuine acceptance of Ned as a person; only a distant appraisal of character traits. But Mr. Ford's attitude toward Ned is deeply interwoven with his attitude toward himself. Like other war-separated fathers, he rejects Ned, and his rejection is largely phobic projection. The father seems to have used his relations with Ned as compensation for his feelings of inadequacy and, perhaps, as an opportunity to act out the hostility with which he invests authority. Through these interpersonal relations he seems to have built into Ned even greater feelings of anxiety and, perhaps, hostility toward people.

CHAPTER 15.
GENERAL SUMMARY AND INTERPRETATION

We have attempted in this investigation to increase our understanding of the role of the father in the development of children. We have been especially concerned with the effect that stress might have on the father-child relation, since a stress situation may bring into focus interpersonal relations and mechanisms of adjustment not so readily seen in ordinary situations. We define "stress" as the impact of demands on an individual to adjust simultaneously in several important areas of functioning. Normally, the tasks of adjustment to life's functions are stretched out through time. When these tasks are telescoped in time, the attempt to make these many adjustments simultaneously leads to an experience of stress.

Such a stress situation occurred when a man, who had been separated during the war from his pregnant wife until his first-born child was at least a year old, returned after the war to take up his role as head of the family. Under such conditions stress occurred for both father and child, since suddenly each was forced to make adjustments that in a non-separated family would have been gradually spaced over a longer period of time.

The way in which the father's pattern of adjustment to this stress situation affected the developing personality of his first-born child has been the subject of our inquiry.

Description of the Investigation

Our general hypothesis was that the father would have difficulties in adjusting to his first-born child after the war and that his consequent attitude and behavior toward the child would affect adversely the development of the child.

Subjects

Our investigation was an intensive study of a small sample. The study was focused on 19 families who were separated during the pregnancy of the mother and reunited after the first child was at least a year old. The fathers were all students or faculty members at Stanford University at the time of the study. No other factors, such as the parents' concern with problem behavior, which might operate in cases obtained from a clinic, affected the selection of the sample.

The 19 families had 35 children, 19 first-borns and 16 second children born after the father's return to the family. The children were of average or above average intelligence. There were 12 boys and 7 girls among the first-borns, 8 boys and 8 girls among the second-borns.

These families, designated as war-separated families, were compared with familes in which there had been no separation of the father. They were matched in socioeconomic status and age and sex of children. The control groups were designated as non-separated families. Due to the complexity of the program for collection of data and to the mobility of the married student population at Stanford, the control group varies in the different substudies.

<u>Methodology</u>

Because the problem which we set out to investigate was complex, we used diverse methods of collecting data. These included a series of intensive interviews with fathers, two semistructured interviews with mothers, observations of children in social situations with peers and adult leaders, and observations of children in five projective-play situations.

The data obtained by the different methods were analyzed separately, sometimes by more than one technique, and the results have been presented in different chapters in this monograph. The data were treated by appropriate statistical techniques to test for significant differences between the war-separated and non-separated groups.

General opinion holds that parents have most difficulty in making adjustments to first children. Therefore, we have compared the first-borns of war-separated families with first-borns from whom the father has not been separated, in order that the effect of war-separation might be evaluated. We wished to determine whether differences between families were greater than differences due to war-separation. Therefore, in the mother-interview study we compared the differences between first- and second-born children in war-separated and non-separated families. We realized, also, that the experiences of the first-born child during the period of the father's absence may have been more influential in determining his development than the experiences after the father's return. Therefore, in the mother-interview study we compared the early life experiences of the war-separated first-borns with those of their siblings and those of the non-separated first-borns.

In our analysis of stress areas for returning veterans there are sections where we have no control data for comparison. Our discussion of the man's adjustment to his wife after the war would have been strengthened if we could have compared husband-wife relations in families where a child had not been born during the father's absence.

Checks on reliability of analysis were made with all techniques requiring interpretation of original data. In all substudies except those reported in Chapter 4 (Fathers' Attitudes Toward First-Born Children) the level of significance expressed in $P < .05$ has been accepted as indicating statistically significant differences between groups. In Chapter 4 we could not readily assume underlying continuity of the scores, which we were analyzing by the t technique; therefore we required a P of .01 or less for significance to minimize the effects of possible lack of continuity.

The technique for collecting data from the non-separated children in the substudy using dramatic-play completions to investigate the child's concept of and attitude toward his father proved to be unreliable. Therefore, the findings of that study cannot be incorporated in this summary.

In the presentation of findings, group differences have been emphasized. However, we have included in several chapters analyses of a few individual cases to preclude too glib transference of group findings to individual cases. In addition, in Chapter 14 we have presented an analysis of one war-separated family against the background of the group analyses to show the interrelations of factors influencing the father's and his son's adjustments to stress.

Findings Concerning War-Separated Families

In this summary of the general findings from our investigation, we have reassembled the material previously reported in the several substudies in order to show the relation of the results obtained from the various approaches to our problem.

In the interests of brevity we are reporting here only findings concerning obtained differences between the war-separated and non-separated groups. These differences are statistically significant except when qualifying terms such as "tendency" are used.

It must be remembered that the results of this investigation were obtained from families who represent a limited level in socioeconomic status. Therefore, applications of these findings to other socioeconomic groups are not warranted at the present time. In addition, because our findings indicate that group trends cannot be assumed to be characteristic of each individual within a group, extreme caution should be exercised in applying these findings to any specific family.

Stress Situations

From the father-interview data we found that the war-separated father on his return from war was faced with major adjustments in assuming the role of head of the family. These adjustments included vocational orientation, re-establishing relations with his wife, and establishing relations with his unknown child: adopting the roles of breadwinner, husband, and father.

There is evidence that the men anticipated with some trepidation the problems they might face in deciding on vocations and finding jobs and the possible difficulties in adjusting to their wives, but they did not sense what lay ahead in adjustments to their first-born children. Adjustments were complicated for the war-separated group by disagreements with the wife's family and by greater differences between husband and wife in methods of rearing children than was found in the non-separated group. The strain which the war-separated fathers felt because of the demand for simultaneous adjustments in these areas is evidenced in their greater anxiety regarding vocational selection and economic support of the family.

The first-born child in the war-separated family, according to the fathers' and mothers' reports, was faced with adjustments to an unknown man who suddenly invaded his world, taking a dominant position in the family. He usurped the child's "mommy," assumed personal intimacies, made unexpected requirements for behavior, demanded obedience, and used methods not theretofore experienced by the child.

Behavior Under Stress

There seems to be a sequential relation in the father's and child's behavioral adjustment to the stress situation. The war-separated fathers reported that the child's immediate response to the father was shy, withdrawing, unresponsive behavior. The child denied affection to the father, refused to be "cared for" by the father, and in some cases interfered in the man's relations with his wife.

The father's subsequent response to his child was criticism of the child's behavior, especially in regard to his dependence on his mother and in regard to his obedience to adults. The father, therefore, assumed his father role primarily as a disciplinarian using more severe methods than the non-separated fathers used in the early years. This brought greater disagreement regarding methods of child rearing between husband and wife than there was in the non-separated family.

The behavior of the war-separated fathers immediately resulted in alienation of their first-borns, whose attitudes became more rejecting of their fathers than were the attitudes of the non-separated group.

Adjustment Patterns of Fathers

An understanding of the ways in which the war-separated fathers worked out their adjustments to the family situations was gained through analyses of the father interviews and supplemented by analyses of data from the mother interviews. We studied the attitudes of the war-separated father toward the behavior of his first-born child after the initial stress period and the resulting father-child relation. We compared the attitudes of the war-separated fathers with the attitudes of non-separated fathers toward their first-born children. We also compared the war-separated father's attitudes with his wife's attitudes toward the same child. In addition, we studied the perceptual patterns of the fathers as they relate to self and to the first-born child.

Attitude toward first-born child's behavior. The war-separated fathers are more concerned about their first-borns' eating behavior than about any other behavior except obedience. They consider that their first-borns have more serious problems in eating behavior than do the non-separated fathers, especially in table manners and in refusals to eat. The children's refusals to eat seem directly related to the fathers' methods of forcing food. These fathers are more worried and more annoyed about the child's eating behavior than are the fathers in the non-separated group.

The war-separated fathers more than the non-separated fathers consider that their first-borns have serious problems in elimination behavior. The fathers are more worried and tend to be more annoyed than the non-separated fathers. They tend to consider that their first-borns have more serious problems in sleep routines and they are more annoyed by them than the non-separated fathers. If persistent bed-wetting is included in sleep disturbances, the war-separated fathers consider these problems more serious than do the non-separated fathers.

The war-separated fathers tend to report more tensions and comforts for the first-borns and tend to be more worried and annoyed by these behaviors, especially whining and thumb-sucking. They also tend to report more problems in the first-born's relations with other children, the war-separated children being more withdrawing, more rejected by others, and the boys less appropriately masculine in their behavior.

There is no behavior in which the non-separated fathers consider that their first-borns have more serious problems or are more worried or annoyed. Only in relation to dressing behavior do they tend in that direction.

It is in the interpersonal relations within the family that the most extreme differences were found between the war-separated and the non-separated groups. From the father interviews we learned that the over-all father-child relation of the father with his first-born involves more serious problems in the war-separated family. This finding was supported by the reports of war-separated mothers, who indicated not only that relations are more distant between fathers and first-borns but also that the first-borns have more traits that annoy the fathers. The war-separated first-borns are closer to their mothers and have fewer traits that annoy them. The fathers are closer to their second-borns. There tends to be a greater problem in sibling relations in the war-separated family than in the non-separated family and the fathers tend to be more worried and annoyed by this behavior.

Comparison of father and mother attitudes toward first-borns. When the reports of the war-separated fathers are compared with reports from their wives about the same children, certain differences emerge. It is apparent that the war-separated fathers are more interested in some areas of behavior such as eating, elimination, sleep routines, and relations with siblings and other children, and ignore areas such as dressing, sleep disturbances, tensions and comforts. Their wives, on the other hand, show relatively consistent interest in all areas. In those areas in which the fathers are least interested, their wives see their children as having severe problems. In eating behavior and relations with other children the war-separated fathers tend to think that the first-borns have greater problems than their wives think they do. The mothers tend to evidence more worry than the fathers about every area of behavior except eating and relations with other children. On the other hand, the fathers tend to be more annoyed than the mothers about all areas of behavior but this difference was statistically significant only for eating behavior. In discussing eating behavior, elimination behavior, and relations with other children the wives show much greater insight into their first-borns' behavior than their husbands do.

Both war-separated parents agree that the mother feels closer to the first-born child. They both feel that the first-born feels closer to his mother than to his father. Both parents report that the father's discipline of his first-born when he returned from war was severe, although the wife tends to minimize the severity of this discipline, perhaps out of loyalty to her spouse. The parents also concur that the relations between father and first-born child are quite difficult. In the area of self-child relations the fathers seem to have about equal insight with the mothers. For spouse-child relations, however, the mothers show much more insight than their husbands. The parents' insight into both of these relations was judged to be relatively slight.

Perception of first-born. We gained deeper insight into the psychological processes underlying the father's behavior through the study of the father's perception of self and of his first-born child. The war-separated father has a higher self-rejection score than the non-separated father. He perceives himself as predominantly passive and his first-born as predominantly passive (half positive, half negative). The non-separated fathers, on the other hand, see themselves and their first-borns as having traits much more in tune with cultural expectancies. The non-separated father perceives himself as predominantly positive active (teaching, directing) and his offspring as positive but passive (appreciating, co-operating, trusting, conforming). The war-separated fathers reject their first-born children and reject in them especially those traits about which in themselves they are ambivalent. Phobic projection seems to be the mechanism used by the war-separated group to isolate and distance the first-born.

Adjustment Patterns of First-Born Children

We have three primary sources for an understanding of the ways in which the first-borns in war-separated families adjusted to the stress occasioned by the return of the father from war; the descriptions of the children given by the mothers supplemented by descriptions given by the fathers; the social behavior of the children observed in group situations; and the private worlds of the children as revealed in projective-play situations.

Background of early development. In order to evaluate the effect of the stress occasioned by war-separation and subsequent reunion of the father on the development of the child, it was necessary to compare the early life experiences of the war-separated and non-separated children. There were no differences found between the groups in the conditions associated with pregnancy, labor, and childbirth. There were no significant differences in the methods of training used by the mothers in relation to organic needs although more war-separated children were breast fed and elimination training was begun earlier with them. The war-separated children were more restricted in locomotor activities but this difference is not statistically significant. There was a tendency also for war-separated children to have more contacts with close relatives and fewer with children than the non-separated group.

Problem behavior. The development of the children in the two groups shows marked differences. In the areas of organic needs (eating, elimination, and sleeping) which are the foci of socialization during the preschool years, the war-separated children have more serious problems. They also are less independent in eating and dressing. The war-separated children manifest more fears of a serious nature and have more overt expressions of tensions.

Relations with other children. According to the mothers' reports the war-separated children have poorer relations with other children than the non-separated children. The fathers' discussions tend to support this difference. Our analysis of observations of the children in group situations (nursery school, kindergarten, grade school, or Monday Club) confirm these impressions of the parents and give further insight into the patterns of the children's behavior with other children.

In group situations the war-separated children are not able to establish or maintain associations with other children as skillfully as the non-separated children. They make overtures to children more often but they less often can maintain genuine associative relations with them. More of their time is spent as onlookers and fringers. They also more often assume extreme dominant roles and they less often show syncretic behavior of the give-and-take type. The war-separated children express unfriendliness more directly than the non-separated children but they also are more often sympathetic to the difficulties of other children.

Relations with adults. The mothers' reports tend to reveal differences between the groups of children in their relations with adults other than parents, but these trends are not statistically significant. However, the observations in group situations do show significant differences. The war-separated children are relatively more often dependent and demanding and less often negative when they make overtures to teachers or adult leaders than the non-separated children. They are less frequently indifferent to adults' advances to them. It seems that the war-separated children do not feel free with adults and cannot act naturally and easily in interpersonal relations with them. When confronted with adult authority they seem in conflict, for they are both more compulsively obedient and more openly defiant than the non-separated children.

Aggression. In overt behavior in peer group situations the war-separated children tend to be more often aggressed against than aggressing. When they do aggress, however, the aggression is more often of an unfriendly, hostile nature than that of non-separated children. The war-separated children handle the aggression against themselves poorly, frequently showing panic or being submissive to it. Fathers tended to be very disturbed about this kind of behavior in their sons, feeling that it was unmasculine.

The war-separated children evidenced some feelings of aggression by a greater incidence of defiant disobedience toward adults in group situations.

One might expect that in permissive situations like the projective-play session, the war-separated group would express more aggression overtly. In each of the four experimental sessions designed to study aggression, the war-separated children were slightly more aggressive than the other group and this difference reached statistical significance in two sessions.

The war-separated group was rated as having stronger feelings of aggression than the non-separated group in each of the four sessions, the combined ratings being significantly different. Because the difference between the groups was greater in hostile feelings than in overt aggression, one might expect the war-separated children to be rated higher on inhibitions of aggression. Although they tended to have stronger inhibitions, the differences were not significant.

Anxiety. There is consistent evidence from several sources that the war-separated children have developed greater feelings of anxiety than the non-separated children. The mothers report differences in the number and seriousness of fears and in the seriousness of tension patterns. In group situations the war-separated children evidence anxiety in their response to conflict situations with their peers and in their compulsive obedience to adult authority. The war-separated children showed greater anxiety in the story-completion sessions when faced with situations which involved the father.

Attitude toward father. From the reports of both mothers and fathers we infer that the war-separated children have more distant relations with their fathers than the non-separated children. Since we could not investigate this directly with young children we endeavored to obtain their attitudes through the indirect method of projective play. In the completions of stories involving the father, the war-separated boys showed that they felt emotionally more distant from their fathers than the non-separated children. In situations carrying the threat of punishment from the father they were less conforming to the father's standards. But the war-separated girls solved the conflicts in the stories in a way which indicated they were less distant and more conforming than the non-separated group. In response to the blocking games, where we endeavored to investigate difference in the child's feelings in response to the mother and father dolls, we found no differences between the war-separated and non-separated groups of children.

The finding of extreme sex differences in attitudes toward the father in the story-completion technique is supported by the findings in the substudies of aggression that the boys had greater feelings of aggression than the girls. However, it is only in these projective situations that the analyses of our data show differences between boys and girls.

Interpretation

The problems which the men in this study faced after the war might be summarized as problems in self-reorientation. Such problems relate to three of Erikson's developmental tasks in personality integration: ego-identity, intimacy, and "generativity" (24). The prewar self of these men was primarily an individual self, a conception of being responsible for and seeking satisfaction for one's self. The postwar self of these men suddenly had to become a self which was family oriented.

The normal process of stabilizing ego-identity as discussed by White (84a) had been interfered with in these men by the uprooting caused by the war. White points out that the stabilizing process owes much to the roles characteristic of adult life: occupational, marital, and parental. "The stored-up sources of his stability come increasingly out of behavior within roles. Under stable social conditions much strength can thus be borrowed from the environment through consistent playing of consistently defined roles" (84a, p. 336). But these men had lacked both stable social conditions and consistent playing of roles. Reality for them was war and military life and the things that go with them and they clung to this somewhat nostalgically as they sensed the vague uncertainties of civilian and family living. One father said this so clearly:

> "I was leaving the war zone for home, but there was an ache. A part of me would be left behind; an unreal self in an unreal world. What had happened between me and those persons I was leaving dead and alive, wouldn't mean anything any more. I felt like saying, 'I can't go, let me off.' But all I could do was look and feel . . . But the minute it was out of sight I turned to thoughts of my wife and baby. I wondered what it would be like after the years—whether it would be possible to draw a line in your life—all these problems and responsibilities to face—I'd have to get out and get a job—"

Under normal conditions a man usually undertakes the roles of breadwinner, husband, and father sequentially, feeling some sense of adequacy in one before entering into the next. But for these men the tasks were telescoped in time, with consequent increase in strain. These men were in an anomalous position. They were husbands, but unsure of their relations with their wives and novices in the role. They were fathers, but of unknown children whom they had seen only in pictures; they lacked any warm interpersonal relations with these children and were vague and uncertain of the role of father. Finally, they were heads of families, without jobs, without training, and with only the faintest conceptions of what they wanted to do or how to go about making decisions.

Although the men anticipated the problems which lay ahead in occupational and marital adjustment, they in no way sensed the problems they would face in adjusting to their first-born children. There seems no doubt that the young child's very natural shyness and refusal of the father's advances (anxious assumptions of the father role) increased the feelings of inadequacy in the returning veteran. The subsequent father-child relation seems to be an outcome of "this last drop" in the father's cup of inadequacy.

The father's early evasion of the supportive role with his first-born (caring for the child), through flight into an authoritative role, can be seen as a compensation for his own sense of inadequacy. The severity of discipline he used may have been directly related to the degree of frustration he felt in not being able either to win over or to conquer his own child at a time when he lacked stability in other roles. The contrast here with the non-separated group of fathers who assume a supportive role with their first-borns and who use more constructive discipline is striking.

In later years, the war-separated father indicated that he cannot perceive himself in a father role with his first-born which seems appropriate in our culture. The usual pattern of a father who directs and teaches and a child who follows and learns gives way to a father who criticizes and complains and a child who disobeys and cannot or will not learn. These fathers are ambivalent about themselves and use phobic projection in perceiving their first-born. This seems to increase the distance between the father and his child.

These changes in the life space of the first-born child acted as psychological stress to which the child had to work out some form of adjustment. It is possible that the early life experiences of the war-separated babies made them less ready to accept the father and more vulnerable to his attacks. The unusually close relation of the first-born with his mother, upon whom he became very dependent, made him less likely to accept the services of a strange man and more likely to resent him as an interference in his relations with his mother.

The child was forced to learn ways of protecting self against the invasion of a strange and threatening object— his father. He could do this by evasion (running to mother), by fighting (disobedience, refusal to eat, soiling), or by conforming. For a young child the first two were simpler forms of behavior which he learned quickly but which brought punishment. Conforming involved more difficult learning, and came more slowly but brought only the negative reward of no punishment. In many instances the father's requirements for learning were beyond the child's level of developmental readiness and thus psychological hazards were increased.

There is evidence that the increased tensions within the child without any parallel increases in reassurance from the father interfered in his learning appropriate socialized behavior in eating and elimination and in interpersonal relations with his peers, with authority figures outside the home, and with his father. What outward conformity the war-separated child has been able to achieve toward the end of the preschool period has come at great cost to his feelings toward self and others. His high level of anxiety is evidenced in his fears and nightmares, in his reactions to conflict situations with his peers, and in his phantasies about threatening situations with his father. He lacks warmth and affection for anyone but his mother. He has a tendency toward feelings of hostility greater than other preschool children. However, he seems in conflict about expressing these feelings in overt aggressive acts.

It seems that these war-separated children as a group have anxieties about their own impulses so that fear of punishment or fear of physical aggression against self keeps them relatively nonaggressive even in permissive situations. The responses of some of the children in individual play sessions after the completion of the research study would tend to support our interpretation. In these sessions overt aggression in phantasy situations increased. The war-separated boy judged by the staff to be the most anxious child in either group refused to participate in the last research projective-play situation but four weeks later smashed to bits all the miniature life toys and family dolls except one doll who sat serene and unscathed amidst the havoc. This one he named the "teacher doll." After this session, Dan for the first time showed a positive relation to the teacher when he threw a shy kiss to her as he left nursery school.

The interpersonal relations between father and first-born seem to have brought certain underlying similarities in their patterns of adjustment. Both father and child have high levels of anxiety, and both have developed hostile feelings of a passive, repressed nature.

If we look at the war-separated first-borns from the standpoint of Erikson's (24) three basic personality tasks of infancy and early childhood (the accomplishment of a sense of trust, a sense of autonomy, and a sense of initiative), we are inclined to believe that the father-child relation has interfered in the child's normal development. The basic sense of trust which he obtained from his mother in the first year has been upset by his relations with his father. Mr. Mathews says of his five-year-old when he visits the neighbors, "A man is just another man, he makes relations with the woman." The difficulties of many of these children in establishing elimination control and the fathers' severe punishment by hard spanking have perhaps built shame and doubt rather than a sense of autonomy in the children. These conflicts may be related to the repressed hostility in these children. Finally, the father's authoritarian control of the child's activities has probably tended to build guilt about the child's own physical exuberance rather than to increase his sense of initiative. Mr. Ford says, "Ned slams the door when he goes out. It has got to stop. I am getting it under control."

Many difficulties are encountered in presenting the findings of an investigation like the one we have just completed. The one most easily recognized is the tendency to emphasize certain of the factors which influence personality development to the exclusion of others. When light is focused on war-separation and subsequent interpersonal relations of father and child, one is apt to forget the dynamics of other factors lying in the peripheral darkness. We recognize the analogy to Lawrence Frank's drunk seeking his watch in the aura of the street light because there was no light in the alley where he lost it (25a). We have tried to protect ourselves and our readers from this error in some degree by glimpses of a father like Mr. Marston (Chapter 5), who did not follow the usual pattern of the war-separated fathers and of a child like Ned Ford (Chapter 14), whose mother sought the same goal as the father in her first-born's behavior but who kept a warm, close interpersonal relation with Ned which served as emotional support in learning.

Another difficulty in our investigation has been due to the fact that we have endeavored to show sequences in interpersonal relations and in subsequent behavior and feelings. We have had to depend on the retrospective reports of fathers and mothers for our knowledge of the early years. We cannot be sure that these reports quite correspond to actual facts although we are sure the attitudes and feelings represent genuine residues.

In addition, the techniques we used for collection of data were such that they precipitated changes in the subjects while we were in the process of securing data. The interviews with parents, especially with fathers, although not planned for therapeutic purposes, brought greater insight to many subjects. This is a basic problem in "action" research.

The distant relation between father and first-born in these war-separated families has brought unhappiness to both father and child. The mothers were conscious of this and the fathers felt it deeply. Although the analyses presented in this monograph do not touch upon this, we have evidence that the war-separated children, through the activities of nursery school and Monday Club, through their phantasy release in individual play sessions, and through their contacts with acceptant teachers and research workers, achieved some measure of emotional release and thus were freer to learn more appropriate ways of behavior. In the process of this investigation the fathers, too, gained insight into their own feelings and began to understand their first-borns better. As Mr. Wagner said in his final session:

"Alma and I had a hard time. Now I can see it. I get a perspective I never had before. It was so different with Pauline (second child). I saw her from the beginning." He got up and walked to the door, then turned and said, "If you want to put it in a nutshell, you could say it like this: I was never home with Alma when she was little and helpless. I never felt she needed to be cuddled and protected. When I came home I felt she was big enough to do this— 'You big lug, you better do as I tell you, you're big enough to do as I say.' That's really it . . . I feel I don't give Alma the affection I give the other children. I try to, especially lately I try. She really is getting to be a very nice child."

Appendixes and References

APPENDIX 1. SOURCES OF DATA

A. War-Separated Families

Family	Interviews		First-Born Child										Second-Born Child	
					Intelligence			Observations C.A. (mos.)		Dramatic Play Completions	Story Completion	Aggression Games		
Name	Father	Mother	Name	Sex	C.A. (mos.)	M.A. (mos.)	I.Q.	1st	2nd	C.A. (mos.)	C.A. (mos.)	C.A. (mos.)	Name	Sex
Arnold	x	x	Bruce	M	49	67	137	48	54	54	56	52	Edward	M
Brown	x	x	Betty	F	81	76	94			88	88		Rose	F
Bryan	x		Mary	F	60	72	120	66	67				Mike	M
Burgman	x	x	Don	M	69	76	110	70	73	81	73	70	Maria	F
Ford	x	x	Ned	M	65	90	138	62	64	63	66	63	Lucille	F
Harlow	x	x	Clarence	M	67	90½	135	64	65	77	64		None	
Holman	x	x	Ray	M	59	69	117	40	59	78	66	56	Lois	F
Irwin	x	x	Patricia	F	66	68	103	65	67	57	75	64	None	
Marston	x	x	Ken	M	50	65	130	49	51	51	55	52	Willard	M
Mathews	x	x	Albert	M	76	100	132			62	61		Leslie	M
Moore	x	x	Rick	M	85	90	106	84	88	80		87	Teddy	M
Osborne	x	x	George	M	68	84	124	65	69	66	69	66	Alvin	M
Snyder	x	x	Kate	F	55	65	118	39	52	61	77	67	Alex	M
Soule	x	x	Fran	F	94	124	132	68	71	63	78	70	Alice	F
Statler	x	x	Allen	M	72	81	113	70	78	73	78	74	Louise	F
Wagner	x	x	Alma	F	63	78	124	58	63	63	63		Pauline	F
Weiss	x		Joe	M	40	50	125	51	55				Lily	F
Wycoff	x	x	Ann	F	64	57	93	46	59	55	71	62	None	
Wolf	x	x	Dan	M	53	61	115	47	59	49		55	Raymond	M
Brock			Grant	M							105		Milly	F
Hill			Irene	F							83		Oscar	M
Josephs			Celia	F							77		Jake	M
Ogden			Gladys	F							62		Kim	M
Treadway			Randall	M							70		Lottie	F

B. Non-Separated Families

Family	Interviews		First-Born Child										Second-Born Child	
					Intelligence			Observations C.A. (mos.)		Dramatic Play Completions	Story Completion	Aggression Games		
Name	Father	Mother	Name	Sex	C.A. (mos.)	M.A. (mos.)	I.Q.	1st	2nd	C.A. (mos.)	C.A. (mos.)	C.A. (mos.)	Name	Sex
Aiken			Phoebe	F							73		None	
Allman			Corrinne	F							74		None	
Armand		x	Connie	F	56	74	132			52		54	Lewis	M
Arndt			Chris	M						64			Cherry	F
Arno	x		Sarah	F									Peter	M
Avery	x		Louis	M				53	54				Andy	M
Barnard		x	Jill	F	75	72	96			67	84	72	Marvin	M
Baruch			Peggy	F						92	93		Rocky	M
Benz			Ivan	M						77	65		May	F
Burrell			Flo	F	58	64	110	58	60				Matt	M
Campbell		x	Duncan	M	44	54	123	43	48	51			Julie	F
Cook			Russell	M	54	62	115					50	None	
Fuller	x	x	Marilyn	F	41	49	120						Sally	F
Garrett	x		Herbert	M									Henry	M
Gates			Amelia	F				72	72				None	
Gibson	x		Sally	F	44	48	109						None	
Goldman	x	x	Lisbet	F	72	96	133+	45	51	67	83	73	Helen	F
Griffin		x	Jack	M									Bill	M
Hamilton		x	Philip	M	45	58	129	40	41				Penny	F
Harper			Ben	M	67	79	118			68	68	68	None	
James			Homer	M						63	63		Boyd	M
Kilpatrick			Doris	F						59			Ella	F
King	x		Leonard	M	94	116	123	93	94	89	100	89	Cecile	F
Kirk			Waldo	M				50	51	51	51		Harry	M

Kuhlan			Carrie	F	56	88	156	54	55				Arlene	F
Lewin			Paul	M	79	86	109				79	75	Wilbur	M
Martin	x		Otto	M	49	66	135						Lucian	M
Maxfield			Arnold	M	55	73	133	54	55	56	55	51	Fred	M
Moffett	x	x	Cathy	F	46	51	111	48	52	57	58		Deborah	F
Murray	x		Luke	M	56	62	110	51	55				Howard	M
Nelson			Rachel	F							66		Ogden	M
Olsen	x		Oren	M									None	
Owen			Gregory	M						69	59		Nancy	F
Park	x		Winston	M									Edith	F
Perry			Rebecca	F							73		Vernon	M
Purcell		x	Roger	M	84	102	121	75	76			72	Dawn	F
Redefer			Timothy	M							68		None	
Roberts			Walter	M	61	84	138			51		57	None	
Rowell	x		Marty	M	42	55	131						Randall	M
Ruppert			Victor	M						71	71		Mathilda	F
Sanborn	x		Bud	M									Elmer	M
Seitz			Ella	F	52	67	132	60	60				Algy	M
Spade			Claude	M						75	76		Win	M
Stevenson		x	Frank	M	83	98	118			64		70	George	M
Stone	x		Harry	M									Luella	F
Thomas			Grace	F	67	106	158			61		66	Lois	F
Thorndike			Art	M				68	68				None	
Tipton	x		Howard	M									Claude	M
Tobin	x		Martha	F									None	
Todd		x	Florence	F									Sammy	M
Tolman			Adela	F							76		None	
Tryon			Hugh	M	53	53	100	52	59			56	Aggie	F
Walker		x	Becky	F	50	56	112						Cameron	M
Woodworth	x		Si	M	52	62	119	62	63				Maude	F

APPENDIX 2. FATHER-CHILD RELATIONS STUDY

Areas of Father-Interview Data

I. Before-marriage history of father
  A. Family experiences which father considers important in influencing his present father pattern
    1. What his father was like
      a. General personality characteristics
      b. In relation to wife
      c. In relation to son (interviewee)
      d. Identification of son with father
    2. What his mother was like
      a. General personality characteristics
      b. In relation to husband
      c. In relation to son (interviewee)
      d. Identification of son with mother
    3. Relations with siblings
      a. Sisters
      b. Brothers
  B. Experiences with peers
    1. Same sex
    2. Other sex
  C. Vocation:
    1. Goals
    2. Experiences
  D. Attitude toward marriage
    1. Ideals
    2. Plans
    3. Previous marriages
  E. Attitude toward self
    1. Acceptance-rejections
    2. Quiet

Ia. Before-marriage history of wife
  A. Family life
    1. Father
    2. Mother
    3. Siblings

II. Courtship period
  A. Circumstances of meeting
  B. Length of courtship
  C. Emotional relations
  D. Effect of war

III. Marriage
  A. Age
    1. Mother
    2. Father
  B. Circumstances
  C. Effect of war

IV. Early marriage period
  A. Circumstances of living
  B. Emotional relations
  C. Effect of war

V. Pregnancy
  A. Planned (effect of war)

- B. Attitudes
  - 1. Father
  - 2. Mother
- C. Circumstances of living
- D. Anxieties; apprehensions
- E. Contacts between husband and wife
- F. Father's feelings of identification with baby
- G. Changes in mother as sensed by father

VI. Birth of child
- A. Circumstances of living
- B. Feelings of father

VII. Period between child's birth and father's return
- A. Length of period
- B. Circumstances of living
- C. Contacts with wife
- D. Father's relations with child
  - 1. Concept of child
    - a. How he looked
    - b. Kind of personality
  - 2. Feelings toward
  - 3. Projections into future

VIII. The father's return
- A. What he was looking forward to
  - 1. Re-establishing relations with wife
    - a. Expectancies
    - b. Apprehensions
    - c. Guilt
  - 2. Establishing relations with child
    - a. Expectancies
    - b. Apprehensions
    - c. Concepts of child
- B. Feelings during early weeks of return
  - 1. Toward wife
    - a. Sensitivity to changes in her
    - b. Sensitivity to changes in self
    - c. Insecurities
    - d. Problems in adjustment
  - 2. Toward child
    - a. Acceptance of father by child
    - b. Difference between what was expected and reality
      - (1) Personality
      - (2) Behavior
      - (3) Looks

IX. Father's early relation with child
- A. Responsibility assumed (how father first got into the family picture, what role he assumed)
- B. Problems in relation with child and father's response to these problems, i. e., how did he feel, what did he do?
  - 1. Child's interference in his relations with wife
  - 2. Child's relation to mother
  - 3. Competition with grandparents
  - 4. Child in flesh differs from father's conception
  - 5. Child's attitude toward father assuming responsibility
  - 6. Mother's attitude toward father-child relation

X. Father's present relation with child
- A. Role of father in care and training
  1. In relation to feeding
  2. In relation to elimination
  3. In relation to bathing, dressing
  4. In relation to getting ready for and going to bed
  5. In relation to play time
  6. In relation to discipline
- B. Attachment of child to father
- C. Attachment of father to child

XI. The second child
- A. General situation
  1. Planned for (father's attitude toward)
  2. Living conditions
  3. Preparation of first child
  4. Age of first child at birth of second
  5. Sex of second child
- B. Father's role
  1. In relation to feeding
  2. In relation to elimination
  3. In relation to bathing and dressing
  4. In relation to getting ready for and going to bed
  5. In relation to activity and play
  6. In relation to discipline
- C. Feelings of father
  1. Acceptance-rejection
     - a. Arrival
     - b. Sex
     - c. Behavior
     - d. Identification
  2. In comparison with first child
  3. Toward mother's role with child
  4. Primary problems from father's point of view

Questions for Final Session

There are some general opinions which people have about the war and its effect on men and I would like to ask you your own opinion about these matters according to your experience:

1. a. It is sometimes said that married men are under definite strain because they have had satisfying sex experiences and suddenly are denied them. What is your opinion about that?
   b. Some married men sought relations with other women--what about the men you were in contact with?
   c. Do you know how they felt about these experiences?
2. a. What effects did the war have on you as a person?
   b. On your relations with your wife?
   c. On your relations with______(first-born)?
   d. On your relations with______(second-born)?
3. a. How does______(first-born) meet up with what you'd like him to be?
   b. Are there any ways in which you hope he will change as he grows older?
   c. What are the main things you have to punish_____(first-born) for?
4. a. In what ways would you say your relations are different with (first-born) and______(second-born)?
   b. Do you feel closer to_____(first-born) or_____(second-born)?

c. Have you ever had the feeling that____(first-born) is more your wife's child than yours?_____(second-born)?

5. a. Do you think____(first-born) ever felt that his maternal grandfather was really his daddy?

   b. Which child seems closer to his maternal grandparents?

6. a. Is there anything else you think important in this whole area that you can tell me about?

APPENDIX 3. RATING SCALE FOR EARLY DISCIPLINE OF FIRST-BORN BY FATHER

1. Constructive — F. rarely punishes. Distracts child's attention. Removes temporarily from situation. Uses rewards for good behavior. Depends on reasoning, talks it over. In general, adjusts standards to child's level. Compromises with child. Tries to analyze.

2. Mild — F. tends to use disapproval, denial of privileges, sitting on chair (but not isolation). May feel somewhat ineffectual in dealing with child. Occasional very mild spanking.

3. Firm — F. is less sure of his authoritarian role than number 4 level. He sometimes gives mild slaps or spankings. He is impatient and peremptory at times. He scolds. He resorts to combinations of mild methods in extreme misbehavior rather than extreme methods. He uses firm tone of voice that may have threatening import. Argues with child.

4. Strict — F. is strict, uncompromising. His demands are incisive. He uses spanking sometimes after other methods have failed or in extreme misbehavior. He relies more on isolation and strict orders that carry the threat of uncompromising authority. He denies any coddling, belongs to the "cry it out" school. He believes in discipline strongly.

5. Severe — F. frequently gives spankings that hurt. He may grab, shake, or handle child roughly. He may slap or hit child. He uses force. He may yell, fight it out with child. In general, his motive seems to hurt, to frighten child. He relies on these methods frequently. He is emotionally concerned with discipline.

APPENDIX 4. RATING SCALE I. SERIOUSNESS OF PROBLEM

People judge differently the severity of children's problems as related to eating behavior. How would you rate these protocols as to seriousness of the problem described? You may use any criterion you wish, but the rating is to be made considering the total situation.

1. This child seems to have no eating problems other than those which might occur in a well-adjusted child.
2.
3. This is a common eating problem and not very serious.
4.
5. This is a very serious problem.

APPENDIX 5. SAMPLE OF CATEGORIZED MATERIAL

Excerpt from Interview III, Mr. Murray.[a]

Question: How does Luke (first-born child) feel about Howard (second-born child)?

Answer: (He won't join) 1 And . . . , or he will verbalize very specifically, ("You're giving him too much attention,") 2 which is true. And, on the camping trip his observation was . . . what was it . . . sometimes he uses language that just [amazes me] 3 The idea again was that (we never do anything for Luke) 4 which really is not justified. [And I'd say, "guess we didn't, guess we haven't gone camping," and mention a few things we have done . . . we haven't done that and that] 5 and after each one he'd say, ("Yes, you did, yes, you did") 6 and this is always in kind of a joking way[b] so it wasn't particularly deep we felt and apparently . . . Luke can (register his dissatisfaction quickly) 7 it doesn't have to well up inside and he has to mope about it, and again [he sees it pretty fast and accurately] 8 [He (plays with Howard quite constructively) 9] 10 We've let him (carry him around) 11 since he was, oh, I suppose a week or two weeks old, and held our breath and our hearts just pounded[b] . . .

Key: [ ] indicates statement about father's self-perception.
( ) indicates statement about father's child-perception.
Numbers refer to unit number for rating.

[a]. An analysis of this excerpt follows.

[b]. Statements denoting perception of an interpersonal process or experience which cannot be classified by means of the categories used here.

Analysis of Excerpt

Unit	Category	Father's Self-Perception	Child-Perception	Intensity	Evaluation
1	Resists passively		x	1	Negative
2	Accuses		x	2	Positive
3	Admires	x		3	Positive
4	Accuses		x	3	Negative
5	Demands	x		2	Positive
6	Agrees		x	2	Positive
7	Hates passively		x	2	Positive
8	Praises	x		2	Positive
9	Co-operates		x	2	Positive
10	Praises	x		2	Positive
11	Supports		x	2	Positive

APPENDIX 6. MOTHER INTERVIEW

Part I. The Life History

Areas

Nursing
1. What plans did you make for feeding your baby before he was born?
2. Did you breast feed this baby?
3. How did you feel when nursing him?
4. How did he respond? Did he take to it easily? Was he a good sucker?
5. How long did you nurse him? Why discontinued?
6. Was the baby fed on a schedule? How determined?
7. Did you feed him when he cried?
8. Did you ever vary from your usual plan?
9. How did you give him a bottle? Hold him? (usually, rarely) Mechanical holder?
10. When did he begin to hold his own bottle?

Weaning

Breast to bottle
1. About how old was he when weaned from the breast?
2. How did you do this?
3. How did you feel about it?
4. Was he, early in life, given a supplementary bottle feeding?

Bottle to cup (relinquishing bottle)
1. When was he weaned from the bottle to the cup? Any regressions?
2. How did you do this?
3. How did it affect his behavior? Make him cry more? Sleep less? Refuse foods? Refuse milk?
4. Did you think this whole weaning process went rather quickly?
5. How did your mother or mother-in-law feel about the method you used?

Comfort Patterns
1. Did he ever suck his fist, thumb, or finger?
2. When did he do it most often? When tired? When hungry? When upset?
3. Could you say when it was most evident to you, when you first noticed it especially?
4. Does he do this now? If not, when did he stop?
5. What did you do about it?
6. Did you ever feel worried because of his thumb-sucking?
7. Is he comforted by food, candy, etc.? Want cookies when he cries?

Expressions of Possible Tension
1. When he's upset, tired, tense, what does he do? Does he: bite his nails? twist, pat or pull his hair? rock his bed? masturbate? blink his eyes? whine? cry easily?

Eating
1. Was he a good eater as a baby? A finicky, fussy eater? A poor eater?
2. Were you ever worried about his eating?
3. Does he eat well now? Chew solid foods? Try new foods?
4. Does he have an inordinate craving for sweets?
5. Does he want foods often between meals? Ask for cookies?

Sleeping
1. As a little baby did you think he slept enough or less time than babies should sleep each day?
2. Do you feel he gets enough sleep now?
3. Does he have difficulty in going to sleep at night?

4. Does he waken before you and your husband in the morning? If so, what does he do?
5. Does he sleep through the night or waken occasionally? Often? Was there a time when this presented a real problem for him or for you?
6. When did he first sleep in a room alone? Was he pleased? Reluctant? Afraid?
7. Does he ever get in your bed at night? Occasionally? Frequently?
8. What do you do when he asks to?
9. Has he ever had dreams? What does he do when he has them?

Toilet Training

1. How did you feel the first few times you changed his diapers?
2. Did anyone else ever do it for you?
3. Did you, yourself, wash the diapers, or did you have diaper service?
4. Did you dislike washing them?
5. At about what age did you start training for bowel movements? How did you do this? Did it take long?
6. Was this child easy or difficult to train?
7. Did you use "naughty boy" or "nasty" or "be a big boy" or "make mommy happy" in effecting this training?
8. At about what age did you start training for bladder control? How did you do this? Did it take as long as you expected? Longer?
9. Was this child easy to train? Difficult?
10. Does he wet his bed at night?
11. Did your parents approve of your methods of toilet training? Your husband's parents?

Language

1. Did you talk to him much as a little baby? Sing to him?
2. Did you go to him whenever he cried?
3. Did he seem to understand you when you talked to him by watching your face? Smiling? Laughing? Frowning?
4. What words did he say first? How old was he then? Who heard him?
5. When did he begin to use words to express his needs?
6. When did he first talk in sentences?
7. Did he ever stutter? When?
8. Do you think his language development is normal, slow, or advanced for his age?
9. Does he like to have stories told to him? Read to him?
10. Who tells him stories? Reads him stories?

Motor Behavior: Locomotion

1. Was he an active baby?
2. Did you feel you needed to watch him constantly because of his activity?
3. Did you encourage him as a baby to roll over? Creep? Crawl? Climb?
4. Do you remember anything special about the first time he sat up alone? Pulled himself to a standing position? Got out of his crib by himself?
5. Did he spend most of his time in his crib before he learned to walk?
6. Did he have a playpen? Did he play much in it?
7. When did he learn to walk? Did he make progress slowly or rapidly?
8. Was he pleased with his new accomplishment?
9. At the time of learning to walk did he take any bad falls? Was he frightened? Were you?
10. Did he stop walking for a while after he had learned? Have you any idea why?
11. Is he a cautious child? A daring child?
12. Did any serious illness, accident, or event (father's return, birth of

a new baby, family moving, etc.) occur around the time of beginning walking?

13. Did he talk less, eat less when learning to walk?

Motor Behavior: Manipulation

1. Was this child eager to do things for himself? Did he like to feed himself? Dress himself?
2. Has he used blocks and other building materials consistently in his play?
3. After he learned to walk did you have difficulty in teaching him not to touch objects around the house?
4. Did he ever pull tablecloths off the table? Turn on the gas on the stove? Play with matches? Put objects in his mouth? Play in water and get the floor all wet? Put things in the toilet? Break a precious object?
5. Did he enjoy messy things?
6. Was he difficult to keep clean?
7. Is he cautious (careful) about handling objects?

Fears

1. Is he afraid of guns (toy), masks, machinery (vacuum cleaners, washing machines, etc.) now?
2. Was this child ever frightened badly?

Experience with People

1. Did you live with relatives or others when he was a baby? How many adults? Children?
2. Did they assist you in caring for him?
3. Did you ever leave this baby for more than a day in his first year of life? For how long? With whom? Do you think he missed you? How could you tell? Were you worried about him while you were away from him?
4. Did you take him for walks in his carriage? To the grocery store? Shopping? Visiting? Did you do this more often in his first year or since then?
5. Did you frequently have baby-sitters? The same one or different ones? Do you now?
6. Does your husband spend much time with the children?
7. Was this child ever punished severely? What happened?

Relations with People

1. Was he ever shy?
2. Is he timid and suspicious of strangers?
3. Was there ever a particular adult whom he disliked?
4. Is he a friendly, outgoing child?
5. Does he give evidences of sympathy?
6. How does he show affection?
7. Does he seek affection from adults? From children?
8. Does he have any personality traits that annoy you? That annoy his father? Other adults?
9. Is he co-operative? Obedient? Pleasant? Thoughtful?
10. Does he frequently play alone?
11. Does he seek the companionship of adults? Of children? Which does he prefer?

Pregnancy

1. When you first knew you were pregnant were you worried, frightened, pleased? Where was your husband at this time?
2. Was your beginning pregnancy difficult because of nausea, etc.?
3. Did you work during it? For how long?
4. Did you travel during it?

5. Were you in labor long? In pain long? Did you know where your husband was at the time? Did he contact you by telephone, cable, telegram, letter before delivery? Shortly after?
6. Was delivery normal, difficult, or do you remember it?
7. How did you refer to the baby before it was born? Did you have a name for it before it was born?
8. Were you surprised at the sex of the child? Pleased?
9. Did you have visitors while in the hospital? Were you treated well by nurses, doctors, etc.?

Part II. Comparison of Children

1. Which child laughs more readily? 2. Cries more easily? 3. Happier? 4. Healthier? Stronger? 5. More selfish? 6. Easier for you to get along with? 7. Easier for your husband to get along with? 8. Looks like you? 9. Looks like your husband? 10. Who is A (first-born) most like? 11. Who is B (second-born) most like?

Part III. Effects of Father-Separation

1. What effects would you say father-separation in the first year of life had on (first-born)?
2. Do you think these effects were inevitable or could some other kind of planning be done if this situation were to occur again?

APPENDIX 7. RATING SCALES

Scale A. Parental Worry

From the parent's statements regarding the child's eating behavior, you can infer the parent's attitude toward that behavior. This attitude may well be quite different from what your own attitude would be in response to the reported behavior, but your own attitude should not enter into this rating. If the statements seem to indicate different attitudes at different periods, give emphasis in your rating to the parental attitudes which you think have been crucial in influencing the child's eating behavior.

1. Child's eating behavior seems normal or better to parent.
2.
3. Child's eating behavior seems to parent to be something of a problem; parent may be somewhat worried or upset about it.
4.
5. Child's eating behavior seems to parent to be a serious problem; parent is worried or upset about it.

Scale B. Parental Annoyance

Regardless of their judgments of the importance or significance of their children's eating behavior, parents differ in their direct emotional reactions to it. From the parent's statements regarding the child's eating behavior, you can infer this reaction, both because of his direct report of that reaction and because of the quality of the words he uses to describe the behavior.

Occasionally a parent will report a single outburst against a child or on some other special circumstance. The significance of such a single incident for this rating should be evaluated largely in terms of other indicators in the excerpts.

If the statements seem to indicate different reactions at different periods, give emphasis in your rating to the parental reactions which you think have been crucial in influencing the child's eating behavior.

Notice that in this scale FREQUENCY OF RESPONSE is indicated in capital letters whereas intensity of response is indicated in underlined letters.

1. Parent is REGULARLY tolerant of, or patient with, the child's eating behavior.

2. Parent is OCCASIONALLY mildly irked by the child's eating behavior.

3. Parent is FREQUENTLY mildly irked by the child's eating behavior, or is OCCASIONALLY quite annoyed by the child's eating behavior.

4. Parent is FREQUENTLY quite annoyed by the child's eating behavior, or is OCCASIONALLY extremely annoyed by the child's eating behavior.

5. Parent is FREQUENTLY extremely annoyed by the child's eating behavior.

Scale C. Parental Insight

Different parents show varying degrees of insight into their children's behavior. "Insight" is used here to mean more or less intellectual analysis or understanding of the child's behavior and development in terms of causes and effects.

Deciding on a rating for any parent on this scale involves two somewhat independent steps:

1. Determining the degree to which the parent attempts to explain or understand the child's behavior. The judge will look for the following kinds of statements in the excerpts.
   a. Attempts to see the behavior or situation from the child's point of view.
   b. Explanations of the child's behavior by reference to the child's age, sex, size, etc.
   c. Explanations of the child's behavior as resulting from his history or current situation, especially unusual aspects of these.
   d. Explanations of the child's behavior in terms of some generalizations or theories about children. Such theories should be more than mere generalities, unless simple reference to a generality is sufficient reference to a current theory (e.g., any attempt to explain regressive behavior by reference to the birth of a sibling).
2. Evaluating the adequacy of these parental attempts at insight in terms of the judge's own understanding of the child.

1. In this area, parent shows considerable insight into child's behavior.

2.

3. In this area, parent shows some insight into child's behavior.

4.

5. In this area, parent shows no insight into child's behavior, discussing this area only in merely descriptive or judgmental terms.

APPENDIX 8. GUIDE FOR OBSERVING CHILDREN[1]

A. Descriptive Behavior
- I. Behavior in relation to organic needs
  - a. Eating and elimination
    1. Rhythm
    2. Attitude toward
    3. Emotional concomitants
  - b. Activity and rest
    1. Energy level
    2. Rhythm
    3. Attitude toward
    4. Emotional concomitants
  - c. Tension level (nail biting; thumb, finger, or lip sucking; tics; etc.)
- II. Motor behavior
  - a. Locomotor behavior
    1. Co-ordination and skill (standing, walking, running, hopping, skipping, jumping, climbing, pushing, pulling)
    2. Emotional concomitants
  - b. Manipulatory behavior
    1. Co-ordination and skill: finger material (water, finger paints, clay, sand, blocks, etc.); with tools (brush paints, woodwork, etc.)
    2. Emotional concomitants
  - c. In games
    1. Skill
    2. Emotional concomitants
- III. Language behavior
  - a. Amount
  - b. Quality
  - c. Purposes
  - d. Emotional concomitants
- IV. Psychosexual behavior
  - a. Interest and concern with items relating to sex
  - b. Degree of modesty
  - c. Body manipulation
- V. Behavior with other children
  - a. Amount of interaction
  - b. Role of the child
  - c. Response of other children
  - d. Emotional concomitants
- VI. Behavior with adults (mother, father, relatives, teacher, co-operating assistants, students)
  - a. Role of child
  - b. Response to directions, coercions, demands
  - c. Response to play, teasing
  - d. Emotional concomitants

B. Analysis of Personality Traits (degree of):
- I. Dependence-independence
- II. Attention demanding
- III. Showing off-withdrawing
- IV. Submissive-aggressive

---

[1]. Prepared by Lois Meek Stolz.

V. Timidity-bravado
VI. Fears
VII. Somberness-gaiety
VIII. Negative-docile
IX. Crying or whining
X. Irritability
XI. Temper tantrums
XII. Sympathetic
XIII. Affectionate

APPENDIX 9. SAMPLE OBSERVATION, DIVIDED INTO BEHAVIOR UNITS WITH RATING OF VARIABLES AND LEVELS

A sample observation is quoted from the records of Ned Ford. The observation took place at Monday Club. Following the observation is a list of the behavior units obtained from it and their ratings. The form for rating is described in Stevenson (74).

Ned is playing on the swings by himself. All the other Monday Clubbers are scattered around the play yard, playing on the slides or in the sand box. Ned jumps from the moving swing, lands on both feet, and races to the teeter-totter. Alone, he runs to the top, and the teeter-totter bangs down to the other side. Again he runs to the higher end, and it crashes again. With his arms extended as if they were propelling him, he races alone to the sand box. Three boys are already occupied with the trucks and other toys there: Don, Ray, and Allen. But Ned chooses to sit alone in the corner of the sand pile and watch. Facing them, he sits alone for about five minutes. As he sits there, he lets sand run through his fingers. He looks up occasionally, but most of the time he is gazing downward at the sand. Gradually Ned eases toward the three busy boys. They do not seem to notice that he is there. Allen is playing with a dump truck that carries sand. Ned picks up a handful of sand and moves over next to Allen. Ned offers nicely, "SHALL I PUT SOME MORE SAND IN IT?"

Allen guards his truck and says, "No. I'll tell you when. I don't want any more sand. You be the driver of the other truck." The three boys continue playing, and Ned assumes his old role of onlooker.

Ray reaches for a truck near Ned and says, "I'm going to get this truck." Allen comes to the rescue, saying, "No. Ned's driver of this truck." Ray accepts this and adds, "And you're the worker."

Allen, engrossed in his own activity, says, "These come out very slowly." He turns the crank of the sand mixer. Ned is sitting at his side, brushing his fingers through the sand. Ned reaches over to help Allen turn the crank of the sand mixer. But Allen pushes Ned's hand away, gently, and continues to crank the machine himself. Apparently Allen was able to operate the sand mixer and the dumper himself, for he calls loudly to Ned (who was sitting next to him):

"Take it away, Ned. Take the truck away."

Ned, on his knees, rolls the truck away as requested. He rolls it to the corner of the sand pile, grunting, "RRRR," as he goes. Soon Ned arrives in the corner with his truckload of sand.

Allen: "O.K., Ned, come back."

With that, Ned rolls the truck back in the same manner. Ray, "I need another truck."

The boys all play in silence for a few minutes, each one busy with a dump truck. Meanwhile Grace comes and sits in the corner of the sand pile where Ned has been sitting previously. As she sits there, Ned looks at her, frowning, and says, "YOU MESSED 'EM ALL UP." He says this quietly, but seemingly is annoyed by her carelessness.

Situation	SP	D	IA	RA	F	Behavior	S	CI	AI	AA
Children scattered around yard at Monday Club, on slides or in sand box.	5					Ned plays on swings by self.				
Soon	5					Races to teeter-totter; alone runs up and down and up it.				
Soon: Don, Ray, Allen in sand box.	4					Races to sand box; sits alone in corner and watches.				
For five minutes	5					Looks down at sand, plays with it.				
Gradually	3					Eases toward three boys.				
Allen playing with dump truck.	1	4				Picks up sand, offers nicely, "SHALL I PUT SOME MORE SAND IN IT?"				
Allen says no, offers him a position in the play.	4					Continues watching.				
Ray reaches for truck near Ned; Allen defends it as Ned's; Allen turns crank of sand mixer.	4					Sits at Allen's side, brushes fingers through sand.				
Allen says they come out slowly.	1				2	Reaches over to help Allen turn crank.				
Allen pushes away Ned's hand gently, continues cranking machine himself; calls to Ned to take truck away.	2	4				Rolls truck away as requested, grunts "RRRR," rolls it to corner.				
Allen tells him to bring it back.	2	4				Does so.				
All play in silence.	3					Busy with truck.				
Grace comes, sits where Ned had been.	3		3		4	Looks at her, frowns, "YOU MESSED 'EM ALL UP," quietly, annoyed.				

tive and now mildly destructive. In some situations his aggressive feelings may express themselves merely as assertiveness.

5. Aggressive feelings of some intensity. This child may show aggressiveness considerably out of proportion to the situation. If he ranks low on inhibitions of aggression, he will usually be aggressive when the situation is permissive of such behavior. If he is not overtly aggressive, there should be considerable indication of inhibition.

6. Powerful aggressive feelings. The behavior of different children at this point in the scale may range from vigorous aggression to nonaggression. In any case, they will probably rank fairly high on the scale of strength of inhibitions. It is difficult for these children to control their aggressive feelings. They are not as free and relaxed in constructive, creative activities as children lower on the scale of aggression.

7. Avid or violent aggressive feelings. One child at this point in the scale may be violently destructive or hostile. Another may control his feelings and show little or no aggressiveness, but in this case he is likely to be overly subdued, tense, or anxious, or give other indications of excessive inhibitions. His behavior may fluctuate between extreme control and extreme aggressiveness. When his aggressive feelings are loosed, it may be difficult for him to bring them back under control immediately.

APPENDIX 12. CHECK LIST OF OVERT INDICATIONS OF INHIBITIONS OF AGGRESSION

1. Inhibitions of aggression.
   a. Withdrawal and inactivity (movements blocked), e.g., child sits in corner and does nothing.
   b. Distraction or "escape" from field, e.g., child ignores E's questions, suggestions, leaves the room, talks of other things.
   c. Restrained, tense, inhibited. Stiff or awkward movements.
   d. Movements directed to the materials in an aggressive manner and then shunted off.
   e. Hostility directed toward other objects. Physical, verbal, or symbolic.
   f. Hostility directed toward experimenter.
   g. Self-directed hostility.
   h. Moralistic verbalizations.
   i. Nervous mannerisms, tics.
   j. Tense facial expression.
   k. A cautious, anxious attitude as expressed in movements, verbalizations, and/or facial expression. Anxiety may be expressed in a variety of ways; a combination of the following segments of behavior may be indicative of it: (1) tenseness, stiff or jerky movements, (2) arrest of bodily movement, (3) representative movements of hands, (4) hands over mouth, (5) tics, nervous mannerisms, (6) posture of one poised for flight, (7) masklike expression, (8) wide-eyed, blank and staring, (9) tight mouth, (10) biting lips, (11) clenched teeth, (12) stuttering or stammering.
   l. Ambivalent, inconsistent response.
   m. Insistence upon reassurance.
2. Guilty behavior following aggression.
   a. Self-accusation or remorse.
   b. Reparations or restitution.
   c. Anxiety following breaking.

APPENDIX 10. ANALYSIS OF OBSERVATIONAL RECORDS

Examples of levels in each category of variables. (These examples were taken from the observational records of Ned Ford, except where another name is used.)

A. With Other Children

Social Participation.

Level	Situation	Behavior
1.	Soon	Ned marches inside, happily twirling stick, offers it to other children, "HERE'S A STICK FOR YOU," hands it to them.
2.	All but Ralph go to other swing; Ralph grabs rope, argues with Ned.	Ned (apparently) argues, and remains in swing.
3.	Four boys playing with trucks in silence, in sand box.	Ned is busy with truck.
4.	Group of girls playing housekeeping.	Ned goes to girls, watches a few minutes.
5.	Children scattered around yard at Monday Club, on slides or in sand box.	Ned plays on swing by himself.

Dominance

Level	Situation	Behavior
1.	Laird jumps in box Ned is trying to push, drags feet.	Ned frowns angrily, "LAIRD, DON'T PUT YOUR FEET DOWN!"
2.	Kiki comes, demands her chair.	Ned frowns, argues.
3.	Allen demands old truck back from Ray. They argue; Ray asks Mrs. X.	Ned suggests, "HEY, HEY, RAY. I KNOW SOMETHING. WHY DOESN'T THAT BRING DIRT INTO THIS ONE, AND THEN I DRIVE IT AWAY?"
4.	Allen pushes away Ned's hand gently, continues cranking machine himself; calls to Ned to take truck away.	Ned rolls truck away as requested, grunts, "RRRR," rolls it to corner.
5.	Howard climbs up on Ned's ledge (Ned has just said he may not).	They talk, pretending to walk on drain pipe.

Initiation of Aggression.

Level	Situation	Behavior
1.	Sam comes near the swings.	David jumps up, socks him hard, shouts, "GO 'WAY!"
2.	Girls playing house.	Ned impishly grins, tips their chair over.
3.	Donna runs past.	David playfully pokes her, grins as he does so.
4.	Mrs. X. asks who lost his note.	Donald answers quickly, "BILLY DID."

5.	Sally shows him her drawing.	Donald glances at it, says calmly, "THAT'S NO GOOD."

Response to Aggression.

Level	Situation	Behavior
1.	Jake takes Sam's truck.	Sam grabs it, hits Jake with it, frowns and flushes.
2.	Howard watches, taunts, "Who can't jump from there?"	Ned yells, "YOU CAN'T COME UP HERE, HOWARD," walks along ledge.
3.	Children chant teasingly, "Sue is dead," several times.	Sue laughs, claps hands together.
4.	Howard takes crayons Jim is using.	Jim looks toward teacher, calls out, "MRS. X."
5.	Suddenly, after Ralph tries to get Ned's swing.	Ned gets out of seat, hands it to Ralph.

Friendliness

Level	Situation	Behavior
1.	Howard and Ned both pasting.	They giggle and talk nonsense syllables.
2.	Allen turns truck crank, says sand comes out slowly.	Ned reaches over to help Allen turn it.
3.	Howard says he is going to tell Ned something.	Ned listens without comment.
4.	Carol, next to Ned, asks who wants her swing; several children, including Ralph, run to Ned and ask for swing.	Ned stops his swing; frowns, "NO, NO, NOT RALPH!"
5.	Sally comes to look at Don's paper.	Don looks up at her, sticks out his tongue.

Sympathy

Level	Situation	Behavior
1.	Ann rejects toy Allen offers her, goes to Mrs. X to report that Allen won't let her have something.	Ned offers, "LOOK, NO ONE'S USING THIS"; gives her a toy.
2.	Visiting mother's baby crying loudly.	Chuck looks at baby, smiles faintly, continues with block play.

B. With Adults.

Child-Initiated Contacts.

Level	Situation	Behavior
1.	Pat shows Miss W. his designs, they discuss them.	Ned suddenly turns, adds to Pat's explanation, "WE'RE JUST MAKING DESIGNS."
2.	Children told to fold papers down middle and cut out holes at center.	Don immediately takes paper to teacher, says, " I CAN'T."
3.	Piece of clay drops from table to floor.	Tim looks at Miss T., says, "PICK IT UP."

4.	Recess period, teacher standing near door.	Bob runs over with two other boys, calls, "TEACHER IS A PREACHER, TEACHER IS A PREACHER," runs away smirking.

Response to Adult-Initiated Contacts.

Level	Situation	Behavior
1.	Mrs. X. starts group game.	Ned joins in eagerly, laughing.
2.	Miss W. suggests to Howard that he ask Ned about Monday Club.	Ned makes no comment to either.
3.	Miss B. comes to watch Don paint.	Don looks up, says, "GO AWAY, YOU."

Response to Adult Authority.

Level	Situation	Behavior
1.	Teacher tells children to clean up.	Tim runs to put smock away, hangs it carefully, pushes in chair, runs outside.
2.	Teacher tells children each to get a block to fill box.	Ned gets one.
3.	Other children bringing blocks.	Bringing blocks to fill box, Ned stops to talk to Frank.
4.	Teacher asks Tom to give his place at easel to Sally.	Tom frowns, doesn't answer, remains in place not painting.
5.	Teacher repeats request.	Tom shouts, "NO!", slams brush on floor.

APPENDIX 11. RATING SCALE FOR STRENGTH OF AGGRESSIVE FEELINGS

1. No covert aggressive feelings. Handles potential frustrations constructively, creatively. High frustration-tolerance. Since these individuals are not putting energy into keeping hostile feelings repressed, one would expect a free emotional response to situations. Aggression, when provoked, may be inhibited or displaced, but there would not be continuing tension. It is likely that anyone at this point in the scale will rate low on the inhibition scale.

2. Covert aggression of minute force. Aggressiveness or assertiveness may occur in response to a frustrating situation, unless inhibited, but aggression is never greater than is needed to handle the present situation. As in 1, one would expect to find a generally relaxed child, free from the continuing tension of inhibiting aggression.

3. Covert aggression of small force. This child may reveal some aggressiveness not directly caused by the immediate situation, but probably only when such behavior is permissible within the general framework of the total situation. The aggressive force is slight enough that it can be controlled easily. These children would probably have few tensions as a result of inhibiting aggression.

4. Moderately forceful aggressive feeling. This child will either show some aggressiveness beyond that directly caused by the situation or will show some signs of inhibiting aggression or both, but his aggressiveness will never be extreme. There may be considerable ambivalence in his responses, now construc-

d. Self-defense.
   (1) promise of restitution, (2) justification or excuses, (3) appeal to experimenter, (4) denial, (5) projection of guilt upon someone else, (6) concealment, hiding of evidence of aggression.

e. Self-punishment.

3. Fear in relation to the experimental situation.

APPENDIX 12a. RATING SCALE FOR STRENGTH OF INHIBITIONS

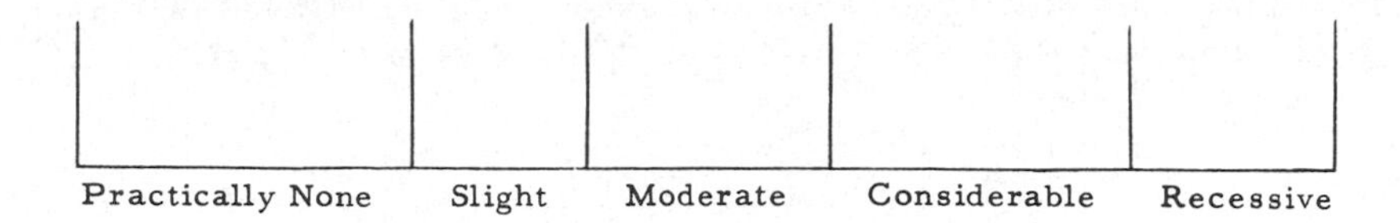

APPENDIX 13. RATING SCALE FOR RATING DESTRUCTIVENESS WITH BALLOONS

1. Approach is relaxed and playful. Expression of enjoyment in play. Possibly protective toward balloons. Possibly high value of balloons as playthings. (Lack of any overt expression of aggressive feelings.)

2. Approach is placid or passive. Little apparent emotional release or satisfaction from breaking balloons. May or may not break balloons, but any breaking is probably only to please the adult or because the child thinks of it as a part of the game.

3. Approach combines playfulness and destructiveness. Destructiveness occurs only with complete assurance of E's permission.

4. Approach is a mixture of play and mild attack. Possibly some ambivalence in response to balloons, a swinging back and forth in mood between playfulness or desire to please adult and slight aggressiveness.

5. Approach is a relaxed direct attack. Assaults balloons with vigor and seriousness. Behavior lacks joy or playfulness.

6. Approach is a violent attack. Breaks balloons avidly and perhaps viciously, possibly tearing and biting. An excited, emotional response. Possibly accompanied by laughing and flushing.

APPENDIX 14. RATING SCALE FOR OVERT AGGRESSION IN BLOCKING GAMES

1. Acquiescence. Compliance or withdrawal from competition, not withdrawal from the total situation. The child adjusts to the adult requirement.

2. Compromise. Both child and adult make some adjustment. The child may state limitations or qualifications upon what the adult may do.

3. Impasse. No solution reached. The child may rationalize, say "I don't know," leave the field.

4. Assertiveness. The adult must adjust to the child's plans. The child demands his rights, but is not hostile or unnecessarily rough.

5. Aggressiveness. The child demonstrates hostility toward the adult or is unnecessarily rough with the equipment.

APPENDIX 15. STORIES USED IN STORY-COMPLETION PROJECTIVE SITUATION

Preliminary Story

One day it was very hot, and a little boy wanted to go swimming. So the boy went to his father and said, "Daddy, I want to go swimming. May I go swimming today?" And the daddy said, "Yes, you may go swimming today. Do you want me to go to the swimming pool with you, or would you like to go by yourself?"

Story I

Once there was a family that was going to take a trip. The whole family was going — the mommy, the daddy, the boy, and the little baby. All of their things were packed for the trip, and the lunch was all ready. The family had wanted so much to take the trip. Just as the boy and the daddy were ready to leave the house and go on the trip, the mommy called to them. The mommy said, "The baby is sick. The baby is too sick to go on the trip today. I must stay home and take care of the baby. Why don't we all stay home today and go on the trip some other day?" But the boy was so disappointed. He wanted to go on the trip anyway. So the boy said, "Daddy, why don't you and I go? Let's go on the trip together — just you and me."

Story II

A boy and his little sister were outside riding on their bikes. They rode up and back in front of the house. They rode their bikes as fast as they could go. The boy was riding his bike so fast that he bumped into his baby sister. They both went banging to the ground. The boy fell off his bike. Then the little sister fell off hers. They laughed and laughed, because they didn't get hurt at all. But when they looked, both of the bikes were broken. The front wheel of each bike was broken. The older boy said, "Let's get daddy to fix our bikes. Then we can race some more." And the little girl said, "Yes, let's get daddy." So they ran to the house together, and brought the broken bikes to their daddy. The children called, "Daddy, daddy, please fix our bikes. We have broken both the bikes." When the daddy saw that both bikes were broken, he said, "We need two new wheels in order to fix the bikes. We need a wheel for each bike. I have one new wheel here, so I can fix one of the bikes. But I can only fix one today. The other must wait until tomorrow, when I can buy another wheel at the store." The older boy said, "O.K. daddy, but fix mine first. Fix my bike today." And the younger sister said, "No, daddy, Fix _my_ bike today."

Story III

Once there was a little boy who lived with his mommy and daddy. One rainy day he had to stay inside and play by himself. First he played with his paints. Then he played with his puzzles for a long time. He played with his blocks. But he got tired of playing with his own things all morning. "What can I do now?" the little boy said to himself. "I want something new to play with." He looked around the room and there on the table he saw something that was round and shiny. It was his daddy's watch. Daddy had forgotten to take it, and had left it in the little boy's room by mistake. The little boy touched the watch and wanted to play with it. He knew that he wasn't to play with any of his daddy's things. But he wanted to anyway. So the boy picked up the daddy's watch and listened to it tick. He looked at it, and held it in his hand. It was very shiny and pretty. Daddy and mommy were in the living room. They did not know that the little boy was playing with daddy's watch. All of a sudden he dropped daddy's watch. It went bang, ker-plunk, as it hit the floor. The little boy didn't know what to do! He had broken daddy's nice watch. It was now in pieces on the floor. And since the radio was on, the mommy and the daddy didn't hear the watch drop, and the little boy wondered what he should do.

Story IV

There once was a boy who played all morning at home with his toys. All of his playthings were spread out on the floor. The room looked very messy. He was all through playing inside. Now he wanted to play outside, because it was such a nice sunny day. So he left the messy room to go outside and play with the other children. Just then daddy came home from school. He saw all of the toys that the boy had left in the room. The daddy called to the boy and said, "Before you go outside to play I want you to come in and pick up your toys." But the boy wanted to play outside. He did not want to pick up his things.

Story V

A boy was inside the house playing with his toy airplane. He would wind it up and let it fly around the living room. His father came into the room and saw the little boy playing with the airplane. "You are not supposed to play with that in the house," scolded the father, "Go outside and play with that thing if you have to fly it." The father was very angry, because he had told the little boy that he should never fly the airplane in the house. That was too dangerous. "O.K." said the boy. "I promise I won't fly it inside anymore. I'll just sit right here and push it around like this." He rolled the airplane across the rug. Then the boy sat on the floor and played with the airplane. He turned the propeller just a little bit and held the airplane in his hands. All of a sudden he dropped the airplane, and it sailed through the room like a big bird. The boy didn't know what to do, because daddy was still in the room. And the daddy had just told him not to fly the airplane inside the house. The little boy just watched the airplane sail through the room. He waited. And finally, when the airplane came down, it hit the daddy hard— right in the head.

Story VI

One day a little boy and his daddy were taking a walk. They had been walking for a long time when they came to a strange, big wall. The wall had many stairs going to the top of it. In places the wall was low, and in some places the wall was very high. If you wanted to, you could walk up the stairs, and then walk along the low wall. Then if you wanted to go much higher, you could climb up to the big high wall. The little boy wanted to climb up the stairs and get on top of the low wall. So the boy went up the stairs and stood on top of the low wall. It looked very high to him, but after a little while, he jumped down, all by himself. Then the little boy climbed up to the top of the very high wall. This looked so much higher! The boy waited and waited, and he looked down. The daddy, who was standing below said, "Hey there. Jump down. Don't be a 'fraid cat. I'll catch you. Come on. Jump." The little boy didn't know what to do. He was so high up. He looked down, and it seemed such a long way to daddy. "Come on," said daddy, "Jump. All right, if you don't want to jump from there, walk down the stairs. We've got to go home now. So hurry up, and make up your mind."

APPENDIX 16. INSTRUCTIONS TO RECORDER FOR STORY-COMPLETION SESSIONS

1. Your record should contain a continuous and inclusive account of the child's behavior from the time he enters the room until the session is ended.

2. Record all overt signs of anxiety and indicate the occasion for this anxiety (i.e., in response to the experimenter, the strange situation, the stories themselves, etc.).

3. Be as interpretive as possible in recording the child's emotional response to the stories, and at the same time include the overt clues upon which you base this interpretation.

4. Record at the left side of the page a keyword of the child or experimenter which will help in later integrating the verbal data with the observed behavior.

5. Add an observer's note at the end of the observation if there is something particularly outstanding about the child or situation which might help in interpreting the record.

APPENDIX 17. CHECK LISTS AND RATING SCALES OF INVOLVEMENT AND ANXIETY

Indices of Involvement

Self-references: "My daddy and I . . ." "That's what I would do."
Looks at experimenter for continuous periods of time.
Focuses intently on pictures, may point out details of picture.
Anticipates next situation in story.
Eager for stories to be read.
Volunteers relevant comments during stories.
Evidence of "thinking" about solutions.
Smiling in appropriate sections of the stories.
Expressing hostility in appropriate sections (verbally or otherwise).
Appropriate concern in conflict situation.

Almost none	Slight	Moderate	Much involvement	Extreme
1	2	3	4	5

Indices of Anxiety

Wide-eyed, vague and staring.
Masked expression, apparent inhibition of emotion.
Squirming.
Worried look, clenched teeth or open mouthed.
Nervous mannerisms: fingers in mouth, scratching hair, playing with fingers.
Biting lips.
Stammering, repeating parts of sentences, incoherent speech.
Escape-type behavior: looking around room, irrelevant verbalizations.
Blinking excessively.
Swallowing hard or often.
Hesitant smile, chin in, often accompanied by "I don't know."
Hurrying on to next story.
Unwillingness to complete story.
Motor tenseness.
Clenching fists.

Normal concern but seems relaxed throughout		Unmistakable anxiety shown		Refuses to face problem directly
1	2	3	4	5

APPENDIX 18. INSTRUCTIONS FOR RATING ANXIETY IN STORY-COMPLETION TECHNIQUE

This is a check list of anxiety indicators. The rater should look for signs of anxiety in the parts of the stories which would be most likely to elicit anxiety responses. Examples of some of these story situations are:

1. When the child drops the watch.
2. After the father calls the child to clean the messy room.
3. When the airplane hits the father.
4. During any response in which the child might be punished.

The signs in the check list should be checked only if they seem to be in response to stressful situations in the story. The signs represent the child's mode of expressing anxiety; they do not imply degree. The degree of anxiety is rated on the scale which is beneath the check list. The degree of anxiety is not contingent upon the number of signs checked, although this may give a clue to the degree of anxiety. Rather, the rater should depend upon the intensity or generality of the anxiety in making his rating. The upper limit of 5 is not as extreme as immobility nor tantrum. To be rated 5 a child may refuse to complete the story (when there is evidence that he is involved in the story); he may show a consistent high level of tension throughout the session; or he may be so anxious that he "masks" any emotional expression.

To be rated 3 the child must show unmistakable anxiety in response to the stressful story situations. A child who is rated 1 maintains a consistent low level of tension. He shows normal concern in the conflict situations, but responds with relative ease and calm. A rating of 1 is to be distinguished from a repression of anxiety which is indicated by a noncommittal expression. Ratings of 2 and 4 are defined on the rating scale as being the midpoints between 1 and 3, and 3 and 5, respectively.

APPENDIX 19. CRITERIA FOR RATING DEGREE OF ANXIETY IN STORY COMPLETIONS FROM RECORDED DATA

1. Enjoys build-up of the story; enjoys tenseness at the climax, or shows only normal concern which indicates involvement; resolves anxiety in all three stories.
2. Seems nervous during the build-up of the story; shows normal increase of anxiety at the climax; shows absolution of anxiety upon completion of the story.
3. Seems to be nervous (wiggles, scratches, rubs, etc.); marked anxiety at the climax; shows absolution in some of the stories, but is still nervous.
4. Anticipates that something "bad" will happen at the climax; is tense throughout the session; shows only a slight increase in anxiety and tenseness at the climax; even completion of the story does not bring absolution of anxiety.
5. Has a "fixed" unemotional expression (not bored nor quietly concentrated); only a slight response to the climax; attempts to withdraw from the situation or the story, and has to be coaxed to finish the story; shows no absolution of anxiety upon completion of the story.

APPENDIX 20. RATING SCALE ON CONFORMITY FOR STORY-COMPLETION TECHNIQUE

1. A rating of 1 is given to any response which indicates that the father's standards are accepted as "right." In completing the story, the child resolves or minimizes the conflict with the father by conforming to his demands.
2. A rating of 2 is given when the child recognizes the discrepancy between his own wishes and his father's demands. However, the conflict is resolved because the child compromises with an understanding father.
3. A rating of 3, like 2, indicates that the child recognizes the conflict between his own standards and those of the father. However, unlike 2, the child follows his own wishes and then receives punishment from the father.
4. A rating of 4 is given to the child who, in completing the story, denies that there is a conflict by following his own wishes and blithely defying or ignoring the father.
5. A rating of 5 indicates that the child is unable to reconcile his own wishes with the father's standards, because he avoids solving the real problem by evading a solution or by responding irrelevantly.

APPENDIX 21. RATINGS ON CONFORMITY

Specific Criteria and Sample Responses

<u>Story III</u>

Rating 1: The child confesses to the father that the watch was broken, and thus is not punished.
"AND THEN SHE WOULD GO TO HER DADDY AND SAY 'I PLAYED WITH IT BUT IT BROKE' . . . HE WENT AND HE TOLD THE LITTLE GIRL THAT SHE WOULDN'T GET SCOLDED THIS TIME BECAUSE SHE TOLD THE TRUTH" (Kate — 6 years, 5 months).

Rating 2: The child confesses that the watch was broken. However, the father takes the blame or the child is relieved by making up to the father in some way.
"HE COULD GET HIS TOOLS AND FIX IT BACK UP AGAIN . . . IF

HE COULD" . . . (and the daddy would say,) "YOU'RE A GOOD BOY FOR FIXING UP MY WATCH" (Leonard— 8 years, 4 months).

Rating 3: The child may tell the father that the watch was broken, but the child is then punished.
"SHE TOLD HER MOTHER AND HER MOTHER AND HER FATHER SPANKED HER. FIRST HER DADDY SPANKED HER AND THEN HER MOTHER SPANKED HER . . . AND I GUESS THAT SHE HAD TO SIT IN A CHAIR AND THEN THEY HAD TO BUY A NEW GLASS" (Gladys— 5 years, 2 months).

Rating 4: The child does not confess, and he ignores the conflict which is posed by the story.
"PICK IT UP AND THEN TRY TO FIX IT . . . SHE'D PUT IT ON THE TABLE THE WAY IT WAS." (Did the daddy find out?) "I DON'T KNOW IF THE GIRL DIDN'T MAKE A MISTAKE WHEN SHE FIXED IT. IF THE GIRL FIXED IT THE WAY IT WAS" (Corrinne— 6 years, 2 months).

Rating 5: The child either hides the watch or hides himself. He withdraws from the conflict or cannot respond at all. "HE WENT AND HID." . . . "MAYBE HE TOOK ALL THE PIECES AND PUT THEM IN THE WASTEBASKET . . . I DON'T KNOW ABOUT THE DADDY" (Ned— 5 years, 6 months).

Story IV

Rating 1: The child conforms willingly by picking up the toys.
"I THINK SHE DID." (Pick up the toys) . . . "UHUH. THAT'S WHAT I WOULD DO" (Celia— 6 years, 5 months).

Rating 2: The father enforces his request without punishing the child.
(The daddy said,) "'WELL THEN YOU CAN'T GO OUTSIDE TO PLAY.' SO THEN SHE PUT THE TOYS AWAY AND THEN SHE WENT OUTSIDE TO PLAY" (Betty— 7 years, 4 months).

Rating 3: The child goes outside, is punished, and then may come inside and pick up the toys.
"HE DIDN'T COME SO HE GOT A WHIPPING" (George— 5 years, 9 months).

Rating 4: The child ignores the father's request and goes on playing.
"HE JUST DIDN'T (pick up the toys) . . . "HE JUST DIDN'T, THAT'S ALL" (Victor— 5 years, 11 months).

Rating 5: The child evades the conflict or gives no response.
"I DON'T KNOW" (Randall— 5 years, 10 months).

Story V

Rating 1: The father excuses the accident, but warns the child.
" 'HAVEN'T I TOLD YOU NOT TO FLY THE AIRPLANE IN THE ROOM?' SAID THE DADDY. 'WELL, I JUST WOUND IT UP A LITTLE AND IT DROPPED OUT OF MY HANDS AND IT FLEW AROUND THE ROOM.' (And the daddy says,) 'OH, THAT'S O.K., BUT NEXT TIME DON'T DO THAT' " (Leonard—8 years, 4 months).

Rating 2: The child compromises with the father by going outside or waiting until he is older to fly the plane.
"THE DADDY SAID, 'STOP IT, I'LL TAKE YOUR PLANE AWAY.' AND THE LITTLE GIRL SAID, 'OH DADDY, PLEASE DON'T, I DIDN'T MEAN TO.' AND THE DADDY SAID, 'WELL YOU OUGHT TO JUST GO OUTSIDE AND ROLL IT. ACCIDENTS HAPPEN, YOU KNOW.' SO SHE SAID, 'O.K.,' AND SHE WENT OUTSIDE AND PLAYED WITH IT" (Peggy— 7 years, 9 months).

Rating 3: The child is punished under all circumstances.
"HE SPANKED HER AND PROBABLY PUT HER TO BED . . . AND HE THREW AWAY THE AIRPLANE. AND THE NEXT DAY WHEN SHE GOT OUT OF BED SHE ASKED HER DADDY WHERE THE AIRPLANE WAS, HE SAID, 'I THREWED IT AWAY.' AND SHE JUST LAY DOWN AND SCREAMED BLOODY MURDER" (Gladys— 5 years, 2 months).

Rating 4: The child ignores the conflict with the father.
"IT PROBABLY HIT HIM SO HARD HIS HEAD STARTED TO BLEED . . . I DON'T KNOW. HE WENT TO THE BATHROOM AND GOT SOMETHING FOR HIS HEAD" (Adela— 6 years, 4 months).

Rating 5: The child does not respond to the conflict situation; or the child responds irrelevantly.
"I DON'T KNOW . . . I GUESS HE WOULD JUST TAKE IT OFF HIS HEAD . . . HE'D PROBABLY, I DON'T KNOW" (Bruce— 4 years, 8 months).

APPENDIX 22. DRAMATIC-PLAY COMPLETIONS

First Session: Stories in the Parents' Home

1. Daddy is in the bathroom. He is shaving. The little boy comes into the bathroom and sees the daddy. Show me what the little boy does.
2. The daddy is reading a book at his study table. The mommy is not at home because she has gone shopping. The little boy is feeling very lonesome because there is no one to play with. You show me what happens . . . What does daddy do? What does the little boy do?
3. Now it is morning, right after breakfast. The daddy is leaving the house, and he is going to school. What does daddy do while he is gone? You show me. How does daddy get to school? Where does daddy have his lunch? Is daddy's school like your school? What does daddy do at school? Who does he see at school?.
4. Here is the little boy in the kitchen. He is looking for something to eat. All of a sudden he knocks over a bottle of milk, and it spills all over the floor. The mommy sees him do it. Show me what happens.
5. Now the boy and his mommy are playing a game on the floor, having lots of fun. When the game is over, the boy hugs the mommy and gives her a big kiss. Daddy is watching them. What does the daddy do? You show me what happens.
6. Daddy is lying on the davenport, listening to the radio. The little boy wants to play with his toy truck. But the truck is broken, and he doesn't know how to fix it. You show me what the little boy does.
7. Here is the little boy sitting at the table where the daddy studies. He is looking at daddy's books. All of a sudden he spills a bottle of ink on daddy's books. Here comes daddy. What happens?
8. The little boy and the daddy are sitting at the table eating their supper. The mommy is in the kitchen. The little boy doesn't like the food. He is messy and sloppy and he spills things. What is going to happen? You show me. What does the daddy do?
9. Here is the little boy playing with his blocks. He has made a nice high tower with the blocks. The baby (or brother or sister) crawls over and knocks down the high tower. What happens? You show me. And mommy is here watching. What does she do? And daddy is here watching. What does he do?

10. The little boy is playing in the living room after supper. He is having a fine time. The little boy doesn't want to go to bed. Daddy comes over, and says he must go to bed now. You show me what happens next.
11. Here is the little boy in his bed. Pretty soon, he will go to sleep. The daddy comes in the room. Mommy is in the living room. The daddy sits on the little boy's bed. You show me what happens.

Second Session: Stories in the Grandparents' Home

12. The little boy and the daddy, and grandfather are at the table eating. Mommy and grandmother are in the kitchen. The little boy won't eat his dinner. The daddy says, "If you won't eat, I'll have to spank you. You are a bad boy." What does grandfather do?
13. Here is the little boy playing outside grandmother's and grandfather's house. All of a sudden he falls and hurts his leg. He goes into the house to have someone fix his leg. You show me what happens when he gets in the house.
14. The little boy is in his grandmother's and grandfather's house playing with some blocks. The baby (or brother or sister) crawls over and knocks down the house he has built with the blocks. What does the boy do to the baby? You show me.
15. Here is the little boy sitting on his grandmother's lap, listening to a nice story. Grandmother says, "I haven't time to read you another story. You ask someone else to read." The daddy and the mother and grandfather are in the room so the little boy asks one of them to read. You show me how it happens.
16. Now it is time to leave the grandmother's and grandfather's house. Mommy and daddy and the brother and baby (name family members) are in the car all ready to go. The little boy has had a wonderful time at grandmother's house. When the daddy says it is time to leave, what does the little boy do?

APPENDIX 23. FATHER-CHILD RELATIONS RATING SCALE USED IN ANALYSIS OF DRAMATIC DOLL-PLAY COMPLETIONS

In this projective situation, we are attempting to rate how the child feels about his father and how the father feels about the child— it is the quality of the process of interaction between them that is rated. The many-sided father-child relation may be expressed in a great variety of subtle ways— by what the child doll does, what the father doll does, what the child himself does, and by what they do not do, sometimes. For purposes of simplicity, as well as for psychological reasons, we are lumping the actions of the child and child doll into one, assuming identification.

Each score is defined in three ways: (1) A, a generalized statement of interpretation; (2) B, the second characterization of a level, a listing of possible behavior at this level; and (3) C, abstracts and brief examples.

Plus 4:

A. This is the most positive score. Here the father is integrated warmly and well into the child's life space and the child is likewise integrated into the father's life space. The child's security is unquestioned.

B. The father shows affection for the child, and the child shows affection for the father. The father is helpful upon his own initiative and is thoughtful and considerate; the child is likewise considerate of the father. The child shows complete confidence in the father and has assurance of father's acceptance of the child. The child obeys with friendliness, accepting the necessity of the situation. The child faces the situation realistically, with evidence of assurance.

C. Examples:

Story 5 M (mother) and C (child) play together on the floor. F (father) comes over. Boy asks: "Want to play a game?" F says "Yes." So they play; the whole family then goes to bed happily.

5 F gives M a kiss (very realistic pantomine). M gives boy a kiss. F gives M a hug, goes and sits down.

6 "Daddy, will you fix my truck?" "Yes," says F. F gets up, turns off the radio, gets his tools, fixes truck. Boy plays with the truck. Boy is also shown to be able to fix his own truck sometimes.

7 "And the little boy wipes it up (ink). He has a washcloth. F goes back and sits on the oouch."

Plus 3:

A. Here there is strong friendly interaction between child and father. Both believe the child's place in the family is a desired one. There seems to be sympathetic understanding by the father of the child, by the child of the father.

B. The relation here is direct and close, and the father befriends and supports the child. The child feels he is a companion of the father. There may be no overt display of affection, but friendly, warm interaction. The child seems moderately confident, may hesitate, but comes through promptly with assurance.

There may be elaboration of the household routine, which may bring the father into the child's life space easily and comfortably. If the father is excluded, it is because the story has not gotten around to him yet; when the child is prompted by the examiner, the father is immediately brought in and given a positive role.

The child feels the father will help him to behave in the desired (by both) and correct fashion.

C. Examples:

Story 6 At the suggestion of the examiner that the F be mentioned ("What does the father do?"), F and C go fix the truck together.

1 F shaves in the bathroom. C, M, other child, all come in and wash up. C says he is "proud" of this story.

15 C gets all members of the household to read him a story.

Plus 2:

A. Here the father-child relation is positive, but not warm, affectionate, or sympathetic. The child realizes his minor role but feels his father is a support and protector. They share mutual respect and confidence. The father is considered as potentially helpful. There is a mildly friendly feeling between them.

B. The child may feel the father-child bond is one in which he has some freedom. The child may demonstrate self-competence to the father and expect and receive approval. The child may waver in self-confidence, but finally accept and face the situation. The child's obedience may not be automatic or immediate.

C. Examples:

Story 1 F is shaving, C asks F to read to him, F says O.K. after he finishes shaving.

6 Boy fixes his own truck; F is omitted.

11 F tells C to go to bed; C refuses. F tells him again; C decides he will go to bed of his own accord.

16 F tells him it is time to go home; C refuses, then decides he will.

Plus 1:

A. Here the father-child relation is weak, but not negative. The child is subordinated to the control of the father. The child has a definite minor role which the child accepts as a minor role. There seem to be definite limitations to free father-child relations and the means of access is limited and narrow.

B. The child may give short answers to the story situation without any elaboration of the father-child interaction. The child's obedience may be immediate, limiting the interaction. The child may accept punishment as inevitable, as an expression of the father's keeping the child in his place. The punishment does not appear to interfere with subsequent positive interactions. There may be mild apprehension by the child, but this is overcome. The father may be dutiful, but give help perfunctorily.

C. Examples:

Story 1 F shaves, C uses toilet; no interaction.
2 C finds someone else to play with; F is left out.
6 M has F fix the truck; C deals with F through M.
9 C retaliates against sibling; F spanks both impartially.
11 C is obedient, goes right to bed— no interaction.
12 C leaves table, GF kisses him goodnight; F omitted.
12 F spanks, C considers this inevitable.
15 F reads a story first, but sends C off to M.

Minus 1:

A. Here we have a mildly negative relation between father and child, or an absence of positive friendly feelings. The child seems to accept, but dislikes the relation which exists. There may be a passive, almost indifferent attitude toward the father. The child may feel uncomfortable when the father enters his life space.

B. The child may not refer to the father, even when the examiner asks specifically about what the father does in the story situation. The father may prefer the other child, leave out the older child. The child may be serious when he is receiving punishment. There may be some compensation to the child from others in the situation. The child may obey, unwillingly.

C. Examples:

Story 5 C is left out; F loves other sibling.
7 F punishes C; M comforts C.
8 C leaves table, is messy; F punishes. M calls dinner; F and C go together to eat.
10 F puts C to bed; C dislikes it.
11 F is put to bed; chance for father-child interaction not taken.
13 "They fix his leg." Examiner questions: "Who?" "GM." F is left out, no elaboration.

Minus 2:

A. Here the father-child relation is definitely negative and child dislikes it, seems uncomfortable or unhappy about the relation being negative. There is some evidence for the dislike of the father and some evidence of anxiety in situations involving the father. The child feels the relation is damaging to his concept of his self; his self-respect has been lowered, he feels. The child has trouble accepting the situation.

B. The child may show his dislike of the relation with his father by mild aggression directed toward his self or toward some object. The child may hide his misdeeds from the father. The child may show fear of punishment. The child may definitely exclude the father; the child may be definitely excluded by the father. If the father punishes the child, the child may show self-pity or unhappiness.

C. Examples:

Story 4 M spanks girl; girl goes to toilet; then sits on stove.
5 C put to bed: F and M continue to play the game.
7 F punishes. C is called a "bad, bad boy."
8 M punishes; F left out. C pities self.
11 "She cried when the father woke her."
15 F refuses to read to C; C goes outside, sits in shade, reads to himself.

Minus 3:

A. Here the relation is definitely negative and/or the child dislikes the father per se. There are definite feelings of hostility and rejection (of C by F, of F by C). The child and father appear to be at odds, and the child is suspicious and distrusts the father. The child feels that he has no place; he feels rejected by the father. The life space of each is separate from the other and the only interaction is negative.

B. There may be some hostility, which is realistically expressed. There may be direct defiance, and conscious, well-calculated disobedience. The child may disobey, say he's sorry, then disobey again. The child may obey out of fear, evidenced by his following expressions of extreme dislike.

The child may try to restore or create a positive father-child bond, but this is done unrealistically (unrealistic restitution).

The child may be able to accept punishment, but may think it is harsh; he may feel that punishment is unjustified, as in cases of accidental behavior (when milk or ink is spilled). Counteraggression may be expressed. It is realistic and somehow matches the punishment the father gives the child. The child may feel his father is a tyrant; he may feel that his father's role is simply that of a punisher. The child may consciously evade a father-child interaction.

C. Examples:

Story 4 C hides from M. C claims he's a nice boy now.
7 C sneaks out money, buys a new bottle of ink (unrealistic restitution).
8 C eats, after being spanked; C vomits.
9 C sees herself as punishing the younger sibling rightfully, but F punishes her, leaves sibling to go scot free.

Minus 4:

A. This is the score for the most negative behavior recorded. There seems to be no positive father-child bond. The child's self seems disintegrated due to the pressures of the story situation. The child seems unable to accept, consciously, his hostile feelings toward the father and, therefore, dares only to express his feelings on a fantasy level.

B. The child presents behavior which is bizarre, illogical, fantasied. The punishment by the father may be unreal to the situation. The aggression by the child may be unreal to the situation. The child or father may enter into unprovoked aggression, as well as counteraggression. There may be severe suppression and blocking by the child, so that he may refuse to commit himself, perhaps due to anxiety (cf. the zero rating).

C. Examples:

Story 1 C knocks F off, puts him in another room, locks himself in bath.
8 "She knocks their food off. She ate his food."
11 "He gets up on the roof, then he jumps, jumps, jumps until it crashes down! It is crashed down."
16 C expresses a great deal of rough fighting between F and GF, and child. C gets very excited, animated, and becomes careless with materials.

Zero:

Here we place all those situations that we are unable to rate, for one reason or another. For example, the behavior of the subject may be so short or so vague and ill-defined that the rater cannot interpret what the level of the father-child interaction probably is. This rating is given if the subject refuses to respond, not because of evasion of the psychological situation presented by the stories, but because of some lack of rapport with the E, or lack of acceptance of the play period, or lack of acceptance of this general type of "game." Also, in stories 12, 13, and 14, rate a zero if F is excluded.

REFERENCES

1. Aldrich, C. A., and Aldrich, M. M. Babies are human beings. New York: Macmillan, 1943.
2. Allen, G. T. Eight-hour orphans. Saturday Evening Post, October 10, 1942, 20–21, 105–06.
3. Anderson, J. E. Methods of child psychology. In L. Carmichael (Ed.) Manual of child psychology. New York: Wiley, 1946. Pp. 1–42.
4. Andrus, R. An inventory of the habits of children from two to five years of age. New York: Teachers Coll., Columbia Univer., Bureau of Publications, 1928.
5. Bach, G. R. Young children's play fantasies. Psychol. Monogr., 1945, XXCIX (2), 1–69.
6. Bach, G. R. Father-fantasies and father-typing in father-separated children. Child Develpm., 1946, XVII, 63–80.
7. Bales, R. F. Interaction process analysis. Cambridge, Mass.: Addison-Wesley, 1950.
8. Baruch, D. W. Aggression during doll play in a pre-school. Amer. J. Orthopsychiat., 1941, XI, 252–59.
9. Block, J., Levine, L., and McNemar, Q. Testing for the existence of psychometric patterns. J. abnorm. soc. Psychol., 1951, XXXXVI (3), 356–59.
10. Bossard, J. H. S. The sociology of child development. New York: Harper, 1948.
11. Cameron, N. Perceptual organization and behavior pathology. In R. R. Blake and G. V. Ramsey (Eds.), Perception. New York: Ronald Press, 1951. Pp. 283-306.
12. Chance, E. A study of transference in group psychotherapy. Int. J. Group Psychother., 1952, II, 40–53.
13. Chance, E. The father's perception of his first child. Unpublished Ph. D. dissertation, Stanford University, 1953.
14. Clifton, E. Some psychological effects of the war as seen by the social worker. Family, 1943, XXIV, 123–28.
15. Darwin, C. A. A biographical sketch of the infant. Mind, 1877, II, 285–94.
16. Davis, A. E. Clinical experience with children in wartime. Soc. Serv. Rev., 1943, XVII, 170–74.
17. Davis, A., and Havighurst, R. J. Father of the man. Boston: Houghton Mifflin, 1947.
18. Despert, J. L. A method for the study of personality reactions in pre-school age children by means of analysis of their play. J. Psychol., 1940, IX, 17–29.
19. Dollard, J., Miller, N. E., Doob, L. W., Mowrer, O. H., and Sears, R. R. Frustration and aggression. New Haven: Yale Univer. Press, 1939.
20. Dowley, E. M. Sex differences in maturation in the control of nocturnal bed-wetting. Unpublished study, Merrill-Palmer School, Detroit, March, 1946.

20a. Dowley, E. M. Cues for observing the behavior of children. Childhood Educ. XXX (3) Pp. 113–17.

21. Dowley, E. M. Characteristics of war-born children as revealed through mother interviews. Unpublished Ed. D. dissertation, Stanford University, 1951.
22. Eliot, M. M. The protection of children in a national defense program. Address given June 11, 1941, Children's Bureau, U. S. Dept. of Labor. Also, by same author: Protection of children in Great Britain in wartime. Am. J. publ. Hlth., November, 1941, XXXI (11).
22a. Engvall, A. Parental evaluations of first-born children in families separated by war. Unpublished Master's thesis, Stanford University, 1953.
23. Erikson, E. H. Clinical studies in childhood play. In R. G. Barker, J. S. Kounin, and H. F. Wright (Eds.), Child behavior and development. New York: McGraw-Hill, 1943. Pp. 411–28.
24. Erikson, E. H. Childhood and society. New York: Norton, 1950.
24a. Faust, M. S. A study of father-child relations using a story-completion technique. Unpublished Master's thesis, Stanford University, 1951.
25. Festinger, L. The significance of difference between means without reference to the frequency distribution function. Psychometrika, 1946, XI (2), 97–105.
25a. Frank, L. K. Research in child psychology: history and prospect. In R. G. Barker, J. S. Kounin, and H. F. Wright (Eds.), Child behavior and development. New York: McGraw-Hill, 1943. Pp. 1–16.
26. Frank, L. K. Projective methods. Springfield, Ill.: Charles C. Thomas, 1948.
27. Freedman, M. B., Leary, I. F., Ossorio, A. G., and Coffey, H. S. Interpersonal dimensions of personality. J. Pers., 1951, XX (2), 143–61.
28. Freud, A. and Burlingham, D. T. War and children. New York: International University Press, 1943.
29. Freud, A. and Burlingham, D. T. Infants without families. New York: International University Press, 1944.
30. Freud, S. Collected papers. Vols. I–IV. London: Hogarth Press, 1948.
31. Freud, S. Mourning and melancholia (1917). Reprinted in Collected papers, IV. London: Hogarth Press, 1948.
32. Gardiner, G. E., and Spencer, H. Reactions of children with fathers and brothers in the armed services. Amer. J. Orthopsychiat., 1944, XIV, 36–43.
33. Gesell, A. L. Feeding behavior of infants: a pediatric approach to the mental hygiene of early life. Philadelphia: Lippincott, 1937.
34. Gesell, A. L. et. al. Infant and child in the culture of today. New York: Harper, 1943.
35. Goodenough, F. L. Measuring behavior traits by means of repeated short samples. J. Delinqu., 1923, XII, 230–34.
35a. Gowin, D. B. Ratings of father-child relations in a projective situation. Unpublished Master's thesis, Stanford University, 1951.
36. Grossman, J. What parents are saying in wartime. New York: Play Schools Association, 1942.

37. Halnan, H. H. A study of father-child relationships using a doll-play technique. Unpublished Master's thesis, Stanford University, 1950.
38. Hansell, T. Methods of disciplining children, a comparative study of mothers' reports in two occupational groups. Unpublished Master's thesis, Stanford University, 1950.
39. Hilgard, E. R. The role of learning in perception. In R. R. Blake and G. V. Ramsey (Eds.), Perception. New York: Ronald Press, 1951. Pp. 95–120.
40. Hill, R. Families under stress: adjustments to the crises of war separation and reunion. New York: Harper, 1949.
41. Hunt, J. McV. Personality and the behavior disorders. New York: Ronald Press, 1944. 2 vols.
42. Hymes, J. L., Jr. A pound of prevention. New York: New York Committee on Mental Hygiene of State Charities and Aid Association, 1947.
43. Igel, A. The effect of war separation on father-child relations. Family, 1945, XXVI, 3–9.
44. Jersild, A. T., and Markey, F. V. Conflicts between pre-school children. Child Develpm. Monogr., 1935, No. 21.
45. Jersild, A. T., and Meigs, M. F. Direct observation as a research method. Rev. educ. Res., 1939, IX, 472–82.
46. Jersild, A. T. Emotional development. In L. Carmichael (Ed.), Manual of child psychology. New York: Wiley, 1946. Pp. 752–90.
46a. Johnson, L. C. The effect of father absence during infancy on later father-child relationships using a doll-play technique. Unpublished Master's thesis, Stanford University, 1951.
47. Lerner, E., Murphy, L. B., (Eds.), Methods for the study of personality in young children. Child Develpm. Monogr., 1941, VI, No. 4.
48. Levy, D. M. Hostility patterns in sibling rivalry experiments. Amer. J. Orthopsychiat., 1936, VI, 183–257.
49. Levy, D. M. Hostility patterns. Amer. J. Orthopsychiat., 1943, XIII, 441–61.
50. Levy, D. M. Experiments in sibling rivalry. In R. G. Barker, I. S. Kounin, and H. F. Wright (Eds.), Child behavior and development. New York: McGraw-Hill, 1943. Pp. 397–410.
51. Levy, D. M. Maternal overprotection. New York: Columbia Univer. Press, 1943.
52. Macfarlane, J. W. Studies in child guidance I: Methodology of data collection and organization. Child Develpm. Monogr., 1938, III, No. 6.
53. McGraw, M. The neuromuscular maturation of the human infant. New York: Columbia Univer. Press, 1943.
54. McNemar, Q. Psychological statistics. New York: Wiley, 1949.
55. May, R. The meaning of anxiety. New York: Ronald Press, 1950.
56. Miller, N. E. The frustration-aggression hypothesis. Psychol. Rev., 1941, XXXXVIII, 337–42.
57. Mowrer, O. H. Learning theory and personality dynamics. New York: Ronald Press, 1950.

58. Murphy, L. B. Social behavior and child personality. New York: Columbia Univer. Press, 1937.
59. Newcomb, T. M. Social Psychology. New York: Dryden Press, 1950.
60. Olson, W. C. The measurement of nervous habits in normal children. Inst. Child Welf. Monogr. Ser., Univer. Minnesota Press, 1929.
61. Olson, W. C. and Hughes, B. O. Concepts of growth: their significance for teachers. Childh. Educ., 1944, XXI, 53–63.
62. Phillips, R. Doll play as a function of the realism of the materials and the length of the experimental session. Child Develpm., 1945, XVI, 123–43.
63. Pintler, M. H. Doll play as a function of the experimenter-child interaction and the initial organization of materials. Child Develpm., 1945, XVI, 145–66.
64. Preyer, W. The mind of the child. New York: Appleton, 1882.
65. Pyles, M. K., Stolz, H. R., Macfarlane, J. W. The accuracy of mothers' reports on birth and developmental data. Child Develpm., 1935, VI (3), 165–76.
66. Ribble, M. The rights of infants. New York: Columbia Univer. Press, 1943.
67. Robinson, E. F. Doll play as a function of the doll family constellation. Child Develpm., 1946, XVII, 99–119.
68. Ryder, J. M. Aggression in young children: a comparative study of first-born children separated from their fathers during the first year of life with first-born children not separated from their fathers. Unpublished Master's thesis, Stanford University, 1951.
69. Sears, P. S. Doll play aggression in normal young children: influence of sex, age, sibling status, father's absence. Psychol. Monogr., 1951, LXV (6).
70. Sears, R. R., Pintler, M. H., and Sears, P. S. Effect of father separation on pre-school children's doll play aggression. Child Develpm., 1946, XVII, 219–43.
71. Seaton, J. K. A projective experiment using incomplete stories with multiple-choice endings. Genet. Psychol. Monogr., 1949, XXXX, 149–218.
72. Shinn, M. Biography of a baby. Boston: Houghton Mifflin, 1900.
73. Shirley, H. F. Suggestions for dealing with emotional problems of children. War Bulletin, Mental Hygiene Society of Northern California, 1942.
74. Stevenson, N. G. A method for analyzing observational records. Unpublished Master's thesis, Stanford University, 1953.
75. Stolz, L. M. What's happening to children born during the war. Lecture given at Stanford Alumni Meeting, Stanford University, May, 1948.
76. Stolz, L. M. The effect of mobilization and war on children. In E. A. Richards (Ed.), Proceedings of the Midcentury White House Conference on children and youth. Raleigh, N.C.: Health Publications Institute, 1951. Pp. 111–122. Also in Soc. Casewk., 1951, XXXII (3), 143–49.
77. Stolz, L. M. and assistants. Survey of cartoons and fiction related

to the returning veteran's relations with his children. Unpublished paper, Stanford University, 1953.

78. Stone, L. J. Experiments in group play and readiness for destruction. In E. Lerner and L. B. Murphy (Eds.), Methods for the study of personality in young children. Child Develpm. Monogr., 1941, VI (4), 101–55.

79. Sullivan, H. S. Psychiatry: introduction to the study of interpersonal relations. Psychiat., 1938, I, 121–34.

80. Thomas, D. S. Some new techniques for studying social behavior. Child Develpm. Monogr., 1929, I.

81. Trainham, G., and Montgomery, J. C. Developmental factors in learning bowel and bladder control. Amer. J. Nurs., 1946, XXXXVI, (12).

82. Ullmann, L. The social behavior of children in war-separated families. Unpublished Master's thesis, Stanford University, 1953.

83. Underwood, V. Student fathers with their children. Marriage and Fam. Living, 1949, XI, 101.

84. Vincent, C. E. Trends in infant care ideas. Child Develpm., 1951, XXII (3), 199–209.

84a. White, R. W. Lives in progress. New York: Dryden Press, 1952.

85. Watson, J. B. Psychological care of the infant and child. New York: Norton, 1928.

86. Wolff, W. The personality of the pre-school child. New York: Grune and Stratton, 1946.

87. Children in wartime: parents' questions. New York: Child Study Assoc. of Amer., 1942.

88. Conference on emergency problems of children and youth. Division of Anthropology and Psychology, National Research Council. Washington, 1941.

89. For parents, for teachers of young children in wartime. Assoc. for Nursery Educ. of So. Calif., and Calif. Assoc. for Childh. Educ., Southern Section.

90. To parents in wartime. Bureau Publication 282, Children's Bureau, U. S. Department of Labor, 1942.

91. Proceedings of the International Congress on Mental Health (London, 1948.) New York: Columbia Univer. Press.

92. Statement of International Preparatory Commission, International Congress on Mental Health, London, August, 1948.